GUARDIANS
OF THE GALAXY
D1176042
TOMORROW'S AVENGERS

COVER ARTISTS: Al Milgrom & Tom Chu

COLLECTION EDITOR: Mark D. Beazley
ASSISTANT EDITORS: Alex Starbuck & Nelson Ribeiro
EDITOR, SPECIAL PROJECTS: Jennifer Grünwald
SENIOR EDITOR, SPECIAL PROJECTS: Jeff Youngquist
RESEARCH & LAYOUT: Jeph York
BOOK DESIGNER: Rodolfo Muraguchi
SENIOR VICE PRESIDENT OF SALES: David Gabriel
SVP OF BRAND PLANNING & COMMUNICATIONS: Michael Pasciullo

EDITOR IN CHIEF: Axel Alonso
CHIEF CREATIVE OFFICER: Joe Quesada
PUBLISHER: Dan Buckley
EXECUTIVE PRODUCER: Alan Fine

Special Thanks to Mary Skrenes & Jeff Christiansen

GUARDIANS OF THE GALAXY: TOMORROW'S AVENGERS VOL. 1. Contains material originally published in magazine form as MARVEL SUPER HEROES #18, MARVEL TWO-IN-ONE #4-5, GIANT-SIZE DEFENDERS #5, DEFENDERS #26-29 and MARVEL PRESENTS #3-12. First printing 2013. ISBN# 978-0-7851-6687-0. Published by MARVEL WORLDWIDE, INC., a subsidiary of MARVEL ENTERTAINMENT, LLC. OFFICE OF PUBLICATION: 135 West 50th Street, New York, NY 10020. $39.99 per copy in the U.S. and $43.99 in Canada (GST #R127032852); Canadian Agreement #40668537. **Printed in the U.S.A**. ALAN FINE, EVP - Office of the President, Marvel Worldwide, Inc. and EVP & CMO Marvel Characters B.V.; DAN BUCKLEY, Publisher & President - Print, Animation & Digital Divisions; JOE QUESADA, Chief Creative Officer; TOM BREVOORT, SVP of Publishing; DAVID BOGART, SVP of Operations & Procurement, Publishing; RUWAN JAYATILLEKE, SVP & Associate Publisher, Publishing; C.B. CEBULSKI, SVP of Creator & Content Development; DAVID GABRIEL, SVP of Publishing Sales & Circulation; MICHAEL PASCIULLO, SVP of Brand Planning & Communications; JIM O'KEEFE, VP of Operations & Logistics; DAN CARR, Executive Director of Publishing Technology; SUSAN CRESPI, Editorial Operations Manager; ALEX MORALES, Publishing Operations Manager; STAN LEE, Chairman Emeritus. For information regarding advertising in Marvel Comics or on Marvel.com, please contact Niza Disla, Director of Marvel Partnerships, at ndisla@marvel.com. For Marvel subscription inquiries, please call 800-217-9158. **Manufactured between 11/14/2012 and 12/24/2012 by R.R. DONNELLEY, INC., SALEM, VA, USA.**

10 9 8 7 6 5 4 3 2 1

TOMORROW'S AVENGERS

WRITERS: ARNOLD DRAKE, STEVE GERBER & ROGER STERN WITH GERRY CONWAY, ROGER SLIFER, LEN WEIN, CHRIS CLAREMONT, SCOTT EDELMAN & STAN LEE

PENCILERS: GENE COLAN, SAL BUSCEMA, DON HECK & AL MILGROM WITH JOHN BUSCEMA

INKERS: MIKE ESPOSITO, FRANK GIACOIA, VINCE COLLETTA, PABLO MARCOS, AL MILGROM, HOWARD CHAYKIN, TERRY AUSTIN & BOB WIACEK WITH DAVE HUNT, JOHN TARTAGLIONE & JOE SINNOTT

COLORISTS: STAN GOLDBERG, PETRA GOLDBERG, GEORGE ROUSSOS, IRENE VARTANOFF, AL WENZEL, GLYNIS WEIN, PHIL RACHELSON, JANICE COHEN & DON WARFIELD

LETTERERS: HERB COOPER, CHARLOTTE JETTER, ANNETTE KAWECKI, DAVE HUNT, KAREN MANTLO, JOE ROSEN, JOHN COSTANZA, DENISE WOHL & IRVING WATANABE WITH JIM NOVAK & SAM ROSEN

ASSISTANT EDITOR: GARY FRIEDRICH

EDITORS: STAN LEE, ROY THOMAS, LEN WEIN, MARV WOLFMAN & ARCHIE GOODWIN

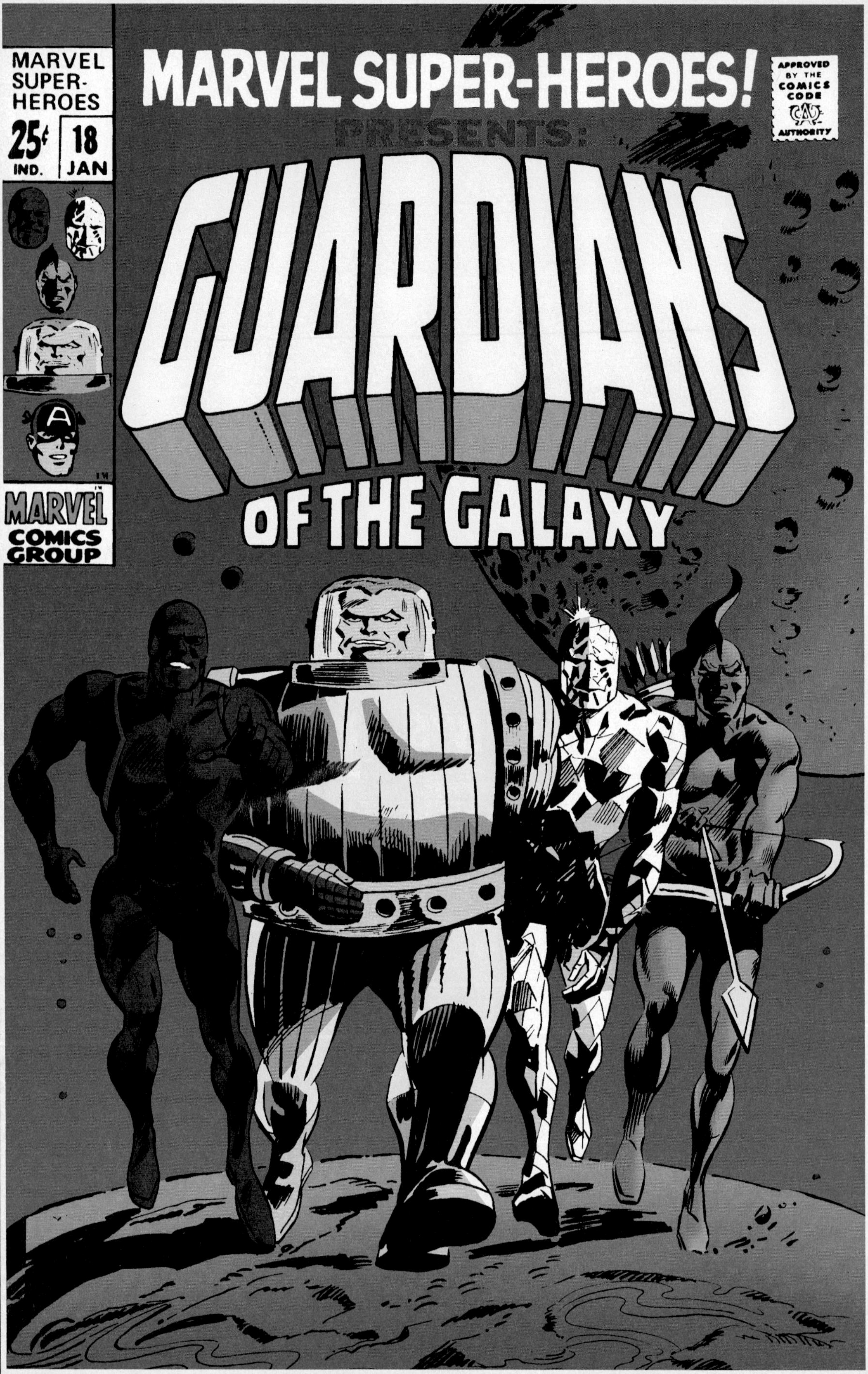

MARVEL SUPER-HEROES

25¢ IND.

18 JAN

MARVEL COMICS GROUP

MARVEL SUPER-HEROES! PRESENTS:

GUARDIANS OF THE GALAXY

APPROVED BY THE COMICS CODE AUTHORITY

A TEN-CENTURY-OLD MAN AND HIS FANTASTIC GUERRILLA LEGION FIGHT TO FREE PLANET EARTH!
EDITED BY STAN LEE
WRITTEN BY ARNOLD DRAKE
PENCILLED BY GENE COLAN
INKED BY MICKEY DEMEO
LETTERED BY HERB COOPER
GUARDIANS OF THE GALAXY!
IT IS THE YEAR 3007! A SINGLE FLAG FLIES OVER U.L.E.--THE UNITED LANDS OF EARTH--AND OVER THE DOZENS OF PLANETS IN THE U.L.E. FEDERATION! WARS AMONG NATIONS LONG AGO CEASED--BUT THE WAR OF THE STAR SYSTEMS HAS ONLY BEGUN...
THIS IS CHARLIE-27, FIFTH GENERATION OF HIS FAMILY BORN ON PLANET JUPITER--AFTER SPACE-MIGRATING FROM EARTH! LIKE ALL PIONEERS, CHARLIE-27'S HUMAN BODY WAS ADAPTED AT BIRTH TO WITHSTAND JUPITER'S CONDITIONS--ELEVEN TIMES THE MASS AND THREE TIMES THE GRAVITY OF EARTH--!
1

AFTER SIX MONTHS OF SOLITARY SPACE-MILITIA DUTY, CHARLIE-27 HAS ROCKETED JOYOUSLY HOME--AND INTO A UNIVERSAL NIGHTMARE FROM WHICH NO HUMAN MAY EVER RETURN ALIVE AND FREE...!
EARTH SHALL
2

WHERE IS EVERYBODY? I LOST RADIO CONTACT TWO MONTHS AGO-- BUT I WAS SURE, ONCE THEY RADAR-SPOTTED MY SHIP, THE WHOLE SQUAD WOULD BE HERE TO WELCOME ME BACK!
THERE'S ALWAYS A PARTY WHEN A MIL-MAN RETURNS FROM SPACE SOLITARY! BUT THIS PLACE IS DEADER THAN A SATURN MOON!
HELLO OUT THERE, FELLOW JOVIANS! HOW ABOUT A FEW ROUSING CHEERS FOR THE CONQUERING HERO?
OVERCOME!
3

THERE WILL BE A MEDAL FOR US, MAZ! WE ARE ABOUT TO CAPTURE THE LAST FREE JOVIAN!
HELLO OUT THERE!!
HALT! IN THE NAME OF THE GLORIOUS EASTERN ZONE COUNCIL!
THE BADOON! THEY'VE REACHED JUPITER ALREADY! THEY MUST HAVE CUT MY RADIO CONTACT!
YOUR REFLEXES ARE A LITTLE SLOW, GENTLEMEN! TRY IT LIKE --THIS!
ARRGH!
HOLY, NEPTUNE! THAT WAS CLOSE! CAN'T HOPE TO STAY THIS LUCKY! MUST STOP THAT BADOON GUARD--ONE WAY OR ANOTHER!
KEEP JUPITER CLEAN
USE THIS
INCENDI - DROP
4

I DIDN'T FIGURE ON THAT! BUT THE BADOON WOULDN'T THINK TWICE ABOUT IT-- SO I CAN'T AFFORD TO, EITHER!
AAAAAACH!
I DON'T KNOW WHEN THEY MOVED IN! THEY MIGHT STILL BE FIGHTING IN THE STREETS! MUST REPORT TO COMMAND HQ ON THE DOUBLE!
DESERTED! NOT A LIVING SOUL! TOO LATE TO REPORT IN NOW! MUST TRY TO MAKE IT TO MY FOLKS! GET THEM OFF OF JUPITER WHILE THERE'S STILL A CHANCE!
BUT, AS CHARLIE-27 APPROACHES HIS HOME...
MY FATHER! THEY'VE GOT HIM! THEY'VE OVERRUN THE ENTIRE PLANET!
MUST FOLLOW THAT TRUCK! THEY'RE NOT GOING TO KILL MY FATHER IN THAT CAMP!
EASTERN ZONE COUNCIL LABOR CAMP-19
HE SWIFTLY FOLLOWS IN A STOLEN ROCKET CAR AND SHORTLY...
THOSE PRISONERS! THEY'RE MINING HIGH-INTENSITY HARKOVITE! WITHOUT PROTECTION, THEY'LL ALL DIE OF RADIOACTIVITY IN FIVE DAYS! CAN'T WAIT! HAVE TO BREAK MY FATHER OUT OF THERE--NOW!
5

RAISE YOUR HANDS, JOVIAN! THE WHOLE FOURTH QUADRANT OF THE EASTERN SECTOR HAS BEEN SEARCHING FOR YOU!
I'M TOO LATE! WE'RE ALL TOO LATE! JUPITER IS LOST!
BUT THEY WON'T PUT ME IN ANY DEATH CAMP! --I'LL DIE HERE-- AND NOW!
WAIT! WHAT AM I DOING--?
STUPID TO SELL MY LIFE SO CHEAPLY! IF I CAN GET OFF JUPITER --I CAN JOIN THE REST OF U.L.E.'S FORCES AND LIBERATE MY PEOPLE! MAYBE IN TIME TO SAVE MY FATHER--IF I LIVE THE LENGTH OF THIS ROAD, THAT IS!
TELE-PORT DEPOT! IF I CAN JUST MAKE IT INTO THERE ALIVE--I CAN RADIO-JUMP TO ANYPLACE IN THE SOLAR SYSTEM!
THEY'RE RIGHT BEHIND ME! GOT TO DIVE FOR THE TELE-TRAN! WOULDN'T GIVE YOU MUCH FOR MY CHANCES!
ZAP!
JUPITER TELE-PORT STATION
LIVING MATTER TRANSMITTER
LIKE A 20TH-CENTURY COMMUTER RUNNING TO CATCH THE 4:57, THE 30TH-CENTURY JOVIAN DIVES FOR A BEAM THAT WILL TRANSMIT HIM THROUGH SPACE!
6

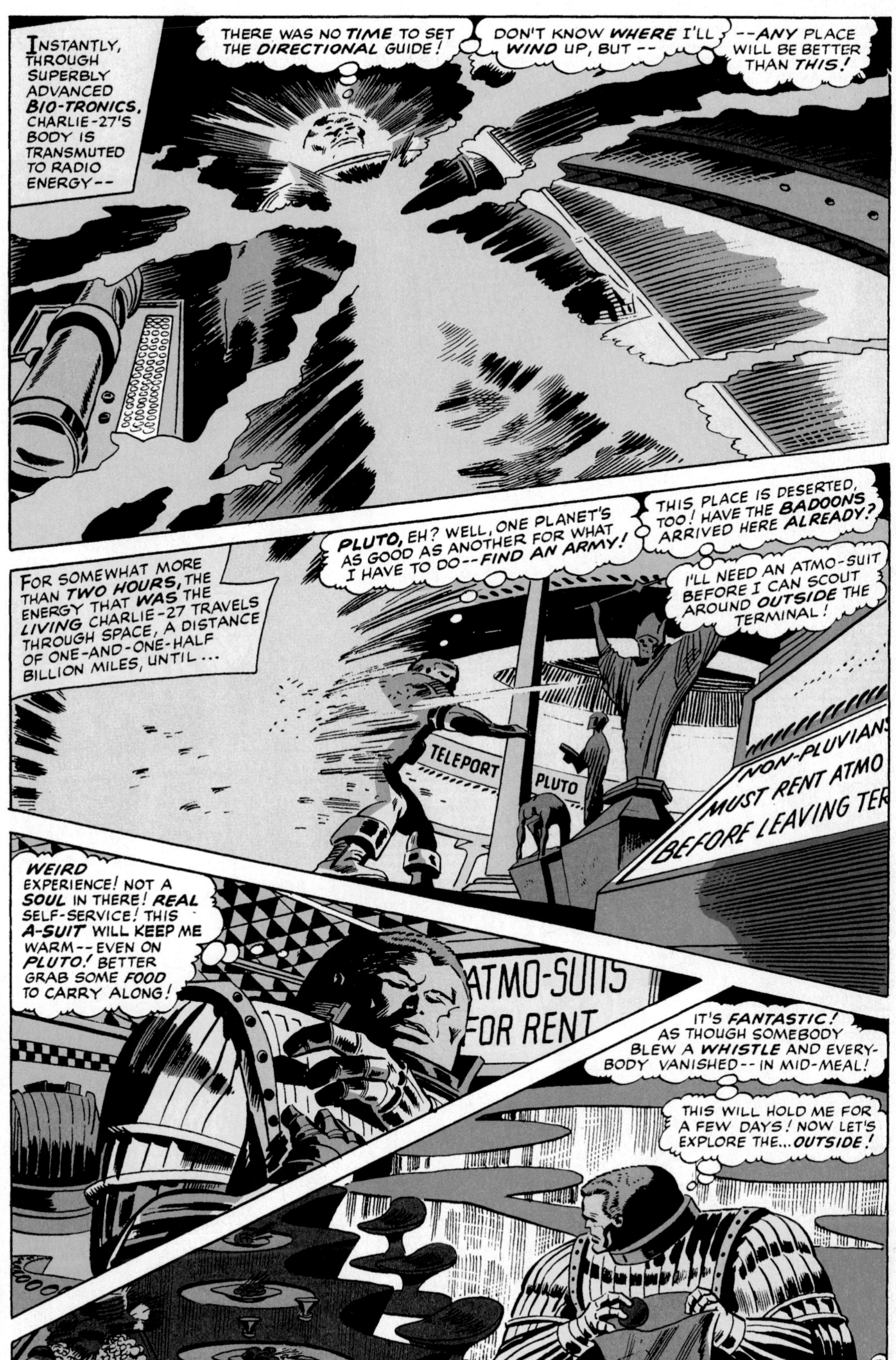
INSTANTLY, THROUGH SUPERBLY ADVANCED BIO-TRONICS, CHARLIE-27'S BODY IS TRANSMUTED TO RADIO ENERGY--
THERE WAS NO TIME TO SET THE DIRECTIONAL GUIDE!
DON'T KNOW WHERE I'LL WIND UP, BUT --
--ANY PLACE WILL BE BETTER THAN THIS!
FOR SOMEWHAT MORE THAN TWO HOURS, THE ENERGY THAT WAS THE LIVING CHARLIE-27 TRAVELS THROUGH SPACE, A DISTANCE OF ONE-AND-ONE-HALF BILLION MILES, UNTIL ...
PLUTO, EH? WELL, ONE PLANET'S AS GOOD AS ANOTHER FOR WHAT I HAVE TO DO--FIND AN ARMY!
THIS PLACE IS DESERTED, TOO! HAVE THE BADOONS ARRIVED HERE ALREADY?
I'LL NEED AN ATMO-SUIT BEFORE I CAN SCOUT AROUND OUTSIDE THE TERMINAL!
TELEPORT
PLUTO
NON-PLUVIANS MUST RENT ATMO BEFORE LEAVING TER
WEIRD EXPERIENCE! NOT A SOUL IN THERE! REAL SELF-SERVICE! THIS A-SUIT WILL KEEP ME WARM--EVEN ON PLUTO! BETTER GRAB SOME FOOD TO CARRY ALONG!
ATMO-SUITS FOR RENT
IT'S FANTASTIC! AS THOUGH SOMEBODY BLEW A WHISTLE AND EVERY-BODY VANISHED--IN MID-MEAL!
THIS WILL HOLD ME FOR A FEW DAYS! NOW LET'S EXPLORE THE...OUTSIDE!
7

MEANWHILE, NOT FAR FROM THE DEPOT...
THE ANIMALS HAVE PICKED UP ANOTHER N-B SCENT!
THAT IS NOT POSSIBLE, YUR! WE KNOW THERE WAS ONLY ONE PLUVIAN LEFT AFTER THE EVACUATION!
I TELL YOU, THEY HAVE FOUND ANOTHER NON-BADOON SCENT! THERE ARE TWO!
THE ANIMALS ARE PULLING TOWARD THE TELE-DEPOT!
THERE HE GOES! ON THE ROOF-- TRYING TO ESCAPE!
RELEASE THE ANIMALS! QUICKLY!
RRROWRRR
GET IN HERE, JUPITER-MAN! UNLESS YOU WANT TO BE A-NUMBER-ONE MEAL!
SATURNIAN HOUND-HAWK! DEADLY-- TOO LATE TO FIGHT!
8

WHO ARE YOU? WHAT IS THIS PLACE? TURN ON SOME LIGHTS SO I CAN SEE!
YOU MAY LEAVE NOW IF YOU WISH, JUPITER-MAN! THE HOUND-HAWKS WILL BE VERY MUCH GLAD TO SEE YOU AGAIN!
BY KARSUS! YOU'RE A CRYSTAL MAN --A PLUVIAN!
YOU MEAN A "ROCK HEAD," DON'T YOU? ISN'T THAT WHAT YOU PEOPLE ALWAYS CALL US? DESPITE THE FACT THAT WE, LIKE YOU ARE DESCENDED FROM EARTHMEN!
THIS IS NO TIME TO FIGHT A RACE WAR! TELL ME WHAT'S HAPPENING HERE!
PLUTO WAS TOTALLY EVACUATED TWO MONTHS AGO! HAVING BEEN LEFT BEHIND TO BLOW UP SOME INDUSTRIAL COMPLEXES, I WAS ABOUT TO MAKE MY ESCAPE--
--WHEN I PULLED THE TROOPS OVER TO THE TELE-PORT AND BLEW YOUR SCHEME! WELL DON'T WORRY-- I'M GOING OUT THERE AND SURRENDER, THEN...
UNNECCESSARY HEROICS, MILITIA-MAN! THIS RADIO TRANSMITTER WILL TAKE CARE OF THE TROOPS!
9

I'VE WIRED MANY ROBOT SERVANTS IN A NEARBY STORE!
THIS TRANSMITTER WILL ACTIVATE THEM!
SENDING THEM SMASHING THROUGH STREETS!
RENT A SERVANT
SWIFTLY, THE STRANGE ALLIES RETURN TO THE TELEPORT...
HURRY, JUPITER-MAN! ROBOT SERVANTS AREN'T MADE FOR FIGHTING BADOON ELITE GUARDS!
THEY'RE DOING GOOD ENOUGH FOR ME!
LE-PORT
10

THERE'S THE TELE-TRAN! HAVE TO DIVE FOR IT! HEY, MILITIAMAN, I FORGET TO ASK-- WHAT IS YOUR NAME?
TELE T
CHARLIE-27! AND WHAT'S YOURS, CRYSTAL MAN?
MARTINEX! PLEASED MEET YOU, CHARLIE-27!
SAME HERE, MARTINEX! NEXT STOP--MOTHER-PLANET EARTH! AND LET'S HOPE THAT IT IS STILL FREE!
11

AT ABOUT THAT SAME MOMENT, ON PLANET EARTH...
THE PRISONERS WILL BOW DOWN BEFORE THE GREAT DRANG--SUPREME COMMANDER OF THE EASTERN SECTOR OF THE BADOON EMPIRE!
AHHHH! SO THIS IS THE ESTEEMED MAJOR VANCE ASTRO, FIRST EARTHMAN TO THE STARS! THE SAGA OF YOUR GREAT ADVENTURE HAS REACHED UNTO OUR WORLD!
AND DID YOU LAUGH, DRANG? DID EVERYBODY HAVE A GOOD LAUGH AT THE ...THOUSAND-YEAR-OLD MAN?!
YOU'LL CHUCKLE OUT OF THE OTHER SIDE OF YOUR FACE IF YOUR ROYAL MURDERERS WILL TAKE THEIR HANDS OFF ME!
12

EVEN YOU MUST ADMIT THERE IS A CERTAIN HUMOR TO THE STORY! MAY WE HEAR IT FROM YOUR OWN LIPS?
NOT IF YOU LIVED TEN TIMES MY THOUSAND YEARS!
INSTANTLY, A GREAT ELECTRONIC HELMET IS LOWERED...
FOOL! WE WILL HAVE IT FROM YOU WILLINGLY OR NOT!
YOU WOULD HAVE DONE BETTER TO TELL IT WILLINGLY, OLD EARTHMAN! THE MEMORY PROBE IS NOT PAINLESS!
IN ANOTHER MOMENT, AS THE MEMORY PROBE BEGINS ITS WORK... AS MAJOR ASTRO IS TURNED TO FACE A CURVED PLASTIC WALL...
"IT WAS THE YEAR 1988! EARTHMEN NOW HAD A SMALL MOON COLONY OPERATING, AND THE FIRST LANDINGS ON MARS HAD TAKEN PLACE--BUT NOW WE WERE STRIKING FOR THE STARS THEMSELVES...!"
MAJOR VANCE ASTRO WILL REPORT TO THE BIO PREP ROOM AT ONCE! COUNT-DOWN WILL COMMENCE IN THREE MINUTES!
13

THIS IS IT, EH, DOCTOR? MY LAST WORDS, MY LAST WAKING VIEW--FOR A LONG WHILE!
THAT'S RIGHT, MAJOR...WE MUST NOW DRAIN YOUR BLOOD AND REPLACE IT WITH THE PRE-SERVATIVE FLUID! WHEN YOU LAND 1,000 YEARS FROM NOW, THE MACHINES WILL AUTOMATICALLY PUMP BACK YOUR BLOOD AND YOU WILL AWAKEN!
EVEN AT OUR PRESENT MAXIMUM SPEED OF 10-6,* YOU STILL COULDN'T REACH THE NEAREST STAR IN TEN LIFETIMES! OF COURSE, IF WE COULD TRAVEL BEYOND THE SPEED OF LIGHT--
FORGET IT, DOC! EINSTEINIAN PHYSICS SAYS THAT'S IMPOSSIBLE!
*TEN TO THE SIXTH POWER-- ONE MILLION MILES AN HOUR! --STAN.
IS THERE ANYTHING ELSE YOU WANT TO SAY--OR HAVE US DO?
YEAH--ONE THING I'D LIKE--
TRIPLE A PRIORITY PHONECALL FOR MAJOR ASTRO-- FROM A MISS BETINA MARSH!
OH, VANCE--I TRIED NOT TO CALL--TRIED NOT TO GET YOU ALL UPSET--BUT I COULDN'T HELP MYSELF!
BUT THAT'S IT! NOW FORGET ABOUT ME! I'D NEVER HAVE WORKED ANYWAY! I'D ALWAYS BE REACHING FOR THE STARS! YOU LIVE, SWEETIE! LIVE! OTHERWISE YOU'LL HAUNT ME--FOR 1,000 YEARS!
"THEN THEY SLIPPED ME THE ANAESTHETIC AND I WENT UNDER...!"
HAVE A GOOD 365,000 NIGHTS' SLEEP, MAJOR ASTRO!
14

"AWAY MY ROCKET ROARED, CARRYING ONE MAN-ON-ICE...!"
"AND THE NEXT THING I KNEW WAS 1,000 YEARS LATER, WHEN MY ALARM CLOCK WENT OFF..."
INCREDIBLE! EVERYONE I EVER KNEW--HAS BEEN DEAD MORE THAN NINE CENTURIES! AND THIS COPPER FOIL WRAPPING--I'VE GOT TO WEAR IT FOREVER! ONE PUNCTURE--AND I'D AGE 1,000 YEARS IN A SECOND!
"SLOWLY, THE SHIP DESCENDED ONTO MY PLANETARY TARGET...
WHAT WILL I FIND OUT THERE? A BARREN WORLD WHERE I'LL STARVE TO DEATH? SOME UN-ENDURABLE CONDITION? OR BONE-CRUSHING BEASTS--OR EVEN PLANT LIFE THAT CAN TEAR ME TO SHREDS?
"BUT, WHEN I OPENED THE SHIPS DOOR..."
♪ --FOR HE'S A JOLLY ♪ GOOD FELLOW--FOR HE'S A JOLLY GOOD FELLOW--THAT NOBODY CAN ♪ DENY! #
THREE CHEERS FOR MAJOR ASTRO!
EARTHMEN! B--BUT IT CAN'T BE! HOW COULD YOU BEAT ME HERE?
HARKOVIAN PHYSICS, OLD MAN! IT REPLACED EINSTEIN'S 800 YEARS AGO!
WELCOME
15

IT WAS DISCOVERED 200 YEARS AFTER YOU LEFT! BUT THERE WAS NO WAY OF INTERRUPTING YOUR JOURNEY! HOWEVER, YOU'VE BEEN A HERO TO EVERY CHILD FOR TEN CENTURIES, MAJOR!
HA HA HA HA HA! IT WAS ALL FOR NOTHING! MY HOME--MY GIRL--MY FRIENDS--HA HA HA!--ALL THROWN AWAY FOR NOTHING!
YOU MUST ADMIT IT IS A FUNNY STORY, MAJOR! BITTER--YET FUNNY!
NOT TO ME, DRANG! IT WILL NEVER BE FUNNY TO--ME! NOW GET TO THE POINT! WHY WERE WE BROUGHT HERE?
YOU KNOW, OF COURSE, MAJOR, THAT YOU ARE THE ONLY EARTHMAN PERMITTED TO NOT WEAR A PSYKE-DISK! WE RESPECT THE SPECIAL KNOWLEDGE OF A MAN WHO HAS LIVED FORTY GENERATIONS!
AND YOU WANT ME TO WORK FOR YOU VOLUNTARILY--THAT'S WHY I'M SPARED YOUR SLAVE DISK!
EXACTLY! WE COULD COMMAND YOU LIKE THOSE POOR WRETCHES OUT THERE!
I SEE WHAT YOU MEAN, DRANG! OKAY, YOU'VE MADE A DEAL! BUT...FOR A PRICE!
YOU SHALL BE WELL PAID FOR BETRAYING YOUR PEOPLE!
PULL HARDER --MISERABLE SLAVES!
MY PEOPLE? YOU'VE GOTTA BE KIDDING! MY PEOPLE DIED... NEARLY 1,000 YEARS AGO! I'M A SHIPWRECK IN TIME, DRANG! AND I TAKE LIP FROM NOBODY!
HMMM! YOU DO HAVE ONE PEOPLE, MAJOR! THIS YONDU--HE IS YOURS?
16

YEAH! NATIVE OF THE PLANET I LANDED ON! DUMBEST PEOPLE THAT EVER LIVED! I KEPT HIM JUST FOR LAUGHS!
THEN, YOU SHOULD NOT MIND--KILLING HIM!
YOU SEE, THE COUNCIL HAS PROCLAIMED SUCH PEOPLE TOO INFERIOR TO SURVIVE!
SO YOU'RE TESTING ME--BY MAKING ME HIS EXECUTIONER! OKAY, BUT--IT'D BE INTERESTING TO DO IT WITH HIS OWN WEAPON! GIVE ME THE BOW ARROW YOU TOOK FROM HIM!
THEN, AS THE STRANGE WEAPON IS BROUGHT FORTH...
SORRY, MY BLUE FRIEND--BUT LIKE WE USED TO SAY BACK IN 1988--THAT'S THE WAY IT MOVES!
YOU CALLED ME--FRIEND! YOU WERE LIAR, COPPER-MAN! GO--KILL!
BUT AS THE SECOND THE ARROW IS FIRED, YONDU EMITS A WEIRD WHISTLE...
SCREEEEE!
SCREEEEE!
ARROW--MADE OF SOUND-SENSITIVE MINERAL FROM HIS WORLD! HE COMMANDS IT WITH HIS WHISTLE! CAN'T GET AWAY--!
AND INSTANTLY, THE ARROW CHANGES COURSE...
17

AND THE UNCANNY MINERAL HAS **MORE** THAN ONE DEADLY SECRET...

TIME TO EXIT--**THE WINDOW!** FOLLOW ME--BUT DON'T STOP **WHISTLING!**
SCREEE!

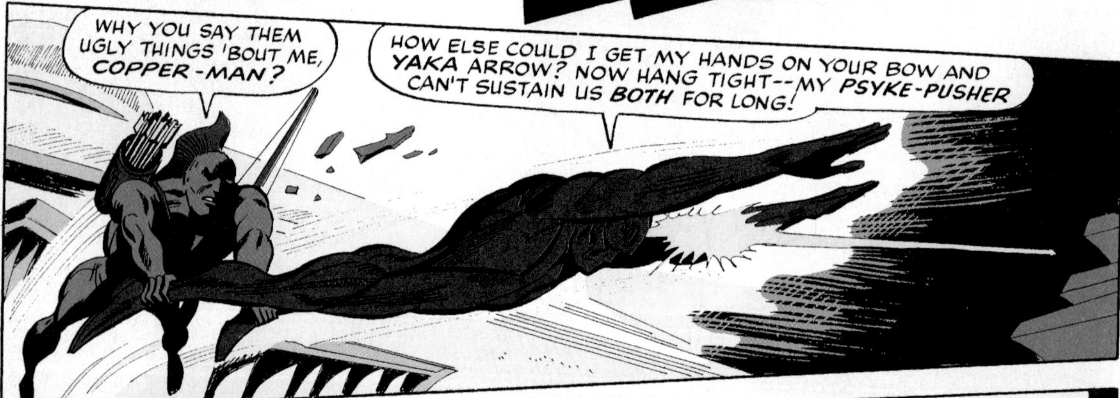
WHY YOU SAY THEM UGLY THINGS 'BOUT ME, **COPPER-MAN?**
HOW ELSE COULD I GET MY HANDS ON YOUR BOW AND **YAKA** ARROW? NOW HANG TIGHT--MY **PSYKE-PUSHER** CAN'T SUSTAIN US **BOTH** FOR LONG!

THAT'S WHAT I HOPED FOR... A **TELE-PORT!** BUT REMEMBER, IT'S **ILLEGAL** FOR ANYONE BUT THE BADOON TO USE THE **JUMP TUBES!** SO THE FIRST BADOON YOU SEE--**START SWINGING!**
18

AT THAT SAME MOMENT, INSIDE THE TELE-PORT, TWO FAR-VOYAGERS HAVE JUST LANDED...
HERE WE ARE, BACK ON MERRY OLD--
HALT! IT IS FORBIDDEN FOR A NON-BADOON TO SPACE JUMP!
YES--WE'RE BACK ON EARTH, CHARLIE-27! BUT IT IS NOT MERRY! HIT THE BADOONS!
TELE-
OVERPOWERING THE SURPRISED GUARDS, THE TWO REBELS STEAL THEIR RAY-GUNS TO MAKE THEIR ESCAPE! SUDDENLY...
MUST BE BADOON GUARDS! GET THEM, YONDU, BEFORE THEY GET US!
HOLD IT! IT'S A MISTAKE!
AGAIN THE SHRILL WHISTLE IS HEARD, AND...
CAN'T SHAKE THAT THING... MARTINEX-- HELP!
SCREEEEEEEEEEE
MY CRYSTALINE BODY STRUCTURE LETS ME CONVERT LIGHT WAVES INTO INTERNAL EXTREMES! WITH MY LEFT HAND, I CAN FREEZE THE VERY AIR!
19

WHERE'VE YOU BEEN? I THOUGHT EVERYBODY KNEW ABOUT--THE 1,000 YEAR-OLD-MAN WHO LEARNED TO HARNESS PSYCHIC-ENERGY!
SURE, WE KNOW WHO YOU ARE, MAJOR ASTRO! BUT WE ALSO KNOW --YOU'VE BEEN BEATIN' OUR BRAINS IN!
CHARLIE-27'S STEELY JOVIAN MUSCLES TURN ASTRO INTO A LIVING MISSILE, AND THEN...
TRYING TO DASH ME AGAINST THE WALL...ALL I'VE GOT TO DO IS REVERSE MY PSYCHIC ENERGY FROM THE SOLES OF MY SHOES...AND...
20

WAIT! YOU'RE NOT A BADOON!
WHA'DYA THINK I'VE BEEN TRYING TO TELL YOU, SIR? WE'RE THE LAST FREE MEN OF JUPITER AND PLUTO, AND WE'RE LOOKIN' FOR A FIGHT --BUT WITH THE BADOON!
SUDDENLY, MORE BADOON GUARDS ENTER...
IT IS MAJOR ASTRO! WE HAVE COUNCIL ORDERS TO KILL--!
NOW ALL YOU'VE GOT TO DO IS MAKE THE ORDER STICK! BUT THAT'S NO SMALL ORDER!
I HAVE HIM--RIGHT IN MY GUN SIGHT!
LIGHT ENERGY, CONCENTRATED BY MY CRYSTAL-TISSUE, DELIVERS...
...EXTREME HEAT THROUGH MY RIGHT HAND! SO MUCH FOR YOUR GUN SIGHT, NO?
21

THE REST OF YOU-- BEAT IT INTO THE JUMP TUBE--
WHILE I TAKE CARE OF--
THESE HONORABLE BADOONS!
WHERE TO, MAJOR? NEW PARIS? NEW MOSCOW? NEW NOME?
NO! THIS IS NO HOLIDAY TOUR, MARTINEX! WE'RE GOING TO FIND THAT FREE COLONY-- OR DIE TRYING!
IN A FLASH ALL FOUR ARE TELE-PORTED THROUGH SPACE TO...
NEW NEW YORK TOOK THE WORST PASTING OF ALL FROM THE BADOON! BUT THEY SAY--
--THAT THE FREE COLONY STARTED HERE! I NOT BELIEVE IT, MAJOR! IS NO FREE COLONY! EVERYBODY DEAD--OR SLAVE!
MY FRIENDS--I'M THE OLD MAN HERE--BY ABOUT TEN CENTURIES! AND I SAY WE CAN FIND THE FREE COLONY!
LISTEN--THERE WAS A STRUGGLE SONG THEY SANG IN MY TIME--IT'S STILL GOOD, IF YOU ALTER IT A BIT! TRY IT WITH ME--
EARTH SHALL OVERCOME! EARTH SHALL OVERCOME! EARTH SHALL OVERCOME --SOMEDAY!!
THUS WERE THEY UNITED ...THUS DO THEY LIVE... AND THUS, PERHAPS, SHALL THEY DIE! BUT WHILE LIFE ENDURES, THEY WILL CHALLENGE THE BANEFUL BADOON... AND ONE DAY, LEGENDS SHALL SPRING UP IN WORLDS YET UNBORN, ABOUT THOSE WHO SHALL BE CALLED... THE GUARDIANS OF THE GALAXY!
THE END--FOR NOW!
22

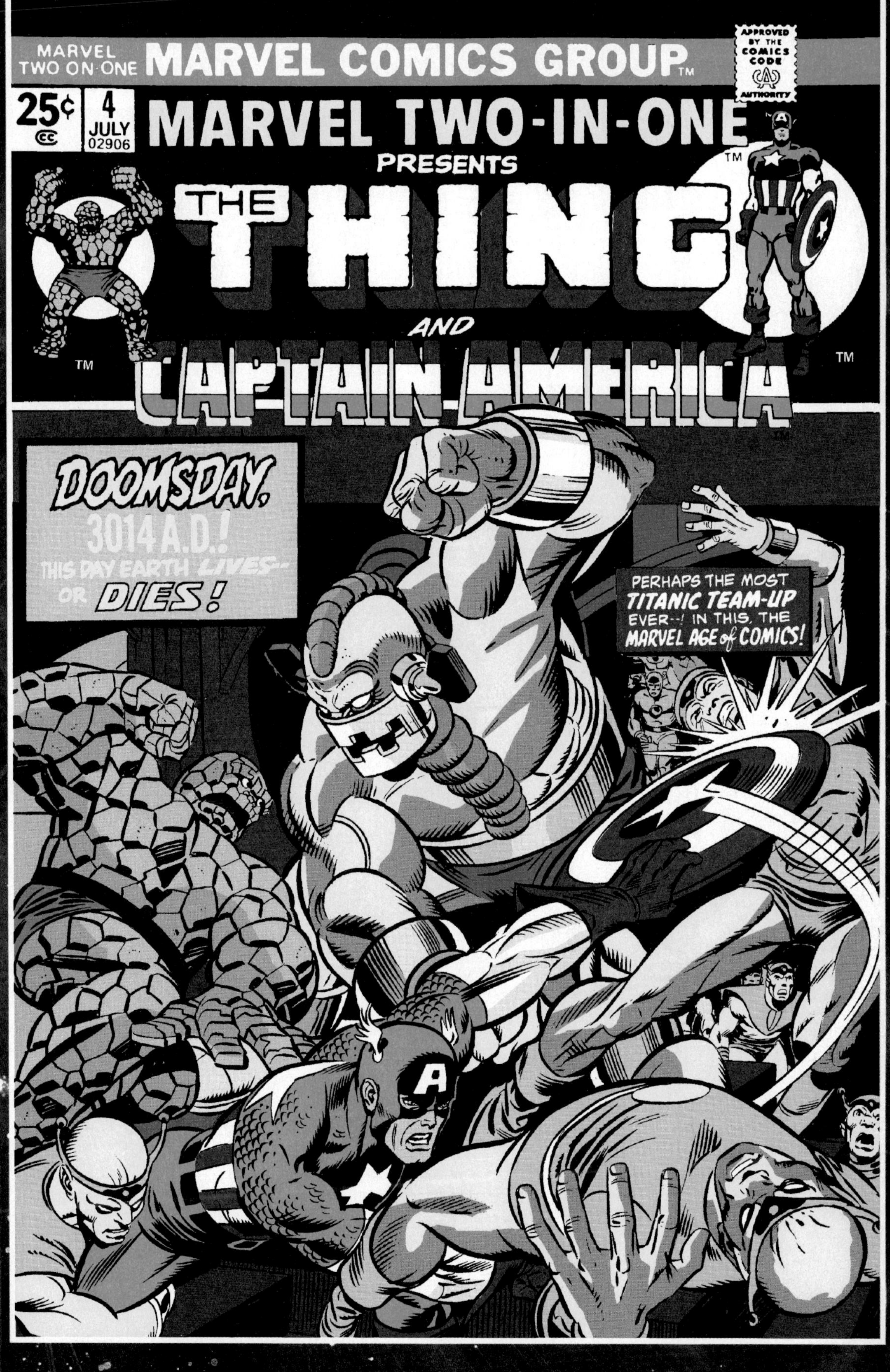
MARVEL TWO ON-ONE
MARVEL COMICS GROUP
APPROVED BY THE COMICS CODE AUTHORITY
25¢
4 JULY 02906
MARVEL TWO-IN-ONE
PRESENTS
THE THING
AND
CAPTAIN AMERICA
DOOMSDAY, 3014 A.D.! THIS DAY EARTH LIVES-- OR DIES!
PERHAPS THE MOST TITANIC TEAM-UP EVER--! IN THIS, THE MARVEL AGE of COMICS!

Stan Lee PRESENTS: The THING and CAPT. AMERICA--TOGETHER!
STEVE GERBER WRITER
SAL BUSCEMA ARTIST
F. GIACOIA INKER
C. JETTER, LETTERER
P. GOLDBERG, COLORIST
ROY THOMAS EDITOR
DOOMSDAY 3014!
CENTRAL PARK ZOO ON A SUNNY SPRING DAY IN NEW YORK.
NOT THE LIKELIEST OF PLACES TO OPEN A TALE OF THE FAR-FUTURE DESTINY OF EARTH AND MANKIND, TRUE. BUT THEN, NEITHER IS OUR PROTAGONIST A LIKELY ONE.
I OUGHTTA HAVE MY HEAD EXAMINED!
HE IS BEN GRIMM--A.K.A. THE THING!

TA THINK--ME, THE EVER-LOVIN' BLUE-EYED IDOL O' MILLIONS--STUCK PLAYIN' NURSEMAID TO A TEENAGE INFANT FROM OUTER SPACE!
LOOKA! LOOKA, UNCA BEN-JEE!
COTTON CANDY
"UNCA BEN-JEE." SHEESH!

AAH, IT AIN'T WUNDARR'S FAULT! REED* SEZ HE MUST'A GROWED UP IN SOME KINDA ISOLATION BOOTH! HE AIN'T STUPID--
HE JUST AIN'T EJJICATED! WE GOTTA HELP 'IM ADJUST.
*REED RICHARDS --LEADER OF THE FANTASTIC FOUR. --ROY.

YA WANT SOME COTTON CANDY, HUH? OKAY, THEN--STAY PUT! I'LL GIT IT!
YA DIG? DON'T MOVE!
WANNA CANDEE, UNCA BEN! CANDEE!

WHUT KIN I DO? I'M STUCK WITH 'IM-- THANKS TA SUB-MARINER!*
GIMME A WAD O' THAT STUFF, MAC.
CANDY
*THE FULL STORY WAS TOLD IN M.T. 2 IN 1 #2. --ROY.
THAT'LL BE FIFTY CENTS, PAL.

ANYWAY, HE AIN'T A BAD KID. I EVEN LIKE 'IM--
--SORTA. BUT HE'S A MENACE!

HE'S STRONG ENUFF TA TEAR THE CITY APART WITH HIS BARE HANDS!
OKAY, FELLA, HERE'S YER--
HUH?!? WHERE--?

RROOAR
AW... NO!

FOR A MOMENT, BENJAMIN GRIMM STANDS SPEECHLESS--
--AS HIS BULGING BABY BLUES GAPE WITH HORROR AT A TRANQUIL SUNDAY AFTERNOON GONE BERSERK!

AND THE CAUSE OF IT ALL?
POOR, INGENUOUS, UNCOMPREHENDING WUNDARR, WHO SIMPLY COULD NOT UNDERSTAND WHY THESE LOVELY BEASTS SHOULD BE CAGED!

I KNEW IT! I KNEW IT! I TURN MY BACK FER A HALF A MINUTE--

--AN' THE BLASTED BRAT RUNS AMOK! WELL, THIS IS THE LAST-- UNNGH
CRIPES--IT'S AN AMBUSH!

LOOK, LEO, NUTHIN' PERSONAL--I'M FER KINDNESS TA ANIMALS AN' ALL THAT--!
BUT THERE'S SUMPIN' ABOUT BEIN' GNAWED ON--

--THAT JEST GITS UNDER MY SKIN!!
SO TA SPEAK.

NUTS! I'M AS LOONEY AS TH' KID--MAKIN' JOKES WHILE HUNNERTS O' LIVES ARE IN--AWP!
BLAST IT, WUNDARR, WHEN I GIT MY MITTS ON YA--!

BUT FOR ALL HIS POWER, THE AUBURN-HAIRED ORPHAN OF SPACE IS STILL A PSYCHOLOGICAL BABE-IN-ARMS.
HE MEANT NO HARM BY WHAT HE DID. SO WHY IS EVERYONE SCREAMING?
IT ISN'T FAIR!

AW, QUIT YER BAWLIN' --BEFORE I REALLY GIVE YA SUMPIN' TA CRY ABOUT!

RATS! THE KID'S REALLY UPSET! AS IF I AIN'T GOT ENUFF TA WORRY ABOUT--
--WITHOUT TRYIN' TA PLAY DR. SPOCK, TOO!

CUT: TO A HAUNTINGLY FAMILIAR COUPLE AND A SOMEWHAT LESS FRENETIC SCENE A SHORT DISTANCE AWAY.
IRONIC, ISN'T IT, SHARON? I HAVE TO TAKE OFF MY MASK--

--TO AVOID BEING RECOGNIZED. I--
HMMM... WHAT DO YOU SUPPOSE THEY'RE RUNNING FROM?

THEY DIDN'T LOOK LIKE CRIMINALS-- MORE LIKE THEY WERE FRIGHTENED BY SOMETHING.
STEVE! IT'S THE ZOO! LOOK!
SOME KIND OF MASS PANIC! WHOLE CROWDS FLEEING!

OH, WELL...SO MUCH FOR OUR QUIET SUNDAY STROLL. LIKE IT OR NOT, I'VE GOT TO CHECK THIS OUT.
AND SO, SHARON CARTER KEEPS A TENSE VIGIL, WHILE STEVE ROGERS BECOMES--

CAPTAIN AMERICA!
THERE'S A FULL-BLOWN RIOT IN PROGRESS UP THERE.
BY NOW, EVEN AN AVENGER MAY BE TOO LITTLE TOO LATE!

MOMENTS LATER--!
SO THAT'S IT! SOME LUNATIC SET THE ANIMALS FREE!
LUCKY THE THING WAS ON THE SCENE.

GRIMM SEEMS TO HAVE THE SITUATION PRETTY MUCH UNDER CONTROL NOW.
NO POINT IN MY HANGING AROUND, I GUESS.
OR... IS THERE?

HOODS--TAKING ADVANTAGE OF THE CONFUSION...LOOTING THE DESERTED CONCESSION STANDS!

AND AS LONG AS I'M HERE, I MAY AS WELL PUT A STOP TO IT!
AM I MISTAKEN, MEN--OR IS THAT MONEY NOT YOURS?

CRUD! THIS PLACE IS CRAWLIN' WITH YOU LONG UNDERWEAR FREAKS!
AN' CRAWLIN' IS EXACTLY WHAT YOU'LL BE DOIN' AFTER I--

UNNGH!
DREAM ON, PUNK!

AND NOW, JUST TO KEEP THINGS FROM GETTING DULL, ENTER THE SUB-MARINER'S COUSIN:
NITA! DON'T! LET'S TURN BACK!
AND MISS WHAT-EVER'S CAUSING ALL THE EXCITEMENT?

GET OFF, ANNIE! YOU KNOW THAT'S NOT MY STY--
OH, WOW! ANNIE! THAT'S WUNDARR--I TOLD YOU ABOUT HIM!
WONDER IF HE'D STILL KNOW ME...?

WUNDARR--IT'S ME. REMEMBER? NITA? I'M YOUR FRIEND! *
NEE-TAH...? NEE-TAH! MY FRIEN'! NEE-TAH!
* THEY MET IN M.T. 2 IN 1 #2. --ROY.

I'M GLAD TA HEAR IT, KIDDO--
'CUZ YER GONNA NEED ALL THE FRIENDS YA CAN GIT! I AIN'T BEEN SO MAD--
MMMAD?
PLEASE, MR. GRIMM-- WHATEVER WUNDARR DID, IT'S NOT HIS FAULT!

AND YOU WON'T HELP MATTERS BY YELLING AT HIM. YOU'VE GOT TO BE PATIENT-- REASON WITH HIM.
LOOK, LADY, CAPTAIN KANGAROO I AIN'T! I'M NOT CUT OUT FER FATHERHOOD!
AND AS FER YOU--

IF YER SO CONCERNED WITH THE KID'S WELFARE, WHY'D YA RUN OUT ON 'IM LAST TIME?
I HAD TO! I HAD AN OBLIGATION TO NAMOR. BUT NOW... I'M GOING TO COLLEGE ON LONG ISLAND...
...SHARING A HOUSE WITH ANN. WE COULD TAKE WUNDARR IN -- TUTOR HIM... IF YOU'LL LET US.
WA-A-A-LL...
FAR OUT! YOU CAN COME VISIT WHENEVER YOU WANT! WE'RE IN THE PHONE BOOK-- UNDER "B. PRENTISS."

YEAH...SURE... I'LL GIVE YA A BUZZ.
TAKE GOOD CARE O' THE KID, Y'HEAR? NOT THAT I'LL MISS 'IM, BUT--
DON'T WORRY. HE'S IN GOOD HANDS.

NO SOONER HAS THE YOUTHFUL THREESOME DEPARTED THAN--
GRIMM-- ARE YOU MAD? YOU'RE LETTING THAT MAN ESCAPE?
SIMMER DOWN, CAP-- HE AIN'T NO VILLAIN. HE JEST NEEDS UNDERSTANDIN'.
WH-A-A-T?

IF YA AIN'T IN A HURRY, I'LL TELL YA ALL ABOUT IT--
--ON TH' WAY BACK TA THE BAXTER BUILDING FER A CUP O' JAVA. HOWZAT SOUND TA YOU, AVENGER?
CAP NODS...AND SUNDAY AFTERNOON IS QUIET ONCE AGAIN.

THUS, SEVERAL BLOCKS AND ONE BIZARRE EXPLANATION LATER, AT THE FABLED HEADQUARTERS OF THE FANTASTIC FOUR--
HEY, REED, MEDUSA! ANYBODY HOME?
WE'RE IN THE LAB, BEN!
I SHOULD'A KNOWN...!

OTHER GUYS PLAY GOLF OR TOSS FRISBEES OR GO FISHIN' ON SUNDAY ...BUT NOT MY PAL, REED!
HUSH, BEN! REED'S IN THE MIDST OF A CRITICAL--
IT'S OKAY, MEDUSA! I'VE MADE THE ADJUSTMENT!

DON'T YOU RECOGNIZE THIS DEVICE, BEN? IT'S IT'S DR. DOOM'S TIME MACHINE. *
I'VE BEEN MAKING SOME MODIFICATIONS ON IT'S 'LAUNCH PAD!'
YEAH? WELL, IF YER DONE, HOW 'BOUT MEDUSA MODIFYIN' SOME COFFEE..
FER OUR GUESTS.
* CAPTURED AFTER F.F. #5--GUESS WHO!

GUESTS? WHO--? CAP! GOOD TO SEE YOU!
HE'S BEEN STANDIN' THERE FER FIVE MINUTES WHILE YUH WUZ YAKKIN', REED!
C'MON, PUT AWAY YER PRINTED CIRCUITS AN' CHEW THE FAT FER AWHILE.

HATE TA ADMIT IT, BUT THIS GIZMO REALLY DOES FASCINATE ME...!
I'LL NEVER FERGIT HOW DOOM SENT US BACK TA TH' DAYS O' THE PIRATES...
...HOW I ACTUALLY WUZ BLACK-BEARD!

WONDER WHUT KINDA MODIFICATIONS REED WUZ DOIN' ON IT, ANYHOO.
POWER FEED
OFF ON
CLIK
AAH, HE'LL GIMME A WHOLE DISSERTATION ON IT LATER, I FIGGER...!

MOMENTS SUCH AS THIS ONE-- QUIET, UNHURRIED MOMENTS, FILLED WITH GOOD FRIENDS AND GOOD CONVERSATION, ARE ALL TOO RARE AMONG MEN AND WOMEN OF THE HEROIC BREED.
SO, WHEN THEY DO OCCUR, THEY ARE SAVORED, RELISHED. THOUGH THE MOOD IS LIGHT, THE TALK IS HEAVY. THE LUXURY OF CHIT-CHAT IS DISPENSED WITH.

BECAUSE THE PEACE NEVER SEEMS TO LAST LONG!
EEEEEEE
WHAZZAT?!
SOUNDED LIKE A SCREAM!

IT CAME FROM THE LAB, BEN! BUT, WHO--?

WELL, I'LL BE..! WHERE'D SHE COME FROM?
TALK, SISTER! WHO ARE YA--HOW'D YA GIT PAST OUR ALARMS--AN' WHADDAYA WANT?
YOU SPEAK ENGLISH? HOW IS THAT POSSIBLE?

WHERE AM I? WHO ARE YOU? I HAVE DONE NOTHING WRONG!
WHY HAVE YOU BROUGHT ME HERE? WHY?

DON'T BE AFRAID. NO ONE'S GOING TO HURT YOU. LOOK...
THAT'S CAPTAIN AMERICA--YOU MUST RECOGNIZE HIM--AND THE FANTASTIC FOUR.

YOU COULDN'T BE SAFER THAN YOU ARE H--OOH!
NO! YOU LIE!
YOU'RE WITH THE UNDER-GROUND! YOU MUST BE!

CAPTAIN AMERICA...THE FANTASTIC FOUR...THEY DIED... MORE THAN A THOUSAND YEARS AGO!
HUH?! WHUT'S SHE TALKIN' ABOUT?

I DON'T KNOW WHY I'M BEING MADE THE OBJECT OF THIS HOAX, BUT--
OH--NO! THE CITY--!

THEN...IT IS TRUE! IT REALLY IS...OOOH...

CHEE! SHE TOOK ONE LOOK AT NEW YORK AN' FAINTED!
WHUT'S WITH THIS CHICK? THE CITY AIN'T THAT UGLY!
AN' WE AIN'T DEAD.. ARE WE?

AS FAR AS SHE'S CONCERNED --YES! YOU MUST'VE ACCIDENTALLY SWITCHED ON THE TIME TRANSPORTER, BEN...AND IT BROUGHT HER HERE-- FROM THE YEAR 3014!
SET HER ON THE SOFA. WE'LL TRY TO REVIVE HER.

MORE THAN AN HOUR PASSES BEFORE...
HER EYES ARE OPENING. SHE'S COMING OUT OF IT.
IT'S ABOUT TIME!
THAT IS NOT AMUSING, BEN!

ASK 'ER WHUT SHE WAS MUMBLIN' IN 'ER SLEEP ABOUT... THE BABOONS!
BADOON... THE BROTHERHOOD OF BADOON...THE RULERS OF THE EARTH...
THEY CAME SEVEN YEARS AGO--IN 3007 --CONQUERED ALL BUT THE FURTHERMOST COLONIES.

MOST OF HUMANITY IS DEAD ON MY EARTH. THOSE OF US LEFT ARE KEPT AS SLAVES.
THAT IS WHY I WAS SO STUNNED TO SEE CAPTAIN AMERICA... OUR SYMBOL OF LIBERTY.
THE GUARDIANS OF THE GALAXY --LEADERS OF THE UNDERGROUND --EVEN NAMED THEIR SHIP AFTER HIM!
NOW, CAP DRAWS A DEEP BREATH AND LISTENS EVEN MORE CLOSELY...

...AS THE GIRL, WHO NAMES HERSELF TARIN, TELLS HER TALE OF A SOLAR SYSTEM ENSLAVED. AND WHEN SHE HAS FINISHED...
RICHARDS... CAN YOU WORK THAT MACHINE IN REVERSE... SEND ME INTO THE FUTURE?
I DON'T KNOW, CAP. THAT'S WHAT I WAS WORKING ON...

C'MON, REED! YOU CAN DO IT! AN' WE'LL ALL GO WITH CAP--LEND THEM GUARDIANS A HAND!
NO, BEN-- MEDUSA AND I CAN'T GO! SOMEONE HAS TO OPERATE THE MACHINE..

..IF IT'S OPERATIVE, THAT IS. I'M NOT SURE. IT'S A CHANCEY PROPOSITION.
BUT IT'S A RISK WE HAVE TO TAKE. IF CAP'S WILLING, I AM.
AND I, TOO, WOULD GO BACK...EVEN TO FACE DEATH ...FOR A CHANCE TO FREE THE EARTH.

THAT SINKS IT FER ME, STRETCH. LET'S GO GIT THEM BABOONS!

REED HASTILY BRIEFS THE FOUR "CHRONONAUTS" ...AND THEN...!
ARE YA SURE ABOUT BRINGIN' SHARON ALONG, CAP?
I'M A TRAINED SHIELD AGENT, MR. GRIMM. I CAN TAKE CARE OF MYSELF.

SAVE THE DEBATE FOR LATER. ARE YOU CERTAIN YOU UNDERSTAND MY INSTRUCTIONS?
YEAH, YEAH--WE GOTTA BE BACK AT THE SPOT WE LAND ON IN 24 HOURS--
--OR WE DON'T GIT A ROUND TRIP!
ONLY...HOW D'YA FREE A PLANET IN ONE DAY?

WE DON'T, GRIMM. THIS IS A SCOUTING MISSION--REMEMBER THAT!
I GOT A FEELIN' YA WON'T LET ME FERGIT!
NUTS--IT WUZN'T BAD ENUFF TAKIN' ORDERS FROM TH' WORLD'S GREATEST EGGHEAD--
NOW I GOTTA LISTEN TO A "SYMBOL O' LIBERTY!"

THEY'RE GONE, MEDUSA...TO WHAT, WE CAN ONLY GUESS.

PERHAPS MR. FANTASTIC CAN ONLY SPECULATE.. BUT WE CAN SEE: THE CITY OF NEW YORK IN THE 31ST CENTURY!
STILL A CITY OF TOWERING SPIRES, OF GLITTERING LIGHTS...BUT IN SHAPES UNDREAMED-OF BY MEN OF OUR DAY. IT IS, IN SHORT, A CITY THAT WORKS.
PLANETARY RADIO-TELEPORT

IT'S BREATH-TAKING! IT'S SO BEAUTIFUL! EVERYTHING HAS CHANGED-- EVERYTHING!
I'LL SAY! THE AIR DON'T EVEN SMELL! BUT WHERE ARE THE PEOPLE?

IT IS LONG PAST CURFEW FOR HUMANS. ALL MUST BE INDOORS BY NIGHTFALL.
WE, TOO, MUST FIND COVER... BEFORE ONE OF THE ZOM PATROLS SIGHTS US.
WHUT THE HECK'S A ZOM PATROL?

THE ANSWER TO THAT QUESTION COMES WITH MIND-WRENCHING SUDDENNESS, AS TWO SHAFTS OF LASER LIGHT LANCE DOWNWARD FROM THE ROOFTOPS--
THAM

--FOLLOWED BY THE MACABRE MARKSMEN THEMSELVES!
THE ZOMS!

THEY WERE MEN ONCE, THESE GLASSY-EYED SERVITORS OF THE BADOON. NOW THEY ARE BUT LIVING MACHINES, PROGRAMMED TO FULFILL A FUNCTION, THEIR CAPACITY TO THINK DESTROYED BY BADOON METHODS OF PSYCHO-SURGERY, TARIN EXPLAINS.
THERE'S NO WAY OUT-- WE'LL HAVE TO MEET THEM HEAD-ON.
NOW YER TALKIN' MY LANGUAGE, PAL!

IT'S CLOBBERIN' TIME!
I DON'T UNDERSTAND... NO MATTER HOW HARD WE HIT THEM... THEY BOUNCE BACK!

"IT'S AS IF THEY DON'T FEEL PAIN!" EXCLAIMS CAP. AND THAT IS PRECISELY THE CASE.
THAT PORTION OF THEIR BRAINS WHICH REGISTERS PAIN HAS BEEN DEADENED.

AND MORE... THEY CANNOT BE RENDERED UNCONSCIOUS!
THE ZOMS CAN BE HARMED...BUT NOT HURT.

THUS, AS CAP AND THE THING SOON REALIZE...

THE ONLY WAY TA STOP 'EM IS TA BREAK EVERY BONE IN THEIR BODIES!
I DON'T LIKE THE IDEA...
IN FACT... IT GITS ME A LITTLE SICK TA THINK ABOUT IT.

BUT IT'S EITHER THAT...OR GIT MAULED OUR-SELVES, SO...!
THE STRUGGLE LOSES ITS NOBILITY AT THAT POINT; BE-COMES A BITTER, UGLY ONE.

AND WHEN VICTORY AT LAST SEEMS IMMINENT, IT IS ACCOMPANIED BY GNAWING REMORSE.
AND BY A HIDEOUS GROWLING NOISE FROM BEHIND!

THE THING WHIRLS--!
--AND LOOKS AWESTRUCK UPON THE ULTIMATE WEAPON OF EARTH'S CONQUERORS...THE UNLIVING BEAST DUBBED THE MONSTER OF BADOON!

I DUNNO WHUT YOU ARE, MELVIN-- BUT IT'S A CINCH YA AIN'T ON OUR SIDE.
SO GUESS WHUT?

WHAMO

BUT TO BEN'S SURPRISE...AND HORROR--!
H-HOLY CRUD...I LANDED MY BEST SUNDAY PUNCH SMACK ON YER FRONT GRILLE....
...AN' YER STILL STANDIN'!!
GRRR

THOSE FEW SECONDS TURN THE TIDE. WATCH NOW...AS A HARD-WON VICTORY CRUMBLES BEFORE YOUR EYES.
SHARON IS STRUCK BY AZOM. SHE CRIES OUT!

NEXT: THE BATTLE TO FREE THE EARTH... AS THE THING AND CAPT. AMERICA ARE JOINED BY-- THE GUARDIANS OF THE GALAXY!!

MARVEL TWO-IN-ONE
MARVEL COMICS GROUP
25¢
5 SEPT 02906
MARVEL TWO-IN-ONE
PRESENTS
THE THING
AND THE
GUARDIANS OF THE GALAXY
IT'S CLOBBERIN' TIME!!
ALL THIS, AND CAPTAIN AMERICA, TOO!
ACTION -- IN THE MIGHTY MARVEL MANNER!

STEVE GERBER WRITER | SAL BUSCEMA ARTIST | MIKE ESPOSITO INKER | A. KAWECKI, LETTERER P. GOLDBERG, COLORIST | ROY THOMAS EDITOR

SEVEN AGAINST THE EMPIRE!

PLANET EARTH--
3014 A.D.

MOST OF HUMANKIND IS DEAD--AND THOSE WHO LIVE, LIVE AS SLAVES OF EARTH'S NEW MASTERS: THE REPTILIAN CONQUERORS CALLED THE BROTHERHOOD OF BADOON!

WHO ARE THEY, EBOR? HOW DID THESE THREE OF ALL MANKIND--

--FIND THE STRENGTH OF WILL TO CHALLENGE MY RULE!

INTO THIS GRIM NEW WORLD HAVE COME SHARON CARTER...CAPTAIN AMERICA... AND THE THING.

AND THEY HAVE BEEN RECEIVED ...LESS THAN GRACIOUSLY.

THE MEANING OF THIS ONE'S COSTUME--THE NATURE OF THE LARGE ONE'S DEFORMITY--
--THE OBJECT OF THEIR MISSION--AND WHO SENT THEM ON IT! I MUST KNOW!

AND YOU SHALL, LORDSHIP DRANG! SPEAK, HUMAN! THE SOVEREIGN WOULD KNOW YOUR IDENTITY...
...AND WHY YOU DARED VIOLATE THE CURFEW FOR THOSE OF YOUR RACE!
I DON'T ...HAVE... A SOVEREIGN. I'M A FREE--

FREE?! THIS IS HOW "FREE" YOU ARE, PINKSKIN! FREE TO DIE--
--FREE TO BE RENT LIMB FROM LIMB IF YOU REFUSE TO COOPERATE!

ENOUGH, INQUISITOR! HE MUST NOT PERISH--YET. NOT BEFORE WE HAVE OUR INFORMATION!
EMPLOY THE MEMORY PROBE!

FROM THE CEILING IT DESCENDS, AMID THE METALLIC CRANKING OF GEARS AND THE SOFT WHIRR OF COMPUTERS.

THE BADOON MEMORY PROBE: NOT NEARLY SO SINISTER IN APPEARANCE ...AS IT IS IN OPERATION.

FOR ITS PURPOSE IS TO ENTER THE PSYCHE... SORT OUT RELEVANT DATA... AND PROJECT SAME FOR ALL TO SEE.
AND THE PROCESS IS... MOST PAINFUL.

THE PROBE'S VOCAL STIMULATOR CLICKS ON, AND DRANG LISTENS, AGHAST AT THE STORY "IT" TELLS:
"MY NAME IS STEVE ROGERS, KNOWN ALSO AS CAPTAIN AMERICA.
"MY COMPANIONS ARE SHARON CARTER, AGENT OF SHIELD, AND BENJAMIN GRIMM, KNOWN ALSO AS THE THING. WE COME FROM WHAT IS TO YOU, EARTH'S DISTANT PAST-- 1974 A.D. OUR MISSION BEGAN WHEN REED RICHARDS' TIME MACHINE ACCIDENTALLY BROUGHT AN EARTHWOMAN NAMED TARIN FROM YOUR ERA INTO OURS.
"AT FIRST, SHE WAS TERRIFIED...REFUSED TO BELIEVE WHAT HAD OCCURRED...UNTIL SHE SAW 20th CENTURY NEW YORK WITH HER OWN EYES... AND FAINTED AT THE SIGHT. WHEN SHE AWOKE, SHE TOLD US OF THE BADOON CONQUEST, OF THE ENSLAVEMENT OF HUMANITY. AND I LEARNED THAT THE MOST PROMINENT FREEDOM FIGHTERS OF THIS ERA--THE GUARDIANS OF THE GALAXY--HAD CHOSEN ME AS THE SYMBOL OF THEIR RESISTANCE--EVEN NAMED THEIR STARSHIP THE "CAPTAIN AMERICA." I WAS TOUCHED... AND ENRAGED.
"I DEMANDED THAT RICHARDS RETURN ME TO THE FUTURE WITH TARIN. BEN AND SHARON INSISTED UPON COMING.
"HERE, WE WERE SET UPON BY THE LOBOTOMIZED, PROGRAMMED HUMAN GUARDS YOU BADOON CREATED--THE ZOMS. IT WAS A BRUTAL STRUGGLE...
"...AND A HUMILIATING ONE, FIGHTING OTHER MEN WHILE YOU WATCHED. AND YET, WE HAD WON...

"...UNTIL YOU UNLEASHED YOUR MONSTER, AND IT TOOK OUT THE THING. WITHOUT HIS STRENGTH, WE FELL TO THE ZOMS' SHEER NUMBERS.

"I AWOKE HERE, MOMENTS AGO. THAT IS ALL I REMEM—"
THE VOCAL STIMULATOR CLICKS OFF.
THE SCREEN GOES BLACK.
AND A GRIM HUSH FALLS OVER THE ROYAL CHAMBER.

UNTIL DRANG CAN CONTAIN HIS HORROR NO MORE--!
MEN OF OLD EARTH! AND NOT MERELY MEN--BUT HEROES!
AND A LIVING SYMBOL OF LIBERTY AT THAT!

LORDSIRE, THEY MUST BE PUT TO DEATH AT ONCE--ALONG WITH THE WOMAN TARIN WHEN SHE IS FOUND!
THEY PRESENT THE FIRST REAL THREAT TO OUR RULE OF SOL-III.

BUSTER--YOU DON'T KNOW HOW REAL!

THE ORANGE-SKINNED ONE--HE'S RECOVERED CONSCIOUSNESS!
FWAM
BETCHA WISH YA COULD SAY TH' SAME FER BIG BOY, HERE!

HIT TH' FLOOR, CAP! HE'S FALLIN' RIGHT ATCHA! AN' IF HE CONNECTS--
CRUNCH
NO! NO!! THE MONSTER'S TORN OPEN THE PROBE'S POWER SOURCE! HE'LL BE--
I'M 'WAY AHEAD OF YOU, BEN!

"--ELECTROCUTED!!"
ZZZAK

ZOMS--CUT THEM DOWN! YOUR LORD-SIRE COMMANDS! THEY MUST NOT ESCAPE!

KILL THEM!!

SORRY, CHUMS--WE DON'T WANT ANY!

NICE WORK, BEN--THEY'LL BE SCRAPING ZOMS OFF THE WALLS FOR WEEKS! BUT THERE ARE MORE OF THEM COMING! WE'VE GOT TO GET OUT OF HERE!
THAT'S JUST WHUT I'M DOIN', PAL! FOLLOW ME!

BEFORE THE TRIO CAN EVEN REACH THE PALACE STEPS, THE MOURNFUL WAIL OF SIRENS SPLITS THE SILENCE OF THE NIGHT...!
WOOOOO

THUS, WHEN THEY DO EMERGE FROM DRANG'S SANCTUM--
UH-OH. LOOKS LIKE WE GOT COMPANY.

SPECIFICALLY: THE BADOON ELITE GUARD AND ANOTHER HORDE (OR TWO) OF MINDLESS, NERVELESS ZOMS, ALL BENT ON THE SAME END...
THERE! THERE THEY ARE! DESTROY THEM!

CRIPES--THERE MUST BE THOUSANDS O' THEM ZOMS AN' BABOONS! BUT THEY AIN'T GETTIN' ME!
BEN--WAIT! YOU DON'T KNOW HOW TO DRIVE THAT CAR!
CAP'S RIGHT, BEN! IT COULD BE DANGEROUS!

MEBBE. BUT, SEE...DRIVIN' IT AIN'T WHUT I HAD IN MIND!

I WUZ THINKIN' MORE OF A FAST GAME O' CATCH!

CAP TURNS HIS ASTOUNDED EYES FROM THE DEVASTATION AND CHAOS THE THING HAS WROUGHT ...BACK TO THE WOMAN HE LOVES.
AND WHEN HE IS ASSURED THAT AGENT 13...

... IS MORE THAN HOLDING HER OWN...
FOOM

...THIS MAN WHO HAD BEEN A LEGEND TO ALL FREEDOM-LOVING PEOPLES SINCE THE DARK DAYS OF WORLD WAR II...
...SWINGS INTO ACTION!

THUS DO THE BADOON EXPERIENCE FIRSTHAND THE STUFF OF WHICH SUCH LEGENDS ARE MADE!
BUT THEY BARELY SEE THE MAN HIM-SELF--ONLY A STREAK OF RED AND WHITE AND BLUE...

...OR A FLASH OF ANGER IN CLEAR AZURE EYES...OR A SILVERY GLINT OF MOONLIGHT ON METAL.

AND THEY HAVE NO TIME TO LOOK AGAIN, MORE CLOSELY.
CHOOM

STILL, IT'S SOON APPARENT...
THERE'S TOO MANY OF 'EM! WE CAN'T FIGHT THE WHOLE BLAMED PLANET!!
LET'S MOVE! TAKE TA THE ALLEYS--IF THERE ARE ANY!

NUTS! THIS CITY'S SO CLEAN--IT'S DISGUSTIN'!
NOT EVEN A TRASH CAN TA HIDE BEHIND!
THIS WAY, BEN--AROUND THIS CORNER --FAST!

WE'VE DONE IT! WE'LL WAIT 'TIL THEY'VE ALL PASSED--

"--THEN MOVE OUT--TRY TO LOCATE TARIN AND, IF WE'RE LUCKY, THE RESISTANCE."
YOU MUST BELIEVE ME! NOW IS THE TIME TO BAND TOGETHER--AND STRIKE! WE DARE NOT DELAY, ZAKKOR!

WE REMAIN... UNCONVINCED, TARIN. THIS TALE YOU BRING US OF CAPTAIN AMERICA, ALIVE AND IN OUR MIDST, IS... DIFFICULT AT BEST TO ACCEPT.
YOU HAVE NEVER BEEN WILLING TO JOIN US BEFORE, YET YOU ASK US NOW TO RISK OUR PEOPLE'S LIVES ON THE BASIS OF THIS WILD STORY.
SPEAKING BLUNTLY, TARIN--WHY SHOULD WE TRUST YOU?

BECAUSE I AM SPEAKING THE TRUTH! I SWEAR IT!
I DID NOT JOIN THE RESISTANCE BEFORE, BECAUSE I THOUGHT YOUR EFFORTS FUTILE. BUT NOW...!

SUDDENLY--!
ZAKKOR! I MUST CONFER WITH YOU AT ONCE!
WHAT--? QARL, THIS IS A CLOSED SESSION! WE ARE--

FORGIVE ME, ZAKKOR, THIS CANNOT WAIT! I HAVE URGENT NEWS--OF A BATTLE ON THE PALACE STEPS...
...BETWEEN THE BADOON GUARDS AND CAPTAIN AMERICA! I'VE GOT IT ON MY VISICORDER, SIR!
WHAT?!

AND WHEN THAT RECORDING HAS BEEN PLAYED...!
TARIN...TRY TO FORGIVE OUR SUSPICIONS. WE SHALL DO AS YOU ASKED: CALL TOGETHER ALL OUR FORCES...AND SUMMON BACK TO EARTH--
--THE GUARDIANS OF THE GALAXY!

THE GUARDIANS OF THE GALAXY: FOUR LONE SURVIVORS OF FOUR LOST WORLDS, EACH PLEDGED TO DESTROY THE BROTHERHOOD OF BADOON!
MAJOR VANCE ASTRO: THE FIRST EARTHMAN TO THE STARS, THE LAST SURVIVOR OF THE 20th CENTURY--A 1000-YEAR-OLD MASTER OF PSYCHOKINESIS.
CHARLIE-27: LAST SURVIVOR OF EARTH'S JUPITER COLONY, BRED TO LIVE ON A PLANET WITH 11 TIMES THE MASS AND THRICE THE GRAVITY OF EARTH--POSSESSED OF SUPERHUMAN STRENGTH.
YONDU: NATIVE OF EARTH-COLONIZED CENTAURI-IV, LAST OF A RACE OF BAR-BARIANS--A MASTER OF WEAPONRY.
MARTINEX: THE CRYSTAL MAN WHOSE BODY CAN CON-VERT LIGHT WAVES INTO BURSTS OF EXTREME HEAT AND COLD; LAST SURVIVOR OF EARTH'S PLUTONIAN COLONY.
VANCE...I'M PICKING UP A COMMUNICATION FROM EARTH--ON OUR FREQUENCY.
IT MUST BE ZAKKOR. ONLY HE KNOWS OUR SHIP IS IN THIS SECTOR OF SPACE.

IT'S A VISICORDER TAPE, HE SAYS... SOMETHING YOU IN PARTICULAR SHOULD WANT TO SEE.
THOSE ARE HIS EXACT WORDS.
PUT IT ON THE SCREEN, MARTINEX. I'LL HAVE A--

--GOOD LORD! IT CAN'T BE!

IT'S HIM--IT'S CAPTAIN AMERICA! I'D KNOW THAT FIGHTING STANCE ANYWHERE! IT'S REALLY HIM!
AND HE'S ALIVE ON EARTH--RIGHT NOW!
IT CAN'T BE A HOAX...ZAKKOR WOULDN'T...IT'S A MIRACLE! THE CHANCE WE'VE WAITED FOR!

THE BADOON ARE PANICKING...THE PEOPLE ARE RISING UP IN ANGER!
VANCE... WAIT! WHAT ARE YOU DOING?

UNLESS ANY OF YOU OBJECT--I'M LAYING IN A COURSE FOR EARTH, MY FRIENDS.
OBJECT? TO MEETING THE BADOON HEAD-ON? NOT ME!
READY TO SWITCH TO HARKOVIAN HYPERDRIVE ANYTIME, VANCE.

NOW, MARTINEX! WE'VE GOT A WAR TO WIN--BACK HOME.
THUS, THE GOOD SHIP "CAPTAIN AMERICA" LEAVES ITS ORBIT ABOUT THE MARTIAN MOON PHOBOS, BOUND FOR EARTH...

--WHERE, SEVERAL HOURS LATER, WE FIND OUR TRIO STILL ENGAGED IN WHAT THEY WERE DOING SEVERAL HOURS AGO.
WE BEEN UP'N'DOWN MANHATTAN FIVE TIMES NOW, CAP. WHUT IF ALL TH' RESISTERS MOVED TA BROOKLYN?!

AAH, MEBBE WE'LL HAVE BETTER LUCK THIS--
OOOPS!
GUESS WHUT I FOUND?

A WHOLE PLATOON O' BABOONS--AN' THEY FOUND US, TOO!
THE MONSTER FROM OLD EARTH! AFTER HIM!

YER CALLIN' ME A MONSTER??
NOW THAT'S WHUT I CALL AN INSULT, MAC!
SAVE THE DEBATE ON AESTHETICS FOR LATER, THING! LAY INTO THEM!
TAKE AIM--FIRE!--THEY CAN'T WITHSTAND YOUR RAY-RIFLES!
COMMANDER OGG WAS A FOOL TO ATTACK THE EARTHMEN WITHOUT REINFORCEMENTS!

HE HOPED TO DEFEAT THEM AND CLAIM ALL THE GLORY FOR HIMSELF... AND HE HAS FAILED.
IT FALLS TO ME TO SOUND THE ALARM!

AND WHEN LORDSIRE DRANG HEARS HOW I--HOW I--I--
URRK

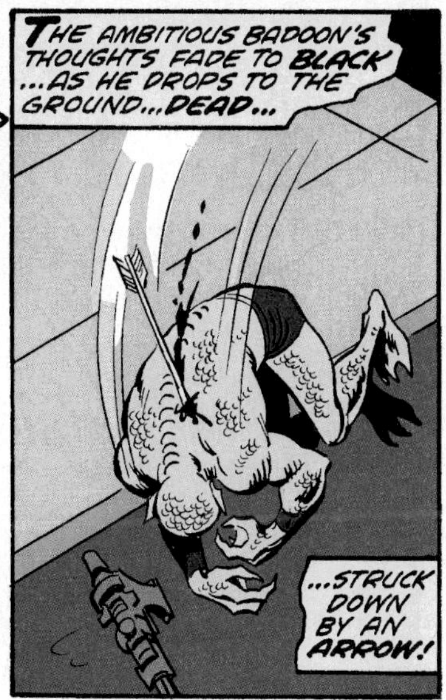
THE AMBITIOUS BADOON'S THOUGHTS FADE TO BLACK ...AS HE DROPS TO THE GROUND...DEAD...
...STRUCK DOWN BY AN ARROW!

THE GUARDIANS OF THE GALAXY HAVE COME EARTH-SIDE--WITH A VENGEANCE!
FOR ALL THE POWER OF THEIR FLASH-GUNS, STILL THEY FLEE FROM MY LIGHTNING BOW!
A COWARD WITH A GUN IS STILL A COWARD, YONDU!
HUH?! WHO IN THE NAME O'--?

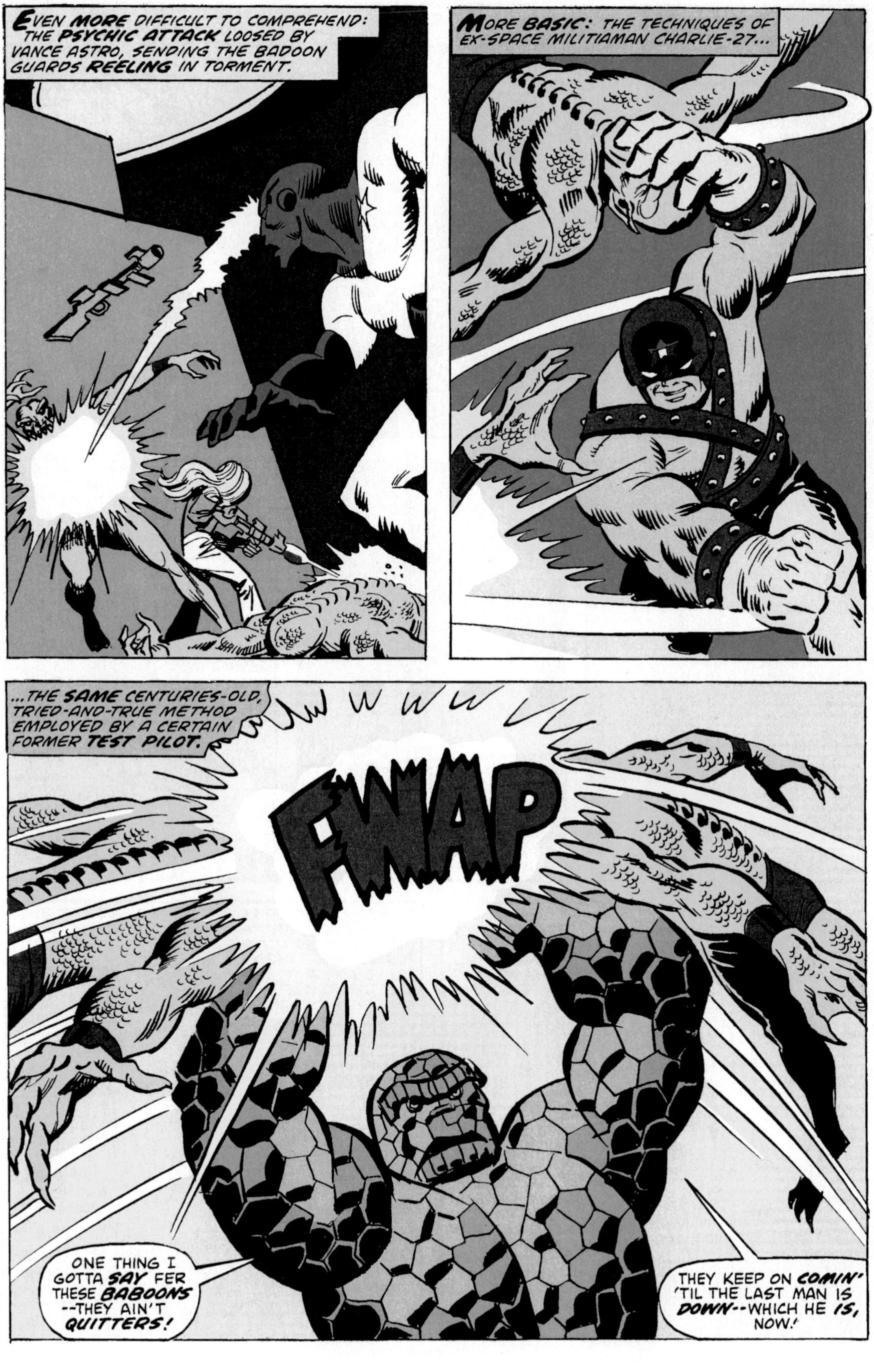

...THE SAME CENTURIES-OLD, TRIED-AND-TRUE METHOD EMPLOYED BY A CERTAIN FORMER TEST PILOT.

FWAP

ONE THING I GOTTA SAY FER THESE BABOONS --THEY AIN'T QUITTERS!

THEY KEEP ON COMIN' 'TIL THE LAST MAN IS DOWN--WHICH HE IS, NOW!

AND THAT BEING THE CASE, I THINK WE CAN AFFORD THE LUXURY OF A FRIENDLY GREETING, AT LEAST.
--THE GUARDIANS OF THE GALAXY, YOU MUST BE. WE'VE LOOKED FORWARD TO THIS MEETING SINCE WE ARRIVED.
I'M MAJOR VANCE ASTRO, CAP. MY COMRADES AND I ARE KNOWN AS--
AND I'VE BEEN WAITING TEN CENTURIES TO SHAKE YOUR HAND.

YOU SEE, YOU WERE MY BOYHOOD IDOL, CAP. I EVEN SAW YOU IN ACTION IN PERSON ONCE, WITH YOUR PARTNER THE FALCON, BACK IN 1972, I THINK.
IN PERSON--? I DON'T UNDERSTAND. HOW--?
I WAS BORN JULY THIRD, 1962, CAP.
WHA-A-AT?? BUT THAT MEANS YER MORE'N A THOUSAND YEARS OLD!

"EXACTLY, MR. GRIMM. BUT I SPENT MOST OF THOSE YEARS ASLEEP, IN SUSPENDED ANIMATION...
...ABOARD THE FIRST AMERICAN ROCKET BOUND FOR THE STARS.

"I LEFT THE EARTH IN 1988, TRAVELLING AT A VELOCITY OF A MILLION MILES PER HOUR.
"EVEN AT THAT SPEED, THE JOURNEY TO EARTH'S NEAREST STELLAR NEIGHBOR REQUIRED A MILLENIUM. BUT A MERE 200 YEARS AFTER I LEFT...

"...A MAN NAMED HARKOV CAME ALONG WITH A NEW THEORY OF PHYSICS THAT MADE FASTER-THAN-LIGHT SPACE TRAVEL A REALITY.
"WHEN I CAME OUT OF MY SHIP ON CENTAURI-IV, A COLONY OF EARTHMEN WAS THERE TO GREET ME!

"I FELT AS YOU MUST HAVE, CAP, WHEN YOU WERE RELEASED FROM THAT ICEBERG BACK IN 1964, AFTER SLUMBERING FOR TWO DECADES.* ONLY I WASN'T AS LUCKY: AS WITH YOU, MY WORLD, ALL THE PEOPLE I'D KNOWN AND LOVED, WERE DEAD AND GONE. BUT YOU HADN'T AGED DURING YOUR SLEEP-- I HAD!
"I AM A PRISONER OF THE COPPER FOIL SUIT THAT SUSTAINS MY LIFE. ONE PUNCTURE, ANY EXPOSURE OF MY SKIN TO FRESH AIR...AND I CRUMBLE INTO DUST. MARTINEX, OUR GROUP'S SCIENTIST, DESIGNED THIS ADDITIONAL OUTER SHELL I WEAR TO PREVENT JUST THAT."
*AVENGERS #4. --ROY.

INCREDIBLE! IF I'D READ THAT STORY AS FICTION, I'D HAVE CALLED IT PREPOSTEROUS. AND YET, YOU'VE LIVED IT! WE MUST CONTINUE THIS CONVERSATION, VANCE...
...AFTER WE'VE GOTTEN WORD TO THE UNDERGROUND TO MARSHAL THEIR FORCES, PREPARE TO--
THAT WON'T BE NECESSARY, CAPTAIN AMERICA!
HUH--?! WHOOZAT??
YOU!!

GREETINGS, GUARDIANS --AND HEROES OF OLD EARTH. I AM ZAKKOR, LEADER OF THE TERRAN UNDERGROUND.
I AND MY FELLOW MEN STAND READY TO FOLLOW YOU INTO BATTLE AGAINST THE BADOON.
AND WE ARE BUT THE FIRST CONTINGENT. WORD OF YOUR ARRIVAL IS SPREADING.
SOON, EVERY HUMAN IN THE NEW YORK SECTOR WILL CONVERGE ON THIS SPOT!

WELL, WHADDAYA KNOW! AN INSTANT ARMY!
NOT SO INSTANT, BEN. THESE PEOPLE HAVE BEEN IN BONDAGE FOR SEVEN LONG YEARS.
AND IT'S TAKEN YOU ALL OF SEVEN HOURS TO MOBILIZE THEM!

WE CAN HAND OUT THE MEDALS LATER, VANCE. RIGHT NOW...
...OUR JOB IS TO FORMULATE A PLAN OF ACTION!
PLAN SCHMAN! YOU FORMULATE! FER ME--

IT'S CLOBBERIN' TIME!

BEN--WAIT! YOU CAN'T JUST-- OH, WHAT'S THE USE?!
LET'S GO!!

THE SUN IS RISING OVER THE CITY AS THE FIRST WAVE OF REBEL FORCES THUNDERS THROUGH THE PALACE GATES.
AND THE SUN WILL RISE THE NEXT DAY, WHETHER THESE MEN AND WOMEN WIN OR LOSE...LIVE OR DIE. YET THEY SEE THE NEW MORNING AS AN OMEN...
THE MONSTER! BRING ON THE MONSTER OF BADOON TO FELL THE ORANGE-SKINNED EARTH-MAN!

...AND EVEN IN THE FACE OF THIS HOR-ROR, THEY FIGHT ON!
HOLY CROW! IT'S STILL ALIVE! I FIGGERED THE ELEC-TRIC SHOCK WASTED 'IM!

THOSE'RE MY FRIENDS YER SHOVIN' AROUND, UGLY!
AN' ONE SHOVE O' YERS IS ENUFF TA KILL 'EM!
SPAK!

IN FACT...YA DON'T DO WON-DERS FER ME, EITHER!
YER STRONGER--AN' MEANER--THAN YA LOOK! AN' BELIEVE ME, THAT AIN'T EASY!
HANG ON, THING! I'M COMING!

TOGETHER, NOW--THREE--TWO--ONE--
THWAMO

THE MONSTER IS DOWNED, AND THE EARTHMEN SWEEP THROUGH THE BADOON PALACE, THEIR BLADES AND BLUDGEONS BLAZING A TRAIL OF REPTILIAN BLOOD TO THE THRONE.
AND NOT ALL THE TERRANS REACH THAT GOAL.
FOR THIS IS WAR... AND PEOPLE DIE IN WARS... BOTH THE BAD GUYS... AND THE GOOD.
THE CONFLICT-- THE DYING-- RAGES ON FOR HOURS.
AND WHOEVER DIES MORE... LOSES.

BUT WHEN, AT LAST, THE FIGHTING IS DONE, "OUR" SIDE IS THE VICTOR.
THIS WAY, "LORDSIRE." YOUR CONQUERORS AWAIT!
IT'S TARIN! SHE'S CAPTURED DRANG!

GLOAT NOW-- WHILE YOU MAY!
YOU'VE SEIZED ONE CITY!

WE CONTROL THE WHOLE PLANET --THE SOLAR SYSTEM--THIS ENTIRE SECTOR OF THE GALAXY!!
YOU'LL NEVER-- URRRK

WHAT DOES IT TAKE TA SHOW YA WE MEAN BIZNESS, DRANG? WE KNOW WE GOT A LONG, HARD FIGHT AHEAD--BUT YER BABOON BROTHERHOOD IS PFFFFT!
DIG?

HE'S RIGHT, DRANG. MAN WON'T SETTLE FOR A FLEETING TASTE OF LIBERTY. WE'RE NOT MADE THAT WAY. THE NEED TO BE FREE IS IN OUR BLOOD. YOUR EMPIRE WILL FALL, BECAUSE IT MUST-- BECAUSE WE ARE HUMAN.

SOMETIME LATER: 24 HOURS AFTER THEIR ARRIVAL IN THE FUTURE, THREE WEARY CHRONONAUTS BID SAD FAREWELLS.
TAKE CARE...ALL OF YOU! AND THANK YOU!
THE TIME TRANSPORTER PLANE DESCENDS... AND IN MOMENTS THEY WILL VANISH INTO THE PAST...BACK INTO LEGEND AGAIN.
SAY "HELLO" TO THE OLD DAYS FOR ME, GUYS.
AND IN THAT BYGONE ERA WE CALL "THE PRESENT," THE THING WILL CONFRONT A NEW AND DIFFERENT MANNER OF MENACE, THE LIKE OF WHICH--AH, BUT THAT IS A TALE FOR NEXT ISSUE, WHEN BEN MEETS...
DOCTOR STRANGE!

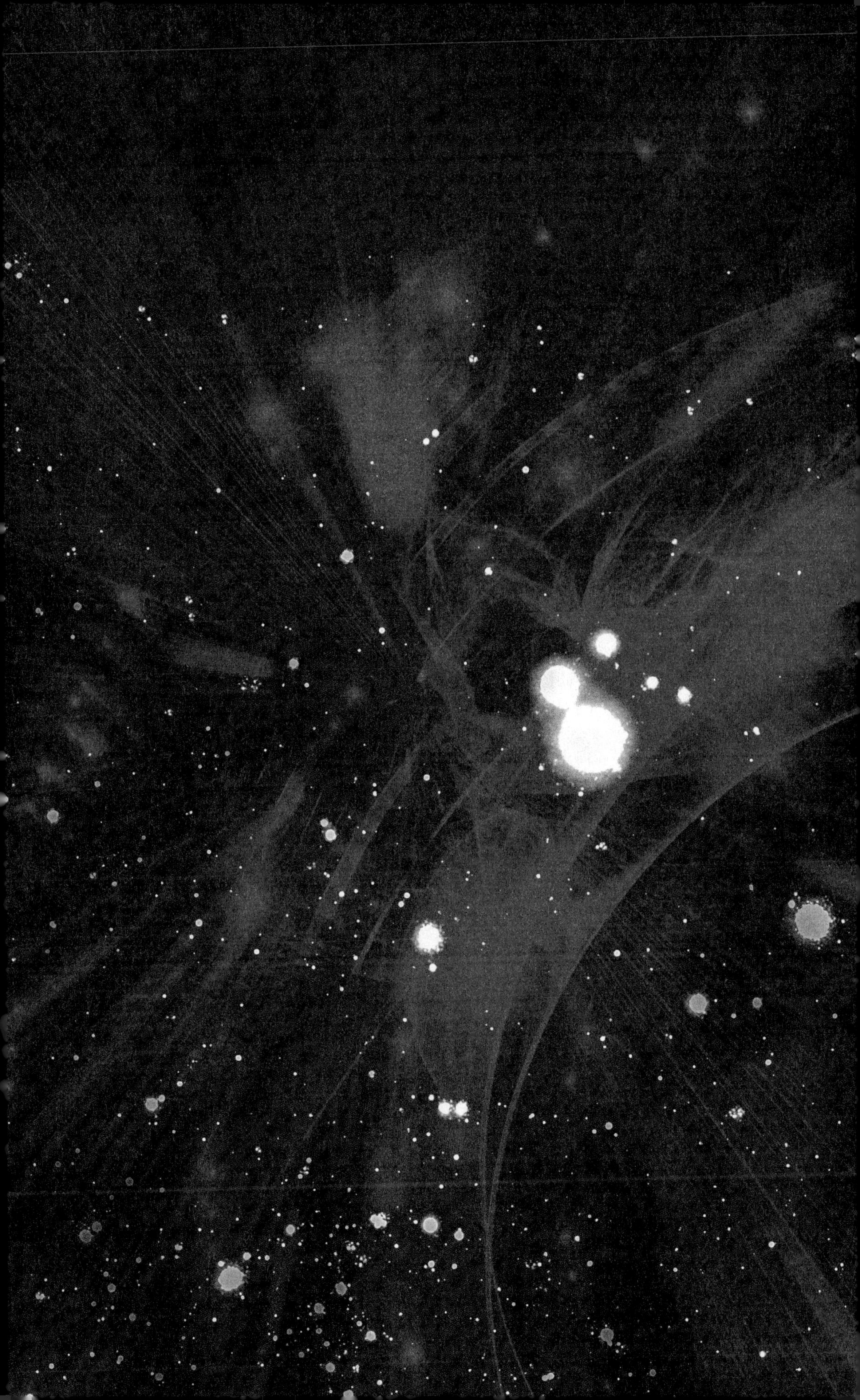

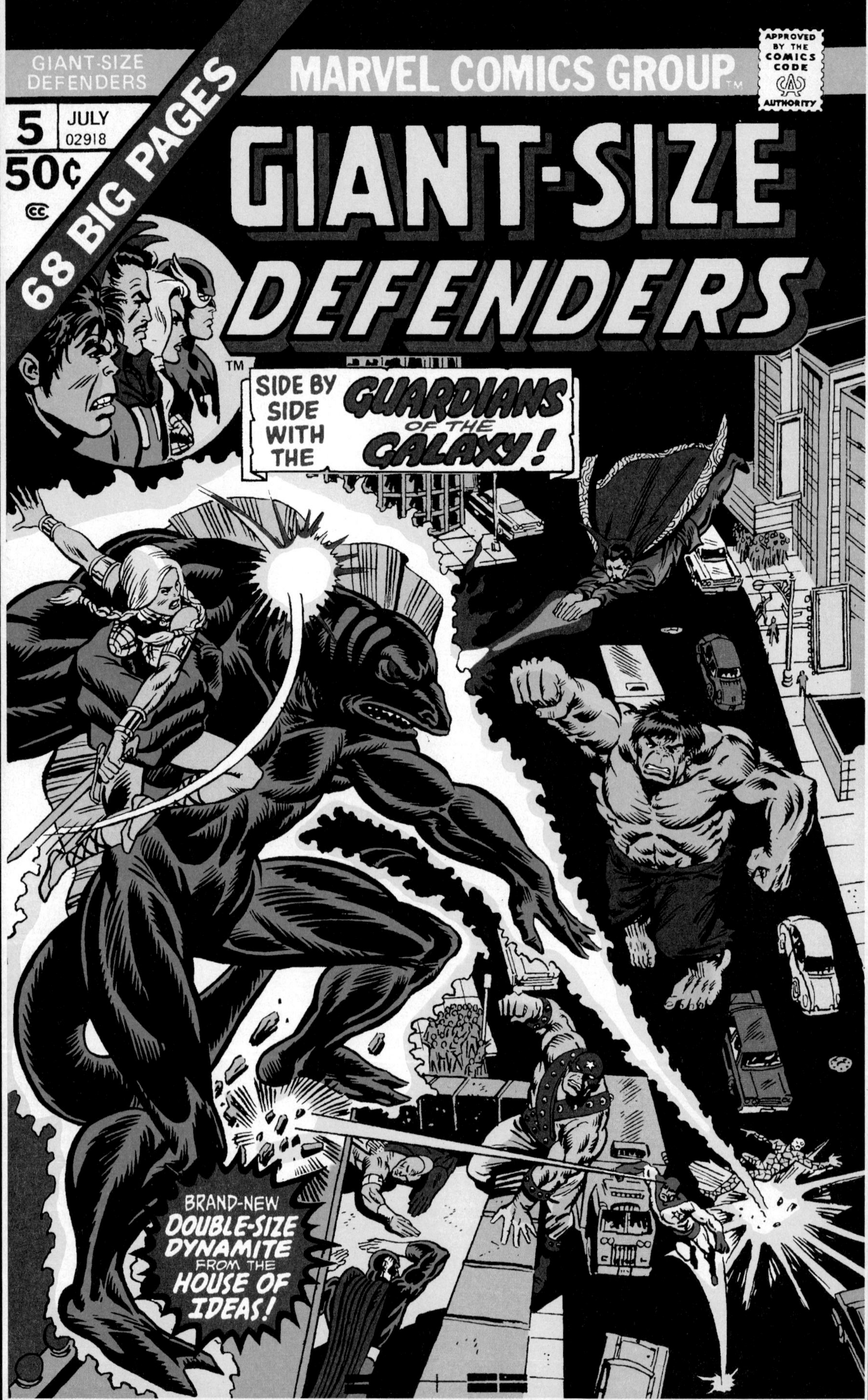
GIANT-SIZE DEFENDERS
68 BIG PAGES
MARVEL COMICS GROUP
APPROVED BY THE COMICS CODE AUTHORITY
5
JULY
02918
50¢
GIANT-SIZE DEFENDERS
SIDE BY SIDE WITH THE GUARDIANS OF THE GALAXY!
BRAND-NEW DOUBLE-SIZE DYNAMITE FROM THE HOUSE OF IDEAS!

Stan Lee PRESENTS: THE DYNAMIC DEFENDERS!™

YOU WON'T BELIEVE THIS, BUT... **STEVE GERBER, GERRY CONWAY, ROGER SLIFER, LEN WEIN, CHRIS CLAREMONT,** AND **SCOTT EDELMAN** PLOTTED THIS TALE. **STEVE** SCRIPTED IT. **DON HECK** DREW IT. **MIKE ESPOSITO** INKED IT. **DAVE HUNT** INKED THE BACKGROUNDS AND LETTERED IT. **G. ROUSSOS** COLORED IT. **LEN** EDITED IT. COFFEE AND MORAL SUPPORT WERE PROVIDED (FOR A PRICE) BY THE LANTERN COFFEE SHOP ON 53RD ST. AND **CARLA** MADE THE MEATLOAF. ONCE YOU'VE READ IT--THE **STORY,** NOT THE MEATLOAF--YOU MAY WONDER **WHY.** ANSWER: WHY NOT?

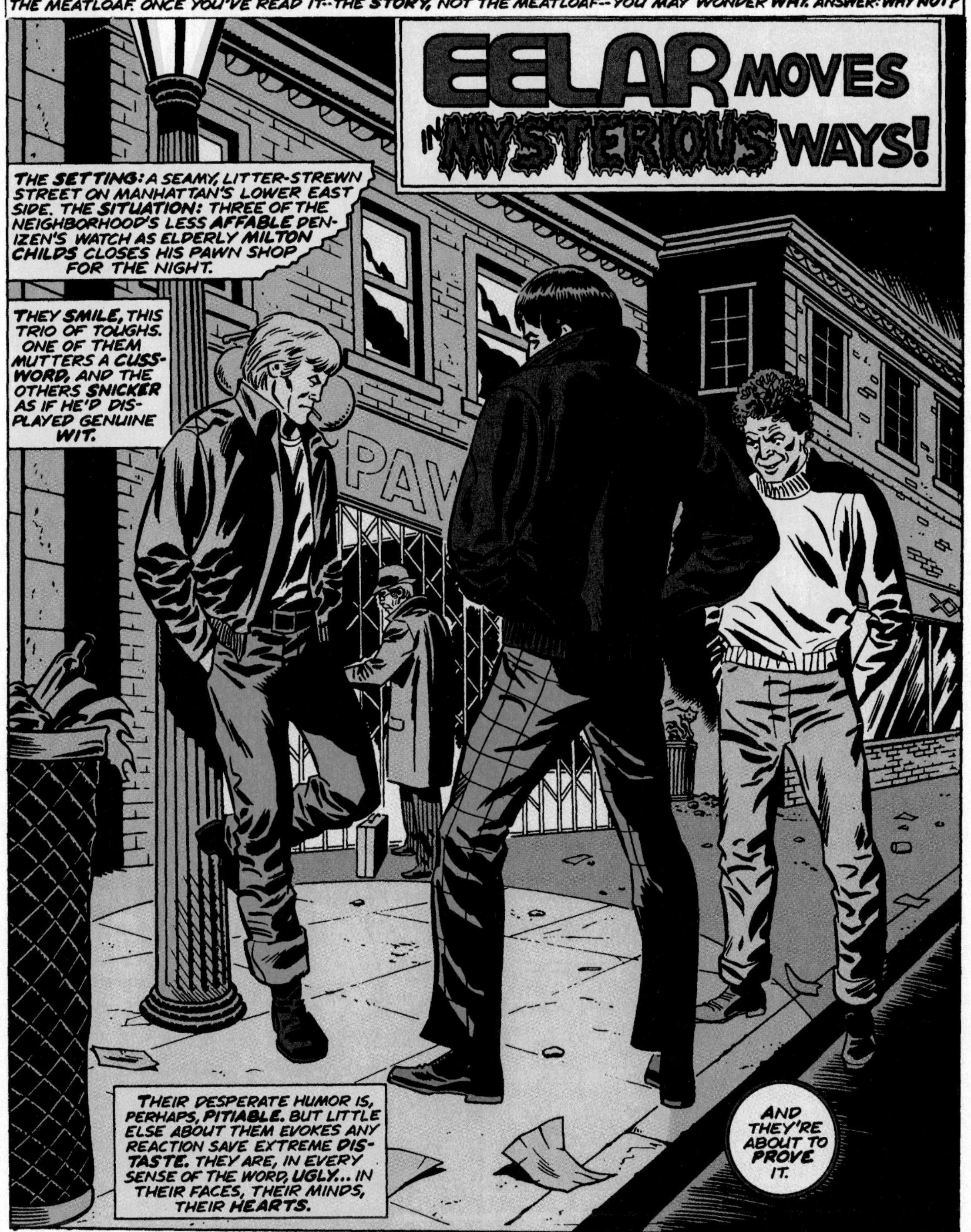

CHILDS SPIES THEM FROM THE CORNER OF HIS EYE.

THEY THINK THAT'S FUNNY, TOO.

HE DEPARTS.

THEY FOLLOW.

HE WALKS FASTER.

SO DO THEY.

HE BOLTS AND RUNS.
SO DO THEY.

HEART POUNDING WILDLY WITH FEAR, HE GLANCES OVER HIS SHOULDER.
THEY ARE THERE.

WHERE'S THE FIRE, POPS? SLOW UP! WE WANNA TALK TA YA!
T-TAKE YOUR HAND OFF ME! I'LL YELL FOR THE POLICE! I SWEAR I WILL!
HEY, HEY...!

THAT AIN'T FUNNY, GRAN'PA. IT AIN'T FUNNY AT ALL.
FIRST YA RUN AWAY FROM US--NOW YA WANNA RING IN THE PIGS--! WHAT IS IT WITH YOU, ANYWAY?
WE WANT YA TA LIKE US--OR WE MAY KILL YA.
CLITCH
HOW 'BOUT IT, OLD MAN? YOU LIKE US?

ENOUGH TA GIVE US SOME MONEY, MAYBE?
SURE, YA DO. STEP INTA THE ALLEY AN' WE'LL DISCUSS IT.
HIGH OVERHEAD, UNAWARE OF CHILDS' PLIGHT, A DECIDEDLY DIFFERENT TRIO PURSUES A SOMEWHAT MORE ELUSIVE AND ESOTERIC OBJECTIVE.
...TEMPORAL DISPLACEMENT VIBRATIONS, HULK. A DISTURBANCE IN THE FLOW OF TIME.
AND WE MUST LOCATE THE SOURCE OF THE DISRUPTION.
TRUTH TO TELL, STEPHEN, I'M NOT CERTAIN I UNDERSTAND, EITHER.
HUH! WHY? SOUNDS DUMB TO HULK!
DR. STRANGE, MYSTIC MASTER--VALKYRIE, WOMAN WARRIOR--THE HULK, BIG GREEN STRONG PERSON...THREE MEMBERS OF THE DYNAMIC NON-TEAM KNOWN AS THE DEFENDERS.
EARTH'S VERY EXISTENCE MAY HANG IN THE BALANCE, VAL.
SHOULD IT GROW IN INTENSITY, SUCH TURBULENCE IN THE TIME-STREAM COULD HURL THE WORLD INTO DARK, COLD LIMBO...
...ENDING ALL LIFE ON THE FACE OF THE PLANET.
AND THERE-- IN THAT GLOWING AREA IN THE HARBOR, WE SHALL, I SUSPECT, FIND THE CAUSE OF THE PHENOMENON.

EVEN AS THE MASTER MAGE SPEAKS, A FERRYBOAT STEAMS TOWARD THE CURIOUS LUMINOSITY.
AND AS THE PROW PENETRATES THE EDGE OF THE GLOW...

THE SEA COMMENCES TO BUBBLE AND CHURN AS THOUGH IN THE GRIP OF ENORMOUS ENERGIES GENERATED BELOW ITS SURFACE.
AND IN THE NEXT INSTANT...

...THE WATERS ERUPT--

--HURLING A VERITABLE GEYSER OF DEAD FISH UP FROM THE SEA BOTTOM ONTO THE DECK--AND PASSENGERS--OF THE FERRY.
UNDERSTANDABLY, THOSE HAPLESS PEOPLE SCREAM... AND PANIC... AND STEP ALL OVER EACH OTHER IN A FUTILE ATTEMPT TO ESCAPE.

BUT THERE'S NOWHERE FOR THEM TO GO--NO PLACE TO HIDE FROM THE TORRENT OF WET, SCALY, FOUL-SMELLING LITTLE CORPSES THAT PELTS THEIR FACES AND BODIES.
IT APPEARS MY NOTION HAS BEEN CONFIRMED, MY FRIENDS. COME--WE MUST OFFER WHAT AID WE CAN.
SO HULK HAS TO FIGHT FISH?! STILL SOUNDS STUPID TO HULK!!

NEVERTHELESS, THE JADE GIANT ACCEDES TO DR. STRANGE'S WISHES. AND WHEN THE SORCERER DROPS HIM ABOARD THE STRICKEN VESSEL...
GET BACK INTO WATER, DUMB FISH!!

STEPHEN-- THESE CREATURES ARE NOT EVEN ALIVE! SOMEONE --OR SOME THING--IS USING THEIR BODIES AS WEAPONS!

INDEED. AND IT SEEMS UNLIKELY THE TEMPORAL DISPLACEMENT ITSELF COULD BE RESPONSIBLE.
SOME OTHER FORCE IS OPERATIVE HERE.
AND BY DIRECTING A MAGICAL PROBE BENEATH THE WAVES...

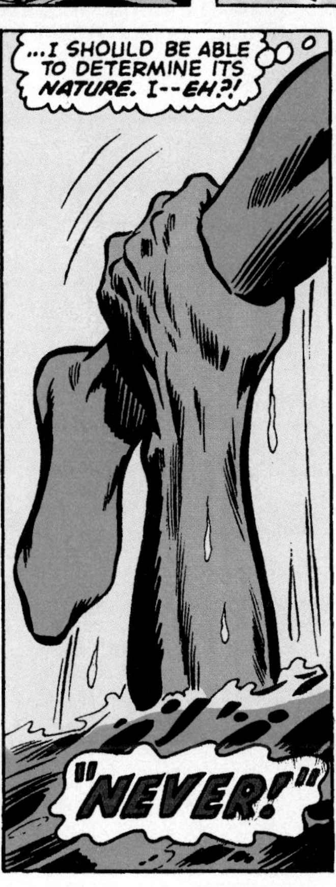
...I SHOULD BE ABLE TO DETERMINE ITS NATURE. I--EH?!
"NEVER!"

BEFORE THE MYSTIC MASTER CAN REALIZE WHAT'S BEFALLEN HIM, THE GREY-BLACK HAND YANKS HIM OUT OF THE SKY--
--DOWN INTO THE WILDLY-THRASHING WATERS!

THE OCEAN IS THICK AND DARK WITH POLLUTION AND COLD WITH THE CHILL OF THE NIGHT...
BUT THE FORM OF STEPHEN STRANGE IS AN INFERNO OF PAIN--HIS MIND, A BRIGHT WHIRL OF CONFUSION. AN ELECTRICAL CHARGE CRACKLES ALONG EVERY NERVE FIBER, ROBBING HIM OF CONSCIOUSNESS.
BUT NOT BEFORE HE SEES THE FACE OF HIS FOE.
NOT BEFORE HE HEARS ITS TELEPATHIC "VOICE".
"EMPIRE IS THE SOLE DESTINY OF OUR RACE! WE SHALL MAKE ANY SACRIFICE, PAY ANY PRICE THAT THAT DESTINY BE FULFILLED!
"WE SHALL SOAR FEARLESSLY AMONG THE STARS, CRUSHING ALL WHO OPPOSE US!"
ABOVE, THE RAIN OF FISH HAS AT LAST SUBSIDED, AND VALKYRIE TURNS HER ATTENTION TO...
STEPHEN, WHAT DO YOU SUPPOSE COULD HAVE-- STEPHEN--?
STEPHEN-- WHERE ARE YOU?!

C'MON, C'MON--WE AIN'T GOT ALL NIGHT, OLD MAN. MOVE IT--BACK OUTTA THE LIGHT.
WE JUST WANNA DO BIZNESS AN' BE ON OUR WAY.
YEAH. WE DON'T WANNA SLICE YA OPEN.

BUT WE WILL, OLD MAN --IF WE DON'T GET WHAT WE CAME FOR. BET ON IT.
LET'S SEE YER WALLET, OLD MAN. WE KNOW YA GOT A BIG FAT ONE.
FORK IT OVER, POPS, OR--

"OR" NOTHING. LET THE MAN BE. LEAVE PEACEFULLY.
BELIEVE ME, IT'S NOT MY DESIRE TO INTERFERE. BUT I'LL BE FORCED TO IF YOU PERSIST IN THIS.
AW CRUD --WE BEEN SPOTTED.

LISTEN, PAL, WE DON'T WANT NO TROUBLE NEITHER. SO WHY DON'T'CHA JUST BUZZ OFF? THIS AIN'T NONE O' YER--
EASE UP, LARRY. LOOK AT THE SIZE O' THAT CLOWN. HE AIN'T SCARED O' YA.
YEAH. AN' SINCE HE WON'T SPLIT --AN' HE'S SEEN OUR FACES--

WE GOT NO CHOICE BUT TA CUT THE OL' GEEZER SO HE CAN'T TALK--
THUT
NO...!
UNNGH

--AN' WASTE THE BIG GUY TOO, HUH, LEO? YEAH. I CAN DIG THAT.
YA SHOULD'A BEAT IT WHEN YA HAD THE CHANCE, FATSO.
CUT THE LIP, AN' LAY INTA HIM, AWREADY!

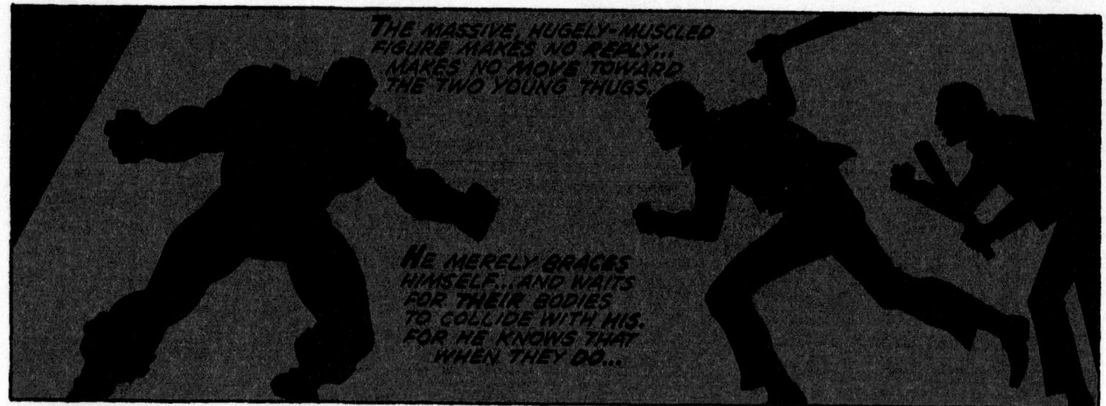
THE MASSIVE, HUGELY-MUSCLED FIGURE MAKES NO REPLY... MAKES NO MOVE TOWARD THE TWO YOUNG THUGS.
HE MERELY BRACES HIMSELF...AND WAITS FOR THEIR BODIES TO COLLIDE WITH HIS. FOR HE KNOWS THAT WHEN THEY DO...

THEY WILL REBOUND PAINFULLY TO THE GRIMY ASPHALT...

...AS SURELY AS IF THEY HAD RUN HEAD-LONG INTO A BRICK WALL.

HE STEPS OUT OF THE SHADOWS, THEN--ONLY BECAUSE HE MUST--ONLY BECAUSE THE LAST OF THE MUGGERS WILL NOT ENTER THE DARKNESS TO MEET HIM.
A LUMP RISES IN THE LITTLE MAN'S THROAT.
H-HEY... C'MON... I GOT NO BEEF WITH YOU. I--
SOMEHOW, HE HADN'T EXPECTED A FOE WHOSE MASS IS 11 TIMES THAT OF AN EARTHMAN'S.

YOU'VE COMMITTED AN ASSAULT ON A FELLOW HUMAN.
VANCE MENTIONED THAT THIS ULTIMATE TREASON WAS NOT UNCOMMON IN THIS ERA...
BUT I NEVER REALLY BELIEVED HIM... UNTIL NOW.

HUH? TREASON? I DIDN'T BURN NO FLAG. I JUST CUT A GUY--THAT'S ALL--

--LIKE I'M GONNA DO TA Y--
ULP

A SINGLE BACKHANDED SLAP--DELIVERED BY MUSCLES BRED TO FUNCTION IN THRICE EARTH'S GRAVITY--SENDS LEO REELING. BUT IT PAINS THE BIG MAN, TOO...
...AT THE DEPTHS OF HIS CONSCIENCE. THE VERY NOTION OF STRIKING TERRAN FLESH IS REPUGNANT TO HIM.
HUMAN LIFE IS SO PRECIOUS WHERE HE COMES FROM...
THAP!
CLUD!

...WHAT WITH THE HUMAN POPULATION DOWN TO A DWINDLING FIFTY MILLION OR SO, AS OPPOSED TO OUR BURGEONING CLAUSTROPHOBIC THREE BILLION-PLUS.
STILL BREATHING.

THERE'S A CHANCE HE COULD BE SAVED, EVEN WITH THIS CENTURY'S PRIMITIVE MEDICINE.

AND EVEN THOUGH IT WILL MEAN REVEALING MY PRESENCE HERE ...I MUST GIVE THIS MAN THAT CHANCE. I COULDN'T LIVE WITH MYSELF IF I DID OTHERWISE.

COULD BE VANCE WAS RIGHT AFTER ALL.
MAYBE HE IS THE ONLY ONE OF US PSYCHOLOGICALLY PREPARED TO DEAL WITH EARTH IN ITS PRE-CIVILIZED PHASE.
MAYBE HE SHOULD'VE BEEN THE ONE TO TRANSPORT DOWN.

ON THE OTHER HAND, MAYBE I NEEDED TO LEARN THERE'S A LITTLE "BADOON"... EVEN IN OUR ANCESTORS.
A.I.B.
CAMBRIDGE

THE CLOAK OF LEVITATION LIFTS THE INSENSATE FORM OF DR. STRANGE TO THE SICKLY-GREEN SURFACE OF THE HARBOR, WHERE VAL SPOTS HIM FROM ABOVE.
STEPHEN!!

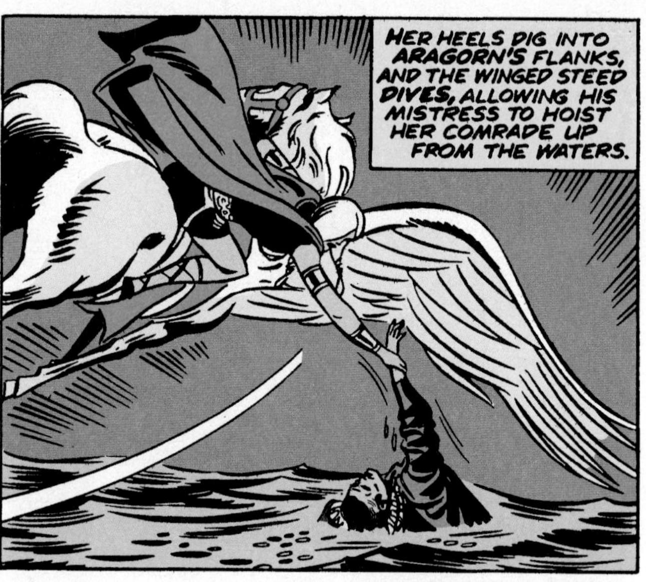
HER HEELS DIG INTO ARAGORN'S FLANKS, AND THE WINGED STEED DIVES, ALLOWING HIS MISTRESS TO HOIST HER COMRADE UP FROM THE WATERS.

WHAT IS WRONG? MAGICIAN LOOKS SICK! WHAT HURT HIM?
I DO NOT KNOW, HULK. HE SEEMS TO BE IN A STATE OF SHOCK. HE IS RECOVERING--BUT SLOWLY.
AND HE KEEPS MURMURING SOMETHING--A NAME, I BELIEVE.

"EELAR." IT MAY BE ONE OF HIS ARCANE DEITIES-- OR THE BEING WHO DID THIS TO HIM. I DO NOT KNOW THAT, EITH--
BUT HULK KNOWS! SEE-- UP THERE!

THAT IS EELAR! HULK JUST KNOWS!
"TO THE CITIES! THE CENTERS OF CIVILIZATION MUST BE FIRST TO FALL!"

I--I "HEARD" HIM-- EVEN AT THIS DISTANCE. HIS INTENT IS TO ATTACK NEW YORK!
WE MUST FOLLOW HIM, HULK--STOP HIM!
UMM. CITY IS NOT HULK'S FRIEND-- BUT MAGICIAN IS-- AND EELAR HURT MAGICIAN.
SO HULK WILL HELP GIRL SMASH EELAR!

UPSTATE NEW YORK:
A SORELY TROUBLED NIGHTHAWK SOARS ABOVE THE THICKLY WOODED AREA NEAR WOODSTOCK AND SAUGERTIES. BUT THOUGH HIS EYES SCAN THE GREEN, ROLLING SPLENDOR ALL ABOUT HIM, HE DOES NOT SEE ITS BEAUTY... ONLY ITS DARK SHADOWS.
BUT PERHAPS THAT'S ONLY NATURAL. LIFE HASN'T BEEN KIND TO HIM THESE PAST WEEKS AND MONTHS.
HE'S FELT BETRAYAL AT THE HANDS OF HIS CLOSEST CONFIDANT, KYLE RICHMOND'S FINANCIAL ADVISER PENNYSWORTH.*
*AS RECOUNTED IN DEFENDERS #25.--LEN.

AND HE'S SEEN A WOMAN HE... LIKED VERY MUCH, MAIMED... HER SPIRIT BROKEN... HER SEEMINGLY UNQUENCHABLE THIRST FOR LIVING AND LOVING RUTHLESSLY, VIOLENTLY SLAKED.

A BOMB PLANTED UNDER THE HOOD OF KYLE RICHMOND'S CAR--THAT'S ALL IT TOOK TO ROB TRISH STARR OF HER LEFT ARM...

...TO HURL KYLE'S FELLOW DEFENDERS INTO A NEEDLESS BATTLE WITH THE SQUADRON SINISTER...

...TO CAUSE THE DOWNCAST MS. STARR TO WALK OUT OF HIS LIFE. THERE WAS NOTHING HE COULD SAY THAT WOULD INDUCE HER TO STAY.*
*GIANT DEFENDERS #4.--L.W.

ADD LONLINESS TO BETRAYAL... AND THE SUM IS A MAN DESPERATE FOR SOLACE...
...OR DIVERSION.

AND HE IS ABOUT TO FIND THE LATTER... IN SPADES!
CHOOM
WHAT--? AN EXPLOSION ABOVE ME?!

GOOD LORD-- SOME KIND OF AIRCRAFT--GOING DOWN IN FLAMES! BUT IT DOESN'T LOOK LIKE ANY JET PLANE I'VE EVER LAID EYES ON.
IT'S GOING TO CRASH-- MILES FROM HERE--

"--IN THE WOODS!"
KROOM

WHAT IS IT WITH ME? EVERYWHERE I GO... ALL I SEE ARE PAIN AND DEATH! I SWEAR... I DON'T EVEN WANT TO INVESTIGATE THAT CRASH. BUT I DON'T HAVE MUCH CHOICE.

THERE COULD BE SURVIVORS.
ADLER SHOES

LOOK UP THERE! DID YOU SEE IT? A FLYING SAUCER-- BLAZING ACROSS THE SKY-- AND NOW--

--A GIANT BIRD--CHASING THE THING! MY GOD, WE'RE BEING INVADED!!
PANIC SPREADS QUICKLY IN THE STREETS... PEOPLE RACING TO THEIR HOMES... TO THE SHERIFF'S OFFICE ...SHOUTING... TREMBLING... ALL THEIR NOTIONS ABOUT THE WORLD SUDDENLY SUNDERED...

...OR, IN ONE CASE, CONFIRMED.
VERPOORTEN'S MEAT MARKET

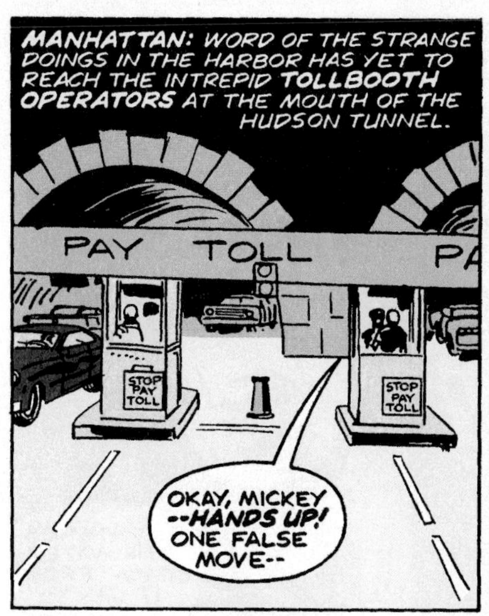
MANHATTAN: WORD OF THE STRANGE DOINGS IN THE HARBOR HAS YET TO REACH THE INTREPID TOLLBOOTH OPERATORS AT THE MOUTH OF THE HUDSON TUNNEL.
PAY TOLL PA
STOP PAY TOLL
STOP PAY TOLL
OKAY, MICKEY --HANDS UP! ONE FALSE MOVE--

--AN' I'LL BLOW YA ALL THE WAY TA TIMES SQUARE! I MEAN IT, MISTER! DON'T MESS WITH OL' DEADEYE!

C'MON, MICKEY-- ADMIT IT! I'M PRETTY IMPRESSIVE WITH THIS ROD, HUH?

YES. I AM IMPRESSED.
N-NOW, WILL YOU PUT THAT THING AWAY, BEFORE YOU KILL SOME-BODY?
I REALLY GOT TO YA, HUH?

SEE--THAT PROVES IT! I OUGHTTA BE OUT ON THE STREETS-- AS A REAL COP. SEE, I'M YER BASIC MAN OF ACTION.
ACTION. RIGHT. PUT IT AWAY.
CHASIN' CROOKS-- FIGHTIN' CRIME-- THAT'S MY BAG.

BAG. RIGHT. PUT IT AWAY--
EEEEEEE

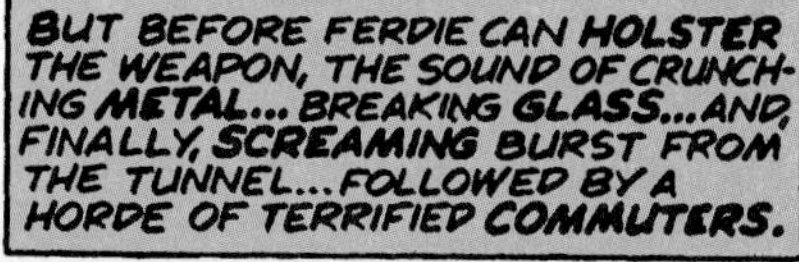
BUT BEFORE FERDIE CAN HOLSTER THE WEAPON, THE SOUND OF CRUNCHING METAL... BREAKING GLASS... AND, FINALLY, SCREAMING BURST FROM THE TUNNEL... FOLLOWED BY A HORDE OF TERRIFIED COMMUTERS.

EXCITEMENT AT LAST! C'MON, MICK, LET'S CHECK IT OUT!

FEARLESSLY, FERDIE CHARGES INTO THE TUNNEL, NOW ILLUMINATED ONLY BY ITS EMERGENCY BACK-UP LIGHTING.
WEIRD-- ALL THESE ABANDONED CARS, HUH?

FERDIE--SLOW DOWN! WE DUNNO WHAT'S UP AHEAD! I MEAN--IT'S GOTTA BE REAL TROUBLE TO KNOCK OUT THE POWER LIKE THIS.
MAYBE WE OUGHTA TURN BACK, Y'KNOW?
NO WAY, MAN.

YOU CHICKEN OUT IF YA WANNA--BUT I'M--HEY! IT'S RAININ' IN HERE!
SPLAT
BUT WHERE'S THE WATER COMIN' FROM? IT CAN'T--

OH, JEEZ--MICKEY--LOOK--THE CEILING'S CRACKIN'! THE RIVER'S POURIN' IN!
WHOM

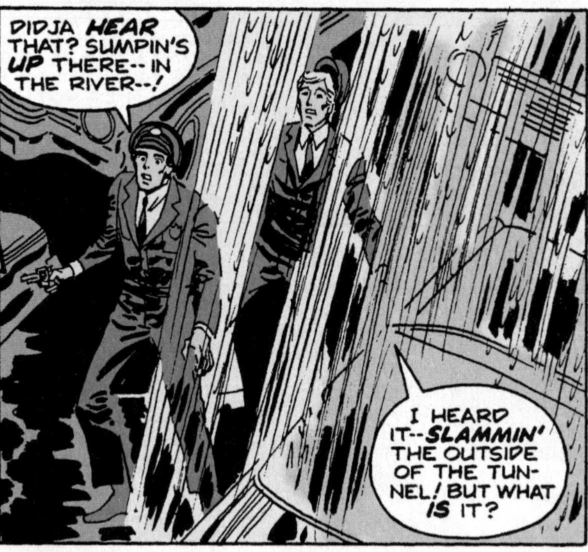
DIDJA HEAR THAT? SUMPIN'S UP THERE--IN THE RIVER--!
I HEARD IT--SLAMMIN' THE OUTSIDE OF THE TUNNEL! BUT WHAT IS IT?

"IT"... IS A THEY. MORE FISH, HUNDREDS OF THOUSANDS OF THEM, MASSED BY EELAR AS A LIVING BATTERING RAM, POUNDING REPEATEDLY AGAINST THE TUNNEL'S CONCRETE ROOF!
"OUR RACE IS SUPREME! CONQUER WE MUST, FOR OUR MIGHT MAKES IT JUST!"
THE WHOLE PLACE IS VIBRATIN' LIKE CRAZY, FERDIE! WE GOTTA GET OUT--

"--BEFORE IT CAVES IN!"
CHASH
FISH!

FERDIE--WHAT'RE YA STARIN' AT? COME ON!
FISH. BUT FISH DON'T SMASH TUNNELS. FISH CAN'T SMASH ANYTHING.

WHALES CAN. BUT THESE'RE JUST FISH. LITTLE, REGULAR FISH. HOW CAN I SHOOT AT FISH?
FERDIE-- THE PLACE IS FLOODIN'!

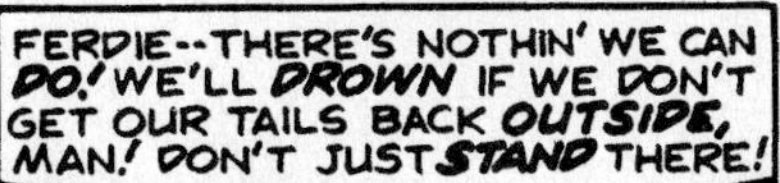
FERDIE--THERE'S NOTHIN' WE CAN DO! WE'LL DROWN IF WE DON'T GET OUR TAILS BACK OUTSIDE, MAN! DON'T JUST STAND THERE!

MOVE IT, FERDIE-- COME ON! LET'S SPLIT FROM THIS--
FERDIE?
FERDIE?

BUT FERDINAND FLYNN, "MAN OF ACTION", IS MESMERIZED, ENTRANCED, PARALYZED BY SHOCK AND DISBELIEF.
FISH.
AND WHEN THAT FACT DAWNS ON HIS PARTNER...

MICKEY HAS NO RECOURSE BUT TO FLEE-- AND PRAY THAT HELP WILL ARRIVE IN TIME.
I-- I'LL FIND SOMEBODY TO COME FOR YA, FERDIE.
HE WON'T HAVE TO LOOK FAR.

FOR THE DEFENDERS, IN PURSUIT OF EELAR, HAVE SPOTTED THE STAMPEDE OF MOTORISTS FROM THE TUNNEL.
STEPHEN --DO YOU BELIEVE EELAR--?
THERE WOULD SEEM TO BE NOWHERE ELSE TO LAY THE BLAME, VAL. THOUGH I CONFESS...
I DO NOT UNDERSTAND WHAT RELATION THE CREATURE COULD HAVE TO THE TEMPORAL DISTURBANCE.
MORE STUPID FISH! FISH EVERYWHERE!

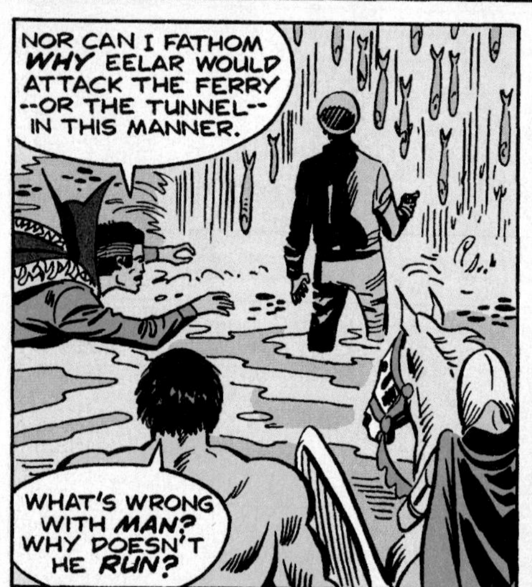
NOR CAN I FATHOM WHY EELAR WOULD ATTACK THE FERRY --OR THE TUNNEL-- IN THIS MANNER.
WHAT'S WRONG WITH MAN? WHY DOESN'T HE RUN?

HE APPEARS TO BE IMMOBILIZED BY SHEER TERROR AND AMAZEMENT.
HUH--?
SCARED STIFF, HULK. BUT WE SHALL DEAL WITH HIS PROBLEM LATER.
FOR NOW, YOU AND VAL MUST KEEP THIS STRUCTURE FROM COLLAPSING.

TOGETHER, YOU TWO-- LIFT THAT AUTOMOBILE AND FOLD IT OVER UPON ITSELF.
KRUNCH
EXCELLENT! NOW--

HULK KNOWS WHAT TO DO NOW--PLUG UP HOLE!
AND THAT DONE, LET US ATTEND TO THE AWE-STRUCK GUARD.

SAUGERTIES: THE BOY WONDERS WHY EVERYONE AROUND HIM WAS TERRIFIED, RATHER THAN JOYOUS.
REAL SPACEMEN! HE COULD HARDLY IMAGINE ANYTHING MORE EXCITING!

MOM! DAD! WAIT'LL YOU HEAR--!
I JUST SAW A UFO--A FLYING SAUCER--A REAL ONE--IT CRASHED--

I DIDN'T HEAR A CRASH, DID YOU, TOM?
DON'T ENCOURAGE HIM, MARY.
IS IT YOUR TURN TO DO THE SPANKING --OR MINE?

TOM, YOU CAN'T SPANK A CHILD FOR HAVING AN OVERACTIVE IMAGINATION.
"IMAGINATION", MY EYE! HE'S LYING, MARY --AND IT'S BECOMING A HABIT WITH HIM!

AND I'VE HAD JUST ABOUT ENOUGH OF IT. LAST WEEK, IT WAS A PYTHON IN THE GARDEN --THEN A GHOST IN THE ATTIC --NOW THIS.
I THINK YOU NEED TO SPEND SOME TIME IN YOUR ROOM, YOUNG MAN.

AND DON'T COME DOWN 'TILL YOU'RE READY TO TELL THE TRUTH.

IT'S A GUT-WRENCHING PLUNGE FROM EUPHORIA DOWN TO DESPONDENCY --AND IT MAY BE MORE HARROWING FOR A 13-YEAR-OLD BOY THAN FOR ALMOST ANY OTHER VARIETY OF HUMAN BEING.
THE ORIGINS OF MARVEL COMICS
STAN LEE

FOR THE SHERIFF IS CONVINCED THAT HIS CONSTITUENTS HAVE FALLEN VICTIM TO A MASS HALLUCINATION... AND THE PEOPLE ARE BEGINNING TO THINK SO THEMSELVES.

CAPTAIN AMERICA

EXCEPT FOR THAT BLOWN-OUT JET TUBE AND A CRUMPLED FRONT END, THE HULL OF THIS THING IS VIRTUALLY INTACT. MAYBE THERE ARE SURVIV--UH-OH.

OH, BROTHER! I THINK I'VE JUST DISCOVERED WHAT THEY MEAN WHEN THEY SAY "STAR TREK LIVES"!

BUT AS FOR BEING FIRST TO ARRIVE AT THE SCENE ...NO. THE WINGED DEFENDER COPS THAT DISTINCTION.

SOME SORT OF PANEL SLIDING OPEN.

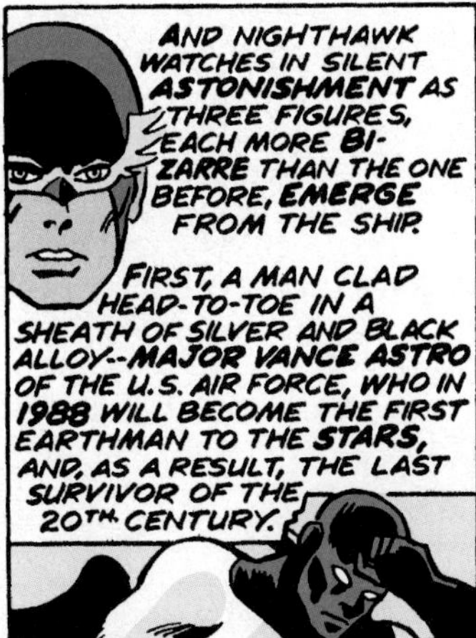
AND NIGHTHAWK WATCHES IN SILENT ASTONISHMENT AS THREE FIGURES, EACH MORE BIZARRE THAN THE ONE BEFORE, EMERGE FROM THE SHIP.
FIRST, A MAN CLAD HEAD-TO-TOE IN A SHEATH OF SILVER AND BLACK ALLOY--MAJOR VANCE ASTRO OF THE U.S. AIR FORCE, WHO IN 1988 WILL BECOME THE FIRST EARTHMAN TO THE STARS, AND, AS A RESULT, THE LAST SURVIVOR OF THE 20TH CENTURY.

THEN COMES YONDU, LAST OF THE BARBARIC BLUE-SKINNED NATIVES OF CENTAURI-IV, THE PLANET OF EARTH'S FIRST INTERSTELLAR COLONY, TO BE ESTABLISHED IN THE DAWNING YEARS OF THE 31ST CENTURY.

BUT THE THIRD MEMBER OF THE SHIP'S CREW IS PERHAPS THE STRANGEST OF ALL: A HUMANOID COMPOSED ENTIRELY OF SILICON CRYSTAL WHOSE BODY CAN CONVERT LIGHT-WAVES INTO BURSTS OF EXTREME HEAT AND COLD.
HE IS MARTINEX, LAST SURVIVOR OF EARTH'S OUTPOST ON PLUTO.

AND TOGETHER, THEY--AND THEIR FOURTH COMRADE, ABSENT AT THE MOMENT, ARE KNOWN AS... THE GUARDIANS OF THE GALAXY!!
BUT, NO, THAT'S INCORRECT. THEY ARE NOT KNOWN AS ANYTHING YET ...NOR WILL THEY BE UNTIL SOME THOUSAND YEARS HENCE.
FOR THEIR SHIP HAS COME NOT FROM SOME FAR STAR... BUT FROM EARTH'S DISTANT FUTURE.
STILL, FOR THE PRESENT, OUR CONCERN MUST BE THE PRESENT, AND SPECIFICALLY...

TIMES SQUARE, MANHATTAN:
EELAR RUNS AMOK, TAPPING THE POWER OF THE FLASHING LIGHTS, ADDING IT TO HIS OWN, UNLEASHING ANOTHER UTTERLY POINTLESS ATTACK.
"FROM OUT OF THE VOID WE SAIL ON THE STARWINDS-- UNFALTERING, UNDAUNTED, UNCONQUERABLE--
"--RAVAGERS OF WORLDS, PLUNDERERS OF SUNS, MASTERS OF THE UNIVERSE!
"WE SHALL BUILD AN EMPIRE ON THE BODIES OF THE LESSER RACES WE ANNIHILATE!"
FWASH

BUT EELAR'S RHYME IS LOST AMID THE DIN OF UNBRIDLED DESTRUCTION HE HAS LOOSED.

CHOOM

EELAR BETTER NOT GET UP-- OR HULK WILL BREAK EVERY BONE IN HIS BODY --IF HIS BODY HAS ANY BONES!
"PLANETS WILL CRUMBLE! NEBULAE WILL BLOW AWAY! WHITE DWARFS AND RED GIANTS, BLUE--"
SHUT UP!!

MY SENTIMENTS PRECISELY, HULK. I THINK IT'S TIME WE DID THE TALKING TO OUR VIOLENT FRIEND... WHILE HE'S DOWN.
EELAR, WE DEMAND--

"THE MOST BRILLIANT SUPERNOVA PALES BESIDE THE GLOW OF OUR GREATNESS!"
I WARN YOU, EELAR --STAY BACK, OR--

"AND OF ALL THE SCUM OF SPACE, WE LOATHE THE YOU MOST OF ALL!"
HUH?

"FOR YOU, TERRANS --YOU PRETEND TO NOBILITY!"
"YOUR POSTURING DISGUSTS US-- AND EMBARRASSES YOU!"

"WE SHALL OBLITERATE YOUR NOISOME RACE!"

FOR ONE UNCOMPREHENDING MOMENT THE DEFENDERS CAN ONLY GAPE AT EELAR'S UTTERLY SENSELESS ATTACK UPON ARAGORN.

BUT AS THE HORSE REARS BACK IN PAIN, VAL DRAWS HER SWORD AND STRIKES--

--ONLY TO BE DOWNED BY THE MAD CREATURE'S ELECTRICAL CHARGE, CONDUCTED ALONG HER OWN BLADE.
SHE DROPS --STUNNED-- GASPING-- TO THE GRITTY ASPHALT.

NOW EELAR HURTS GIRL! GIRL IS HULK'S FRIEND TOO!!
CHUD
HULK HATES EE--OW!

HULK'S HAND--BURNS--LIKE HULK HIT FIRE, NOT FISH!
HIS ELECTRICAL CHARGE IS EVEN MORE POWERFUL THAN WE SUPPOSED.

STILL, YOU MANAGED TO STAGGER HIM, HULK, AND MY SPELLS SHOULD--
"YOU ARE COSMIC FLOTSAM-- THE REFUSE OF THE UNIVERSE!"
THEY SHOULD... BUT THEY DO NOT. EELAR'S CRACKLING ENERGY FIELD CAUSES THE SORCERER SUPREME'S MYSTIC BOLTS TO DISSIPATE ON CONTACT.

REMARKABLE. VANCE TOLD ME, TOO, ABOUT THE MANY SUPER-BEINGS THIS ERA PRODUCED...
...BUT I NEVER THOUGHT I'D SEE ANYTHING LIKE THIS! THAT CAPED MAN'S POWER IS ASTOUNDING!
AND YET, FOR ALL THEIR MIGHT, THEY'RE LOSING THIS STRUGGLE.
I'VE NEVER SEEN ANYTHING QUITE LIKE THEIR FOE, EITHER. BUT THERE'S SOMETHING ODDLY FAMILIAR ABOUT HIS TELEPATHIC "SPEECHES."
I'M TEMPTED TO JUMP INTO THE FRAY... TRY TO HELP... BUT THAT WOULD ONLY LEAD TO MORE QUESTIONS. I CAN'T RISK IT...!

I THINK WE CAN RISK IT, VANCE. CHARLIE'S TRACKING DEVICE IS FUNCTIONING... MY SCANNERS HAVE PINPOINTED HIS LOCATION...

...AND THE RADIO-TELEPORT SYSTEM IS FULLY OPERATIVE ON THE "SEND" CIRCUIT.
NO QUESTION. I CAN TELEPORT YOU AND YONDU TO CHARLIE WHENEVER YOU WISH.
BUT YOU CAN'T 'PORT US BACK--AND OUR COMMUNICATIONS ARE DEAD.
HOW DO WE GET BACK HERE ONCE WE'RE CERTAIN HE'S SAFE?
I THINK THE LINE GOES: "I'M NIGHTHAWK --FLY ME."

I MUST BE OUT OF MY MIND--BUT I BELIEVE YOUR STORY ABOUT COMING FROM EARTH'S FUTURE. SO I CAN BE YOUR GUIDE BACK TO THE SHIP.
BUT ONE QUESTION--SUPPOSE WE FIND YOUR FRIEND IN A PUBLIC PLACE? YOU WERE NERVOUS ABOUT TELLING ME...
CHARLIE-27 WAS A SPACE MILITIAMAN, NIGHTHAWK...

FOLLOWING ORDERS IS AS NATURAL AS BREATHING TO HIM. AND HE WAS INSTRUCTED...
...TO KEEP OUT OF SIGHT AT ALL COSTS. TRUST ME-- HE OBEYED.

MARTINEX ACTIVATES THE TELEPORT CONSOLE. A SOFT HUM FILLS THE CHAMBER...
AND THE ATOMS OF ASTRO, YONDU, AND NIGHTHAWK'S BODIES ARE DISSEMBLED AND BROADCAST INTO THE ETHER.

HIS COMRADES AND HIS NEWFOUND ALLY GONE, THE PLUVIAN SCIENTIST TURNS HIS ATTENTION TO THE REPAIRS WHICH MUST BE MADE. BUT BARELY HAS HE PRIED OPEN THE CONSOLE'S "RETRIEVE" CIRCUIT, WHEN...
CLACK
FOOTSTEPS ON THE METAL FLOORING--AN INTRUDER!

OF A SORT... YES.
OH, WOW...!
IF THAT MEANS WHAT I THINK IT DOES... I CONCUR.

BUT IF MARTINEX IS STARTLED BY THE SIGHT OF THE YOUNG MAN, IMAGINE HIS FELLOW GUARDIAN'S --AND NIGHTHAWK'S-- ASTONISHMENT...
...UPON THEIR ARRIVAL...
...AT THE "SECLUDED" SPOT WHERE CHARLIE HAS CHOSEN TO SECRETE HIMSELF!
BY THE THREE SUNS! MAJOR, WHAT--?
TIMES SQUARE-- IN THE MIDST OF SOME KIND OF RIOT!
A TELEPORT MALFUNCTION--IT'S GOT TO BE--!
HUH?! DOC! VAL! HULK!
VANCE! YONDU!! HERE--I'M OVER HERE!!
NEW YORK'S CROWDS AREN'T NOTED FOR THEIR POLITENESS... BUT AT THE SOUND OF THE JOVIAN'S BOOMING VOICE, THE THRONG STEPS RESPECTFULLY ASIDE, CLEARING A PATH...

...ALLOWING HIM TO REJOIN HIS AWED, SPEECHLESS COMRADES.
INDEED, THE AWE AND SPEECHLESSNESS SEEM TO BE CONTAGIOUS. THE EIGHT HEROES CAN DO LITTLE BUT STARE AT ONE ANOTHER WHILE THE BEFUDDLED CROWD GAPES AT ALL OF THEM.
UNTIL...

EELAR, ALL BUT FORGOTTEN IN THE CONFUSION, PROPELS HIMSELF ALOFT ONCE MORE.
"PARAMECIA-- GALACTIC BACTERIA--"
"--THAT IS WHAT YOU ARE!"

"AND NOW THAT WE HAVE CONQUERED YOU, YOU SHALL BE OUR SLAVES!"
EELAR IS GETTING AWAY! HULK WILL FOLLOW!
DOC-- WHAT IS GOING ON HERE? WHEN DID THAT-- WHATEVER IT IS--CONQUER US?
NO ONE HAS BEEN CONQUERED, KYLE --BUT EELAR MUST BE STOPPED.

YOU AND VAL ACCOMPANY THE HULK--GO AFTER HIM-- NOW--
--WHILE I CONSULT WITH THE FOUR--

--STRANGERS.
GONE!

AND I AM CERTAIN--I SENSED IN ONE OF THEM THE SOURCE OF THE TEMPORAL DISRUPTION! WHICH MEANS...EELAR IS BUT A BY-PRODUCT OF THE DISTURBANCE.
THUS, EELAR'S OWN POWER...
...MUST EMANATE NOT FROM THE TIME-FLOW... BUT FROM SOMETHING IN THE SEA!

WHILE, BLOCKS AWAY, IN THE ALLEY WHERE THIS WHOLE FURSHLUGGINER GIANT-SIZE MESS BEGAN...!
CHARLIE, ARE YOU SURE THIS IS THE SPOT WHERE YOU LANDED? MARTINEX IS GOING TO HAVE TO RUN A CHECK ON HIS SENSOR BANKS.

UNLESS... THE OLD MAN'S SUIT-CASE...
SUPPOSE I OPEN IT PSYCHO-KINETIC-ALLY... JUST OUT OF CURI-OSITY...

WELL, WHAT DO YOU KNOW--?! SOMEBODY PAWNED WHAT WE CROSSED TEN CENTURIES TO FIND!

LET'S JUST HOPE IT CONTAINS THE INFORMATION WE'RE AFTER. WITH ALL WE'VE BEEN THROUGH, I FIGURE WE DESERVE AT LEAST A CHANCE AT SAVING OUR EARTH.
WE'LL KNOW IN A MOMENT, VANCE. I'VE SWITCHED IT ON BUT...

...NOTHING! IT'S A GENUINE BADOON MENTO-PROGRAM-MER-- BUT IT'S TAPES ARE EMPTY! BLANK!
WE'VE COME ALL THIS WAY--FOR NOTHING!

I SUSPECTED AS MUCH. IN OUR HASTE TO PURSUE EELAR WE FAILED TO NOTICE-- THIS AREA OF THE HAR-BOR IS STILL AGLOW.
THEN EELAR IS A DIRECT PRODUCT OF THIS PHENOMENON-- WHICH ITSELF IS A BY-PRODUCT OF THE TIME DISPLACEMENT.

SOME FORCE OR MECHANISM 'NEATH THE SUR-FACE WAS ACTI-VATED BY THE TEMPORAL DISTURBANCE.

AND MY SPELL HAS DREDGED UP THAT DEVICE.

ALL OF WHICH OFFERS LITTLE RELIEF FROM PUZZLEMENT FOR THE HULK, VALKYRIE, AND NIGHTHAWK, WHO CONVERGE UPON EELAR IN CENTRAL PARK...
...TO FIND THE BESTIAL BERSERKER ENGAGED IN COMBAT...

...WITH A TREE.
"BEHOLD OUR POWER, TERRAN-- AS YOU DIE!!"
EELAR IS... CRAZY! TREE CAN'T FIGHT!
DON'T KNOCK IT, GREENIE.

BETTER HE POUNDS ON THAT TREE THAN ON ONE OF US. BUT, WHY--?

I BELIEVE I CAN FINALLY ANSWER THAT ALL-IMPORTANT QUESTION, NIGHTHAWK--AND THIS ODD HELMET IS THE KEY TO THE MYSTERY.
YOU SEE, EELAR WAS CREATED BY THIS DEVICE.
DUMB HAT MADE EELAR? MAGICIAN IS CRAZY TOO!

NEARLY EXHAUSTED, PERHAPS, EMERALD ONE --BUT NOT DEMENTED YET.
BEHOLD!

AS HE SPEAKS, DR. STRANGE LOOSES A MYSTIC MENTAL PROBE, WHICH, BEING OF A NEUTRAL NATURE, SLIPS PAST EELAR'S ELECTRICAL FIELD...

...INTO THE SEASPAWN'S BRAIN. THERE, THE ENERGY SWIMS ABOUT HIS CONSCIOUSNESS, SEEKING TO DISCERN THE CREATURE'S PATTERN OF THOUGHT AND ACTION.

AND WHAT THE PROBE REVEALS IS... EELAR HAS NONE. NO PATTERNS. NOT EVEN ANY REAL THOUGHTS. THE PROBE EMERGES UNCHANGED FROM EELAR'S HEAD.

THE CREATURE IS UTTERLY MINDLESS... ACTING WITHOUT REASON... ATTACKING ANY CONVENIENT TARGET, BECAUSE IT IS PROGRAMMED TO DO SO.
PROGRAMMED BY THAT HELMET, NO DOUBT.
INDEED.
AND YOU THREE ARE, APPARENTLY, RESPONSIBLE FOR ACTIVATING THE DEVICE.
THEY MADE EELAR? THEN THEY ARE HULK'S ENEMIES?
I DO NOT THINK SO, HULK. MY SURMISE IS... THEY ARE TIME TRAVELERS... FROM EARTH'S FUTURE.

AND THEIR APPEARANCE IN OUR ERA SET IN MOTION THE TEMPORAL FORCES WHICH ACTIVATED THE HELMET.
BUT THE HELMET IS ONLY A PLAYBACK DEVICE FOR RECORDINGS. HOW--?

IT WAS ALSO THE HOME FOR A NEST OF ELECTRIC EELS. AND THE UNIQUE RADIATION WHICH POWERS IT MUTATED ONE OF THOSE EELS... AND PROGRAMMED THE NON-INTELLIGENT BEAST WITH THE INFORMATION CONTENT OF THE RECORDING.

BADOON WAR PROPAGANDA --ANCIENT STUFF --PRE-EMPIRE-- I KNEW I'D HEARD IT BEFORE!

THEN IT ALL FITS--HE CAN'T THINK, BUT HE'S BEEN TAUGHT TO BE THE ULTIMATE "GOOD SOLDIER":
VICTORY AT ANY PRICE--EVEN IF THERE'S NO WAR! HE'S BEEN FIGHTING ANYTHING AND EVERYTHING... AT RANDOM!

PRECISELY. YOU FUTURE-MEN STILL HAVE MANY QUESTIONS TO ANSWER...
BUT THOSE WILL WAIT. FOR NOW I SUGGEST WE UNITE TO REMOVE THIS MENACE? AGREED?
THE GUARDIANS NOD. AND THE SEVEN HEROES ALL TURN THEIR ATTENTION BACK TO EELAR--

...WEAPONRY MASTER YONDU FIRES HIS MYSTERIOUS YAKA-ARROW... AND BREAKS INTO A WHISTLE!

NO, NOT SOME CENTAURIAN FOLKSONG... BUT A SERIES OF TONAL COMMANDS TO THE WEIRD "LIVING" SHAFT.

AND, IN RESPONSE, THE ARROW TURNS IN MID-FLIGHT, CIRCLES THE CONFUSED EELAR...

...DRAWING HIS LIMITED ATTENTION AWAY FROM THE DEFENDERS AND GUARDIANS...

...SO THAT THE COMBINED PSYCHIC MIGHT OF VANCE ASTRO AND DR. STRANGE...

TZZZATK

...MAY BE TURNED TO DISPELLING EELAR'S ELECTRICAL FIELD!

AND SINCE ONLY THAT CHARGE PROTECTED EELAR FROM THE HULK'S POWER...

...WHAT REMAINS OF THE MATTER IS DEALT WITH BRUTALLY...
KRAK

WHAP
...AND EFFICIENTLY.

I SUPPOSE THE FINAL STROKE MUST BE MINE.
A PITY, THOUGH ...AS HE WAS TRULY BLAMELESS...
NO, VAL--STOP.

BUT, STEPHEN--WILL NOT THE CREATURE'S POWER REGENERATE? SURELY WE DARE NOT ALLOW ANOTHER SUCH EPISODE AS--
THAT IS NOT THE ONLY ALTERNATIVE, VAL.

VALKYRIE STEPS ASIDE...THE SORCERER SUPREME CONCENTRATES, CONJURES, INVOKES THE NAMES OF THE ETERNAL VISHANTI...

...AND EELAR IS SUDDENLY, IRREVOCABLY TRANSFORMED.
IT IS DONE. EELAR HAS REVERTED TO HIS ORIGINAL STATE.

WHICH LEAVES US ONLY THE SMALL TASK OF RETURNING HIM TO THE SEA.
AND LEARNING THE TRUTH ABOUT THE FUTURE-MEN.

AND AT THE MYSTIC'S GREENWICH VILLAGE SANCTUM, AFTER THE FIRST HAS BEEN ACCOMPLISHED...!
...SO THE EARTH WAS--OR WILL BE --CONQUERED IN 3007 A.D. BY THE RACE CALLED THE BA-DOON.
WE'VE MANAGED TO RECAP-TURE NEW YORK, THOUGH--*
--AND EXAMINING THEIR HISTORICAL RECORDS, WE LEARNED THAT THEY HAD AT-TEMPTED TO SEIZE THE EARTH ONCE BEFORE--UNSUC-CESSFULLY.**
BUT THE RECORDS WERE INCOMPLETE --PARTS WERE APPARENT-LY LOST WHEN THE BA-DOON FLED. OUR MISSION TO THE PAST WAS TO FIND THOSE LOST RECORDS.
*MARVEL 2-IN-1 # 5. **SILVER SURFER # 2.--LEN.

AND WE FAILED. WE MAY NEVER KNOW HOW HU-MANITY WAS SAVED THE FIRST TIME. UNLESS...YOU CAN TELL US.
I CANNOT. SO FAR AS I REMEMBER ...SUCH AN IN-VASION NEVER TOOK PLACE.*
* IN FACT, NO ONE BUT THE SURFER AND THE BADOON EVEN KNEW ABOUT IT.--L.W.

DOC--THE EARTH HE'S DESCRIBED--I DON'T WANT THAT FOR HUMANITY. ISN'T THERE SOMETHING WE CAN DO?

HULK KNOWS WHAT TO DO-- SMASH STU-PID BADOONS! TAKE HULK TO THEM, AND HULK WILL--
I'M AFRAID THAT'S IMPOS-SIBLE, HULK...!
PERHAPS... AND PER-HAPS NOT. BUT OUR FIRST CONCERN MUST BE RETURNING YOU TO YOUR OWN TIME--AT ONCE.

BUT WEIRD AS ALL THAT MAY SOUND, CONSIDER THIS:
BUT YOUR PLANET-- WHAT'S IT LIKE? HOW FAR IS IT? WHAT'S YOUR NAME?
I'VE TOLD YOU --I CAN'T ANSWER THOSE QUESTIONS.

NOW, PLEASE, YOUNG MAN-- YOU MUST GO. THE REPAIRWORK--
Y'KNOW, I'M GONNA BE AN ASTRONAUT SOMEDAY. MY NAME EVEN SOUNDS LIKE "ASTRONAUT."

IT'S ASTROVIK. BUT I'M GONNA CHANGE IT WHEN I GROW UP... JUST MAKE IT "ASTRO"...
...VANCE ASTRO!
END.

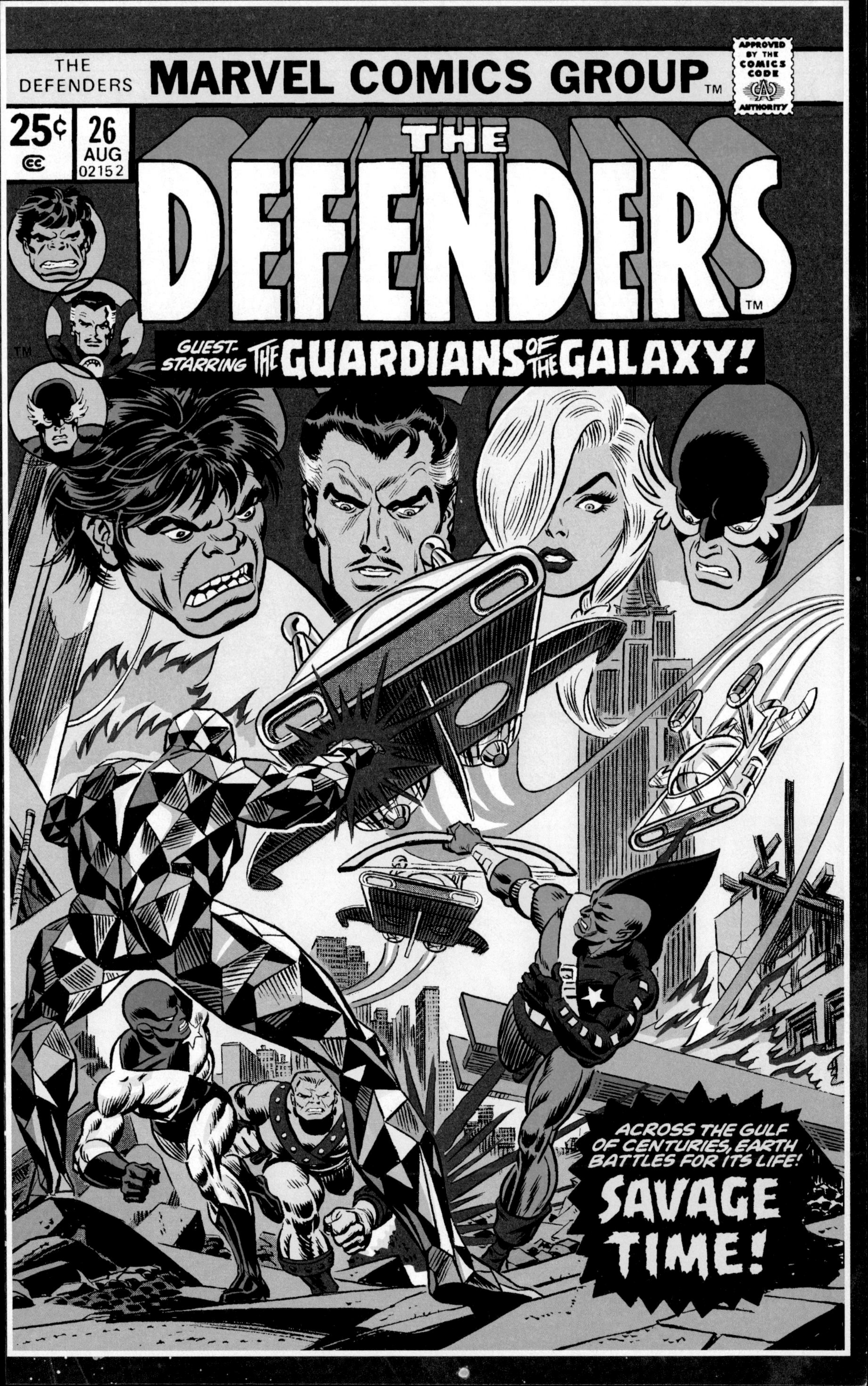

THE DEFENDERS **MARVEL COMICS GROUP**™

TM

GUEST-STARRING THE GUARDIANS OF THE GALAXY!

ACROSS THE GULF OF CENTURIES, EARTH BATTLES FOR ITS LIFE!

SAVAGE TIME!

STAN LEE PRESENTS: THE DYNAMIC DEFENDERS!™

STEVE GERBER, WRITER | SAL BUSCEMA & V. COLLETTA, ARTISTS | K. MANTLO, LETTERER; I. VARTANOFF, COLORIST | LEN WEIN, EDITOR

THE PERSONALITY OF BARBARA NORRISS HAS BEEN SUBMERGED 'NEATH MY OWN BY THE MAGIC OF THE ASGARDIAN ENCHANTRESS.
I AM WHAT I AM-- THE WOMAN WARRIOR, THE DEFENDER. AND YOU, MR. NORRISS, ARE A STRANGER TO MY EYES AND TO MY HEART.
BARBARA NORRISS IS GONE--FOREVER-- AS THOUGH SHE NEVER EXISTED. YOU MUST ACCEPT THAT.
ACCEPT THAT MY WIFE HAS GONE CRAZY? THAT SHE BELIEVE'S SHE'S A FEMALE ERIK THE RED ON A FLYING HORSE?!
I'M SORRY BARB, I CAN'T--

YOU MUST. FOR NEITHER OF US CAN ALTER MATTERS. NEITHER OF US CAN RESURRECT BAR-BARA... OR THE LIFE YOU HAD WITH HER.
IT'S BEST YOU FORGET--
FORGET?! HOW CAN I FORGET WHEN YOU'RE RIGHT HERE IN FRONT OF ME?
DO SOMETHING MY WAY FOR ONCE. INSTEAD OF FOR-GETTING--

--LET'S TRY TO REMEMBER!
MMPH
WITHOUT WARNING, JACK PULLS HER TOWARD HIM, PRESSES HIS LIPS HARD AGAINST HERS.

YET FOR ALL ITS PASSION, THE KISS LASTS BUT A SINGLE, CHILLING MOMENT.
DIDN'T YOU FEEL IT? DIDN'T YOU FEEL ANYTHING?
NO.
NOTHING.
AND I ADVISE YOU NEVER TO FORCE YOUR-SELF UPON ME AGAIN...
...IF YOU VALUE YOUR LIFE.

NOW, THEN... IF YOU'VE NOTHING MORE YOU WISH TO DISCUSS... I SUGGEST WE BE ON OUR WAY.
BACK TO GREENWICH VILLAGE...?
I SHALL TAKE YOU WHEREVER YOU WISH.

I MUST JOIN THE OTHER DEFENDERS AT OUR HEAD-QUARTERS. STEVEN HAS TAKEN THE GUARDIANS OF THE GALAXY THERE TO KEEP THEM SAFE FROM PRYING EYES.
GUARDIANS? THOSE OTHER THREE--?

I CAN TELL YOU NO MORE. I AM PLEDGED--
HRREEEEEE
ARAGORN, WHAT--? HELA'S GHOSTS! THE CLIFFS--!
GOOD LORD-- IT FEELS LIKE--

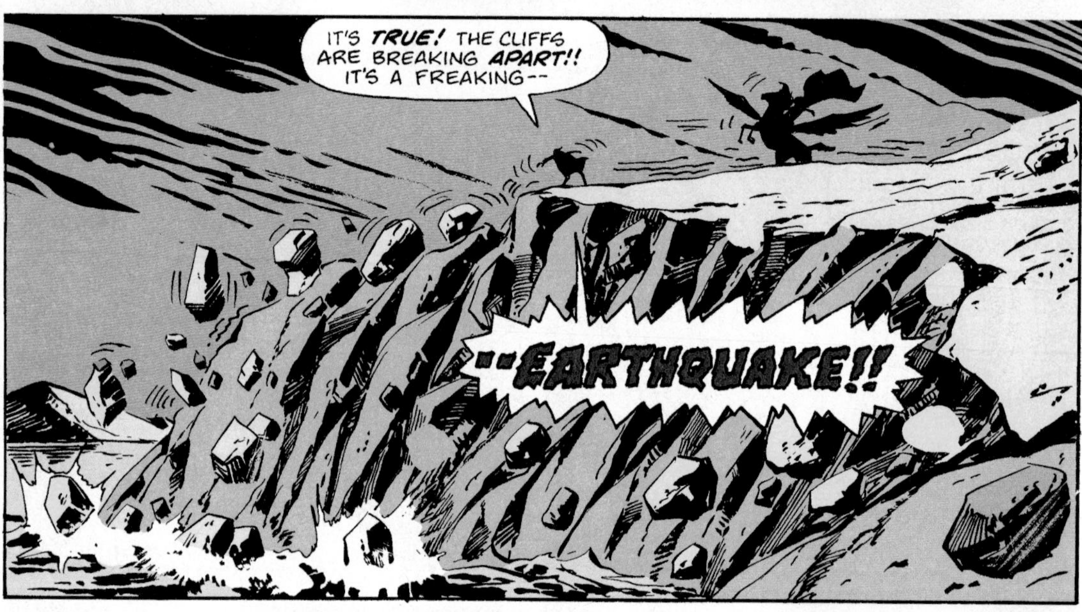
IT'S TRUE! THE CLIFFS ARE BREAKING APART!! IT'S A FREAKING--
--EARTHQUAKE!!

B-BUT THIS CAN'T BE HAPPENING! IT'S IM-- MY FEET-- SLIPPING--CAN'T BALANCE--!
MR. NORRISS --HERE! CLIMB UP BEHIND ME!

I--I CAN'T!! VIBRATIONS--TOO STRONG! I'M--
--FALLING!!

AS JACK TUMBLES BACKWARD, VAL PUTS THE DISAGREEABLE EXPERIENCE OF A MOMENT AGO OUT OF HER THOUGHTS.

A MAN'S LIFE IS IN DANGER...

... AND SHE ALONE CAN EFFECT A RESCUE.

AS SHE HAULS JACK ASTRIDE THE WINGED STEED, NORRISS CANNOT HELP BUT WONDER WHICH IS MORE ASTOUNDING -- THE QUAKE, OR HIS WIFE'S PRODIGIOUS STRENGTH?
PREFERING NOT TO CONSIDER THE LATTER, PERHAPS FOR REASONS OF SELF-ESTEEM...
TH- THIS IS INSANITY! THERE ARE NO EARTHQUAKE FAULTS IN NEW JERSEY!!

IT'S HAPPENING ALL OVER, DOC. A TIDAL WAVE SWEEPING TOWARD ENGLAND... TORNADOES IN THE BAHAMAS... AND NOW AN EARTH TREMOR ON THE PALISADES.
THE WEATHER'S GONE COMPLETELY HAYWIRE...
...JUST AS YOU PREDICTED.

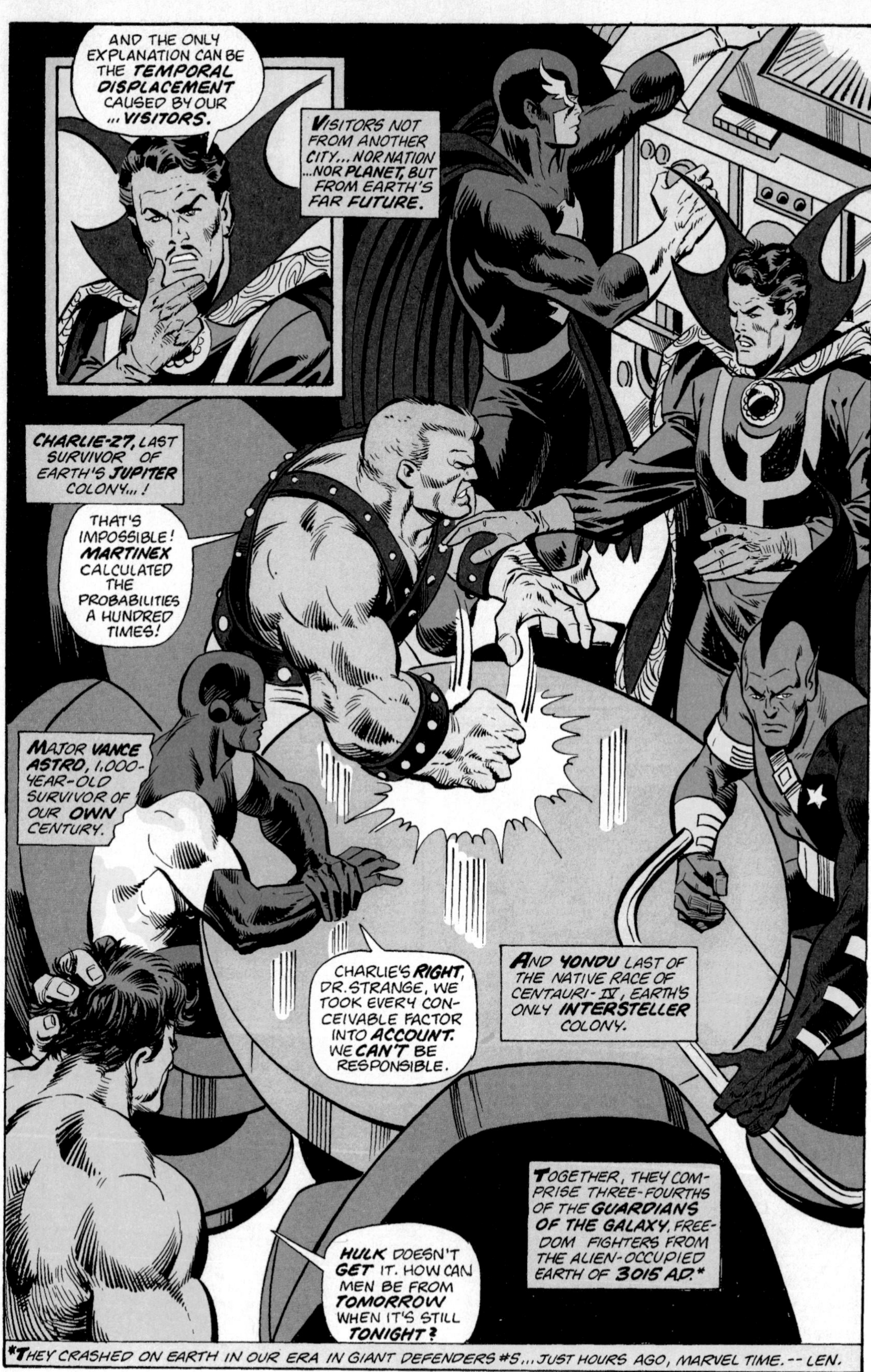
AND THE ONLY EXPLANATION CAN BE THE TEMPORAL DISPLACEMENT CAUSED BY OUR ...VISITORS.
VISITORS NOT FROM ANOTHER CITY... NOR NATION ...NOR PLANET, BUT FROM EARTH'S FAR FUTURE.
CHARLIE-27, LAST SURVIVOR OF EARTH'S JUPITER COLONY...!
THAT'S IMPOSSIBLE! MARTINEX CALCULATED THE PROBABILITIES A HUNDRED TIMES!
MAJOR VANCE ASTRO, 1,000-YEAR-OLD SURVIVOR OF OUR OWN CENTURY.
CHARLIE'S RIGHT, DR. STRANGE, WE TOOK EVERY CONCEIVABLE FACTOR INTO ACCOUNT. WE CAN'T BE RESPONSIBLE.
AND YONDU LAST OF THE NATIVE RACE OF CENTAURI-IV, EARTH'S ONLY INTERSTELLER COLONY.
TOGETHER, THEY COMPRISE THREE-FOURTHS OF THE GUARDIANS OF THE GALAXY, FREEDOM FIGHTERS FROM THE ALIEN-OCCUPIED EARTH OF 3015 AD.*
HULK DOESN'T GET IT. HOW CAN MEN BE FROM TOMORROW WHEN IT'S STILL TONIGHT?
*THEY CRASHED ON EARTH IN OUR ERA IN GIANT DEFENDERS #5... JUST HOURS AGO, MARVEL TIME. -- LEN.

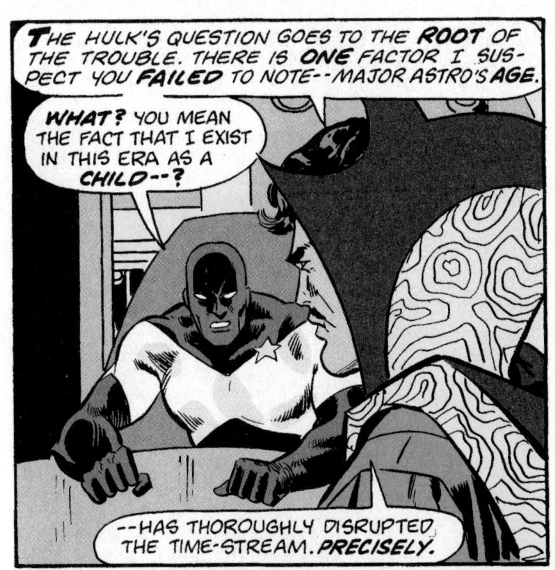

"WHAT YOU'RE SEEING IS A GENUINE U.F.O., A SHIP PRESUMABLY OF EXTRATERRESTRIAL ORIGIN WHICH CAME CRASHING TO EARTH HERE IN UPSTATE NEW YORK A FEW SHORT HOURS AGO.

"AS YOU CAN SEE, THE STRANGE CRAFT HAS BEEN CORDONED OFF BY A CONTINGENT OF NATIONAL GUARD TROOPS. AND WITH GOOD REASON.

WXYZ

"IT SEEMS THE PILOT OF THIS SPACECRAFT HAS SURVIVED THE SHIP'S PLUMMET FROM SPACE AND IS CONCEALING HIMSELF INSIDE.

BUT PERHAPS THE MOST PUZZLING ASPECT OF THE SHIP IS IT'S INSIGNIA. FOR INSCRIBED IN ENGLISH ON THE HULL ARE THE WORDS "CAPTAIN AMERICA."
GENERAL, YOU CAUGHT A GLIMPSE OF THE ALIEN. WOULD YOU CARE TO--
NO COMMENT.

GENERAL! HE'S COMIN' OUT! THE SPACEMAN'S COMIN' OUT-- LOOK AT 'IM--HE'S A WALKIN' DIAMOND!
AN' HE'S GOT A KID WITH 'IM!!

DIAMOND HE IS NOT--BUT RATHER SILICON. AND HIS NAME IS MARTINEX, LAST SURVIVOR OF EARTH'S COLONY-TO-BE ON PLUTO.
D- DON'T SHOOT HE'S NOT AN ENEMY --REALLY!

DR. STRANGE-- THE BOY WITH MARTINEX--
--IT'S ME!!
I DON'T UNDERSTAND ... WHY CAN'T I... STRANGE, DO SOMETHING!

AT ONCE. SHOULD ONE OF THOSE GUARDSMEN BECOME UNNERVED... A STRAY BULLET COULD PLUNGE ALL ETERNITY INTO IRREPARABLE CHAOS!

AND BY THE HOARY HOSTS OF HOGGOTH, THAT MUST NOT COME TO PASS!

UP AND AWAY FROM THE NASSAU/SUFFOLK HEADQUARTERS OF THE DEFENDERS, THE BOLT OF ENCHANTMENT SOARS...

...TRAVERSING HUNDREDS OF MILES IN SCANT SECONDS...

...THEN ARCING DOWNWARD...

...STRIKING THE STARSHIP...AND MARTINEX... AND YOUNG VANCE ASTROVIK... AND ENVELOPING ALL IN A BURST OF CLEAR WHITE LIGHT.

AND WHEN NEXT THEY APPEAR... THE SIGHT THAT GREETS THEIR EYES IS A FAR DIFFERENT ONE.
OH, MAN --FAR OUT! WHO ARE THEY?

GOOD FRIENDS -- THREE OF THEM. AND THE OTHER NEWFOUND ALLIES, I'D SURMISE.
QUITE CORRECT, MARTINEX. WE ARE PLEASED TO SEE YOU SAFE.

BUT WE HAVE LITTLE TIME FOR PLEASANTRIES, I'M AFRAID. HOW LONG WILL YOU REQUIRE TO REPAIR THE SHIP? IT IS URGENT THAT I KNOW.
I CAN HAVE HER SPACEWORTHY IN A FEW HOURS...
BUT SHE'S NOT DESIGNED FOR INTRA-ATMOSPHERIC FLIGHT. WE CAN'T LAUNCH HER WITHOUT...

LEAVE THAT TO ME.
MERELY ATTEND TO YOUR REPAIR WORK-- QUICKLY. EACH SECOND IS PRECIOUS.
YOU SEE, THE EARTH IS GRINDING TO A HALT ON ITS AXIS BECAUSE OF YOUR PRESENCE IN THIS ERA.

BEFORE ANY OF THE DEFENDERS OR GUARDIANS CAN BRING HIMSELF TO COMMENT FURTHER, YOUNG VANCE'S UNADULTERATED WONDER EASES THE TENSION.
CRIPES, ARE ALL OF YOU SPACEMEN? ARE YOU ALL FROM THE SAME PLANET?
IF YOU TRACE THE GENEALOGY BACK FAR ENOUGH...!

YOU SEEM ODDLY AMUSED, NIGHTHAWK. WHAT IS IT?
I WAS JUST THINKING... ALL THE GOOD ADVICE I COULD GIVE MYSELF ... IF I MET A KID NAMED KYLE RICHMOND.

MARTINEX WOULDN'T TELL ME ANYTHING ABOUT YOUR PLANET AT ALL. WHERE IS IT? HOW FAR AWAY? WHAT'S IT LIKE?
I'D ONLY BE IN THE WAY WHILE CHARLIE AND MARTINEX MAKE THE REPAIRS...
WHY DON'T WE TAKE A WALK... AND I'LL GIVE YOU A HISTORY LESSON.

YOU MEAN-- THE HISTORY OF YOUR OWN PLANET? WOW...
I CONFESS TO A CERTAIN CURIOSITY ABOUT "YOUR PLANET'S" CHRONOLOGY MYSELF, MAJOR.
HOW MUCH CAN YOU TELL US ABOUT IT?
FOR ONE THING-- WE HAVEN'T ANY WILDFLOWERS THERE.

WE USED TO... ABOUT A THOUSAND YEARS AGO. BUT THEY WEREN'T CONSIDERED ESSENTIAL AFTER THE OZONE CATASTROPHE.
ALL THE INDOOR AGRICULTURAL SPACE HAD TO BE GIVEN OVER TO FOOD CROPS ... OR WE'D HAVE STARVED TO DEATH.
OZONE? INDOOR FARMS? I'M AFRAID I DO NOT--
WE WEREN'T MUCH FURTHER ADVANCED IN SCIENCE THAN YOU ARE WHEN IT HAPPENED.
WE MADE A VERY FOOLISH CHOICE, THAT'S ALL.

"WE DECIDED WE VALUED DRY **ARMPITS** AND THE 3-BILLION-DOLLAR **AEROSOL** INDUSTRY ...OVER OUR FLOWERS, OUR FOOD, AND ULTIMATELY OUR **HEALTH**. OH, THE SCIENTISTS **WARNED** US...!

"THEY SAID THE GAS IN THOSE CANS WOULD BREAK DOWN THE **OZONE** LAYER -- THE WORLD'S PROTECTION FROM THE SUN'S ULTRAVIOLET RAYS-- BUT WE DIDN'T **BELIEVE** IT. NOT UNTIL THE FIRST **SKIN CANCER** EPIDEMIC IN 1982.

"NOT UNTIL A WALK IN THE SUN BECAME SO **DEADLY** THAT EVEN TO CROSS THE STREET, WE NEEDED PROTECTIVE **CLOTHING** OVER EVERY SQUARE INCH OF OUR **BODIES**.

"IN 1988, OUR **SPACE PROGRAM** ENDED WITH A BANG. WE SENT A MAN ON A THOUSAND-YEAR JOURNEY TO THE **STARS**. AND IT TOOK THE **LAST** OF OUR FUNDING.

"AT LAST, WE WERE GOING TO WORK TOGETHER-- AND WE TURNED OUR TECHNOLOGY AWAY FROM THE MINDLESS PROLIFERATION OF WEAPONRY, PUT IT TO WORK FOR PEOPLE INSTEAD OF AGAINST THEM. THE CITIES SLOWLY BEGAN TO SMILE AND LAUGH AGAIN. HUMANKIND UNITED-- IT WAS THE REALIZATION OF A DREAM.

"BUT THAT DREAM WAS CRUELLY OBLITERATED IN THE YEAR 2001, WHEN WE WERE INVADED BY THE MAR--BY OUR NEIGHBORING PLANET.

"OUR POPULATION WAS ALL BUT DEC-IMATED. THOSE CREATURES ACTUALLY BRED HUMANS TO EAT.

"THE CITIES CRUMBLED. OUR SCIENCE DIED. OUR CIVILIZATION COLLAPSED. IN A WORD, WE WERE CONQUERED.

"THERE ARE NO RELIABLE HISTORIES OF THE PERIOD OF OCCUPATION. LEGEND HAS IT THAT A BAND OF 'FREEMEN,' LED BY A CHARISMATIC FIGURE KNOWN AS KILLRAVEN BEGAN THE REVOLT AGAINST THE INVADERS.
"ALL WE CAN SAY FOR CERTAIN IS THAT BY 2075, THE ALIENS HAD ABANDONED OUR WORLD. WE MAY NEVER KNOW EXACTLY WHEN OR WHY.

"WE DO KNOW THAT THE NEXT 500 YEARS WAS A BARBARIC PERIOD, WITH SCIENCE HIGHLY CENTRALIZED IN FEUDAL CITY-STATES RULED BY THE SO-CALLED TECHNO-BARONS ... WHO EVENTUALLY WENT TO WAR WITH EACH OTHER -- FOR POSSESSION OF THE MOON.

"THAT WAS THEIR UNDOING.
"THE SERFS DIDN'T WANT TO FIGHT THEIR WAR. THEY REBELLED. AND WITH THE EXECUTION OF THE TYRANT KWAAL IN 2525, THE REIGN OF THE TECHNO-BARONS ENDED.

"COMMUNICATIONS WERE RESTORED BETWEEN THE CITY-STATES -- A SECOND WORLD FEDERATION WAS ESTABLISHED -- WE WERE ON OUR WAY UP ONCE AGAIN. AND THIS TIME, WE WOULD REACH FOR THE STARS.

"GENETIC ENGINEERING, DEVELOPED UNDER THE TECHNO-BARONS, ALLOWED US TO BREED SUB-SPECIES OF HUMANS TO COLONIZE OUR SOLAR SYSTEM, FROM THE PLANET NEAREST THE SUN...

"...TO THE WORLD FURTHEST FROM ITS LIGHT AND WARMTH. THERE, ONLY THE SILICON-MEN OF MARTINEX'S SPECIES COULD SURVIVE.
"BUT EVERY-WHERE, MEN WERE STUDYING, LEARNING ABOUT THEIR UNIVERSE AS NEVER BEFORE.

"IN TIME, WE EVEN OVERCAME THE CONSTRAINTS OF GRAVITY.
"TO STUDY THE GAS GIANTS OF OUR SOLAR SYSTEM, WE BUILT CITY-SPHERES THAT HUNG IN THOSE PLANETS' POISONOUS METHANE-LADEN ATMOSPHERES.

"AND WE POPULATED THOSE SPHERES WITH THE MEN AND WOMEN OF CHARLIE'S RACE, WHOSE MASS AND DENSITY WERE ADAPTED TO THRIVE UNDER THOSE CONDITIONS.

"IT ALL TOOK HUNDREDS OF YEARS, OF COURSE, BUT BY THE MID-2900'S WE'D UNDER-TAKEN CONSTRUCTION OF OUR FIRST STARSHIP FLEET.

"AND BY 2960, WE'D REACHED THE NEAREST STAR-SYSTEM TO OUR OWN...
"...AND ESTABLISHED OUR FIRST FRIENDLY CONTACT WITH AN ALIEN RACE.

"THE YEAR 3000 WAS CELEBRATED WITH THE JOINING OF ALL THE COLONIES AS CO-EQUAL PARTNERS IN A UNITED FEDERATION. THE MILLENIUM HAD COME... AND ONLY A THOUSAND YEARS LATE.
FEDERATION OF EARTH
"AND SPEAKING OF LATE -- REMEMBER THAT GUY THEY SENT INTO SPACE BACK IN 1988?

"WELL, IN 3006, HE LANDED -- A 1000-YEAR-OLD PRISONER IN A SUIT OF COPPER FOIL -- A SUIT HE COULDN'T DISCARD, BECAUSE CONTACT WITH THE AIR WOULD REDUCE HIM TO DUST. HIS INTERSTELLAR VOYAGE HAD BEEN MADE A FARCE. MAN WAS ALREADY THERE TO GREET HIM.
"POOR SLOB. HE WAS GIVEN A HERO'S WELCOME ... BUT SOMEHOW, HE JUST COULDN'T MAKE HIMSELF CARE.

"AT LEAST, NOT UNTIL 3007 ... WHEN, BELIEVE IT OR NOT, IT HAPPENED ALL OVER AGAIN. A RACE CALLED THE BADOON, THIS TIME. THEY CAME OUT OF NOWHERE, QUESTING FOR GALACTIC EMPIRE.
"AND AGAIN OUR CIVILIZATION WAS WRECKED.

"TEN CENTURIES OF HUMAN STUGGLING, A THOUSAND YEARS OF PAINFULLY CLAWING OUR WAY UP FROM THE DREGS -- WIPED OUT IN WHAT SEEMED A MERE INSTANT. WE WERE SLAVES--FOR THE THIRD TIME.

"THE BADOON GOT ALL THE COLONIES AND FINALLY CAPTURED THE HOMEWORLD. AND SINCE THEY HAD NO USE FOR US-- ONLY OUR RESOURCES AND OUR LABOR--THEY ERADICATED MOST OF THE POPULATION. BUT WE FOUR SURVIVED -- MARTINEX, CHARLIE, YONDU AND MYSELF.

"AND WE VOWED TO TAKE OUR WORLD BACK! AND OVER EIGHT YEARS, WE'VE HAD A FEW TRIUMPHS -- LIKE SEIZING THE LAST REMAINING SHIP OF THE STAR FLEET TO USE AS OUR TRAVELLING BASE.

"AND TOGETHER WITH THE HOMEWORLD UNDERGROUND -- AND SEVERAL HEROES WHO MYSTERIOUSLY APPEARED OUT OF OUR PLANET'S PAST* -- WE'VE MANAGED TO REGAIN CONTROL OF ONE MAJOR CITY."
*THE THING AND CAPT. AMERICA. SEE MARVEL 2-IN-1 #5. --LEN.

BUT WE'VE STILL A LONG FIGHT AHEAD OF US-- TEN PLANETS TO RECLAIM--AND FIFTY MILLION HUMANS TO RELEASE FROM BONDAGE. BUT WE'LL--
I--I'M SORRY IT'S JUST... ALL THAT STUFF... IT COULD HAPPEN HERE, TOO --COULDN'T IT?
VANCE-- WHAT'S THE MATTER? ARE YOU CRYING?

IT COULD, VANCE ...YES. BUT IT DOESN'T HAVE TO. IT'S DIFFICULT TO EXPLAIN... BUT NO WORLD'S FUTURE IS PREDESTINED. ONLY THE PAST IS ABSOLUTE.
I CAN'T CHANGE THE HISTORY OF MY WORLD. BUT YOU CAN ALTER THE SHAPE OF THINGS TO COME.
AND THAT WOULD BE TRUE... EVEN IF YOUR FUTURE WERE MY PAST.

IS THAT TRUE, DOC? IS AST-- THE MAJOR'S STORY JUST ONE POSSIBLE DESTINY?

PARADOXICAL THOUGH IT MAY SEEM ...THAT IS CORRECT. SO TAKE HEART, VANCE. EARTH NEED NOT SUFFER THE FATE OF THAT OTHER WORLD.
C-CAN YOU SEND ME HOME NOW, MISTER? MY FOLKS'LL BE WORRIED ABOUT ME...!

I WAS ABOUT TO SUGGEST PRECISELY THAT. MERELY CLOSE YOUR EYES... ENVISION THE HOUSE WHEREIN YOU DWELL...

...AND BY THE POWER OF THE ETERNAL VISHANTI, YOU SHALL BE THERE!

HAVE NO FEAR, MAJOR. THE BOY WILL REMEMBER NOTHING OF WHAT YOU TOLD HIM. MY SPELL SAW TO THAT.
I SHOULD'VE KNOWN. THANKS, STRANGE.

SUDDENLY, THE SOUND OF MASSIVE PINIONS SLAPPING AGAINST THE NIGHT AIR DIRECTS ALL EYES SKYWARD TO...
VAL-- AND HUBBY! THE HONEY-MOONERS RETURN.

I WOULD ADVISE YOU EMPLOY SOME OTHER NICKNAME FOR MR. NORRISS IN HIS PRESENCE, NIGHTHAWK. WE HAVE TROUBLES ENOUGH.
STEPHEN-- WHAT IS THIS? WHY IS THAT SPACECRAFT HERE--?
THAT, VAL, IS A LONG STORY.

AND WHEN THE TALE HAS BEEN TOLD...
WE ARE WAITING NOW FOR THE REPAIRS TO BE COMPLETED. THEN...

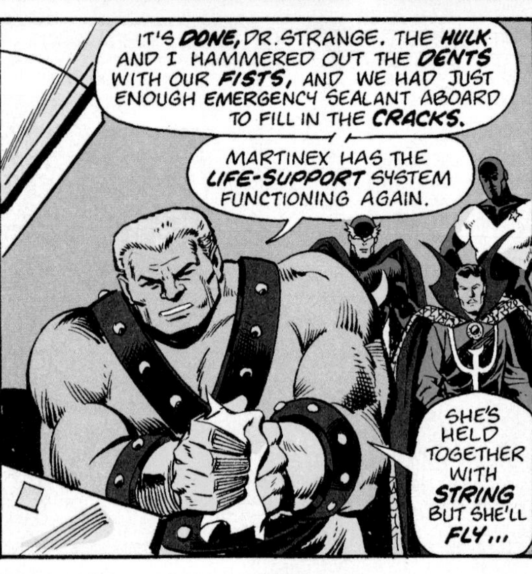
IT'S DONE, DR. STRANGE. THE HULK AND I HAMMERED OUT THE DENTS WITH OUR FISTS, AND WE HAD JUST ENOUGH EMERGENCY SEALANT ABOARD TO FILL IN THE CRACKS.
MARTINEX HAS THE LIFE-SUPPORT SYSTEM FUNCTIONING AGAIN.
SHE'S HELD TOGETHER WITH STRING BUT SHE'LL FLY...

...IF WE CAN GET HER INTO SPACE.
AND THAT I SHALL DO, ONCE WE ARE ALL ABOARD.

BARBARA-- HOLD IT! WHERE DO YOU THINK YOU'RE GOING?! THAT CRAZY THING WON'T FLY!!
LOOK AT THEM! THESE PEOPLE ARE ALL INSANE! YOU CAN'T--!
I CAN-- AND SHALL, IF I SO CHOOSE.

AND I SHAN'T ASK YOU NICELY AGAIN-- TO KEEP YOUR HANDS OFF ME!!
NOW WILL YOU KINDLY REMOVE YOURSELF FROM MY LIFE?!

MOMENTS LATER, WITHIN THE SHIP...
YOU ARE COMING WITH US, DOCTOR-- YOU AND YOUR FRIENDS?
WE'VE NAMED OURSELVES EARTH'S DEFENDERS, YONDU. IF WE WOULD BE TRUE TO THAT MISSION, WE COULD NOT DO OTHERWISE.
ALL SYSTEMS OPERATIVE, STRANGE. WE'RE READY WHEN YOU ARE.
THOUGH AS A SCIENTIST, I CAN'T BELIEVE THAT A FEW ESOTERIC UTTERANCES--

" --CAN LAUNCH US INTO ORBIT."
"BEHOLD YOUR VIEW-SCREEN, CRYSTAL-MAN --AND YOUR DOUBTS SHALL BE BANISHED."
UH, STRANGE... AREN'T YOU FORGETTING SOMETHING? LIKE THE TIME BARRIER? WITHOUT BOTH ENGINES WE'RE STILL STUCK IN YOUR ERA. WE--
AND NOW, LET US PREPARE OURSELVES TO BATTLE THE--

THAT, TOO, HAS BEEN DEALT WITH, MAJOR. AGAIN OBSERVE THE SCREEN.
AND LOOK WELL, ALL OF YOU... AT THE SIGHT OF AN EARTH ENSLAVED.
LOOK VERY WELL--FOR BEFORE WE HAVE GONE...
...THAT SIGHT SHALL BE NO MORE!
THE MIGHT OF THE DEFENDERS, TURNED AGAINST THE SAVAGE EMPIRE OF THE BADOON --BUT NOT BEFORE YOU MEET THE MYSTERIOUS BEING KNOWN ONLY AS--
The STARHAWK!

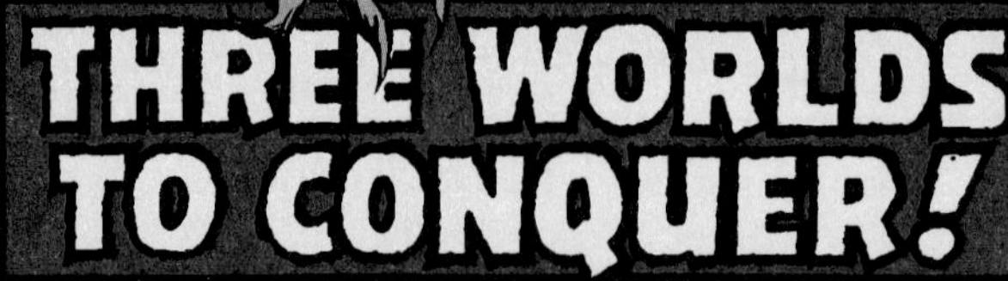
THE DEFENDERS
MARVEL COMICS GROUP
APPROVED BY THE COMICS CODE AUTHORITY
25¢
27 SEPT 02152
THE DEFENDERS
THE BADDOON WOMEN ARE FAR MORE SAVAGE THAN THEIR MEN!
UNLESS I STRIKE SWIFTLY, HULK AND VALKYRIE ARE DOOMED!
THREE WORLDS TO CONQUER!

Stan Lee PRESENTS: THE DYNAMIC DEFENDERS!™

STEVE GERBER Writer | SAL BUSCEMA & V. COLLETTA Artists | JOE ROSEN Letterer AL WENZEL Colorist | LEN WEIN Editor

PLANET EARTH, 3015 A.D.: MOST OF HUMANKIND ARE **DEAD**, AND THOSE WHO LIVE, LIVE AS SLAVES OF EARTH'S **CONQUERORS**--THE BANEFUL **BROTHERHOOD OF BADOON**. YET, SMALL THOUGH ITS NUMBERS MAY BE, HUMANITY'S LONGING FOR **FREEDOM** HAS NOT PERISHED. AND AT THE VANGUARD OF MAN'S STRUGGLE STANDS THE INTERPLANETARY GUERILLA BAND KNOWN AS... **THE GUARDIANS OF THE GALAXY!**

BUT THE JADE GIANT REMAINS SKEPTICAL-- OR PERHAPS CLAUSTROPHOBIC-- DESPITE THE REASSURANCE OF THE GUARDIANS AND THEIR AFOREMENTIONED "PASSENGERS": HULK'S FELLOW DEFENDERS!

I DON'T SEEM TO BE GETTING THROUGH TO HIM, DR. STRANGE. PERHAPS IF YOU TRIED--!

HIS UNEASE STEMS FROM A MISTRUST OF TECHNOLOGY, MARTINEX.

HE'S RARELY SEEN IT EMPLOYED FOR HIS BENEFIT.

I SUGGEST YOU CONTINUE YOUR PROCEDURE. NIGHTHAWK AND I SHALL DEAL WITH OUR EMERALD-HUED TEAMMATE.

I DON'T KNOW, DOC-- CHARLIE SEEMS TO BE DOING THE BEST OF ANY OF US.

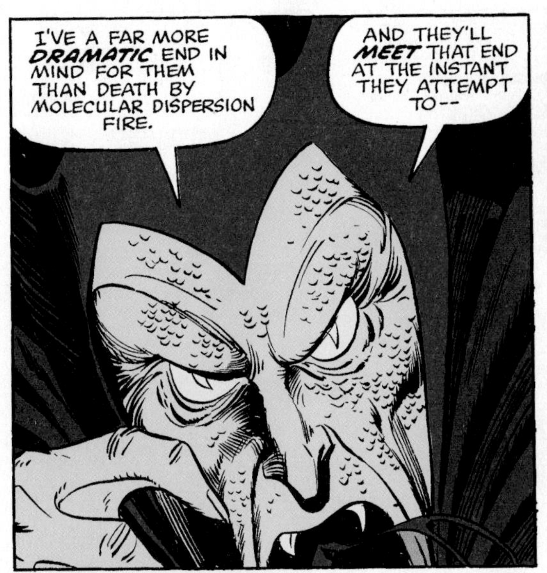

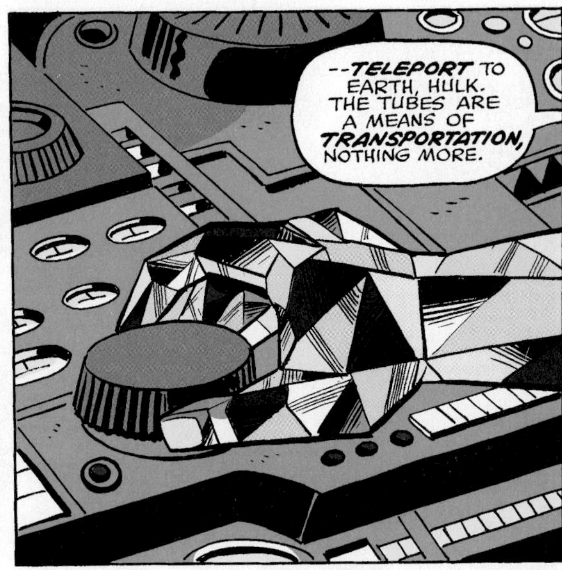

HULK **STILL** DOESN'T LIKE IT.

MAYBE GREEN-SKIN **RELATES** BETTER TO ANOTHER TWO-LEGGED **MACK TRUCK.**

I'LL ASSUME THAT'S A **COMPLIMENT,** NIGHTHAWK--

--SINCE I'VE NO IDEA WHAT A MACK TRUCK **IS.**

BUT LIKE VALKYRIE, VANCE ASTRO, AND YONDU-- THE GREEN BEHEMOTH UNDERSTANDS (IF **MINIMALLY**) THE ENORMITY OF THE **TASK** BEFORE HIM-- AND **SUBMITS.**

CRYSTALLINE FINGERS ADROITLY MANIPULATING THE DIALS OF THE CONTROL CONSOLE, THE LAST SURVIVOR OF EARTH'S PLUVIAN COLONY ACTIVATES THE TELEPORT "SEND" CIRCUIT.
AND FOUR SETS OF ATOMS ARE BROADCAST TO EARTH.

BACKTRACK SEVERAL SECONDS: THE TELEPORT CIRCUITS REACH MAXIMUM POWER OUTPUT... SENSORS REACT ON EARTH... DROOM'S WEBBED HAND COMES DOWN HARD ON A BRIGHT RED BUTTON...

...AND ANOTHER HIGH-INTENSITY DIRECTIONAL RADIO WAVE LANCES UP INTO SPACE...

...TO BISECT AND DEFLECT THE FOUR BEAMS FROM THE "CAPTAIN AMERICA"...
...HURTLING THE SCRAMBLED MOLECULES OF THE GUARDIANS/ DEFENDERS TEAMS ON A JOURNEY AWAY FROM EARTH...
...INTO THE TRACKLESS VOID OF SUB-SPACE!

I-- I DON'T UNDERSTAND IT-- THE CIRCUIT WAS FUNCTIONING PERFECTLY-- AND YET--
I'VE LOST THEM!!

WHAT DO YOU MEAN-- "LOST"? YOU KILLED THEM, DIDN'T YOU? YOU MURDERED THEM!!
BY THE VISHANTI-- HOW--?
WHO IS THAT MAN? HOW DID HE GET ABOARD?

"THE LATTER I CANNOT ANSWER. BUT HIS NAME IS JACK NORRISS-- AND HE IS HUSBAND TO THE VALKYRIE!"
AND I WANT TO KNOW WHAT YOU'VE DONE WITH MY WIFE!
WHERE IS SHE? WHERE'S BARBARA?!

THE ANSWER TO THAT QUESTION WOULD LIKELY NOT PLEASE JACK NORRISS. FOR THE WARRIOR-WOMAN AND THE 1,000-YEAR-OLD MASTER OF PSYCHO-KINESIS HAVE RE-INTEGRATED-- KNEE-DEEP IN SOME FETID MARSHLAND.

THE WATERS ARE BLOOD RED AND MURKY... THE VEGETATION, A TANGLE OF DEEP PURPLE AND GOLD... THE ENTIRE GESTALT: ALIEN AND FRAUGHT WITH PERIL.

WH-WHAT IS THIS PLACE? SURELY THIS CANNOT BE--?

IT ISN'T. WE WERE SUPPOSED TO 'PORT DOWN IN NEW YORK. AND, VAL--

--WE'RE NOT EVEN ON EARTH!

...AND THE DUO IS SUDDENLY UNDER ATTACK!
UP FROM THE MUCK... DOWN FROM THE BRANCHES OF THE TREES, THEY COME IN DROVES, SLIMY-HAIRED LIZARD-THINGS...

...SAVAGE, MINDLESS, AND UNCONTROLLABLY VIOLENT. AND THOUGH THEIR CLAWS CANNOT PENETRATE ASTRO'S PROTECTIVE METAL SHEATH...

...THEIR SHEER WEIGHT IS SUFFICIENT TO FORCE HIS GLITTERING FORM DOWN INTO THE MIRE...
...TO DROWN.

VAL'S MAGIC-SPAWNED STRENGTH IS GREATER. SHE STANDS FIRM AGAINST THE CRUEL ASSAULT.

SHE EVEN STRIKES BACK.
BUT AS SHE DOES SO... A WAVE OF NAUSEA SWEEPS OVER HER.

HER THRUSTS GROW WEAKER, MORE AWKWARD. HER WILL TO SURVIVE SEEMS PITTED AGAINST SOME OTHER, EQUALLY POWERFUL INSTINCT...
...UNTIL HER BARE FLESH IS TORN OPEN BY THE SWIFT, STINGING SWIPE OF REPTILIAN CLAWS.

THEN SHE STABS WITHOUT THOUGHT, WITHOUT FURTHER QUESTION...
EEGAAAH

...AND REAPS AN UNEXPECTED SIDE-EFFECT.
IT IS... AS IF... I'D INFLICTED... THE FATAL WOUND... UPON MYSELF! PAIN... CANNOT STAND...

PAIN SUCH AS SHE HAS NEVER KNOWN SEARS HER EVERY NERVE, BLAZING A FIERY TRAIL TO HER BRAIN. SHE DOUBLES OVER...CRIES OUT... FALLS FACE-FORWARD INTO THE CRIMSON-CLOUDED WATERS.
AND THE BEASTS SURGE TOWARD HER CONVULSING FORM.

WHILE, MERE YARDS AWAY...
VAL-- HAVE TO GET TO HER-- HELP HER-- SUMMON UP-- CONCENTRATION--

--AND --BLAST --THESE --BERSERKERS--
--AWAY!!

FREE OF THE BEASTS' ENORMOUS WEIGHT, HE STRUGGLES TO HIS FEET, RAVENOUSLY GULPING IN THE HUMID AIR...
...CASTING HIS EYES LEFT AND RIGHT FOR SOME SIGHT OF--
VAL!! GOOD LORD--THEY'RE POUNDING HER INTO THE GROUND!

ONCE MORE, HE REACHES DEEP INTO HIS CONSCIOUSNESS ...GATHERING TOGETHER SPARKS OF PSYCHIC FORCE... FUSING... FOCUSING... HURLING THEM OUTWARD THROUGH THE PSYKE-PUSHER DISC CONCEALED 'NEATH HIS METALLIC HOOD.
OFF-- GET OFF-- HER--

NOW!

VAL-- HERE-- LET ME HELP YOU UP. ARE YOU ALL RIGHT? CAN YOU STAND?
I-- AM NOT SURE. FELT-- SUFFOCATING-- FACE IN MUD-- MY SHOULDER-- I THINK-- IT IS BLEEDING. WHAT WERE THEY? WHY--?
I ONLY WISH I KNEW...!

THEY RESEMBLE THE BADOON...SAME PHYSICAL CONFORMATION... BUT UNLESS THEY'RE SOME PRIMITIVE OFFSHOOT...
THERE WILL BE TIME FOR SPECULATION LATER, MAJOR.
WHAT-- ANOTHER HUMAN?

OR SOMETHING SIMILAR.
THE WOMAN IS IN NEED OF AID. BRING HER THIS WAY. FOLLOW ME.

WHILE, BACK IN EARTH-ORBIT...!
MARTINEX-- YOU'VE TAKEN THAT PANEL APART AND PUT IT BACK TOGETHER HALF-A-DOZEN TIMES, NOW!
TELL US, ALREADY-- WHAT WENT WRONG?!
WITH OUR CIRCUITRY-- NOTHING. SOME OUT-SIDE FORCE CAUSED THE MALFUNCTION. THERE'S NO OTHER EX--
AND OUR FRIENDS-- WHAT'S BECOME OF THEM?
THEY COULD BE ANYWHERE: ON EARTH. ON SOME OTHER WORLD. OR... DEAD, ADRIFT IN SPACE.

MY GOD-- HE ADMITS IT!!
HOW CAN YOU ALL JUST STAND THERE-- AND LET THIS ROCK-HEADED FREAK GET AWAY WITH MURDER?!
YOU CALL YOURSELVES "HEROES." I'LL SHOW YOU HOW TO BE--

ENOUGH, MR. NORRISS.
WE SHALL HAVE NO VIOLENCE HERE. IS THAT CLEAR?

WHAT-- WHAT DID YOU DO TO ME? I-- I CAN'T MOVE!
I SHALL LIFT THE SPELL WHEN YOU THINK YOU CAN CONTROL YOURSELF, SIR.

MY APOLOGIES, MARTINEX, FOR MR. NORRISS' LANGUAGE AND BEHAVIOR. I'M AFRAID HIS NOTIONS ABOUT REALITY ARE STILL SOMEWHAT-- SHALL WE SAY, LIMITED.
UNDERSTOOD. LET'S RETURN TO THE PROBLEM AT HAND.
LOCATING OUR FOUR STRAYS. AGREED. I HAVE AN IDEA--!

"TAKE ME TO YOUR SENSOR BANKS," THE MYSTIC ENJOINS. AND A PUZZLED BUT INTRIGUED MARTINEX COMPLIES.
AND EVEN AS THEY STRIDE THE STARSHIP'S METAL CORRIDORS...
...YONDU, LAST OF THE CENTAURI-IV PRIMITIVES, AND THE HULK, FIRST OF THE GAMMA-RAY-BORN PRIMITIVES, MATERIALIZE AMID A BIZARRE BACCHANALLIAN REVEL...ON A WORLD NEITHER HAS EVER SEEN.
REVOLTING! GROGGED OUT OF THEIR MINDS-- ALL OF THEM!
EVER THE NOBLE SAVAGE, YONDU'S VERY SENSE OF DECENCY IS OFFENDED BY THE SIGHTS AND SOUNDS OF THE RECKLESS ABANDON THAT SWIRLS ALL ABOUT HIM.

REAL OR IMAGINED, HIS WILDERNESS-BRED INSTINCTS DETECT A SINISTER QUALITY ABOUT IT. HE MUST KNOW MORE.
YOU-- HO! I HAVE NEED OF DIRECTIONS. WHAT IS THE NAME OF--

GOOZOT! HOGLO NOROSEM ZEBU. GROTNIK?
I SHOULD'VE EXPECTED IT. THE LANGUAGE IS AS ALIEN AS THE PLACE ITSELF.
MAN DOESN'T TALK RIGHT!

NOTHING IS RIGHT HERE! PEOPLE LAUGH-- DANCE-- SING--!
BUT PEOPLE LOOK STUPID-- NOT HAPPY!
YOU SENSE IT, TOO, THEN. THE SADNESS IN THE AIR-- THE ODOR OF--

EEEYAAAAAAA
--DEATH.
WOMAN SCREAMS! BUT WHERE FROM?

THIS WAY, HULK! HURRY!

HERE-- DOWN THIS PASSAGE-WAY! I PRAY WE'RE IN TIME TO HELP!
HOW COME NOBODY ELSE RUNS WITH US?
EEEEE

ARE HULK AND FLAG-HEAD ONLY ONES WHO HEAR NOISE?
I DOUBT THAT, HULK. AND YET--
BY THE THREE SUNS!!

THEY MEAN TO HACK HER TO PIECES! THEY--
STOP! GET AWAY FROM HER! ARE YOU ALL MAD?

BUT THE SWORDSMEN, APPARENTLY, ARE AS DEAF AS THE REVELERS -- SO YONDU RESORTS TO OTHER MEANS TO DISPERSE THEM:

THE YAKA ARROW AND A SHRILL WHISTLE--

--TO WHICH THE WEIRD SHAFT OF "LIVING" METAL RESPONDS BY LOOPING AND DIVING AROUND AND AMONG THE WOMAN'S ATTACKERS...

...SENDING THEM RACING IN PANIC FROM THE ALCOVE.
IT APPEARS WE'VE FOUND A LANGUAGE THEY UNDER-STAND.

AND PERHAPS THE WOMAN CAN PROVIDE THE INFORMATION WE NEED.
LET US HELP YOU UP. YOU MUST BE OVERCOME WITH FRIGHT.

GOOZOT! NURK RETS LAVAN SKOO!
SWAT

WOMAN HITS FLAG-HEAD FOR HELPING HER?! WOMAN IS STUPID, TOO!

I CONFESS-- THE CUSTOMS OF THIS RACE DO-- OH, NO!
HUH? NOW WHAT?!

HALT-WHERE-YOU-STAND. YOU-ARE-CHARGED-WITH-DISRUPTION-FESTIVAL-OF-DEATH. YOU-MUST-BE-BROUGHT-TO-JUSTICE.

TIN MEN WANT TO FIGHT HULK?
WAIT, MY FRIEND-- THEY HAVE WEAPONS! AND WE DO NOT KNOW WHAT POWERS THEY MAY POSSESS...!
GOOD!! HULK NEEDS SOMETHING TO SMASH!

HULK DOESN'T CARE!
CHOOM
HULK JUST WANTS TO HIT SOMETHING-- BEFORE STUPID PLACE DRIVES HULK CRAZY!!

Y-YOU'VE DESTROYED ALL OF THEM-- I DIDN'T REALIZE YOU--
NO! HULK DID NOT CRUSH THEM ALL! LOOK!
THERE IS ONE MORE!

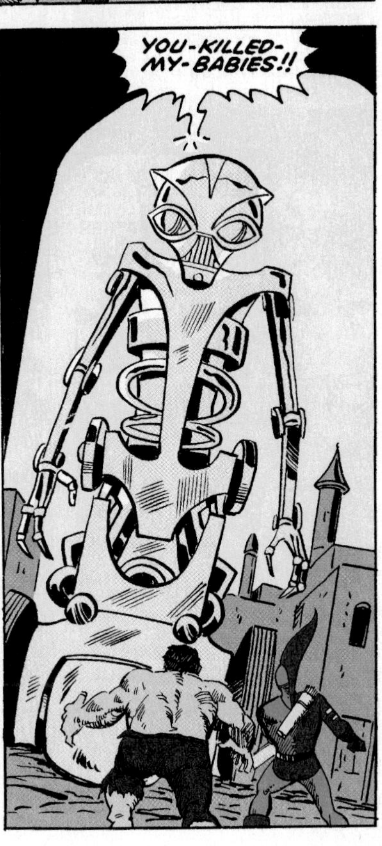
YOU-KILLED-MY-BABIES!!

AND-BY-SO-DOING-YOU-HAVE-SEALED-YOUR-FATE. YOU-ARE-ADJUDGED-GUILTY- --

--AND-HEREBY-PLACED-IN-THRALL.

THE WIRING IS COMPLETED NOW, STRANGE. TO ALL INTENTS AND PURPOSES--
--YOU'RE PART OF OUR COMPUTER SYSTEMS.
THEN LET US COMMENCE WITH THE SEARCH.

ARE YOU CERTAIN YOU WANT TO ATTEMPT THIS? IF YOU CAN'T MANAGE THE VOLTAGE COURSING THROUGH YOU--!
HAVE NO FEAR FOR ME, PLUVIAN. PRAY RATHER THAT YOUR CIRCUITS ARE UP TO THE TASK.

WHATEVER YOU SAY. I'VE PROGRAMMED THE SENSOR BANKS FOR WIDE SCAN, AS YOU REQUESTED.
AND I'M ENGAGING THE COMPUTER--
--NOW!

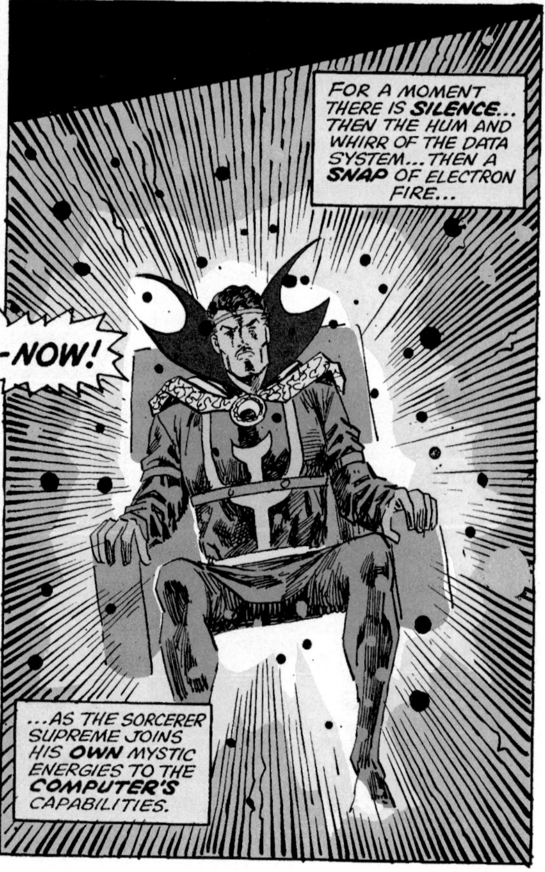
FOR A MOMENT THERE IS SILENCE... THEN THE HUM AND WHIRR OF THE DATA SYSTEM... THEN A SNAP OF ELECTRON FIRE...
...AS THE SORCERER SUPREME JOINS HIS OWN MYSTIC ENERGIES TO THE COMPUTER'S CAPABILITIES.

THE RESULT IS A **FUSION** OF MYSTICISM AND TECHNOLOGY: A SORCERER WHO CAN PROCESS AND EVALUATE **DATA** INPUT WITH MACHINE **PRECISION** AND SPLIT-SECOND **RAPIDITY**...

...AND A COMPUTER THAT IS **ONE WITH THE UNIVERSE.**

TOGETHER THEY REACH OUT, PROBING, SEEKING, TOUCHING, TRAVERSING THE INTERSTELLAR VOID... INTUITION GUIDING LOGIC... EXAMINING WHOLE STAR-SYSTEMS AT NERVE-IMPULSE CLIP...

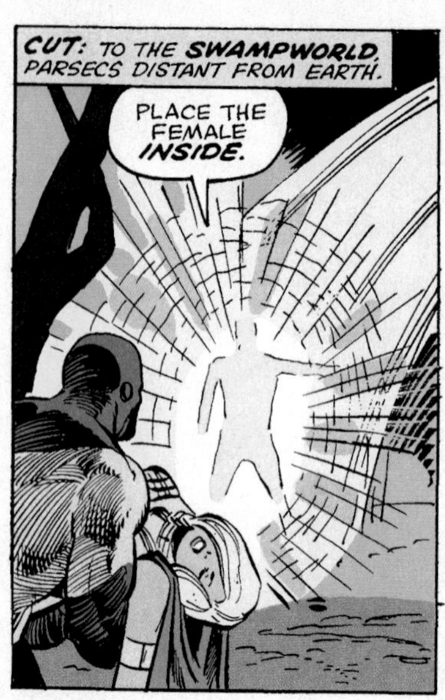
CUT: TO THE SWAMPWORLD, PARSECS DISTANT FROM EARTH.
PLACE THE FEMALE INSIDE.

SHE'S LOST A LOT OF BLOOD. DO YOU HAVE MEDICAL SUPPLIES? ANTI-SEPTICS? GAUZE?
BLAST IT-- ANSWER ME!
STAND ASIDE, PLEASE.

I SHALL BE HER HEALER... I WHO AM THE LIGHT...!

FOR THE LIGHT MENDS ALL WOUNDS... OF THE SPIRIT AND OF THE FLESH... AND I AM THE GIVER OF THE LIGHT.
INTO THE STRICKEN ONE FROM ME DOES THE LIGHT FLOW...

...THAT SHE MAY RISE INTO THE WORLD, WHOLE ONCE MORE.
I DON'T BELIEVE IT--!

A MOMENT AGO YOU WERE SPRAWLED AT DEATH'S DOOR, AND NOW--
I AM WELL. I FEEL NO PAIN... NO WEAKNESS... AND MY WOUNDS HAVE VANISHED!

HOW DID YOU DO IT? WHO-- OR WHAT-- ARE YOU?
ARE YOU A NATIVE OF THIS PLANET? YOU LOOK HUMAN, AND YET...

THESE THINGS DO NOT CONCERN YOU.
WHAT MATTERS NOW IS THAT I HAVE SAVED THE WOMAN...
...AND YOU AND SHE ARE IN MY DEBT.

WHILE, AT THE OPPOSITE END OF THE GALAXY...
WELL, WELL... LOOK WHAT THE "CAT" DRAGGED IN, GOOZOT.*
DISGUSTING. HAVE THEM DISMEMBERED.
AND LET US WATCH.
NOW, GIRLS... DON'T BE HASTY. WE SHOULD FIRST LEARN WHO THEY ARE.
*ENOUGH IS ENOUGH. WE'RE TRANSLATING FOR YOU.--MARV.

ZINNIA, DARLING... TELL US. WHERE DID YOU FIND THEM? WHAT IS THEIR CRIME?
DISRUPTION-OF-DEATH-FESTIVAL. INFANTICIDE.
THEY-KILLED-MY-BABIES.

BABIES? GOOZOT, WHAT DOES IT MEAN?
MERELY A CLEVER BIT OF PROGRAMMING, DEAR... TO INSTILL IN ZINNIA A SENSE OF DUTY.
HER TWO CAPTIVES... HOW ODD THEY LOOK. SURELY THEY ARE NOT OF US.

PERCEPTIVE, MY DEAR. I WOULD SURMISE THEY ARE... GIFTS, OF A SORT... FROM OUR ALLIES, THE BADOON.
INTERESTING SPECIMENS, THESE.

THEY'LL BE FUN... IN THE GAMES. TAKE THEM TO THE STUDIO, ZINNIA.
BUT BEFORE WE LET THE PEOPLE VIEW THEM... DO FIND SOME MORE SUITABLE ATTIRE FOR THE GREEN PERSON, EH?

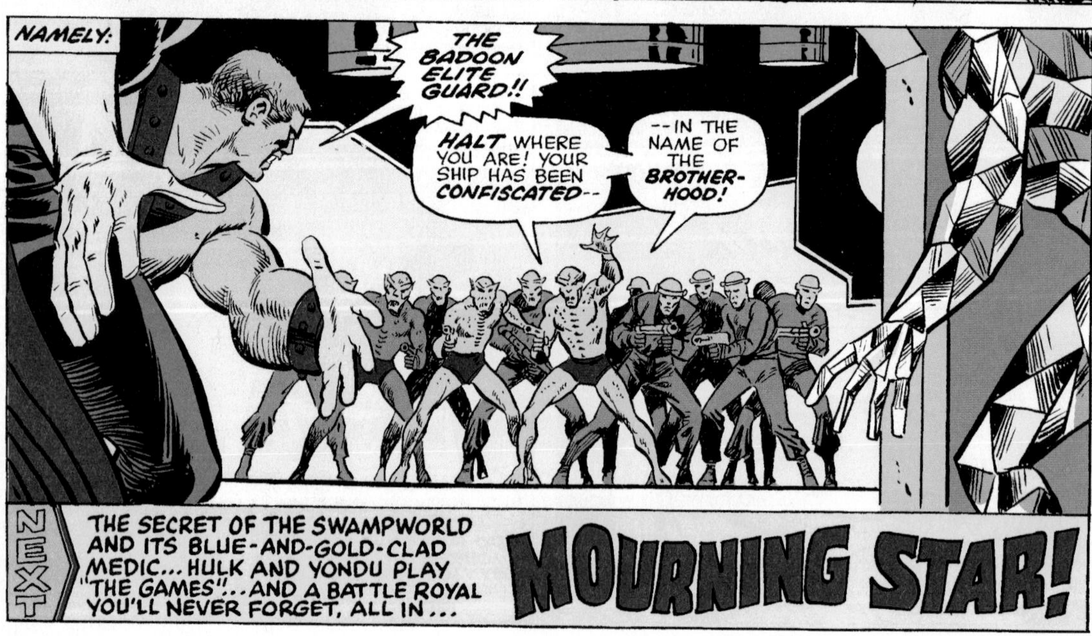

NEXT

THE SECRET OF THE SWAMPWORLD AND ITS BLUE-AND-GOLD-CLAD MEDIC... HULK AND YONDU PLAY "THE GAMES"... AND A BATTLE ROYAL YOU'LL NEVER FORGET, ALL IN ...

MOURNING STAR!

THE DEFENDERS MARVEL COMICS GROUP™

APPROVED BY THE COMICS CODE AUTHORITY

25¢ 28 OCT 02152

THE DEFENDERS™

ENTER: STARHAWK!

WITH A COVER LIKE *THIS* ONE, NEED WE SAY ***MORE?***

Stan Lee PRESENTS: THE DYNAMIC DEFENDERS!
TM
STEVE GERBER WRITER
SAL BUSCEMA ARTIST
FRANK GIACOIA & JOHN TARTAG EMBELLISHERS
JOE ROSEN LETTERER
AL WENZEL COLORIST
MARV WOLFMAN EDITOR
MY MOTHER, THE BADOON!
QUICKIE SYNOPSIS: THE DEFENDERS HAVE JOURNEYED TO THE ALIEN-OCCUPIED EARTH OF 3015 A.D., ALONG WITH THE GUARDIANS OF THE GALAXY, FREEDOM-FIGHTERS OF THAT ERA. HOWEVER, EARTH'S CONQUERORS, THE LIZARD-LIKE BROTHERHOOD OF BADOON, INTERCEPTED THE TELEPORT SIGNAL CARRYING FOUR OF THE HEROES TO THE PLANET'S SURFACE, THEREBY...
...STRANDING VANCE ASTRO AND VALKYRIE ON A WEIRD SWAMPWORLD...
...AND MAROONING HULK AND YONDU ON A PLANET OF DRUNKARDS AND ROBOT SLAVES.
DR. STRANGE, TIED IN TO THE COMPUTER OF THE GUARDIANS' STARSHIP, MYSTICALLY SEARCHES FOR HIS MISSING ALLIES, UNAWARE THAT...
THE SHIP'S BEEN BOARDED--
--BY THE BADOON ELITE GUARD!!

AND SINCE THAT'S WHERE WE LEFT OFF... THAT'S WHERE THE MADNESS BEGINS ANEW!
YOU HAVE ON BOARD THIS VESSEL SOME NEW POWER SOURCE--
--A SENSOR PROBE MORE POTENT THAN ANY KNOWN WEAPON IN YOUR WORLD'S ARSENAL.
WE'VE COME TO CONFISCATE IT-- AND YOU, REBELS!

SENSOR--? HE MEANS THE SHIP'S COMPUTER-- AND--
--AND DOC, RIGHT? HIS MAGIC IS THE "POWER SOURCE" THEY'RE AFTER!
BUT THE COMPUTER HOOK-UP'S ALREADY TAXING HIM TO HIS LIMITS.
TRUE. ANY TAMPERING WITH THE MECHANISM WOULD MEAN HIS DEATH.

AND THAT, MY FRIENDS, WOULD INDICATE--
-- WE'VE A FIGHT ON OUR HANDS!

TWIN BURSTS OF HEAT AND COLD FLY FROM THE CRYSTALLINE HANDS OF MARTINEX, SOLE SURVIVOR OF EARTH'S COLONY ON PLUTO.
CRACK
FLAM

AND CLOSE BEHIND... THE RAMPAGING FORM OF CHARLIE-27, LAST OF EARTH'S JOVIAN COLONISTS...
...LIKE MARTINEX, A PRODUCT OF ADVANCED GENETIC ENGINEERING...

...BUT WITH ELEVEN TIMES THE MASS OF HIS TERRAN ANCESTORS.
AND EVEN THE NERVELESS, MINDLESS ZOMS, HUMAN SLAVES TO THE BADOON, NOTICE THE DIFFERENCE.

TO HIS SURPRISE, NIGHTHAWK, THE LONE DEFENDER IN THE FRAY, FINDS THAT THE ETERNAL DARK OF SPACE DOUBLES HIS STRENGTH AS SUNSET DOES ON EARTH. AND YET...
WHAT'S WITH THESE CREEPS? THEY LOOK HUMAN-- BUT NO MATTER HOW HARD I HIT 'EM--
--THEY BOUNCE BACK FOR MORE!

THE ZOMS DON'T FEEL PAIN, NIGHTHAWK! THEY'VE BEEN LOBOTOMIZED BY THE BADOON-- PROGRAMMED TO HATE THEIR FELLOW EARTHMEN!
KRUNCH

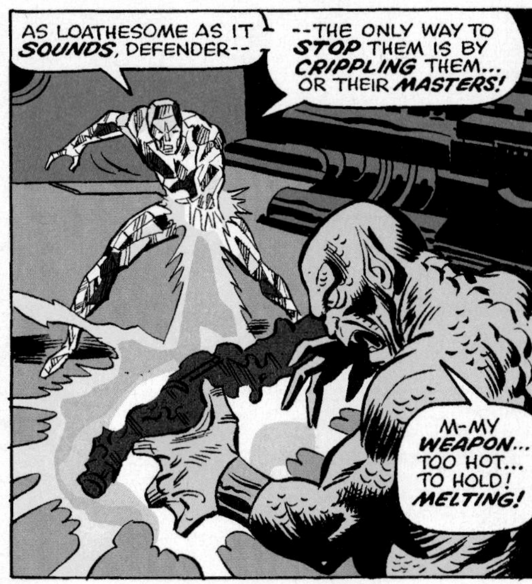
AS LOATHESOME AS IT SOUNDS, DEFENDER--
--THE ONLY WAY TO STOP THEM IS BY CRIPPLING THEM... OR THEIR MASTERS!
M-MY WEAPON... TOO HOT... TO HOLD! MELTING!

THE BADOON HAVE DONE IT ALL, THEN, HAVEN'T THEY--
--EVEN FOUND A WAY TO TURN HUMAN AGAINST HUMAN.

WELL, IF THEY CAN DO IT--
CLUD
--SO CAN I !!

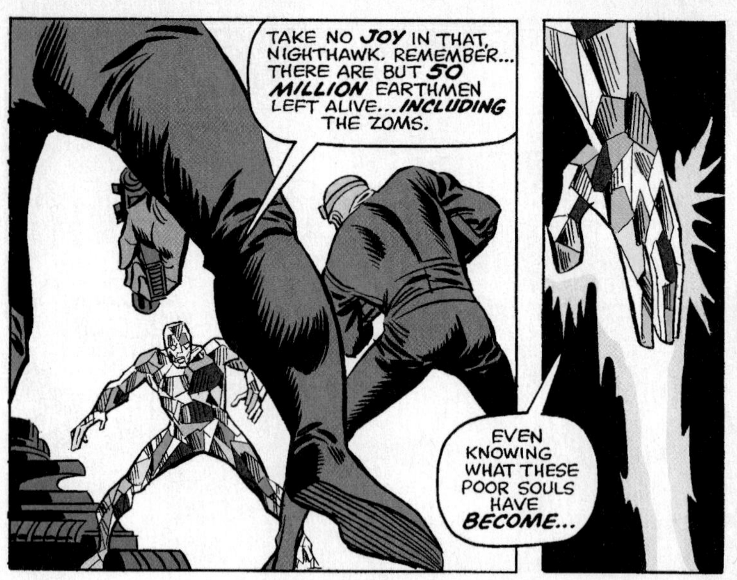
TAKE NO JOY IN THAT, NIGHTHAWK. REMEMBER... THERE ARE BUT 50 MILLION EARTHMEN LEFT ALIVE... INCLUDING THE ZOMS.
EVEN KNOWING WHAT THESE POOR SOULS HAVE BECOME...

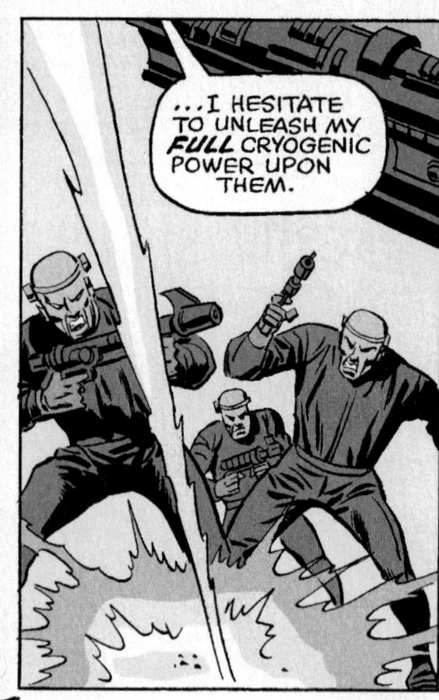
...I HESITATE TO UNLEASH MY FULL CRYOGENIC POWER UPON THEM.

BETTER TO ACT INDIRECTLY... TO PRESERVE HUMAN LIFE... EVEN IN THIS HIDEOUS FORM, THAN--
YEOW!
ZZAT
ZOMS-- THE WING-CAPED ONE HAS BEEN DISABLED! UPON HIM-- AT ONCE--
--BEFORE HE RECOVERS FROM THE STUN!

SILENTLY, FOR THEIR VOICES HAVE BEEN STOLEN WITH THEIR THOUGHTS, THE ZOMS CONVERGE ON THE TOTTERING NIGHTHAWK.
AND THOUGH HE STRUGGLES VALIANTLY...
...HE STRUGGLES IN VAIN. SAPPED OF HIS STRENGTH, HE IS HELPLESS IN THEIR GRASP.

CRYSTAL MAN-- JOVIAN-- LET THE BATTLE CEASE!
UNLESS, OF COURSE, YOU'D CARE TO HASTEN YOUR COMRADE'S DEMISE!

MY ORDERS ARE TO SEIZE THIS VESSEL INTACT. I'VE THUS EMPLOYED ONLY THE MOST MILD WEAPONRY.
BUT EVEN A BADOON STUN-PISTOL AT SUCH CLOSE RANGE AS THIS...!
YOU NEED SAY NO MORE. YOUR POINT HAS BEEN MADE.
EXCELLENT! THEN I SUGGEST WE PROCEED AT ONCE TO YOUR MYSTERIOUS POWER SOURCE!

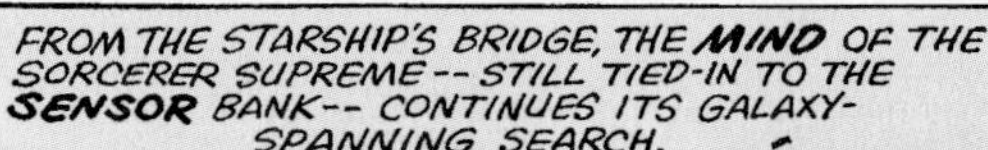
FROM THE STARSHIP'S BRIDGE, THE MIND OF THE SORCERER SUPREME -- STILL TIED-IN TO THE SENSOR BANK -- CONTINUES ITS GALAXY-SPANNING SEARCH.

PROBING... ANALYZING DATA WITH COMPUTER RAPIDITY... REACHING OUT INTO THE CLUSTERS OF STARS... THIS SUN TOO HOT... THIS ONE, TOO COOL... THAT ONE... THAT ONE...

...CONTACT!!

FAMILIAR VIBRATIONS... PLANET LOCATION: CAPELLA SYSTEM... HE'S FOUND THEM!... SECOND PLANET FROM SUN... WITH A STRANGER... READINGS INDICATE RESIDUE OF SOLAR-TYPE ENERGY IN THIRD LIFE-FORM...!
THE WOMAN SEEMS WELL ENOUGH TO TRAVEL. LET US BEGIN THE TREK.

NO, VALKYRIE... DO NOT DRAW YOUR SWORD. YOU SHALL HAVE NO NEED OF IT, I PROMISE YOU.
BUT THE LIZARD-BEASTS...!
UNLESS YOU WOULD RELISH ANOTHER ATTACK OF NAUSEA... DO AS I SAY.

YOU FORGET...I KNOW ALL ABOUT YOU, WARRIOR-WOMAN: THAT YOUR BODY ONCE HOUSED BARBARA DENTON... THAT ALL HER MEMORIES ARE LOST TO YOU...THAT YOUR NEW PERSONA IS THE ENCHANTRESS' CREATION...

...AND THAT YOU ARE POWERLESS TO DEFEND YOURSELF AGAINST A FOE OF YOUR OWN GENDER.
WHAT?! WHAT HOW--?

NO MATTER. I KNOW. AND THAT IS THAT.
THE SWAMP CREATURES... WERE ALL FEMALES? IS THAT WHAT YOU'RE SAYING?

YOU ASTONISH ME, MAJOR ASTRO.
CAN IT BE YOU GUARDIANS OF THE GALAXY HAVE LEARNED SO LITTLE OF YOUR WORLD'S CONQUERORS?
HAVE YOU NEVER QUESTIONED HOW A BADOON BROTHERHOOD COULD EXIST...
...WITHOUT A SISTERHOOD?

YOU CAN'T MEAN-- THOSE MINDLESS ANIMALS--?!
MAJOR... YOU YOURSELF REMARKED ON THE RESEMBLANCE WHEN THEY FIRST ASSAULTED US.

ALL IS NOT WHAT IT SEEMS ON THIS SWAMPWORLD, MAJOR. THE CREATURES YOU ENCOUNTERED WERE NOT SAVAGES AT ALL.
BEHOLD--!
HELA'S GHOSTS--!

"VENESIA-- CITY OF THE SISTERHOOD OF BADOON!"

A METALLIC METROPOLIS-- AFLOAT ON THE SWAMPWORLD'S SHALLOW WATERS-- WITH CANALS AS THOROUGHFARES--

--AND THE SWAMP CREATURES WHOM WE BATTLED... AS INHABITANTS!

A WORK OF ART, WOULDN'T YOU SAY? HARDLY THE DOMAIN OF MINDLESS BEASTS.

VAL AND ASTRO'S INCREDULITY IS FULLY MATCHED BY THAT OF A CERTAIN BADOON COMMANDER, BACK IN EARTH-ORBIT...!
BUT I SEE NO GENERATORS... NO CIRCUITRY... ONLY AN OUT-LANDISHLY-GARBED HUMAN...
...WHO IS HIMSELF THE POWER SOURCE YOU SEEK.

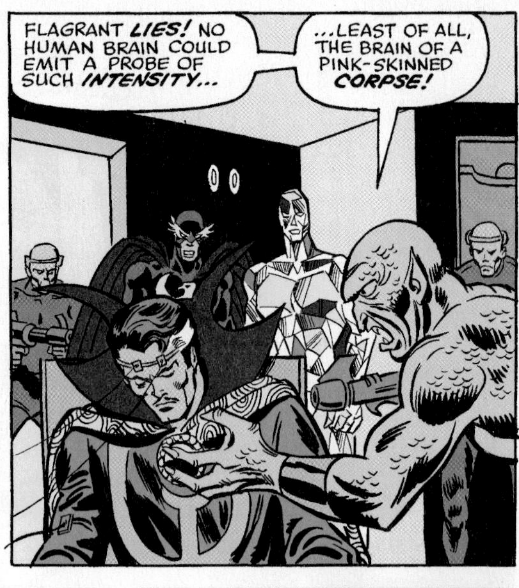
FLAGRANT LIES! NO HUMAN BRAIN COULD EMIT A PROBE OF SUCH INTENSITY...
...LEAST OF ALL, THE BRAIN OF A PINK-SKINNED CORPSE!

CORPSE!?!
NO! IT CAN'T BE! YOU'RE TRYING TO TRICK US! YOU--

AH, THEN HE WAS ALIVE AT SOME POINT... AND APPARENTLY BURNED HIMSELF OUT. INTERESTING.
WE'LL WANT A CLOSER LOOK AT HIS CRANIUM LATER, I'M SURE.

BUT OUR MEDICAL TEAMS CAN FETCH THE HEAD FOR US ANYTIME.
YOU THREE ARE A MORE IMMEDIATE PROBLEM.
ZOMS! SHOW THEM BACK TO THE TELEPORT CHAMBER.

"WE'LL TAKE THIS TRIO OF REBELS TO SOL-III... TO FACE THEIR EXECUTIONERS!"
AND SO THE TELE-PORT WAVES STAB PLANET-WARD...

...WHILE A GHOSTLY FIGURE, THE ASTRAL FORM OF DR. STRANGE, OBSERVES THE ODD DOINGS WITH... AMUSEMENT?
SO. THEY'VE MISTAKEN MY PHYSICAL BODY'S DECELERATED METABOLISM --FOR NO LIFE PROCESS AT ALL.
EXCELLENT!

I BELIEVE I CAN TRUST IN MY ALLIES' RESOURCEFULNESS TO KEEP THEM ALIVE ON EARTH--
--WHILE I HASTEN TO THE AID OF OUR FOUR STRAYS.

"FOR IF THE COMPUTER'S CALCULATIONS WERE **CORRECT**, I CAN LOCATE THE **HULK** AND **YONDU**--

"--BY PROCEEDING PRECISELY THE SAME **DISTANCE** AT PRECISELY THE OPPOSITE **ANGLE** FROM THE COURSE WHICH WILL LEAD ME TO VALKYRIE AND VANCE ASTRO."*

THAT **SECOND** TRAJECTORY, WHEN AND IF DR. STRANGE **FOLLOWS** IT, WILL TAKE HIM TO A **DRUNKARDS'** WORLD RULED BY THE SLACK-JOWLED **EMPEROR GOOZOT**, MASTER OF THE GAMES... A WORLD OF BIZARRE TECHNOLOGICAL **INTERMIX**, WHERE **ROBOTS** COEXIST WITH MEDIEVAL **DUNGEONS**...

...WHERE, EVEN NOW, THE **JADE GIANT** OF THE DEFENDERS AND THE **WEAPONS MASTER** OF THE GUARDIANS, ARE BEING **GROOMED** TO BATTLE FOR THEIR LIVES.

*"WHA--?"--MARV.

VOICE OVER: "MON-TEE, FACING THE ULTIMATE GIVEAWAY ON OUR SHOW TONIGHT, WE'RE PROUD TO PRESENT NOT ONE, BUT TWO GIFT-CONTESTANTS FROM OUR FRIENDS, THE BROTHERHOOD OF BADOON!

"MEET MISTER GREEN AND MISTER BLUE!"

1 2 3 4

SUPER-DEATH SWEEPSTAKES

AND ONE LOOK IS ALL IT TAKES, FOLKS, TO TELL YOU WE'VE GOT ONE HECKUVA SHOW FOR YOU TONIGHT!

ALRIGHTEE, PANELISTS, IT'S TIME TO CHOOSE A DEATH FOR MR. BLUE!
HAVE YOU REACHED YOUR DECISION?
WE SURE HAVE, MON-TEE. WE WANT-- DEATH BY IMPALEMENT!
TER-RIFIC, PANEL!

IMPALEMENT IT IS! NOW WATCH AS OUR SUPER-DEATH TOTALIZER FLASHES MR. BLUE AWAY TO A SOUNDPROOF ROOM NEARBY!
SWASH
THERE HE GOES-- TO BE TOTALLED!*
*WE'RE TRANSLATING TO EARTH-EQUIVALENT COLLOQUIALISMS, OF COURSE.-- M.W.

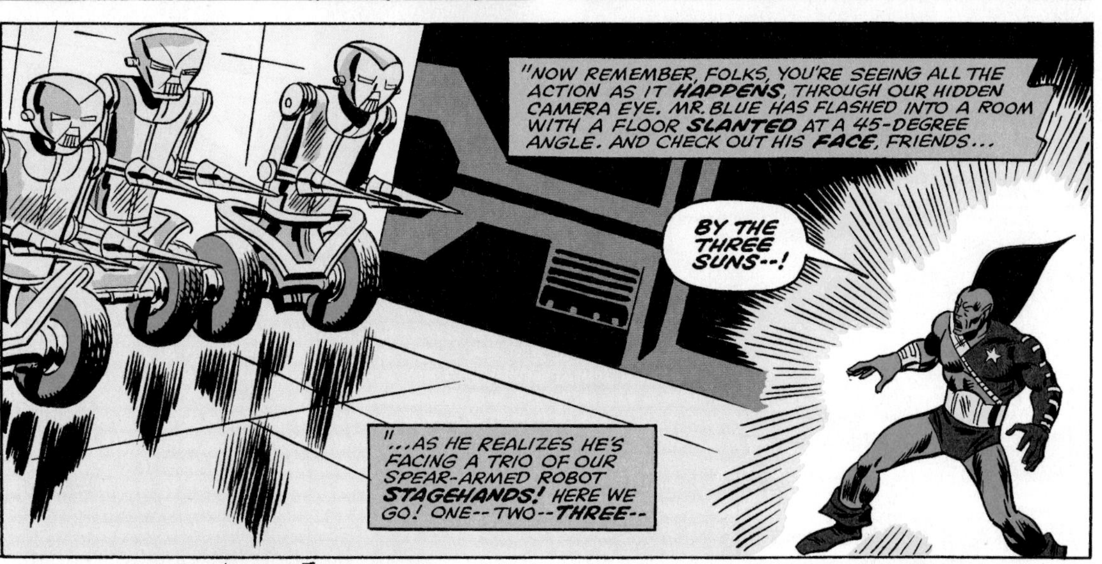
"NOW REMEMBER, FOLKS, YOU'RE SEEING ALL THE ACTION AS IT HAPPENS, THROUGH OUR HIDDEN CAMERA EYE. MR. BLUE HAS FLASHED INTO A ROOM WITH A FLOOR SLANTED AT A 45-DEGREE ANGLE. AND CHECK OUT HIS FACE, FRIENDS...
BY THE THREE SUNS--!
"...AS HE REALIZES HE'S FACING A TRIO OF OUR SPEAR-ARMED ROBOT STAGEHANDS! HERE WE GO! ONE--TWO--THREE--

CHUGACHUGA
"--DEATH!"
MAYBE...

...AND THEN AGAIN, MAYBE NOT.
CHANG
TRULY, THIS IS A PLANET OF MADMEN!!
FOR YONDU, THE SAVAGE GUARDIAN, BRED IN THE WILDERNESS OF CENTAURI-IV, IS A TAD MORE AGILE THAN THE TYPICAL CONTESTANT.

ONE OF THE ROBOT ASSASSINS-- HELD FAST IN THE METAL WALL!
BUT THE OTHERS ARE TURNING--
CREEK
--CHARGING AT ME AGAIN!!
"YEP, SO THEY ARE!
"BUT FOR HAVING SURVIVED ROUND ONE, MR. BLUE, YOU'VE EARNED A CHANCE-FOR-LIFE BONUS!
SPING
ANTHOS BE PRAISED!
ZWIT
ZWIT
TO THEIR DISMAY, THE BETTORS REALIZE THAT YONDU'S HAND IS NO STRANGER TO THE MACE.
"WELL, FOLKS, HE'S GOT HIS CHANCE-- LET'S SEE NOW IF HE KNOWS WHAT TO DO WITH-- UH-OH."
AND BEFORE THEIR STARTLED EYES, HE LAYS WASTE TO HIS FIRST MECHANIZED ASSAILANT.
CHOOM
HOWEVER...
THAT BLOW SEPARATES THE MACE FROM ITS CHAIN LEAVING THE CENTAURIAN DEFENSELESS AGAINST NUMBER TWO!
STILL, THE ROBOT MANAGES ONLY TO PIN YONDU'S AZURE FORM TIGHT TO THE WALL-- RENDERING THE ROBOT ITSELF INCAPABLE OF MOVEMENT.
CHANG
A STALEMATE, THEN?

IT APPEARS SO... UNTIL THE METAL MAN OPENS ITS "MOUTH" AND STICKS OUT ITS "TONGUE": A SILVERY-BRIGHT ALLOY BLADE ON AN ACCORDION HINGE...
...MOVING INCH-BY-INCH TOWARD YONDU'S THROAT!

THIS IS IT, FOLKS-- THE MOMENT YOU'VE ALL BEEN WAITING FOR! WATCH CLOSELY--
YOU'RE ABOUT TO SEE A GENUINE DEATH TAKE PLACE LIVE ON YOUR SCREEN!

"YES... YES, THE POINT'S COMING CLOSER! IT'S GOING TO-- NO, WAIT! LOOK AT MR. BLUE STRUGGLE, LADIES AND GENTLEMEN!

"HE'S TENSED THE CHAIN ON THE ROBOT'S NECK! HE'S PUSHING --PUSHING WITH ALL HIS MIGHT TO HOLD THE BLADE BACK!

"AND NOW-- GREAT GNAXOS, FOLKS-- HE'S TORN THE ROBOT'S HEAD CLEAN OFF!
CLONCH

"HE'S WON THE SUPER-DEATH SWEEPSTAKES! LET'S BRING HIM BACK TO THE STUDIO--"

--AND GIVE THE MAN A ROUSING ROUND OF APPLAUSE, WHAT DO YOU SAY?
GUARDS!! SURROUND HIM AT ONCE!

CUT:
TO THE PALACE ROYAL OF THE SISTERHOOD OF BADOON, ON THE SWAMPWORLD.
HAIL, QUEEN TOLARIA!

HAIL TO YOU ALSO, STARHAWK-- AND TO THE TERRANS, THE SISTERHOOD EXTENDS ITS WELCOME.

THIS IS INSANITY! A CITY AS TECHNOLOGICALLY ADVANCED AS ANY ON EARTH-- BUILT BY SAVAGES! A BADOON QUEEN, BIDDING AN EARTH-MAN "WELCOME"?!
WHAT'S GOING ON HERE?!

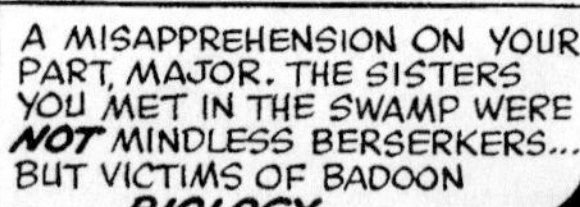
A MISAPPREHENSION ON YOUR PART, MAJOR. THE SISTERS YOU MET IN THE SWAMP WERE NOT MINDLESS BERSERKERS... BUT VICTIMS OF BADOON BIOLOGY.

BUT I SENSE YOU ARE NOT CONVERSANT WITH THE HISTORY OF OUR RACE.
MAY I ENLIGHTEN YOU, MAJOR?

"THE BADOON EVOLVED ON THIS VERY WORLD, MANY MILLIONS OF YOUR YEARS AGO.
"INDEED, OUR RACE IS OLDER THAN THE KREE... OLDER THAN THE SKRULLS ...AND YET WE REACHED TECH-NOLOGICAL MATURITY ONLY RECENTLY, COSMICALLY SPEAKING...
"...DUE TO AN INBORN GENETIC DEFECT:

"THE MALE BADOON HATED THE FEMALE-- AND VICE VERSA. THE RESULT, OF COURSE, WAS AN ONGOING WAR OF THE SEXES SUCH AS YOUR WORLD HAS NEVER KNOWN.
"MATING WAS ACCOMPLISHED ONLY THRU FORCE. PROGRESS OF ANY SORT WAS IMPOSSIBLE.
"NATURE COMPENSATED BY ALLOWING THE MATING URGE TO STRIKE ONLY ONCE IN EACH BADOON'S LIFESPAN. BUT WHEN IT DOES, WE ARE REDUCED--MALE AND FEMALE ALIKE--TO ANIMALS.

"THOUGH FIERCER AND STRONGER THAN THE MALES OF OUR SPECIES, WE BADOON FEMALES LACKED THEIR CUNNING, THEIR SLYNESS.
"AND SO, IN TIME, WE WERE OVERCOME, PLACED IN BONDAGE.

"AND WHILE WE TOILED WITH OUR HANDS, GUARDED BY AND SEGREGATED FROM THE MALES EXCEPT FOR MATING PURPOSES... THEY SET ABOUT EVOLVING A TECHNOLOGY. AND THAT WAS THE STATE OF AFFAIRS FOR A FEW THOUSAND SUN-CYCLES, AS THE BROTHERHOOD PROGRESSED FROM SPEARS...

"...TO SPACESHIPS.
"AND THEN THE ULTIMATE SEGREGATION OCCURRED.
"THE MALES DESERTED THIS WORLD...

"...RETURNING ONLY ONCE EACH SUN-CYCLE IN GIANT SPACE ARKS, BEARING THOSE WHOM THE MADNESS HAD STRICKEN...
"...TO PROPAGATE THE RACE.

"WHEN THE MATING IS DONE, THEY REMAIN TO COLLECT. AND CODE THE EGGS FROM WHICH THE INFANT BADOON WILL EMERGE.

"AND THOSE EGGS ARE TRANSPORTED TO THE PLANET-HOME OF THE BROTHERHOOD, WHERE THEY ARE HATCHED IN INCUBATORS.
"BY THEIR OWN CHOOSING, OUR MALES HAVE ASSUMED RESPONSIBILITY FOR THE PROCESS OF CHILDBIRTH.

"OF COURSE, THEY HAVE NEITHER THE DESIRE NOR THE BIOLOGICAL INCLINATION TO REAR THE OFFSPRING WHICH HATCH AS FEMALES. AND SO THESE ARE RETURNED TO THE SWAMPWORLD... AND THE SISTERHOOD, TOO, IS PERPETUATED."

IT IS NOT A BAD SYSTEM, REALLY. INDEED, FOR US, IT MAY HAVE BEEN THE ONLY SOLUTION.
THE BROTHERHOOD KNOWS NOTHING OF OUR ADVANCES SINCE THEIR EXODUS, SO WE APPEAR NO THREAT TO THEM.

SO YOU'VE REMAINED SLAVES TO THE MALES' SYSTEM. IT'S NICE AND SAFE AS LONG AS YOU STAY CONFINED TO THIS WORLD AND NO QUESTIONS ARE ASKED.
HAS IT NEVER OCCURRED TO YOU... TO REVOLT? TO THROW OFF THE CONSTRICTIONS PLACED UPON YOU?

WHY? OUR EXISTENCE HERE IS ALL WE DESIRE... PEACE AMONG OURSELVES AND WITH THE MALE OF OUR SPECIES.
AND IF THE REST OF THE MILKY WAY WANTS YOU DEAD --THAT DOESN'T MATTER?

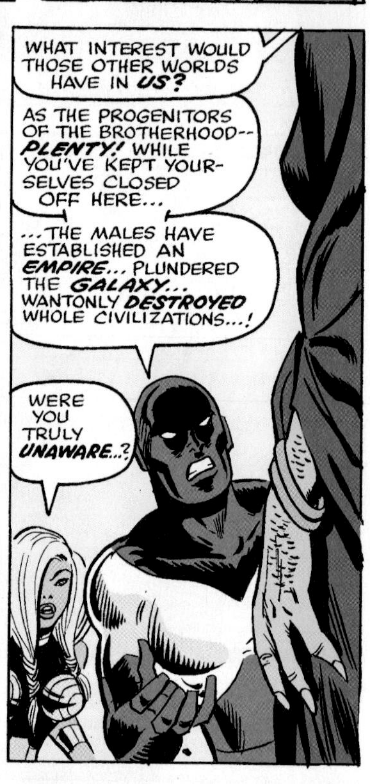
WHAT INTEREST WOULD THOSE OTHER WORLDS HAVE IN US?
AS THE PROGENITORS OF THE BROTHERHOOD-- PLENTY! WHILE YOU'VE KEPT YOURSELVES CLOSED OFF HERE...
...THE MALES HAVE ESTABLISHED AN EMPIRE... PLUNDERED THE GALAXY... WANTONLY DESTROYED WHOLE CIVILIZATIONS...!
WERE YOU TRULY UNAWARE...?

WE HAD ASSUMED... THE BROTHERHOOD'S CULTURE HAD PROGRESSED IN A SIMILAR FASHION TO OUR OWN.
THE MALES' TREATMENT OF US WAS A PHYSIOLOGICAL NECESSITY. WE NEVER BELIEVED...!
EVEN ON THIS WORLD, IT NEVER EXTENDED TO OTHER SPECIES.
THEY WERE A GENTLE BREED, ACTUALLY. WE RATHER ENVIED THE COURTESY THEY ACCORDED THEIR PETS AND BEASTS OF BURDEN.
STARHAWK... DOES THIS TERRAN SPEAK THE TRUTH? ANSWER-- AS ONE WHO KNOWS.
HE DOES NOT LIE.

BUT I MAY SAY NO MORE, GOOD QUEEN.
IT IS MY TIME NOW...TO DEPART.
THE SEED OF EARTH'S SALVATION HAS BEEN PLANTED... MY MISSION FULFILLED.

NOW THE STARWINDS BECKON ME AGAIN. I FEEL THEIR TUG AT MY SOLAR SAILS.
I HEAR THEIR CALL TO RETURN TO THE VOID.

THUS UNTIL SUCH TIME AS THE SEED'S HARVEST SHALL BE REAPED...I MUST CAST MY LOT WITH THE COLD AND DARK.

SO SAYING, THE GOLDEN-WINGED MYSTERY-MAN HURTLES PAST THE SKY OF THE SWAMPWORLD, OUT INTO THE TRACKLESS REACHES OF SPACE...
...OBSERVED ONLY BY THE STARTLED ASTRAL EYES OF DR. STRANGE.
FASCINATING... A HUMAN WHO VOYAGES UNAIDED THROUGH SPACE IN PHYSICAL FORM.

MORE FASCINATING... I'M CERTAIN HE SENSED MY APPROACH FROM THIS PLANET'S SURFACE... AND THAT MY COMING WAS THE STIMULUS FOR HIS DEPARTURE.
YET I DETECTED NO SORCEROUS ENERGIES WITHIN HIM...ONLY THE MEREST TRACE OF PSYCHIC ABILITY.
CURIOUS. BUT I CANNOT ALLOW MYSELF THE LUXURY OF REFLECTION UPON IT...

--WATCHING AS YOU PAY THE PRICE FOR DEFIANCE OF THE FAR-FLUNG EMPIRE OF BADOON!

"GUARDIANS OF THE GALAXY," YOU CALL YOURSELVES? KEEPERS OF THE FLAME OF FREEDOM?

THEN LET EARTH SEE ITS GALAXY LEFT IMPERILED-- ITS FLAME EXTINGUISHED!

BROTHERS OF THE EMPIRE-- TAKE AIM!!

NEXT

LET MY PLANET GO!

THE DEFENDERS

MARVEL COMICS GROUP™

25¢ 29 NOV 02152

THE DEFENDERS™

EARTHLINGS, UNLESS YOU INSTANTLY SURRENDER--

--YOUR PLANET DIES!

THIS IS IT! THE FINAL BATTLE BETWEEN THE DYNAMIC DEFENDERS AND THE BANEFUL BADOON!

Stan Lee PRESENTS: THE DYNAMIC DEFENDERS!™
STEVE GERBER WRITER | SAL BUSCEMA & VINCE COLLETTA ARTISTS | JOHN COSTANZA, letterer, GLYNIS WEIN, colorist | MARV WOLFMAN EDITOR
LET MY PLANET GO!
UP AGAINST THE WALL: NIGHTHAWK OF THE DEFENDERS... MARTINEX AND CHARLIE-27 OF THE GUARDIANS OF THE GALAXY.
PREPARED TO BLAST THEM INTO THE WALL: A FIRING SQUAD OF THE BROTHERHOOD OF BADOON, EARTH'S ALIEN CONQUERORS, FOR THIS IS THE YEAR 3015 A.D., AND THESE THREE HAVE DARED DEFY THE RULE OF HUMANITY'S NEW MASTERS.
ON PLANETWIDE VIDEO, MEN AND WOMEN HUDDLED IN SLAVE CAMPS WATCH IN HORROR. FOR THIS IS MORE THAN AN EXECUTION OF MEN. A DREAM OF FREEDOM IS ABOUT TO BE PUT TO DEATH.

THERE MAY BE A SUBTLER WAY OF HANDLING THIS--ONE THAT WOULDN'T REVEAL OUR PRESENCE.
BUT I CAN'T AFFORD TO WAIT 'TIL IT OCCURS TO ME. NO TIME...!

HAVE TO FIRE THE PSYCHOKINETIC BLAST-- NOW!
A BOLT OF PURE FORCE LEAPS FROM THE BRAIN OF MAJOR VANCE ASTRO, SLICING THROUGH THE METAL CASINGS OF THE BADOON MOLECULAR DISPERSION RIFLES.
MOON OF ELOS--!
KRRRAAAAATAK

HOW THE--? WELL, WHAT DO YOU KNOW? THE CAVALRY'S ARRIVED!
VANCE! AND YOUR FELLOW-DEFENDER, THE WOMAN WARRIOR VALKYRIE!

LET US PRAY I CAN BE WORTHY OF THAT APPELLATIVE, MARTINEX.
I, TOO, WOULD RECOMMEND PRAYER, FEMALE.
FOR ARMED ONLY WITH THAT BLADE, YOU'VE NOT A CH--

YEAAAGH
THAT MIGHT BE SO... WERE YOUR MARKSMANSHIP EQUALLY DEADLY AS YOUR WEAPON.
HOWEVER...

VAL-- LEAVE THE TROOPS TO ME! PUT YOUR SWORD TO WORK ON OUR FRIENDS' RESTRAINTS!
MY POWER CAN'T HELP THEM... THE DEVICES WORK ON A MIND-DEADENING PRINCIPLE...

THAT'S WHY CHARLIE AND MARTINEX HAVEN'T BROKEN FREE ALREADY... NERVOUS SYSTEMS WON'T RESPOND TO THEIR BRAINS' ORDERS TO USE THEIR POWERS...!
I'D WONDERED ABOUT THAT!
LISTEN... I'M AS INTERESTED AS ANYONE IN BADOON TECHNOLOGY...

...BUT FOR NOW, COULD WE SKIP THE CONVERSATION...
...AND JUST RUN FOR OUR LIVES?!

YOUR MILITIAMAN'S INSTINCTS HAVE FAILED YOU, CHARLIE. WE SHOULD'VE PAUSED TO CONSIDER--
...WHAT WE MIGHT BE RUNNING INTO!
HALT!
ANOTHER SWARM OF BADOON!

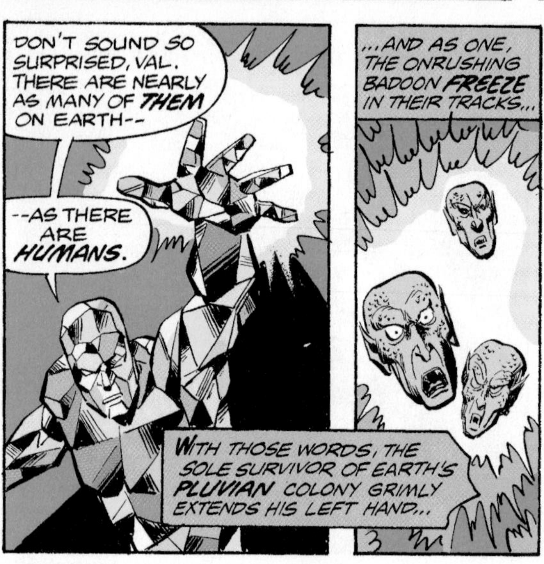
DON'T SOUND SO SURPRISED, VAL. THERE ARE NEARLY AS MANY OF THEM ON EARTH--
--AS THERE ARE HUMANS.
WITH THOSE WORDS, THE SOLE SURVIVOR OF EARTH'S PLUVIAN COLONY GRIMLY EXTENDS HIS LEFT HAND...
...AND AS ONE, THE ONRUSHING BADOON FREEZE IN THEIR TRACKS...

...LITERALLY.
NOW CAN WE GET OUT OF HERE?
WITH ALL DUE HASTE NIGHTHAWK-- YES.

WE SHOULD BE SAFE HERE FOR A TIME.
LONG ENOUGH TO HEAR HOW VAL AND VANCE GOT BACK TO EARTH, I HOPE.
WE DON'T KNOW HOW.

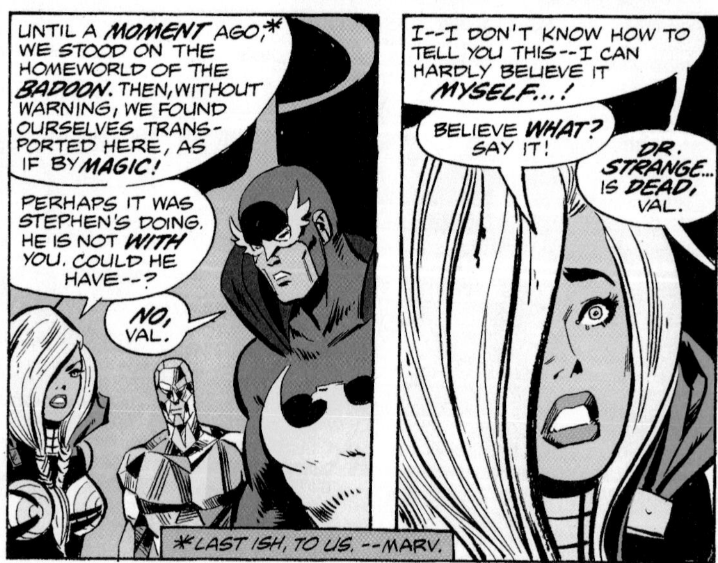
UNTIL A MOMENT AGO,* WE STOOD ON THE HOMEWORLD OF THE BADOON. THEN, WITHOUT WARNING, WE FOUND OURSELVES TRANSPORTED HERE, AS IF BY MAGIC!
PERHAPS IT WAS STEPHEN'S DOING. HE IS NOT WITH YOU. COULD HE HAVE--?
NO, VAL.
*LAST ISH, TO US. --MARV.
I--I DON'T KNOW HOW TO TELL YOU THIS--I CAN HARDLY BELIEVE IT MYSELF...!
BELIEVE WHAT? SAY IT!
DR. STRANGE... IS DEAD, VAL.

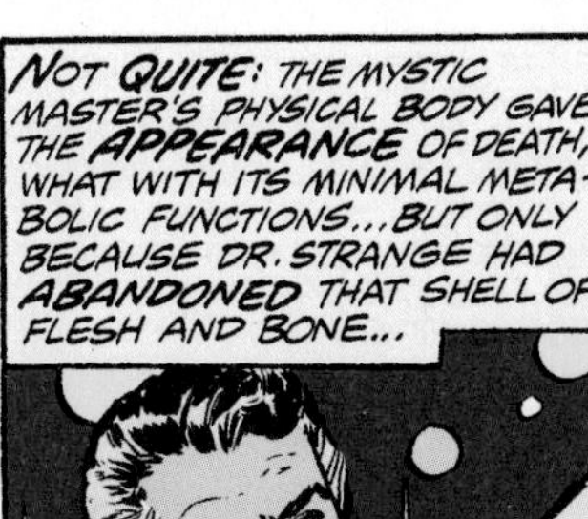
NOT QUITE: THE MYSTIC MASTER'S PHYSICAL BODY GAVE THE APPEARANCE OF DEATH, WHAT WITH ITS MINIMAL METABOLIC FUNCTIONS... BUT ONLY BECAUSE DR. STRANGE HAD ABANDONED THAT SHELL OF FLESH AND BONE...

...TO ROAM THE COSMOS IN HIS ASTRAL FORM.

IN TRUTH, HE WAS RESPONSIBLE FOR VAL'S RESCUE. AND NOW, WITH THE SPEED OF THOUGHT...
...HE RACES THROUGH THE DARK VOID TO A SECOND WEIRD WORLD...
...TO PLUCK BACK TWO MORE VICTIMS OF THE SAME TELEPORT MISHAP.

IT'S A PLANET OF DRUNKARDS AND MADMEN, WHERE A FUTURISTIC TECHNOLOGY COEXISTS WITH BARBARIC DISDAIN FOR THE VALUE OF LIFE, A WORLD WHERE DEATH IS A FESTIVAL... AND A GAME.
R-DEATH SW
IT'S HERE THAT YONDU OF THE GUARDIANS AND HULK OF THE DEFENDERS ARE STRANDED.
OKAY, PANEL-- MR. BLUE SURVIVED. IT'S TIME TO CHOOSE A DEATH FOR MR. GREEN.

WAIT, FOLKS--IT'S EMPEROR GOOZOT HIMSELF WITH A NEW CONTESTANT FOR US!
A FORMER WIFE OF MINE, MON-TEE. BUT FROM WHAT I OVERHEARD IN THE DUNGEON...
SHE'D PREFER MR. GREEN AS HER MATE.

I WISH THEM TO DIE TOGETHER, MON-TEE.

"YOU HEARD THE EMPEROR'S COMMAND, LADIES AND GENTLEMEN. THAT MEANS MR. GREEN AND HIS PRETTY FRIEND HAVE WON A TRIP TO--

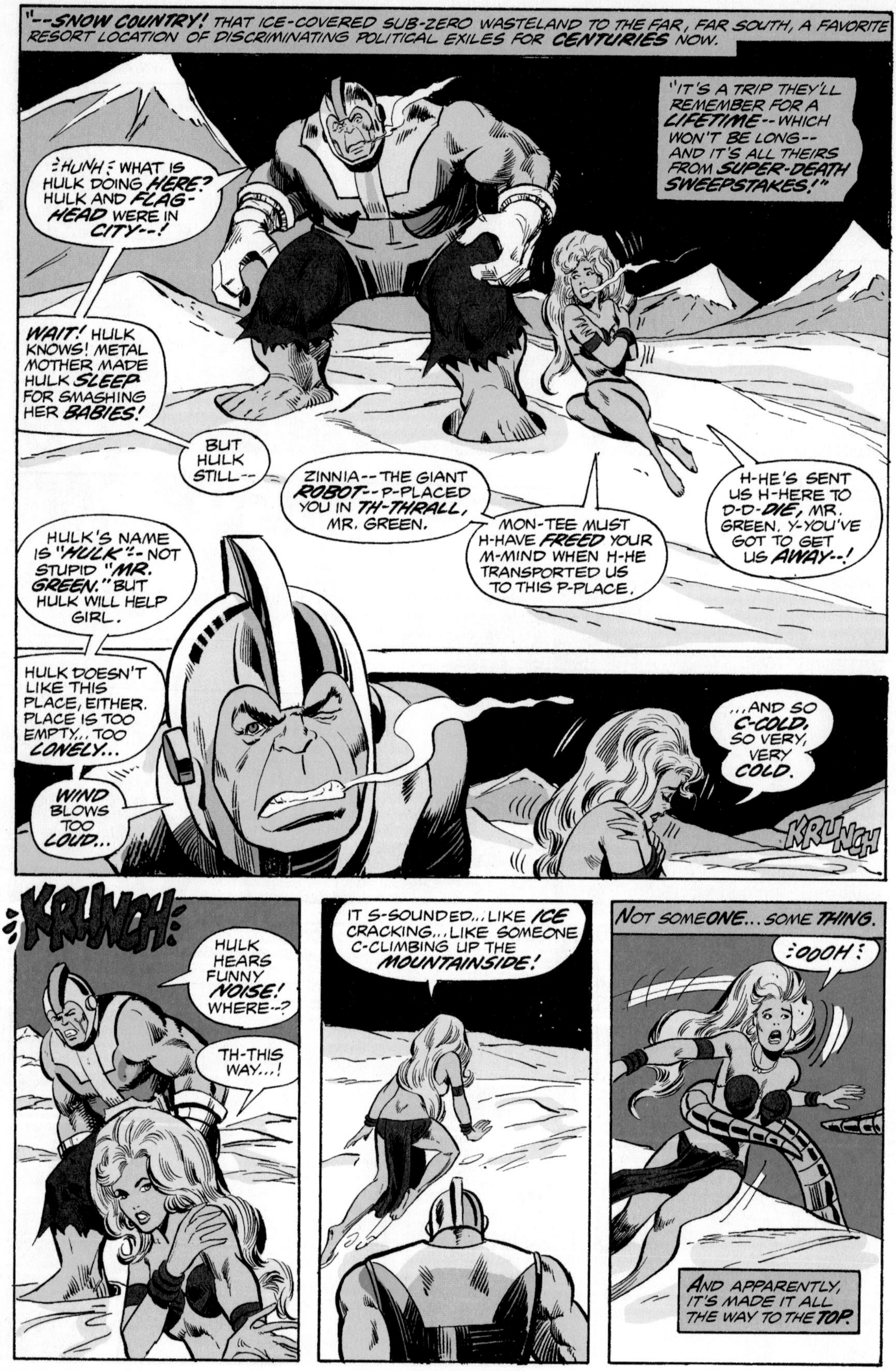

"--SNOW COUNTRY! THAT ICE-COVERED SUB-ZERO WASTELAND TO THE FAR, FAR SOUTH, A FAVORITE RESORT LOCATION OF DISCRIMINATING POLITICAL EXILES FOR CENTURIES NOW.

"IT'S A TRIP THEY'LL REMEMBER FOR A LIFETIME--WHICH WON'T BE LONG--AND IT'S ALL THEIRS FROM SUPER-DEATH SWEEPSTAKES!"

HUNH! WHAT IS HULK DOING HERE? HULK AND FLAG-HEAD WERE IN CITY--!

WAIT! HULK KNOWS! METAL MOTHER MADE HULK SLEEP FOR SMASHING HER BABIES!

BUT HULK STILL--

ZINNIA--THE GIANT ROBOT--P-PLACED YOU IN TH-THRALL, MR. GREEN.

MON-TEE MUST H-HAVE FREED YOUR M-MIND WHEN H-HE TRANSPORTED US TO THIS P-PLACE.

H-HE'S SENT US H-HERE TO D-D-DIE, MR. GREEN. Y-YOU'VE GOT TO GET US AWAY--!

HULK'S NAME IS "HULK"--NOT STUPID "MR. GREEN." BUT HULK WILL HELP GIRL.

HULK DOESN'T LIKE THIS PLACE, EITHER. PLACE IS TOO EMPTY... TOO LONELY...

WIND BLOWS TOO LOUD...

...AND SO C-COLD, SO VERY, VERY COLD.

KRUNCH

EMERALD EYES WIDE, THE JADE GIANT STALKS FORWARD TO THE EDGE OF THE SLOPE, THERE TO BEHOLD...
BUGS!

NOT THE BUNNY. A TRIO OF MONSTROUS METALLIC ANTS...AND THE TERRIFIED WOMAN WRITHING IN THEIR CLUTCHES.

HOLD ON, GIRL! HULK WILL SMASH--
NO! STAY BACK! THERE'S NOTHING YOU CAN--

--DO.
CHOOM

IN THE DUNGEON, HULK'S MASSIVE MUSCULATURE-- SO DIFFERENT FROM THE SOFT, WINE-SOAKED BODIES OF THE MEN SHE KNEW-- AROUSED HER CURIOSITY. NOW HE EVOKES FROM HER NOTHING LESS THAN AWE.
IT'S THE VERY SAME FEELING THAT SWEEPS OVER GREENSKIN HIMSELF, AS HE LIFTS HIS GAZE FROM THE METAL BODY HE HAS BROKEN, AND SEES...
MORE BUGS!! A WHOLE ARMY OF BUGS TO KILL HULK AND GIRL!!

ONE MEMBER OF OUR CAST, AT LEAST, IS NOT IN DEADLY DANGER AT THE MOMENT.
THE BEING KNOWN AS STAR-HAWK SAILS THE SPACEWINDS HOMEWARD.

HOME IS NOTHING FANCY, REALLY-- JUST A HUNK OF ROCK, A CABIN, TREES, GRASS, AND A HORSE.
BUT, AS HE ENTERS THROUGH THE AIRLOCK AND HEARS THE JOYFUL SHOUTS OF THE CHILDREN...

...HE IS REMINDED AGAIN WHY HE HAS LONGED FOR THIS SIMPLE PLACE.
TARA, SITA, AND JOHN ARE THEIR NAMES.

HOW LONG WILL YOU BE HERE? ARE YOU HOME TO STAY?
I CANNOT SAY-- UNTIL I'VE CONSULTED ALETA, TARA.

I AM THE LIGHT... AND THE GIVER OF LIGHT... AND THE TWO MUST DECIDE JOINTLY.
ALL THAT I AM... ALL I CAN BE...

"...FLOWS FROM HER."
THE CABIN'S INTERIOR IS SUDDENLY LIT WITH A FIERY PRESENCE ON THE COM-PUTER'S VISUAL PANEL.
SHE SPEAKS NOT A WORD; NOR DOES STARHAWK.

BUT WHEN THE IMAGE FADES, HE KNOWS WHAT HE MUST DO... AND GRIEVES AT THE THOUGHT.
IT IS NOT YET MY TIME. THE STARS BECKON, AND I HAVE NO CHOICE BUT TO JOURNEY...

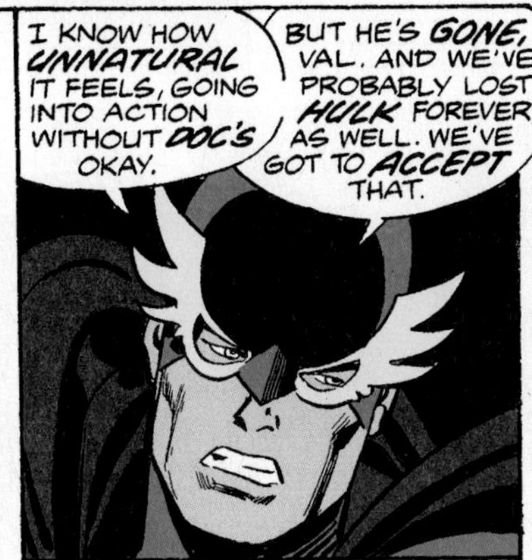

SOMETHING I LEARNED IN THE SPACE MILITIA: A LITTLE RIGHTEOUS ANGER GOES A LONG WAY TOWARD EVENING THE ODDS.
THESE ARE DR. STRANGE'S MURDERERS-- ALL OF THEM. THINK OF THEM THAT WAY-- AND NO OTHER WAY, AND JUST--
--CHARGE!!

THERE'S A RING OF AUTHORITY IN THE JOVIAN'S DEEP, MUSCULAR VOICE. AND HE'S GIVEN NO COMMAND--
--BUT RATHER, OFFERED A CHALLENGE. AND THE WARRIOR-WOMAN RESPONDS.

FISTS POUNDING, BLADE SLASHING, THEY LUNGE TOGETHER PAST THE RING OF GUARDS, UP THE STAIRS, TO SHATTER THE STEEL DOORS...

...AND INTO THEIR ENEMIES' MIDST.
AW, GEE-- LOOKS LIKE WE WEREN'T EXPECTED!
ARM YOURSELVES! CUT DOWN THE INTRUDERS! THEY'RE TERRANS! THEY'RE--

"--ANTS!!"
KLONG
CLANK

BUGS ARE TOO MANY!
HULK SMASHES BUGS--BUT ALWAYS THERE ARE MORE!
WHAT CAN WE DO? EVEN YOU CAN'T HOLD THEM OFF FOREVER! EVENTUALLY YOU'LL TIRE, AND--

HUH! HULK NEVER GETS TIRED! BUT HULK IS SICK OF FIGHTING STUPID BUGS!
HULK JUST WANTS TO GO AWAY-- SO HULK WILL!
N-NO! YOU C-CAN'T LEAP OFF A M-MOUNTAIN! WE'LL BE--

DUMB GIRL! HULK IS JUMPING UP, NOT--
KRAZZK
--DOWN.

UH-UH-UH! NO FAIR BOUNDING AWAY! THE RULES SAY YOU WIN OR DIE... WHERE YOU STAND!
CLUD

HULK DOESN'T CARE ABOUT RULES! HULK'S RULES ARE HULK'S OWN!

AND HULK WILL PROVE IT!
IF HULK CAN'T GO AWAY FROM MOUNTAIN--

--HULK WILL MAKE MOUNTAIN GO AWAY FROM HIM!!

TELEVISION SCREENS ON THE DRUNKARDS' WORLD GO MOMENTARILY GREY, AS ALL THE ORBITING SATTELITE CAMERAS CAN RECORD IS A SHOWER OF NEWLY-CRUSHED GRAVEL.
AND WHEN THOSE SCREENS CLEAR ONCE AGAIN, THE GREEN BEHEMOTH AND HIS PETITE COMPANION STAND ON FLAT GROUND AMID THE DUST-LADEN BODIES OF WHAT FEW ROBOT ANTS ARE LEFT UNBURIED.
IF THE GIRL WAS AWED BEFORE... SHE IS STUPE-FIED NOW, INCAPABLE EVEN OF SPEAKING.

NOT THAT OUR EVER-EFFERVESCENT EMCEE WOULD ALLOW HER A WORD IN EDGEWISE, ANYWAY...!
THEY'RE BACK, FOLKS! GIVE 'EM A HAND!
CLAP
CLAP

IT'S AN HISTORIC MOMENT HERE ON S.D.S., FOLKS-- NOT ONE, NOT TWO, BUT THREE SURVIVORS ON THE SAME EDITION OF OUR GAME!

ARE YOU ALL RIGHT, MY FRIEND?
HULK... FEELS... SWELL...

...BUT HULK IS GOING TO MAKE FAT-FACE FEEL VERY BAD!!
:UPH: WE FORGOT TO PUT MR. GREEN BACK IN THRALL...
FAT-FACE WON'T FORGET AGAIN...!

FAT-FACE WON'T HAVE HEAD TO FORGET WITH!
G-GUARDS..?
HEEDLESS OF THE ONCOMING SQUAD OF ROBOTS, HULK DRAWS BACK HIS HUGELY-SINEWED ARM... AND SWINGS!

BUT THE PUNCH NEVER CONNECTS. BOTH THE JADE GIANT AND THE BLUE BOWMAN VANISH AT THAT INSTANT.

AND HULK'S MASSIVE FIST LANDS HARD...ON THE SCALY FLESH OF A BROTHER OF BADOON!
VAL!! LOOK!
KWAF
HELA'S GHOSTS! THE HULK-- HERE?!

MILES ABOVE, THE GUARDIANS' STARSHIP "CAPTAIN AMERICA" STILL ORBITS THE EARTH, THE HAUNTING SILENCE IN ITS CORRIDORS BROKEN AT LAST BY THE CAUTIOUS FOOTSTEPS...
...OF JACK NORRISS, VALKYRIE'S HUSBAND.
TERRIFIC. STRANGE'S HEX WEARS OFF ME... I GO BACK INTO HIDING... AND NOW THAT I'M READY TO SHOW MY FACE AGAIN...
... THERE'S NOBODY TO SHOW IT TO! I'M ALONE ON THIS SHIP.

AT LEAST I HAD TIME TO THINK... AND EVEN REACH A CONCLUSION OR TWO.
LIKE: SINCE STUMBLING BACK INTO BARBARA'S LIFE, I'VE ACTED LIKE A FLAMING --UH-OH.

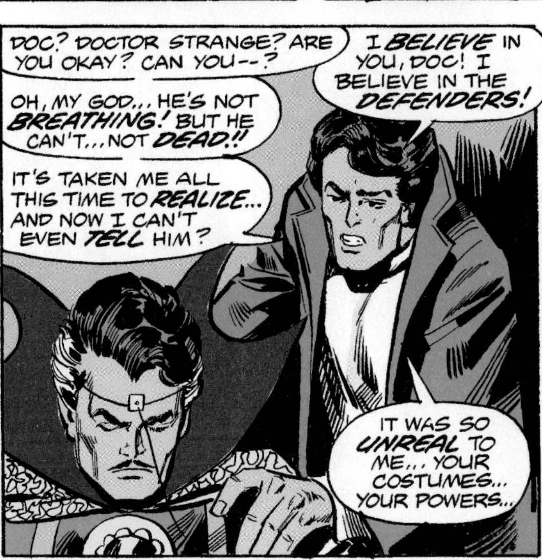
DOC? DOCTOR STRANGE? ARE YOU OKAY? CAN YOU--?
OH, MY GOD... HE'S NOT BREATHING! BUT HE CAN'T... NOT DEAD!!
IT'S TAKEN ME ALL THIS TIME TO REALIZE... AND NOW I CAN'T EVEN TELL HIM?
I BELIEVE IN YOU, DOC! I BELIEVE IN THE DEFENDERS!
IT WAS SO UNREAL TO ME... YOUR COSTUMES... YOUR POWERS...

BUT I THINK I UNDERSTAND NOW-- WHY YOU'VE KEPT THE TEAM A SECRET, MOSTLY-- WHY--
--YEEOW!! YOU'RE ALIVE!!
PLEASE, MR. NORRISS-- NOT TO SHOUT UNTIL I'VE READJUSTED TO MY PHYSICAL SENSES.
IT DOES REQUIRE A MOMENT OR TWO.

I CAUGHT PART OF WHAT YOU SAID. I'D LIKE TO HEAR MORE-- WHEN I RETURN FROM EARTH.
...
IS BARBARA DOWN THERE? TELL ME--!
SHE IS. YES.

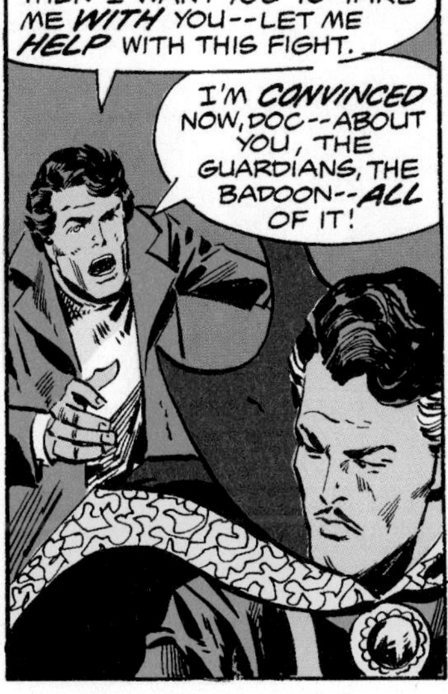
THEN I WANT YOU TO TAKE ME WITH YOU--LET ME HELP WITH THIS FIGHT.
I'M CONVINCED NOW, DOC--ABOUT YOU, THE GUARDIANS, THE BADOON--ALL OF IT!

IT'S MY PLANET, TOO! I'VE THE RIGHT--!
I'M FRANKLY SKEPTICAL OF THIS SUDDEN CONVERSION, MR. NORRISS. BUT PERHAPS--
YES. VERY WELL. LET'S PUT IT TO THE TEST.

YOU WERE RIGHT, VANCE--THIS IS THE COMMUNICATIONS CENTER!
AND THE CREEP WITH THE HEAD-DRESS MUST BE DROOM!

CAREFUL--DON'T DAMAGE--EQUIPMENT--USE YOUR SKILL--

SAME WAY--I USE PSYCHE-BLAST--CLEAR BADOON--
--AWAY!!

FOOLS! YOUR ENTIRE SPECIES SHALL PAY FOR THIS WITH THEIR LIVES!!
A QUINTET OF MADMEN CANNOT DEFEAT THE BROTHER-HOOD OF--

OH SHUT UP, WILLYA?! YOU ALL LOOK ALIKE--YOU ALL TALK ALIKE--I'VE HAD IT UP TO HERE WITH YOU!!

GET THAT CALL THROUGH FAST, VANCE! EVEN WITH HULK AND YONDU BACK--

"--THE OTHERS CAN'T LAST LONG WITHOUT HELP!"
FORTUNATELY, THAT WON'T BE NECESSARY.
AID HAS ARRIVED... IN THE MOST UNEXPECTED FORM OF ALL.
STEPHEN! ALIVE!!

JACK GRIMACES. HIS ARRIVAL HAS GONE UNNOTICED, EVEN BY HIS OWN SPOUSE. BUT THE MASTER MAGE EVINCES NO EMOTION WHATEVER.

HE MERELY LOOKS UPON THE RAMPANT VIOLENCE...DEEMS IT DISTASTEFUL... AND, WITH A GESTURE AND AN UTTERANCE, TERMINATES IT.
THE BADOON HAVE BEEN PARALYZED, AS SIMPLY AS THAT.

IS THIS SORT OF MIRACLE ROUTINE FOR YOU, DR. STRANGE-- RISING FROM THE DEAD?
OR ARE WE TO SURMISE YOU WEREN'T--?

IT WAS MORE CONVENIENT, MARTINEX, TO ALLOW THE BADOON TO BELIEVE WHAT THEY CHOSE... 'TIL THE PROPER MOMENT.
NOW THAT MOMENT IS NIGH, WHEN ALL EARTH SHALL BE MADE FREE FOR ALL TIME.
I'VE CHOSEN JACK TO AID IN MY PART OF THE EFFORT.

WE TRUST YOU'LL BE ABLE TO MANAGE MATTERS HERE UNTIL WE RETURN.
FWASH

THIS IS ONE OF THE BADOON PRISON CAMPS, JACK.
MAY I RELY UPON YOUR MARKSMAN-SHIP...?

NO PROBLEM, DOC. I'M USED TO A 20-GAUGE SHOTGUN.
AND THIS RAY-RIFLE FROM THE SHIP'S ARSENAL DOESN'T EVEN HAVE A RECOIL.

AS JACK DISPENSES WITH THE GUARDS, THE SORCERER SUPREME CAUSES THE FENCES TO DEMATERIALIZE...

...AND CALLS TO THE CAPTIVES TO THROW OFF THEIR SHACKLES.

...UNTIL ALL FIFTY MILLION TERRAN MEN, WOMEN AND CHILDREN HAVE BEEN LIBERATED... WITH PREDICTABLE RESULTS. A BLOODBATH ENSUES, AS THEY RUN WILD AGAINST THEIR FORMER MASTERS.

CHOOSH

FROM THE PARAPET OF THE BADOON FORTRESS IN CHICAGO, DR. STRANGE VIEWS WHAT HE HAS WROUGHT.

WE'LL REJOIN THE OTHERS SHORTLY, JACK. I NEEDED A MOMENT HERE FIRST...

...TO CONVINCE MYSELF OF THE NECESSITY OF WHAT I'VE DONE.

WHAT WE DID, DOC...

...EVEN THOUGH I'M SURE MY CONTRIBUTION WASN'T A NECESSITY.

YOU COULD'VE ZAPPED THE BADOON OFF THE FACE OF THE EARTH ALL BY YOURSELF, COULDN'T YOU? WHY--?

IT WOULD HAVE RENDERED ALL THE YEARS OF ENSLAVEMENT MEANINGLESS ... EVEN IF IT WERE WITHIN MY POWER.

PERCEPTIVE, DR. STRANGE. FREEDOM MUST BE EARNED TO BE VALUED.
HUH--?! WHO IN THE WORLD--?

I SUSPECT HE IS NOT OF THIS WORLD, JACK...
"...THOUGH HE HAS CHOSEN TO PLAY SOME ROLE IN ITS DESTINY. I'VE SEE HIM BEFORE, DEPARTING THE SWAMPWORLD OF THE BADOON, HAVING AIDED VALKYRIE AND VANCE ASTRO THERE."
THEN YOU OUGHT BE CERTAIN...
I AM NO ENEMY OF EARTH...
...AND THAT YOU MAY TRUST IN WHAT I SAY.

YOU AND YOUR DEFENDERS HAVE DONE ALL YOU CAN HERE. YOU MUST RE-TURN TO YOUR OWN ERA.
IT IS TRUE...I FIND NO ENMITY IN YOU. BUT NEITHER HAVE I EVIDENCE THAT YOU ARE A SEER.
WE PLEDGED TO SEE EARTH FREE BEFORE WE DEPARTED.
WHO ARE YOU TO ASK THAT WE DO LESS?

I AM... ONE WHO KNOWS.
TELL HIM, JACK NORRISS.

D-DOC... I HAVEN'T BEEN RIGHT ABOUT MUCH LATELY...TOO MANY NEW EXPERIENCES BOMBARD-ING MY HEAD... BUT...
I RECOGNIZE SOMETHING IN THIS GUY... SOMETHING OF ME... AND OF BARBARA.
I KNOW THIS SOUNDS CRAZY... BUT HE'S LIKE ALL OF US... AND NONE OF US. I THINK HE'S RIGHT.

THE MASTER OF THE MYSTIC ARTS HAS RECOGNIZED IT, TOO: THE SYNTHESIS OF OPPOSITES WITHIN THIS BEING.
HE LOOKS DEEPLY INTO STAR-HAWK'S EYES...
...AND NODS.

WE SHALL GO... BUT NOT WITH-OUT ONE FINAL GESTURE.

HE CALLS UPON THE ETERNAL VISHANTI, AND FROM HIS HANDS FLOWS A MULTI-HUED QUILTWORK OF MYSTICAL ENERGIES THAT BLANKETS THE CITY, DROPS LIKE A SHIMMERING CLOAK OVER ITS SILVERY SPIRES.

AND IN THE FLAME-LIT STREETS BELOW, THE BANEFUL BROTHERS OF BADOON FALL... ASLEEP.

THIS ONE CITY, AT LEAST, SHALL BE TAKEN WITH-OUT FURTHER BLOODSHED.
THOSE WAGING THE WAR ARE, AFTER ALL, LIVING BEINGS...
...NOT PHILOSOPHICAL CONSTRUCTS. IF I'VE FORSAKEN ONE BELIEF TO AFFIRM ANOTHER, SO BE IT.
YOU SAVED A LOT OF LIVES, DOC, LET IT GO AT THAT.

THERE IS A KIND OF UN-TUTORED WISDOM IN THIS YOUNG MAN, DR. STRANGE.
IN ME?! YEAH. YOU BET. I'M "MR. SMARTS" OF--LORD, WHAT YEAR IS THIS?

STARHAWK!!
APPEARING OUT OF NOWHERE, JUST LIKE LAST TIME--WHEN THE FIGHT IS OVER!

BUT WE'LL WONDER ABOUT HIM LATER.
RIGHT NOW, I'M JUST GLAD YOU'RE BACK WITH US, DOC. WE'VE GOT A LONG FIGHT AHEAD...!
NOT "WE", VANCE. YOU... YOUR FELLOW GUARDIANS... AND THE ONE YOU CALL STARHAWK.

DOC! WHAT ARE YOU SAYING?! DON'T! YOU CAN'T--
STEPHEN! HAVE YOU GONE MAD? WE MUST REMAIN TO--
FAREWELL, YOU FIVE--MAY OSHTUR WATCH OVER YOU ALWAYS.

THEY'RE GONE-- AND SOMEHOW I DOUBT WE'LL SEE THEM AGAIN.
STRANGE REFERRED TO US AS "FIVE", THOUGH. DOES THAT MEAN YOU INTEND TO JOIN US AGAINST THE BADOON?
JUST WHAT DO YOU INTEND STARHAWK... FOR US... AND FOR EARTH?
BUT THAT IS A STORY FOR ANOTHER TIME.

AND SPEAKING OF ANOTHER TIME, HOW ABOUT RIGHT NOW-- 1975-- AT THE DEFENDERS' SUBURBAN HEADQUARTERS?
--DO THIS!!
--FINISH THE FIGHT!

HAS THAT CLOAK OF YOURS LEVITATED YOUR MIND AWAY?!
SEEMS LIKE WE WENT THROUGH AN AWFUL LOT TO ACCOMPLISH HALF A MISSION!
WHY--?

I CANNOT ANSWER IN A MANNER YOU WOULD UNDERSTAND, KYLE.
I SUGGEST YOU ASK MR. NORRISS.
ASK HUBBY??

I KNOW YOU DON'T THINK MUCH OF ME, NIGHTHAWK. I KNOW BARBARA DOESN'T THINK OF ME AT ALL.
BUT DOC AND I BOTH SAW SOMETHING IN STARHAWK.
FOR ME, IT WAS... AN ULTIMATE FUSION... CREATIVITY AND DESTRUCTIVENESS... PASSION AND LOGIC. WHATEVER, IT'S SOMETHING EARTH WILL FINALLY WANT...
...A MILLENNIUM FROM NOW.
-FINIS-

MARVEL PRESENTS

MARVEL COMICS GROUP™

APPROVED BY THE COMICS CODE AUTHORITY

25¢ 3 FEB 02113

MARVEL PRESENTS:™

GUARDIANS OF THE GALAXY™

NOW IN THEIR OWN BRAND-NEW SERIES AT LAST!

FEATURING-- THE POWER OF STARHAWK!

UNIVERSE-SPANNING ACTION IN THE SPECTACULAR MARVEL MANNER!

Stan Lee PRESENTS: BY POPULAR DEMAND--! THE BEGINNING OF THE MOST STAR-SPANNING SERIES OF THEM ALL...!
SOMETHING YOU HAVE TO KEEP IN MIND: IN A KNOWN UNIVERSE OF PERHAPS 100-BILLION GALAXIES, NOTHING MUCH HAPPENS THAT'S BIG ENOUGH TO MATTER.
TAKE THE MILKY WAY, FOR EXAMPLE. HERE'S THE SPAWNING PLACE OF THE KREE, THE SKRULLS, THE WATCHERS--A SPIRAL OF 250-BILLION STARS. AND YET IT'S ONLY ONE PUNY GALAXY. THERE ARE 99,999,999,999 MORE JUST LIKE IT.
SO WHO CARES IF, A THOUSAND YEARS FROM NOW, A BUNCH OF LIZARDS ARE ITS RULERS?
AND IF THE ENTIRE GALAXY IS OF NO GREAT IMPORT--WHY WOULD ANY SENSIBLE BEING CARE WHAT BECOMES OF THE EARTH? A LITTLE DIRT, A LITTLE WATER--COSMICALLY, IT DOESN'T QUALIFY AS A SPITBALL.
WHAT DIFFERENCE WOULD IT MAKE IN THE TOTAL SCHEME OF THINGS IF THIS WORLD JUST VANISHED?
NONE. NONE AT ALL.
UNLESS YOU HAPPEN TO LIVE HERE.
JV 154
Just Another Planet Story!
STEVE GERBER WRITER | AL MILGROM ARTIST | PABLO MARCOS INKER | DENISE WOHL LETTERER | PHIL RACHE COLORIST | MARV WOLFMAN EDITOR

IN THE YEAR 3015 A.D., COMPARATIVELY FEW PEOPLE DO-- LIVE HERE, THAT IS. MOST OF HUMANKIND IS DEAD, SLAIN BY EARTH'S CONQUERORS, THE AFORE-MENTIONED LIZARDS, THE BANEFUL BROTHERHOOD OF BADOON.
UNTIL RECENTLY, THE 50 MILLION OR SO SURVIVORS TOILED AS SLAVES TO THEIR REPTILIAN MASTERS. THEN, THE DEFENDERS-- TIME TRAVELING HEROES FROM EARTH'S PAST--FREED THEM FROM BONDAGE.*
SINCE THEIR LIBERATION, WAR HAS RAVAGED THE FACE OF THE GLOBE, AS TERRAN MEN, WOMEN, AND CHILDREN FOUGHT TO REGAIN SUPREMACY ON THEIR OWN WORLD.
*IN DEFENDERS #'S 26 THRU 29. --MILLENIUM MARV.

THIS IS THE FINAL CONFLAGRATION--IN THE STREETS OF NEW MOSCOW, CAPITAL OF THE WORLD GOVERNMENT.
AND HERE, AS IN EACH PREVIOUS BATTLE, FOUR FLAMBOYANT FIGURES STAND AT THE VANGUARD--
THE GUARDIANS OF THE GALAXY!™

MAJOR VANCE ASTRO: FIRST EARTHMAN TO THE STARS, LAST SURVIVOR OF THE 20th CENTURY.
AT AGE 1053, HE'S OLD ENOUGH TO REMEMBER HOW REVOLUTION WAS ROMANTICIZED IN OUR ERA...

...OLD ENOUGH, TOO, TO HAVE NOTICED THAT HOWEVER NOBLE THE CAUSE, WAR IS STILL A KIND OF MADNESS.
AND THE KILLING ISN'T MADE ANY PRETTIER BY LOFTY IDEALS.

NOR IS THE MADNESS PARTICULARLY CHOOSY ABOUT ITS VICTIMS.
A TERRAN PHALANX RUSHES TO THE STEPS OF FEDERATION HALL, AND BLINDED BY ITS FERVOR...
...FAILS TO NOTE WHAT ITS MYRIAD FEET MAY TRAMPLE.

THE CHILD IS FIVE, PERHAPS SIX YEARS OLD--BORN BEHIND PRISON FENCES, FOR THE BADOON ARRIVED ON EARTH BEFORE HE DID.
THIS IS HIS FIRST TASTE OF FREEDOM. SO FAR, HE DOESN'T LIKE IT MUCH.

IN THE SKULL OF VANCE ASTRO, NERVE IMPULSES MASS, SPARKS OF THOUGHT CONGEAL.
FROM HIS BRAIN LEAPS A PSYCHOKINETIC BURST--PURE FORCE OF MIND.

THE MOB IS SCATTERED, THE CHILD IS SAVED. BUT PRECIOUS MOMENTS HAVE BEEN LOST.

THERE IS NO PLACE OF SAFETY ON THIS NEW EARTH, NOWHERE THE CHILD CAN WAIT OUT THE HOLOCAUST.
SO HE CLINGS TO ASTRO'S SILVERY BODY-SHEATH... AND BECOMES PART OF THE CHARGE AS IT RESUMES.

CHARLIE 27: LAST OF EARTH'S JUPITER COLONY, GENETICALLY-ENGINEERED TO WITHSTAND THE ENORMOUS GRAVITY AND RAMPANT RADIATION OF THE JOVIAN ATMOSPHERE.

AND ROLLING ON DRIVERLESS, THE MINDLESS MAMMOTH...

...BECOMES THE INSTRUMENT OF DESTRUCTION FOR ITS OWN CREATORS.

ONE SKIRMISH, THOUGH, DOESN'T DECIDE A WAR. CHARLIE HAS BARELY A MOMENT TO GLOAT BEFORE--!
KZZZAT!
DEATH FROM ANOTHER DIRECTION: THE BADOON LUNGES FORWARD, DRAWING A BEAD ON THE JOVIAN.
NO ESCAPE THIS TIME. WHEN THE TRIGGER IS SQUEEZED...!

BUT THE TRIGGER NEVER GETS SQUEEZED. A GLEAMING SHAFT SLICES THE AIR... AND THE THROAT OF THE WOULD-BE ASSASSIN.

A YAKA ARROW, LOOSED FROM THE BOW OF YONDU, LAST OF THE NATIVES OF CENTAURI-IV, SITE OF EARTH'S ONLY INTER-STELLAR COLONY.
"THANKS" ISN'T ENOUGH-- BUT I CAN'T THINK OF ANYTHING ELSE TO SAY, FRIEND.

THEN DO NOT SPEAK. WAIT WHILE I RECOVER MY SHAFT...
...AND WE WE CAN JOIN VANCE INSIDE FEDER-ATION HALL.
UNGH WAS THAT REALLY NECESSARY?

THE "LIVING METAL" YAKA IS FOUND ONLY ON MY HOME-WORLD, CHARLIE. I DARE NOT WASTE--
THE LOGIC OF THE PRIMITIVE. I SHOULD'VE KNOWN.
ONCE THE BADOON WAS DEAD YOU COULDN'T EVEN SEE HIM, COULD YOU?

"WHAT," ASKS YONDU, IS THERE TO SEE ONCE THE SPIRIT HAS DEPARTED THE PHYSICAL FORM? THERE ARE CERTAIN RITUALS OF MY PEOPLE I MIGHT PERFORM...
"... BUT I'VE NO WISH TO HAVE THAT SPIRIT DWELL FOREVER IN ANTHOS."

"ANTHOS. THAT'S WHAT YOUR PEOPLE CALLED HEAVEN, ISN'T IT?" CHARLIE INQUIRES.
"IT WAS OUR WORD FOR PEACE, AS WELL," THE CENTAURIAN ANSWERS GRIMLY.

ATTENTION ALL SECTORS! THIS IS KOORD, BADOON GOVERNOR OF SOL-III. EMERGENCY AT LOCUS PRIME!

THE COMMUNICATIONS SYSTEM HAS BEEN TEMPORARILY DISABLED, KOORD.

EH? WHO--?
THE PLUVIAN--MARTINEX!
THIS LAST LIVING MEMBER OF EARTH'S COLONY ON PLUTO MAKES NO REPLY, BUT POINTS AN ACCUSING FINGER AT THE CHIEF EXTERMINATOR OF HIS PEOPLE.

IT IS MORE THAN AN ACCUSATION, HOWEVER--IT'S AN EXECUTION.
FROM THE CRYSTALLINE HAND ISSUES A BLAST OF EXTREME HEAT.
AN INSTANT LATER, KOORD IS NO MORE. AND THE SCIENTIST-MEMBER OF THE GUARDIANS SLIPS AWAY, A GRIM SMILE ETCHED UPON HIS FEATURES OF FACETED SILICON.

IN THE MAIN ROTUNDA OF FEDERATION HALL-- LATELY THE BADOON THRONE CHAMBER, BUT NO MORE-- THE LAST SYMBOLIC VESTIGES OF THE REPTILES' TYRANNY COME CRASHING TO THE MARBLE FLOOR. THE WAR IS OVER. THE VICTORS ARE HUMAN.
VANCE! CHARLIE! YONDU!
MARTINEX! WE'VE DONE IT! THE LAST OF THE BADOON ARE BEING ROUNDED UP IN THE STREETS!
THE EARTH IS FREE!
ALL THAT'S LEFT IS TO FIND KOORD AND MAKE THE SURRENDER OFFICIAL.
THAT WON'T BE POSSIBLE, VANCE. KOORD IS... NO LONGER WITH US.
YOU COOKED HIM? CONGRATULATIONS, MISTER--!
THE DARK NIGHT OF EVIL IS ENDED THEN. DAWN IS COME.
UH-HUH! ALL THAT POETIC STUFF. WHICH REMINDS ME: ANYBODY SEEN STARHAWK?
AS USUAL OUR MASTER RHETORICIAN HAS BEEN ABSENT DURING MOST OF THE ACTION.
"PRETTY ODD BEHAVIOR-- FOR A GUY WHO SEEMED SO INTENT ON HELPING US DEFEAT THE BADOON.
"BUT THEN... EVERYTHING ABOUT STARHAWK IS PRETTY ODD, ISN'T IT?"

"HE WON'T CONFIDE IN US WHO HE REALLY IS, WHERE HE CAME FROM OR EVEN WHAT HIS MOTIVES ARE.
"HE'S JUST THE SORT OF ENIGMA EARTH DOESN'T NEED; ALL THAT POWER, COUPLED WITH ALL THOSE QUESTIONS.

"'ONE WHO KNOWS,' HE CALLS HIMSELF," ASTRO MUTTERS. "KNOWS WHAT?"
LEAD 'EM TO THE SQUARE. WE'LL KILL 'EM ONE BY ONE...!
MAIM 'EM, I SAY! AN EYE HERE, AN ARM THERE... LIKE THEY DID TO US!
NO, TERRAN. YOU SHALL DO NEITHER.

THE HUMANS HAVE BEATEN THE BADOON. IT REMAINS TO BE SEEN WHETHER THEY WILL TRIUMPH OVER THEIR OWN BASEST EMOTIONS.
IF THEY CANNOT, THEIR NEW WORLD ORDER HASN'T A PRAYER OF SURVIVAL.

AND SO THEY'LL SIMPLY NOT BE ALLOWED TO RUN AMOK, MAD FOR VENGEANCE.
THEY'LL BE FORCED TO REBUILD THEIR CIVILIZATION ON A FOUNDATION OF DIGNITY, NOT HATRED.
FOR THE BROTHER-HOOD OF BADOON SHALL BE WHISKED FROM THEIR MIDST BY MORE FITTING DISCIPLINARIANS:
THE FEMALES OF THEIR OWN SPECIES!

QUICK! OUTSIDE--MORE OF THEM--SPACE-FLEET LANDING--BADOON REINFORCEMENTS--!

WHA-A-AT?!

STARHAWK! HE'S BETRAYED US!!

HE MUST'VE BEEN A BADOON AGENT ALL ALONG! HE--

CALM YOURSELF, MY FRIEND. THINK IT THROUGH!

WOULD SUCH AN AGENT PERMIT US TO DEFEAT HALF THE BADOON--MERELY TO UNLEASH THE OTHER HALF UPON US?

AND GET THE WOMEN, TOO! AND THAT CLOWN IN THE BLUE PAJAMAS!

WHO'S HE TO TELL US HOW TO RUN OUR WORLD?

HOW DO WE KNOW HE'S EVEN HUMAN?

"THE TERRANS DO NOT SEEM FAVORABLY DISPOSED TOWARD THE SOLUTION WE'VE PROPOSED, STARHAWK," THE QUEEN OBSERVES.

"THEIR ABILITY TO EVALU-ATE ALTERNATIVES LOGIC-ALLY, MAJESTY, IS VASTLY HAMPERED BY THEIR EMO-TIONAL BENT," THE MYSTERY MAN EXPLAINS.

THE MALES HAVE DISHONORED OUR NAME THROUGHOUT THE GALAXY.

IF THE TERRANS WISH THEM DEAD-- SO BE IT. I SHALL AWAIT THEIR DECISION.

NO! YOU MUSTN'T LEAVE! DON'T--!

PEOPLE-- LISTEN TO ME! STOP!! YOU'RE RUINING EVERYTHING! THERE'S NO NEED--
REASON WON'T PENETRATE, MAJOR THE HOSTILITY RUNS TOO DEEP...
BLAST IT, TAKE YOUR HAND OFF ME! WHERE WERE YOU AND YOUR PHILOSOPHICAL BULL DURING THE FIGHT-- WHEN WE NEEDED YOU?
I AM NOT ACCOUNTABLE TO YOU, MAJOR, FOR MY WHEREABOUTS.
MY DUTY LIES WHERE I DETERMINE I AND ONLY ONE OTHER.
UH-HUH! I SUPPOSE HE SPEAKS TO YOU DIRECTLY.
I WAS NOT REFERRING TO YOUR DEITY. SHIELD YOUR EYES, MAJOR.
FOR YOUR OWN PEACE OF MIND, ACCEPT THAT YOUR INTERESTS AND MINE ARE COMPLEMENTARY...
...AND THAT ANY ACTION I TAKE WILL REFLECT THAT COMPATIBIL-ITY OF PURPOSE.
I CAN'T SEE! I CAN'T SEE!
THE BLUE GUY-- HE'S BLINDED US!

"Do you find my tactics unnecessarily abusive, Major...or can you agree that your people were *already* quite blind? " Starhawk queries.

Reluctantly, Astro nods.

"If need be," Starhawk continues, "we shall repeat this scenario in every city on the face of the globe, until all of the Brotherhood has been evacuated. When your humankind opens its eyes once more, they shall have only one another to look upon.

"We shall give reason its chance, Major. We shall afford earth every opportunity to exercise its *creativeness* and to reject the course that leads to self-destruction.

"If even then humanity chooses the latter---that is what they *deserve.*

"Harsh though it may sound, your race's period of oppression cannot be permitted to excuse whatever excesses it may commit."

A chill racing up his spine, Astro nods again. Man has the means to reach the stars now, and this motivation for conquest, this suspicion and mistrust of—things extraterrestrial, this predilection for violence must not travel with him.

So Vance and Charlie and Yondu and Martinex resolve, at least for the present, to cooperate with this One Who Knows. And in the ensuing days, what *must* be done *is* done, sometimes without resistance, usually not.

Within a week, earth has been deprived of its potential scapegoat. Whatever future is to come , men and women will be its cause, with only themselves to praise or blame for its triumphs and its failures.

...and there are a goodly number of *both* in the months that follow.

AUTUMN: BRED IN THE WILDERNESS OF HIS OWN WORLD, YONDU SEEKS HIS SPIRIT IN WHAT MEAGER WOODLAND IS LEFT ON OURS.
THE WATERS FLOW... THE TREES AND GRASS OBEY THE SEASONS AND LIVE AND DIE AND LIVE...
...BUT SOMETHING... HAS BEEN LOST.

THERE IS NO CHALLENGE HERE, NO MEANS, NO PLACE FOR THE LIFE-FORCE TO BE UPLIFTED...
...ONLY HOLLOW REPETITION OF WHAT HAS GONE BEFORE.

IT IS HERE, ON THIS WORLD, I MUST DWELL... FOR I'VE NOWHERE ELSE TO GO...
AND YET THERE'S NO REASON TO LIVE ON A WORLD WHOSE SOUL IS DEAD!

NO REASON TO LIVE... AT ALL. THE GHOSTS OF MY PEOPLE SPEAK TO ME. AND THEIR VOICES SAY...

...IT IS MY TIME TO DIE.
HIS MIND EXCLUDES ALL THOUGHTS BUT THAT ONE. HIS HEARTBEAT SLOWS.

I WOULD NOT HAVE ACTED TO SAVE MY LIFE IF MY DEATH WAS TRULY WHAT THE SPIRITS DESIRED.
I'VE NOT LOOKED DEEP ENOUGH, OR FAR ENOUGH, THEN.
I SHALL NURSE THIS HUMAN BACK TO HEALTH... THEN PURSUE MY QUEST... WHEREVER IT SHALL LEAD.

WINTER: IN THE CITY CALLED BERLIN: MARTINEX AND A FELLOW SCIENTIST WORK TO WADE THROUGH THE REMAINS OF EARTH'S MOST EXTENSIVE TECHNICAL LIBRARY.
NOTHING! THE COMPUTERS BEYOND REPAIR--THE TAPES WEATHER-DAMAGED, INCOMPLETE!
THE BADOON TOOK BETTER CARE OF THIS COMPLEX THAN--
THERE WAS NO CHOICE. THE CITY WAS ALL BUT DESTROYED. WE COULD CONSTRUCT SHELTER FOR PEOPLE OR FOR TAPES ...BUT NOT BOTH!
BUT THE KNOWLEDGE THAT WAS STORED HERE-- HOW CAN MAN SURVIVE WITHOUT IT?
I KNOW HOW YOU FEEL. SCHOLARS EVERYWHERE ARE CONCERNED. BUT THERE ARE OTHER LIBRARIES. WE--
YOU WITHDREW YOUR HAND. WHY?
WHA? I DON'T KNOW... I JUST...
I AM NOT AN ALIEN, YOU KNOW. YOU'RE AWARE THAT MY GRANDPARENTS WERE CARBON-BASED HUMANS LIKE YOURSELF?
Y-YES...
BUT YOU'RE STILL REPELLED BY ME, AREN'T YOU? EVEN THOUGH THE FIRST OF MY RACE WAS BIRTHED HERE-- IN THIS VERY LABORATORY--
--FROM THE ALTERED GENES OF AN EARTHMAN!
IT'LL BE... DARK SOON. GETTING COLD. I'D BEST BE GOING.
G-GOOD LUCK WITH YOUR DIGGING. HOPE YOU FIND SOMETHING...
NO. THERE'S NO USE LOOKING FURTHER. I'VE UNCOVERED TOO MUCH ALREADY.

LOS ANGELES: THERE BEING NO SPACE MILITIA NOW, CHARLIE TURNS HIS TALENTS TO THE MASSIVE TASK OF RECONSTRUCTION. AND, BEING NEW TO THE WORK, HE FINDS CERTAIN ASPECTS OF IT... IRRITATING.
C'MON, YA GORILLA! MOVE! GET THOSE GIRDERS OVER HERE! AN WATCH WHERE YER GOIN'-- LOOK OUT FER THEM BRICKS--
I'D APPRECIATE IT... IF YOU'D ADOPT A DIFFERENT TONE... SIR.
HE'S ACCUSTOMED TO OBEYING ORDERS. NO PROBLEM THERE. BUT HE'S SERVED UNDER THE FINEST ADMIRALS IN THE SPACE FLEET AND HE HAD THEIR RESPECT.
DON'T WISE-MOUTH ME, CHUNKY! YOU'RE NO HERO HERE, SEE?!
YOU AIN'T SPECIAL AT ALL, JUST ANOTHER WORKHORSE--
--THAT NEEDS ME TO BE ITS BRAIN.
IS THAT SO?
THEN PUT YOUR GENIUS TO WORK ON GETTING YOU OUT OF THIS-- AND SHUT UP!!
NO! DON'T!!
WHEEEOOOO
WHAT'RE YA-- WHERE YA GOIN'? COME BACK!!
YOU HEARD THE WHISTLE, BOSS, IT'S QUITTIN' TIME.
SO--I QUIT!
THUS ENDS "THE DAY CHARLIE TOLD OFF HIS BOSS."

SAN FRANCISCO, AFTER HOURS: IN A TINY, CROWDED CABARET, VANCE ASTRO INDULGES IN A BIT OF INTROSPECTION.
WHY DO I DO THIS TO MYSELF? WHY DO I KEEP COMING HERE-- STARING AT THE SWEAT ON THAT DANCER'S HIPBONES?
I MEAN... I'M TRAPPED IN THIS METAL BODY STOCKING FOR THE REST OF MY LIFE, RIGHT?

ANY CONTACT WITH THE AIR, AND MY 1000-YEAR-OLD SKIN TURNS TO DUST, SO--
HEY, PAULA, OVER HERE!
SIT WITH ME, PAULA--
THIS WAY, LUSCIOUS!!
OH, NO. PLEASE!

MAY I JOIN YOU?

I'D, UH, RATHER YOU DIDN'T. BELIEVE ME, THERE'S NO FUTURE IN IT FOR EITHER OF US.
YEAH, HON-- NOTHIN' YOU CAN DO FOR HIM-- OR HIM FOR YOU!
SOME BIG HERO! SOME REAL MAN!

CRASH
EEYAAAAAAGH

TOUCHY ABOUT THAT, HUH?
YEAH, JUST A LITTLE.

SO WHERE DOES ALL THIS GET US? WHAT DO I DO NOW?
I SUPPOSE THERE'S ALWAYS ANOTHER CABARET, OR SUICIDE, IF THEY'RE ALL CLOSED.
SUDDENLY...
WHAT IN--? THE TELEPORT BEAM?
AN INSTANT LATER, ASTRO'S ATOMS RE-INTEGRATE ABOARD THE GUARDIANS' STARSHIP "CAPTAIN AMERICA," TO BE GREETED BY...
WELL. THE THREE UGLIEST FACES I KNOW.
I TAKE IT YOU FOUND POSTWAR EARTH AS FRUSTRATING AS I DID!
NOT IN QUITE THE SAME WAY... BUT YES.
THERE'S NOTHING FOR ANY OF US DOWN THERE.
WHICH IS WHY, MAJOR, I'VE PROPOSED YOU FOUR UNDERTAKE A MISSION WITH ME. AND YOUR COMRADES HAVE CONSENTED.
STARHAWK?! HERE--?
WHAT MISSION? WHAT IS THIS??
"WE'RE LEAVING EARTH-ORBIT, MAJOR. I'VE ALREADY PLOTTED OUR COURSE AND LOCKED IN THE AUTO-NAVIGATIONAL SYSTEMS.
"WAITAMINIT--I HAVEN'T CONSENTED TO ANYTHING!"
"YOU'LL FIND THIS FAR MORE FULFILLING THAN THE SUICIDE YOU'D CONTEMPLATED, MAJOR. I GIVE YOU MY WORD--AS ONE WHO KNOWS."
NEXT: JOURNEY TO THE CENTER OF THE GALAXY!

Beginning with our third issue, this sector of magazine space will be reserved for your comments, questions, and criticisms regarding the GUARDIANS OF THE GALAXY. It thus behooves us to recall at this juncture one of the immutable laws of physics: for every action, there is an equal and opposite reaction.

Translation: you have to act (by writing letters) before we can react (by making nasty replies in bold type). Otherwise, we won't have a letters page. So take a hint, huh, space-pilgrim? Hitch your typewriter or ballpoint— no crayons, please— to a starship, shift into Harkovian creative drive, and WRITE!!

(Or, so help us, we'll get even more sickeningly cutesy the next time we're forced to remind you. And that's no idle threat. You've no idea the linguistic atrocities we're capable of committing.)

Okay, now *that* we've got that out of our propulsion systems...!

A word or two is in order about the earth of 3015 A.D., the far-future era in which our GUARDIANS tales are set.

As you've no doubt noticed, it's a very different world from our own. There are no food shortages, no gas shortages, no inflation or unemployment. Primarily because there's also no problem with overpopulation: the only resource in short supply, thanks to the Badoon, is *people.*

Fifty-million human beings are left alive— more than enough for a softball game, true, but a mere *one-sixtieth* of earth's present population.

But before the coming of the Badoon, not only was earth itself teeming with life— earth *colonies* had been established on three of our nine planets and on the fourth planet in orbit about the nearest star, Alpha Centauri.

Mercury, the smallest planet in our solar system and the nearest to the sun, became a mining colony, inhabited by genetically-altered humans able to withstand the enormous heat of the Mercurian day (temperatures approaching 400 degrees centigrade) and the brittle cold of its month-long nights. Tiny though the planet is, its importance to humanity's progress in that future era was tremendous: here was found in sufficient quantities the fuel that made the Harkovian hyperdrive work. Its discovery on Mercury made faster-than-light space travel a reality and set man on his course to the stars.

So far as is known, every member of the Mercurian colony met his death during the Badoon invasion.

Neither Venus nor Mars was ever colonized. Venus, with its enormous atmospheric pressure and its surface temperatures approaching 800 degrees centigrade, proved too great a challenge even for the genetic engineers. Mars, as terrans learned to their sorrow back in 2001, was already inhabited. (Check out any issue of KILLRAVEN if you doubt us.)

The surface of Jupiter, too, proved too difficult an environment to colonize. But "floating cities" contained in plastiglass bubbles were constructed in the planet's atmosphere, and from this vantage point the scientists of Charlie-27's race were able to study Jupiter itself and the other giant planets, Saturn, Uranus, and Neptune.

Perhaps the greatest feat of earth's geneticians was the creation of the silicon-based humanoids who inhabited earth's colony on Pluto, the solar system's last outpost. These crystalline men and women, though created in man's own image, had virtually nothing in common with their earthborn ancestors. Their method of reproduction, their patterns of growth were vastly different from those of earthmen— and just *how* different will become clear when we delve into Martinex's "youth" in issues to come.

Centauri-IV, as luck would have it, was an earthlike world, inhabited by a race of blue-skinned primitives whose lifestyle resembled, though hardly duplicated, that of the American Indian before the arrival of the Europeans. That culture survives now only in Yondu, the weapons master, the natural hunter of the Guardians. The rest of his people were wiped out, along with the terran colonists, by the Badoon.

Which brings us back to the Homeworld, an earth which has known scientific advances far beyond our imagination, which has savored the thrill of interplanetary exploration...and which, for eight years, has worn the yoke of slavery. It's an embittered planet now, in 3015 A.D. Its people are weary. And whether it can rise up from the ashes of its conquest and liberation is an open question.

The future, it seems, even 1040 years from now, is only beginning.

MARVEL VALUE STAMP

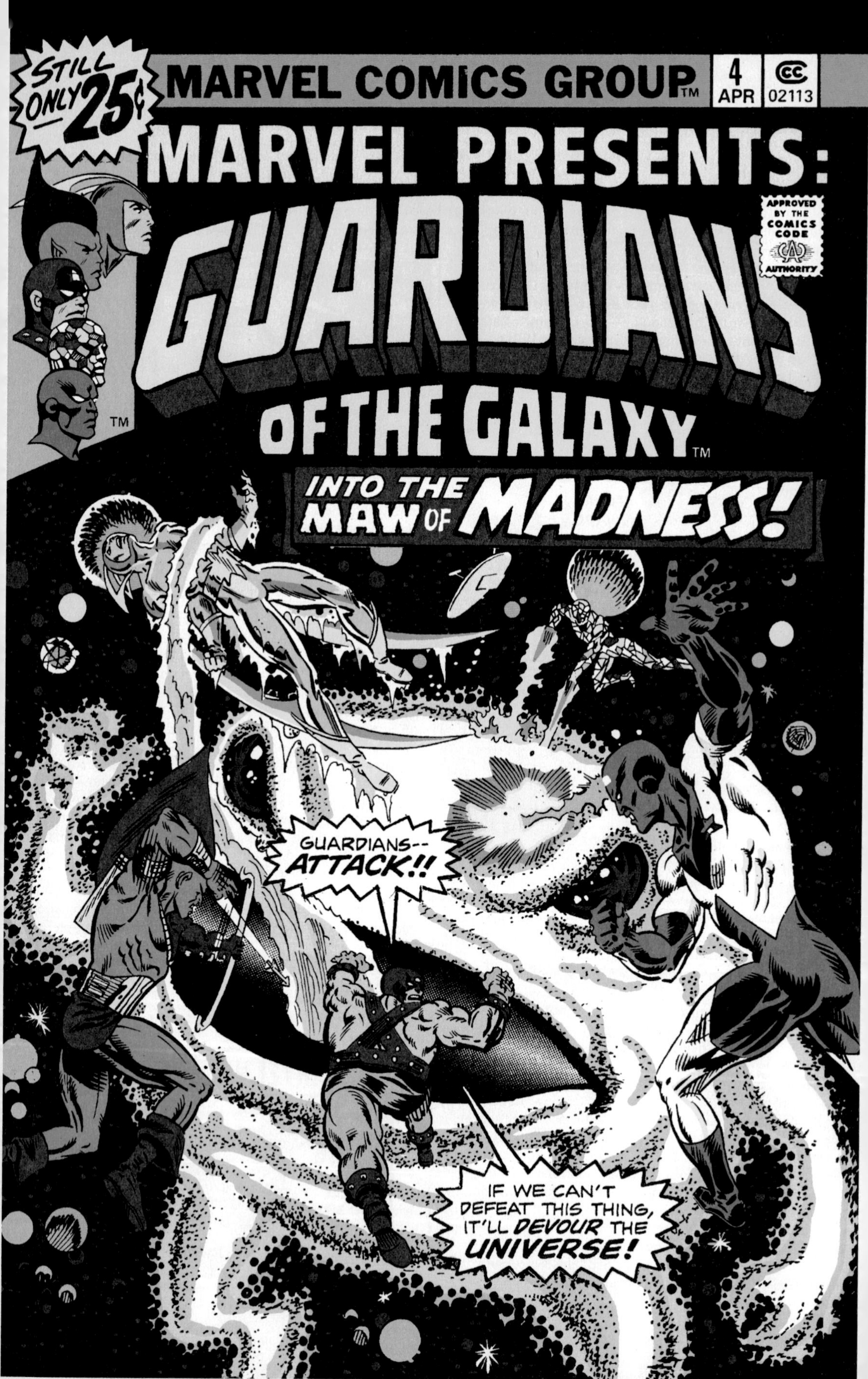
STILL ONLY 25¢
MARVEL COMICS GROUP
4 APR
CC 02113
MARVEL PRESENTS:
GUARDIANS OF THE GALAXY
APPROVED BY THE COMICS CODE AUTHORITY
INTO THE MAW OF MADNESS!
GUARDIANS-- ATTACK!!
IF WE CAN'T DEFEAT THIS THING, IT'LL DEVOUR THE UNIVERSE!

Stan Lee PRESENTS:
The GUARDIANS of the GALAXY TM
STEVE GERBER WRITER
ALLEN MILGROM ARTIST
JANICE COHEN, Colorist
IRV WATANABE, Letterer
MARV WOLFMAN EDITOR
INTO THE MAW OF MADNESS!
YOU MEAN WE TOOK A DETOUR FROM A VOYAGE TO THE CENTER OF THE GALAXY--
--JUST SO YONDU COULD COME WORSHIP AT THE PLANET OF HIS CHOICE?
HE FELT IT NECESSARY TO CONSULT THE GODS OF HIS RACE BEFORE UNDERTAKING SO URGENT A MISSION AS OURS, MAJOR ASTRO.
AND HE COULD ONLY ACCOMPLISH THAT HERE-- ON HIS NATIVE CENTAURI-IV.
HE'S THE ONLY CENTAURIAN TO SURVIVE THE BADOON INVASION, VANCE--THE ONLY LIVING PRODUCT OF HIS CUSTOMS AND CULTURE.
ANTHROPOLOGICALLY--
JV/83

THE **REMAINDER** OF THE EX-SPACE-MILITIAMAN'S COMMENT IS RENDERED **INAUDIBLE** BY THE DIN OF **THUNDER**--THE CRACKLING OF ELECTRIC **FIRE**.

THE PLANET SEEMS TO **SHUDDER** AT ITS VERY **CORE**.

THE ELEMENTAL SPIRITS HAVE **ANSWERED** YONDU'S CALL.

FROM THE SKY OF THE DEAD WORLD, LIFE-GIVING **RAIN** POURS IN TORRENTS.

NATURE'S **TEARS**. THE PLANET, LIKE YONDU, **MOURNS** ITS MURDERED PEOPLE.

IT IS THE WORD OF ANTHOS: I AM NOT TO ABANDON OUR QUEST.
MY TIME IS NOT COME TO JOIN THE UNSEEN WORLD.
FOR CRYING OUT LOUD, I COULD'VE TOLD YOU THAT-- WITHOUT ALL THIS MUMBO-JUMBO!
IT ISN'T "MUMBO-JUMBO," VANCE--THAT'S ONE OF THE FIRST THINGS THE EARTH'S COLONISTS LEARNED.
THERE WAS A STRANGE, ALMOST MYSTICAL RELATIONSHIP BETWEEN THE LAND AND THE PEOPLE OF CENTAURI-IV.
SOME SORT OF LINK THAT EARTHMEN LOST LONG AGO...
ONE MOMENT...
COMPUTER: EXECUTE PRE-PROGRAMMED TELEPORT...
...AS I WAS SAYING, A LINK LOST LONG AGO, WHEN WE BROKE OUR TIES TO NATURE, AND CHOSE THE TECHNOLOGICAL ROUTE.
EVEN AS CONFIRMED AN EMPIRICIST AS I RECOGNIZES THE VALUE OF MAN'S INTUITIVE KNOWLEDGE, VANCE.
OH, SWELL. SUDDENLY I'M TRAVELING WITH THE GURUS OF THE GALAXY!
GOO-WHAT...?
SKIP IT. AN ARCHAISM. I KEEP FORGETTING-- I'M THE ONLY THOUSAND-YEAR-OLD IN THIS CROWD.
LISTEN--I THINK I'M FEELING MY AGE. THE WEATHER PLANETSIDE MADE MY BONES ACHE. IF YOU NEED ME, I'LL BE--

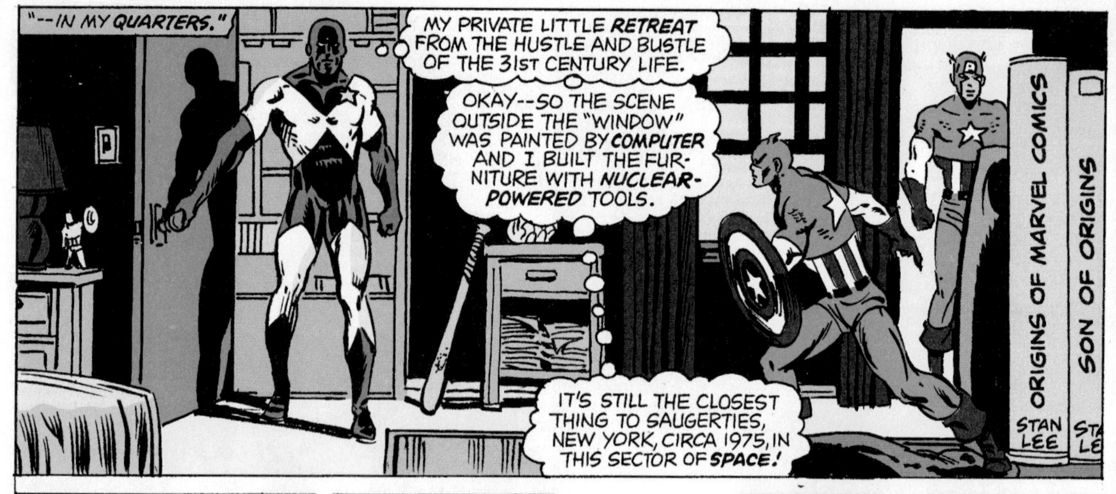

--A LANCE OF **PURE MENTAL FORCE** WHICH, UPON STRIKING THE MYSTERIOUS **STARHAWK**, CREATES A CURIOUS EFFECT INDEED.

THESE DISPLAYS--OF TEMPERAMENT--ARE BECOMING--IRRITATING, MAJOR. NEED I--REMIND YOU--?
I'VE THE POWER--TO VAPORIZE--YOUR GLEAMING ARMOR--ALLOW THE AIR TO REDUCE YOUR ANCIENT FLESH--TO COARSE, STALE DUST?
YEAH. RIGHT. REMIND ME. IT SLIPPED MY MIND.
I'VE KILLED BEFORE, MAJOR--AND ONLY ONCE WITH ANY SLIGHT REMORSE.
I'VE NO DESIRE TO SLAY ANY BEING OF WORTH. AND SO I'VE TOLERATED YOUR HOSTILITY THUS FAR.
AS ONE WHO KNOWS... I OWE YOU THAT!
I AM THE LIGHT... AND THE GIVER OF LIGHT... BUT I CAN ALSO STEAL THAT LIGHT AWAY.
IN YOUR VERNACULAR MAJOR: DO NOT PRESS YOUR LUCK.
UH-HUH. I'M IMPRESSED.
BUT NOT BY YOUR TOUGH TALK, "O INSCRUTABLE ONE." WHAT INTERESTS ME IS --WHO WAS THAT LADY I SAW YOU WITH?!
AND THIS "ONE WHO KNOWS" IS ALL-TOO ACUTELY COGNIZANT OF THAT FACT.
OUTSIDE IN THE SHIP'S CORRIDOR, ALONE, HIS STOLID VENEER CRACKS EVER SO SLIGHTLY.
QUITE BY ACCIDENT, VANCE ASTRO HAS SEEN BENEATH THE SURFACE OF THINGS, AND THE BEING CALLED STARHAWK ...IS DISTURBED...
FOR IT IS NOT HIS NATURE TO BE KNOWN, AND YET, HE SEEMS TO BE THE TOPIC OF CONVERSATION EVERYWHERE.
WE'RE BACK ON COURSE TO THE HUB OF THE GALAXY. BUT, MARTINEX...
YOU'RE GROWING IMPATIENT TO LEARN WHAT TROUBLE STARHAWK EXPECTS TO FIND THERE.
AS WOULD I, IF NOT FOR THIS OPPORTUNITY TO SCAN THE VARIOUS STAR-SYSTEMS ON OUR WAY FOR--
MARTINEX--CHARLIE--THERE IS SOMETHING--AN OBJECT--BEFORE US IN OUR PATH. LOOK HERE.

HOLY HARKOV--WE'RE UNDER ATTACK--CLICK ON THE FORCE SCREENS, MARTY--FAST!
SCREEN'S ON! AND I'M GETTING A SENSOR-FIX ON OUR ASSAILANT, AS WELL.
UNFORTUNATELY...THE READINGS MAKE NO SENSE AT ALL.
IT'S AN EARTHSHIP--FOUR-MAN PERSONAL CRAFT OF THE TYPE OWNED BY SOME WEALTHIER BUSINESSMEN BEFORE THE BADOON INVASION.
WE'RE BEING HIT BY ITS METEOR-DEFLECTOR BEAMS!
WE'VE NO TIME FOR AN ALTERCATION. EMPLOY YOUR TRACTOR BEAMS. BRING THE CRAFT ABOARD.
LET'S MEET THE FOE FACE-TO-FACE.
MARTINEX NODS HIS APPROVAL. CHARLIE'S THUMB FALLS ON THE PROPER BUTTON. AND A CALL GOES OUT TO GREET THE CAPTURED CRAFT IN THE STARSHIP'S HOLD.
D-DON'T COME ANY CLOSER! STOP RIGHT WHERE YOU ARE--OR I'LL BLAST YOUR ATOMS HALFWAY TO ANTARES! I SWEAR I WILL!
GOOD LORD--! A MERCURIAN? AND A KID, NO LESS! THERE WEREN'T SUPPOSED TO BE ANY OF YOU LEFT!
THERE WON'T BE ANY OF YOU LEFT IF YOU TAKE ANOTHER STEP TOWARD ME!
NO BADOON IS GOING TO--
BADOON?! C'MON--DO I LOOK LIKE A LIZARD?
YOU'RE A--A ROBOT, THEN--THE BADOON SEIZED ALL OF EARTH'S STARSHIPS--
NOT THIS ONE. BUT THEN, PERHAPS YOU HAVEN'T HEARD OF THE GUARDIANS OF THE GALAXY!
N-NO...BUT I KNOW A PLUVIAN...AND A JOVIAN...WHEN I SEE 'EM.

"**I'M** AS QUALIFIED 'TO GUARD THE GALAXY' AS ANY OF YOU CLOWNS. MAYBE **MORE** SO.

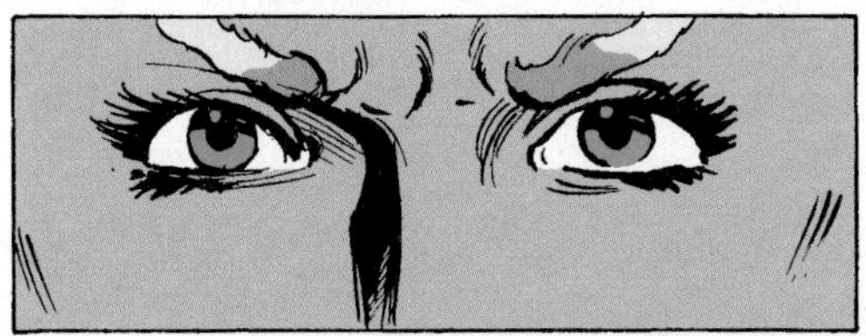

"LIKE, **SURVIVAL'S** BEEN MY BUSINESS, MY **ONLY** BUSINESS, SINCE THE BADOON DEMOLISHED THE MERCURIAN MINING COLONY-- **SEVEN YEARS AGO.**

"UH-HUH. I WAS **ELEVEN** EARTH-YEARS OLD WHEN MY PARENTS WERE **CUT DOWN** RIGHT IN FRONT OF MY EYES...

"...WHEN I HAD TO CHOOSE BETWEEN **DYING** WITH THOSE I LOVED...

"...OR TAKING THE HELM OF MY OWN FATE, NOT TO MENTION THE FAMILY SPACECRAFT, AND GETTING OUT **ALIVE.**

"OBVIOUSLY, I DECIDED MERCURY DIDN'T NEED ANOTHER **MARTYR.**

"I KNEW **HOW** TO PILOT THE SHIP...BUT NOT **WHERE.** IF THE BADOON HAD REACHED MERC, THEY'D ALREADY HAVE GOTTEN PAST **EARTH.**

FOOD CONC. PROTIEN VITA C

"SO I HEADED **AWAY...** NOWHERE SPECIAL... JUST **AWAY.** AND HOPED I'D HAVE ENOUGH TO **EAT** 'TIL I GOT THERE.

"I DIDN'T. AND I BARELY GOT PAST THE SOLAR SYSTEM WHEN THE **GENERATOR** BLEW. I WAS **DRIFTING...** 'TIL I SPOTTED A DEAD **CARGO SHIP...**

"...AND TOOK MY FIRST LITTLE STROLL **OUT THERE.** SOME FUN. I WAS SCARED STIFF.

"THE CREW OF THAT **DERELICT** WAS STIFF, TOO. FAILED LIFE-SUPPORT SYSTEMS DID 'EM IN. PRETTY UGLY. IF I HADN'T ALREADY SEEN A WHOLE **PLANET** SNUFFED, I MIGHT'VE BEEN A LITTLE **QUEASY**.

"INSTEAD, I SAW THE **BRIGHT SIDE**. THERE WERE SPARE PARTS AND ENOUGH FOOD FOR AN **ARMY** ON THAT OLD HULK. AND I'D PROVED TO MYSELF I COULD **MAKE IT** ALONE IN SPACE.

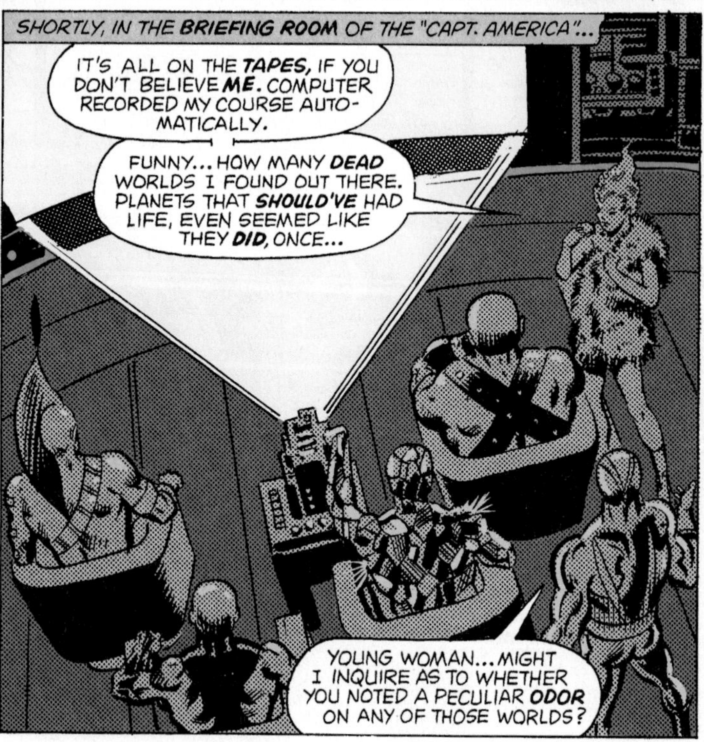

WHA-A-AT? RIGHT. ALL THOSE PLANETS SMELLED MILDEWED! HAVE YOU--?
ACCORDING TO YOUR LOG TAPES, THE PLANETS YOU'RE DESCRIBING LAY DIRECTLY ALONG OUR COURSE TO THE GALAXY'S CENTER.
I PRESUME, STAR-HAWK, THAT MORE THAN COINCIDENCE IS AT WORK HERE.
THAT IS CORRECT. YES.
WHY-- THAT'S RIGHT! THAT'S IT EXACTLY. EVERY ONE OF THEM SMELLED LIKE DAY-OLD LAUNDRY!
THOSE WORLDS DID SUPPORT LIFE AT ONE TIME. BUT FOR CENTURIES NOW, AN ALIEN FORCE HAS BEEN GNAWING ITS WAY THRU THE STAR-SYSTEMS...
...CONSUMING THAT LIFE.
SO WHAT ARE WE CHASING-- GALACTIC TERMITES?
NIKKI...
VANCE... HOLD YOUR MOUTH IN CHECK.
THE REST OF US HAVE BEEN WAITING TO HEAR STARHAWK'S EXPLANATION...WITHOUT INTERRUPTION.
OH! WELL! FAR BE IT FROM ME TO SHOUT DOWN THE KAHLIL GIBRAN OF THE STARS...!
THE FORCE YOU MOCK IS LESS AKIN TO A HOUSEHOLD PEST THAN TO A VAMPIRE.
IT IS INFINITELY OLD, INCALCULABLY POWERFUL, AND INSATIABLY HUNGRY.
"EVEN I HAVE BEEN UNABLE TO DETERMINE ITS EXACT NATURE. BUT FROM ALL I'VE DEDUCED, THE PLANETS IT'S CONSUMED THUS FAR HAVE MERELY WHETTED ITS APPETITE.
"I FEAR, MY FRIENDS...IT SUSTAINS ITSELF ON THE ENERGY OF EXPLODING GALAXIES."

HAVING SPOKEN HIS PIECE, STAR-HAWK BOWS HIS HEAD AND STANDS IN STONY SILENCE.

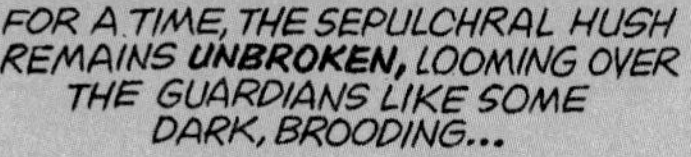
FOR A TIME, THE SEPULCHRAL HUSH REMAINS UNBROKEN, LOOMING OVER THE GUARDIANS LIKE SOME DARK, BROODING...

...SHADOW.
TARA--SITA-- LOOK!!
WH-WHAT IS IT?
IT'S BLOTTED OUT THE DAY!

WHAT'LL WE DO? WHAT IF IT TRIES TO GET INSIDE?
I--I DON'T KNOW! I'M GOING TO PUNCH UP ALETA! MAYBE SHE CAN HELP US!
SHE'LL HAVE TO-- IF STARHAWK ISN'T HERE.

ALETA HAS JUST AS MUCH POWER AS STARHAWK. YOU'LL SEE.
SHE CAN DO ANYTHING HE CAN--AND HE CAN'T DO ANYTHING WITH-OUT HER.
C'MON, DON'T TAKE SIDES, NOW. HIT THOSE BUTTONS, TARA!

SHE DOES. AND A MOMENT LATER, THE INTERIOR OF THE CABIN IS BATHED IN BRIGHT LIGHT.
AFTER THE DARKNESS OUTSIDE, THE WOMAN'S APPEAR-ANCE IS NEARLY BLINDING--SUCH IS THE BEAUTY OF HER VISAGE, THE ENERGY OF HER PRESENCE.

AND, PARSECS DISTANT, THAT EXPENDITURE OF ENERGY IS FELT.
YOU MUST...EXCUSE ME, MY FRIENDS. WE SHALL DISCUSS THE MATTER FURTHER WHEN--
ONE BLASTED MINUTE, MISTER! YOU CAN'T BAIT US WITH A LINE LIKE THAT AND THEN EXIT STAGE LEFT!
COME BACK HERE!

TARA, SITA, AND JOHN STAND TRANSFIXED BY ALETA'S SERENE LOVING GAZE.
THEY KNOW THEY NEED NOT SPEAK FOR HER TO UNDERSTAND THEIR DISTRESS.

NOR NEED SHE UTTER A WORD...TO ALLEVIATE THE UPSET.
A SINGLE FLASH OF BRILLIANCE, PENETRATING TO THE CHILDREN'S SOULS...

...AND ALL IS CALM ONCE MORE.
SUDDENLY, IT IS BEDTIME, AND THE CHILDREN FILE TO THEIR BUNKS.

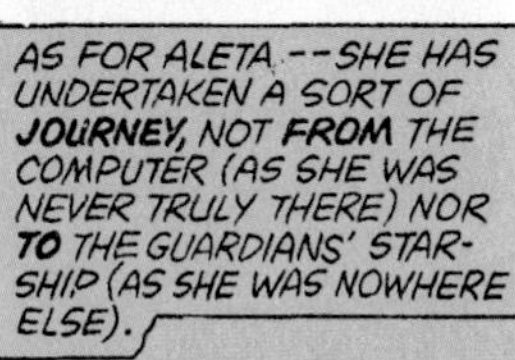

AS FOR ALETA --SHE HAS UNDERTAKEN A SORT OF JOURNEY, NOT FROM THE COMPUTER (AS SHE WAS NEVER TRULY THERE) NOR TO THE GUARDIANS' STARSHIP (AS SHE WAS NOWHERE ELSE).

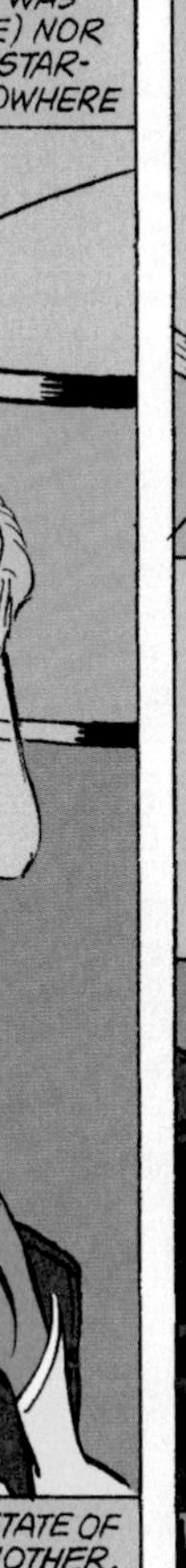

...BUT FROM ONE STATE OF EXISTENCE TO ANOTHER.

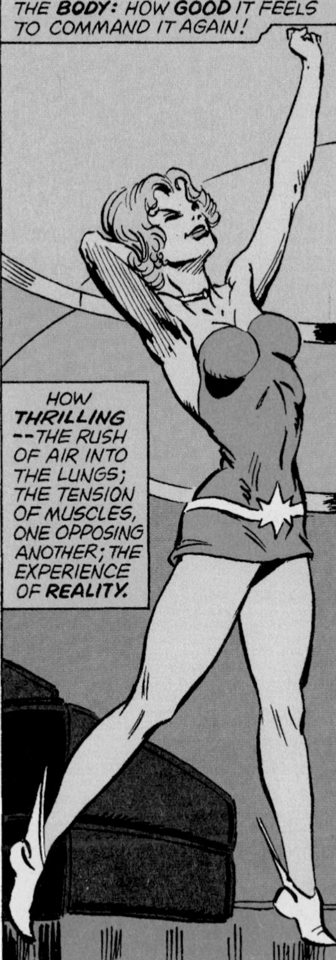

THE BODY: HOW GOOD IT FEELS TO COMMAND IT AGAIN!
HOW THRILLING --THE RUSH OF AIR INTO THE LUNGS; THE TENSION OF MUSCLES, ONE OPPOSING ANOTHER; THE EXPERIENCE OF REALITY.

BUT THERE IS NO TIME TO SAVOR THE SENSATIONS OVERLONG. SHE IS HERE TO COMMUNICATE A MESSAGE.
BUT SEARCHING, SHE FINDS NO IMPLEMENTS FOR WRITING --NO DEVICES FOR RECORDING.
THE QUARTERS OCCUPIED BY STARHAWK ARE BARE.

IT WAS, PERHAPS, TO BE EXPECTED. THE ONLY TRACE HE EVER LEFT BEHIND WAS THE MEMORY OF HIM. HIS TRACKS WERE ALWAYS COVERED.
PSSST-- BIG BLUE?
ALMOST ALWAYS.

HOP DOWN OFF THE PEDESTAL.

YOU'VE BEEN HOLDING OUT ON US, HAVEN'T YOU--PAPA?

SPARE ME YOUR TEDIOUS ATTEMPTS AT HUMOR, MAJOR.
YOU HAVE A MESSAGE TO RELAY, DO YOU NOT?
ALL IN GOOD TIME. FIRST, CLUE ME IN ON--
STARHAWK! VANCE! TIE IN TO THE BRIDGE--
ASTRO HERE. AND THIS BETTER BE GOOD. YOU'VE NO IDEA WHAT YOU'VE INTERRUP--
GET UP HERE, VANCE--FAST! AND BRING STARHAWK WITH YOU.
AND HURRY, MAN...
"WE'VE FOUND OUR 'TERMITE'!"
I DON'T GET IT. WE'RE NOWHERE NEAR THE GALAXY'S HUB. WHAT'S THIS THING DOING HERE?
I TOLD YOU, MAJOR--IT'S TRUE NATURE IS INDETERMINATE. IT MAY BE THAT THIS IS ONLY PART OF THE CREATURE. OR PERHAPS ITS SPAWN.
AND WE CANNOT EXCLUDE THE POSSIBILITY THE CREATURE CAN OCCUPY MORE THAN ONE PLACE AT ONE TIME.
WE SHALL KNOW MORE... AFTER I INVESTIGATE.

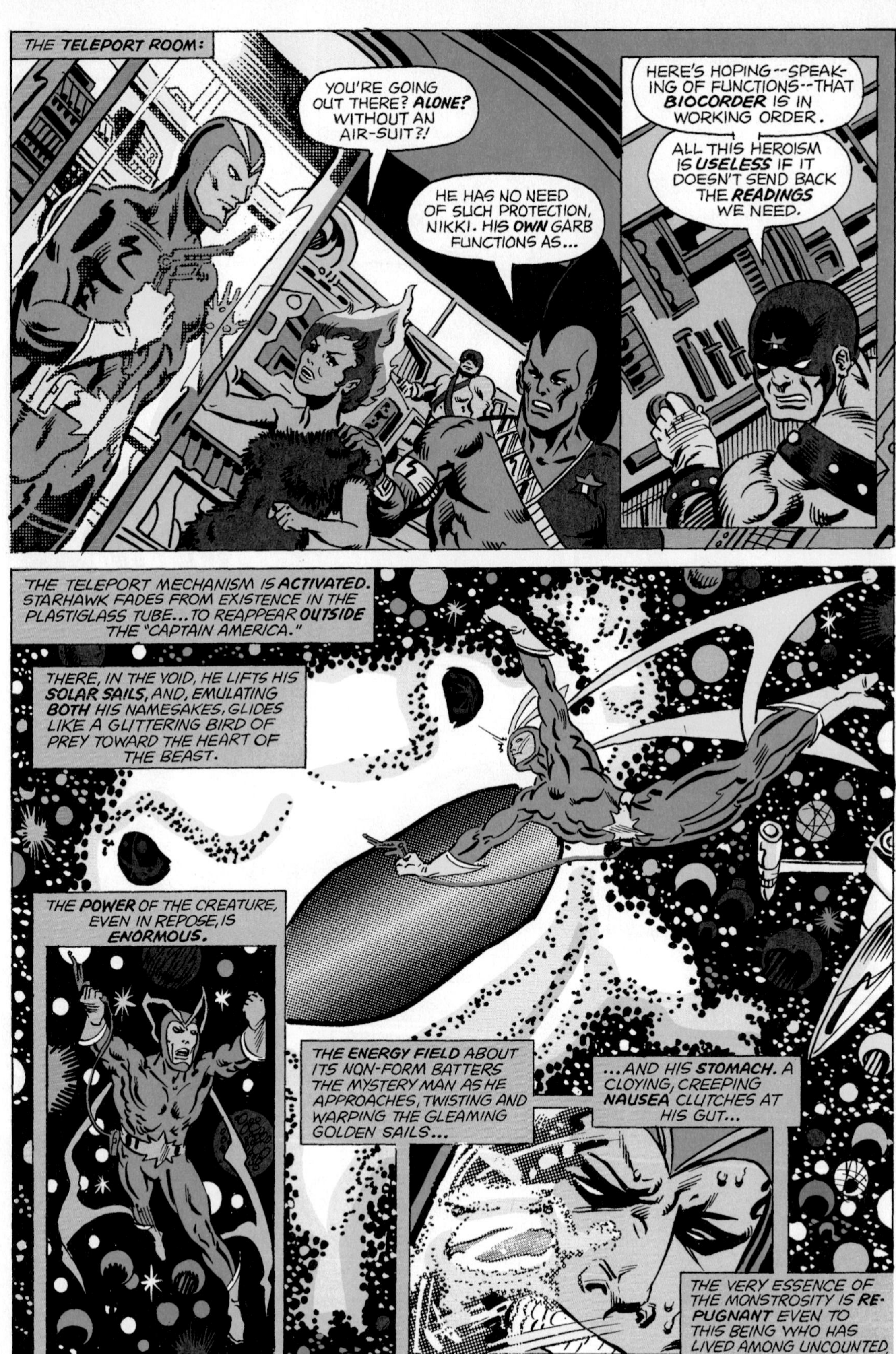
THE TELEPORT ROOM:
YOU'RE GOING OUT THERE? ALONE? WITHOUT AN AIR-SUIT?!
HE HAS NO NEED OF SUCH PROTECTION, NIKKI. HIS OWN GARB FUNCTIONS AS...
HERE'S HOPING--SPEAKING OF FUNCTIONS--THAT BIOCORDER IS IN WORKING ORDER.
ALL THIS HEROISM IS USELESS IF IT DOESN'T SEND BACK THE READINGS WE NEED.
THE TELEPORT MECHANISM IS ACTIVATED. STARHAWK FADES FROM EXISTENCE IN THE PLASTIGLASS TUBE...TO REAPPEAR OUTSIDE THE "CAPTAIN AMERICA."
THERE, IN THE VOID, HE LIFTS HIS SOLAR SAILS, AND, EMULATING BOTH HIS NAMESAKES, GLIDES LIKE A GLITTERING BIRD OF PREY TOWARD THE HEART OF THE BEAST.
THE POWER OF THE CREATURE, EVEN IN REPOSE, IS ENORMOUS.
THE ENERGY FIELD ABOUT ITS NON-FORM BATTERS THE MYSTERY MAN AS HE APPROACHES, TWISTING AND WARPING THE GLEAMING GOLDEN SAILS...
...AND HIS STOMACH. A CLOYING, CREEPING NAUSEA CLUTCHES AT HIS GUT...
THE VERY ESSENCE OF THE MONSTROSITY IS REPUGNANT EVEN TO THIS BEING WHO HAS LIVED AMONG UNCOUNTED, UN-HUMAN, ALIEN SPECIES.

YES, I'M SURE. THE BIOCORDER'S WORKING PERFECTLY. IT'S JUST...
THIS CREATURE ISN'T ENERGY OR MATTER ...SOLID OR LIQUID... ALIVE OR DEAD!
YOU'RE DESCRIBING-- NOTHING.
KARANADA.

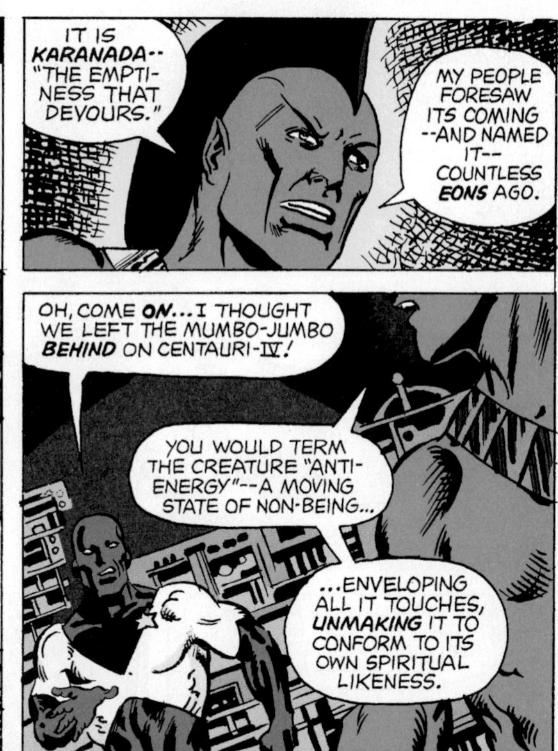
IT IS KARANADA-- "THE EMPTINESS THAT DEVOURS."
MY PEOPLE FORESAW ITS COMING --AND NAMED IT-- COUNTLESS EONS AGO.
OH, COME ON...I THOUGHT WE LEFT THE MUMBO-JUMBO BEHIND ON CENTAURI-IV!
YOU WOULD TERM THE CREATURE "ANTI-ENERGY"--A MOVING STATE OF NON-BEING...
...ENVELOPING ALL IT TOUCHES, UNMAKING IT TO CONFORM TO ITS OWN SPIRITUAL LIKENESS.

"IT IS PURE COLD," YONDU CONTINUES, "NOT MERELY THE ABSENCE OF HEAT.
"IN THE TALES OF MY PEOPLE, IT IS TO COME UPON THE UNIVERSE BOTH SLOWLY AND SUDDENLY, UNNOTICED, YET WREAKING HAVOC.
"IT EXISTS TO PUT AN END TO EXISTENCE. IT HAS NO OTHER PURPOSE.
"IT IS TOTAL PARALYSIS, CESSATION OF MOVEMENT NOT MERELY IN THE LIMBS --BUT THE SOUL, AS WELL.
"AND THOSE WHO DO NOT POSSESS WITHIN THEMSELVES THE ESSENTIAL ELEMENT OF SPIRIT--KARANADA'S OPPOSITE--

"--ARE DOOMED TO BE ITS VICTIMS. FOR THEM, THERE CAN BE NO ESCAPE."

I'VE LOST STARHAWK! THE BIOCORDER'S STOPPED TRANSMITTING! NO SIGNAL AT ALL--!
IT DIDN'T BURN OUT. IT JUST--DIED. LOST ENERGY UNTIL IT GAVE UP.
KARANADA.

WHATEVER...WE'VE NO CHOICE, AT LEAST FOR NOW, BUT TO ASSUME THAT STARHAWK HAS PERISHED.
HE LEFT INSTRUCTIONS WITH ME...A PRECAUTION AGAINST THIS EVENTUALITY. HE--

CHOOM

THE SENSOR BANKS--MASSIVE OVERLOAD--HOW--?
THE VIEWSCREEN--LOOK AT THE SCREEN--!

THAT'S HOW!!
GOOD LORD--THE THING'S COMING AFTER US! WE'VE GOTTA GET THE SHIP OUT OF ITS ATTACK RANGE--
--IF THERE'S A PLACE IN THE UNIVERSE FAR ENOUGH! EVERYBODY TO YOUR STATIONS! MOVE!!

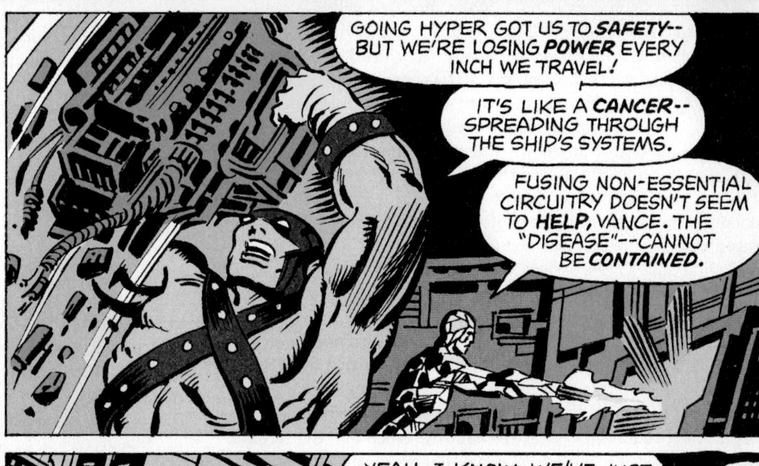

NEXT: PLANET OF THE ABSURD!

c/o MARVEL COMICS GROUP, 575 MADISON AVE. N.Y.C. 10022

AN OUTLINE COURSE IN WORLD HISTORY

1975-3015 A.D.
by **Steve Gerber**

(In DEFENDERS #26, we presented in capsule form the strange and somewhat terrifying tale of what's in store for our planet between now and the Guardians' era. Since that initial presentation, we've been deluged with letters asking to hear the story again, this time in greater detail. So we've called upon Marvel's expert future-historian—"expert" because he made it up!—to fill in the gaps left in that first telling. However, we caution readers *not* to apply the following account to any other Marvel mags which take place in the futures. This history is accurate only along the Guardians' time-line. —Trained Armadillo)

The rapid disintegration of Western Civilization began with the economic depression of the 1970's, an irreversible erosion of the quality of life coupled with an upward-spiraling of the cost of living, both of which the political leaders of the time chose to ignore. Rather than encouraging the populace to cut consumption, these leaders opted instead for the proliferation of nuclear fission plants to power more factories to produce more inferior goods from quickly-dwindling natural resources. The result was chaos.

Acting against the advice of scientists, governments refused to outlaw aerosol cans, deeming the industry's three-billion-dollar yearly gross more important than the ecological threat posed by the fluorocarbon gases these containers released into the atmosphere. In 1982, the first effects of this decision were made manifest. The gases had broken up earth's *ozone layer,* the world's atmospheric protection from the sun's ultraviolet radiation. That radiation, reaching the ground unfiltered, resulted in a massive epidemic of *skin cancer.* The enormous *crop failures* followed not far behind, plunging the planet into near-famine.

Monies were averted from social welfare and non-essential scientific programs into the development of *bionics,* mechanical replacements for human limbs eaten away by the cancerous sunlight. Farms were moved indoors.

In 1988, the United States' space program concluded with the launching of Major Vance Astro on a thousand-year journey to the nearest star. He left behind a world at war, as armies of the bionic man-machines swept over the globe, battling for their nations' possession of the fast-vanishing food supply.

These Bionics Wars continued until 1995, when a fission plant exploded, rendering the western half of Canada uninhabitable. This sudden, undeniable, highly visible catastrophe resulted in worldwide public outcry, a plea for sanity from the masses, coupled with the threat of violent revolution should the nations not come to their senses. That same year, the leaders complied, and the Treaty of Peking was signed, establishing the first *Confederation of Nations.* Reconstruction of the cities was begun in a spirit of cooperation between peoples.

The harmony was disrupted in 2001 A.D. when earth was invaded and conquered by its neighboring planet Mars. The human population was all but obliterated, as the Martians bred men and women for consumption as foodstuff. No reliable records exist of the period of occupation, but legends tell of a band of Freemen headed by a charismatic figure known as *Killraven,* who led the first attempts at insurrection against the invaders. All that is known for certain is: by 2075, the aliens were gone from earth. Whether they abandoned their conquest or were defeated may never be ascertained.

The next five hundred years were a barbaric period with science and its power highly centralized in feudal city-states ruled by the so-called "Techno-Barons." During this time, a physicist known as Harkov made the theoretical breakthrough that would, in centuries to come, prove Einstein wrong and make interstellar faster-than-light travel a reality. The theory was lost, however, in the serfs' revolt against the "Techno-Barons," a clash precipitated by the rulers' attempts at conscription to fight a war for po.\ ssion of the moon.

The serfs were successful. Communications were re-established between the city-states, and by 2530, the second World Federation had been established.

Man turned his energies to exploring the solar system—and, in time, colonizing it. Genetic engineering, developed under the Techno-Barons, made possible the breeding of sub-species of humanity: the heat- and radiation-resistant Mercurians; the silicon-based Pluvians; the Jovians, whose mass and molecular density were many times that of their Terran ancestors.

Venus, with its immense atmospheric pressure and surface temperatures of up to 900°, was left uninhabited but heat-throttle thermo-electric plants placed on its surface provided power for earth and its Luna colony by means of laser relay satelites.

By the year 2800, Pluto had been colonized, teleport service was in use between the inner planets, and the first space Militia was inaugurated to safeguard interplanetary trading.

Fifty years later, Harkov's papers were uncovered in an archeological dig. The secret that had eluded mankind for centuries had at last been found— but without means for practical application. And it took another fifty years before the fuel to power the Harkovian hyperdrive, the mechanism that would propel man to the stars, was discovered in quantity at Mercury's core.

The first terran starship, "Andromeda," was constructed in 2908, but perished on its maiden voyage, upon entering the Proxima Centauri anti-matter star-system. It was in the year 2940 that the first successful instellar voyage was made—to Alpha Centauri—and the first terran interstellar colony was founded on Centauri-IV, Yondu's native world.

By 3006, when Vance Astro's millenium-old ship landed on that same planet, the United Federation of Earth, an alliance of all the nations of earth and all her colonies, had been established, and our world had entered a "Golden Age." But in that same year, the Centauri-IV colony was attacked and destroyed by the reptilian race known as the Brotherhood of Badoon.

In less than a year, earth, too, had fallen, as well as the Mercurian, Jovian, and Pluvian colonies. By late 3007, the last survivors of the colonies had banded together as the Guardians of the Galaxy.

The rest of the story has been recounted in MARVEL TWO-IN-ONE # 5-6, GIANT-SIZE DEFENDERS # 5, DEFENDERS # 26-29, and MARVEL PRESENTS # 3: the Guardians' seizing of the starship *Captain America:* the battle to free New York; first contact with the Sisterhood of Badoon; and the eventual expulsion of the Badoon from our solar system in the year 3015.

But the war is far from over. The Badoon had plundered not merely our own tiny star-system, but the greater part of the Milky Way Galaxy. Their empire has begun to fall: the Sisterhood, aligned with the conquered worlds, is aiding in the effort for freedom. But the Guardians will be encountering the Badoon again. And if the rumors were true— the atrocities this alien race perpetrated on earth were mild by comparison to those effected against other races, other cultures, in the early days of their push for empire, when they (the Badoon) were still unsure of their power.

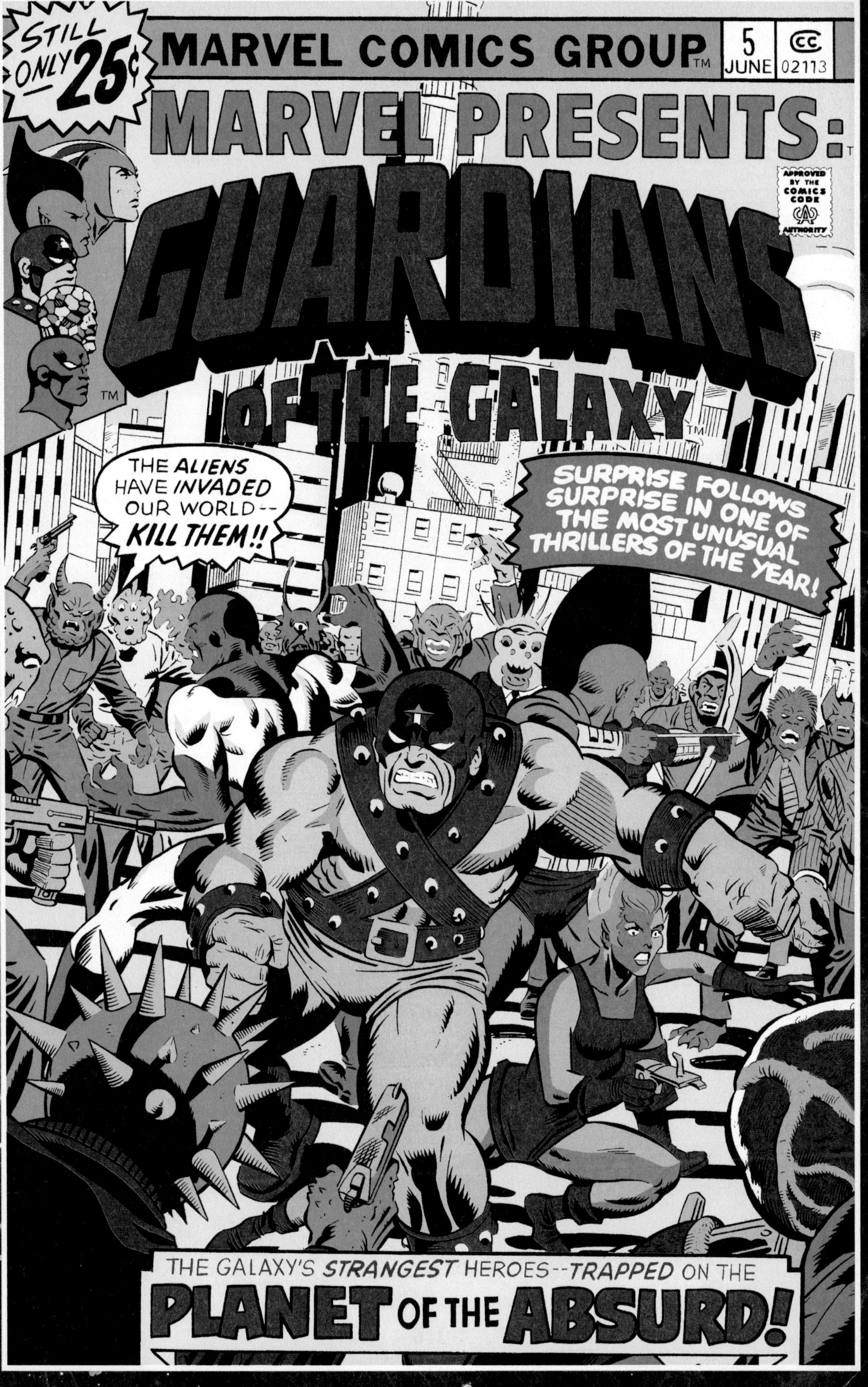
STILL ONLY 25¢
MARVEL COMICS GROUP
5 JUNE
CC 02113
MARVEL PRESENTS:
GUARDIANS OF THE GALAXY
APPROVED BY THE COMICS CODE AUTHORITY
THE ALIENS HAVE INVADED OUR WORLD-- KILL THEM!!
SURPRISE FOLLOWS SURPRISE IN ONE OF THE MOST UNUSUAL THRILLERS OF THE YEAR!
THE GALAXY'S STRANGEST HEROES--TRAPPED ON THE
PLANET OF THE ABSURD!

Yondu, from Centauri-IV. Charlie 27, from Jupiter. *Martinex,* from Pluto. And Earth's thousand-year-old survivor, *Vance Astro.* Ten centuries from now, these last survivors of their worlds will see planet Earth from the grasp of the *Badoon.* Together with the mysterious being known as *Starhawk,* they roam the universe!

Stan Lee PRESENTS: THE GUARDIANS OF THE GALAXY!™

JV260

STEVE GERBER WRITER / A. MILGROM & H. CHAYKIN ARTISTS / K. MANTLO • LETTERER J. COHEN • COLORIST / M. WOLFMAN EDITOR

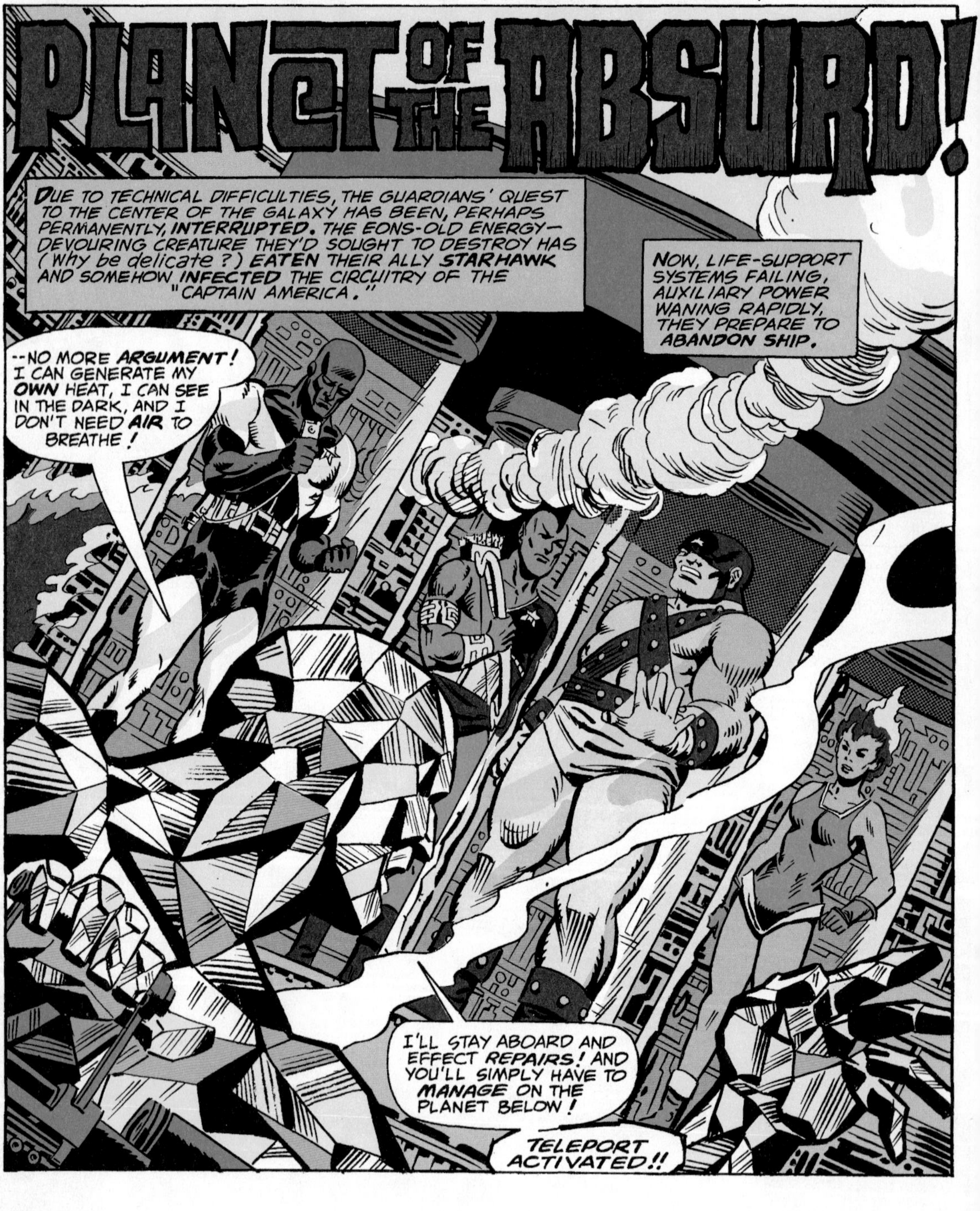

PLANET OF THE ABSURD!

DUE TO TECHNICAL DIFFICULTIES, THE GUARDIANS' QUEST TO THE CENTER OF THE GALAXY HAS BEEN, PERHAPS PERMANENTLY, **INTERRUPTED.** THE EONS-OLD ENERGY-DEVOURING CREATURE THEY'D SOUGHT TO DESTROY HAS (*why be delicate?*) **EATEN** THEIR ALLY **STARHAWK** AND SOMEHOW **INFECTED** THE CIRCUITRY OF THE "CAPTAIN AMERICA."

NOW, LIFE-SUPPORT SYSTEMS FAILING, AUXILIARY POWER WANING RAPIDLY, THEY PREPARE TO **ABANDON SHIP.**

--NO MORE **ARGUMENT!** I CAN GENERATE MY **OWN** HEAT, I CAN SEE IN THE DARK, AND I DON'T NEED **AIR** TO BREATHE!

I'LL STAY ABOARD AND EFFECT **REPAIRS!** AND YOU'LL SIMPLY HAVE TO **MANAGE** ON THE PLANET BELOW!

TELEPORT ACTIVATED!!

"YOU SHOULD MATERIALIZE SOMEWHERE IN THIS WORLD'S LARGEST CITY... BUT I COMPUTED YOUR 'PORT COORDINATES RATHER HURRIEDLY.
"I ONLY HOPE I HAVEN'T SET YOU DOWN IN THE MIDDLE OF A WALL."
NO PROBLEM ON THAT SCORE, MARTY. BUT A SHARPSHOOTER YOU'LL NEVER BE!
IT--IT'S A FOREST!
NO!

THE GREYISH COLOR OF THE SKY... THE SCENT OF SULFUR ON THE WIND... THE TOO-PALE GREEN OF THE LEAVES...
THESE PLANTS, PERHAPS THIS ENTIRE WORLD, IS... STRANGLING. I FEEL IT...
WHAT A KILLJOY. IF--
HALT!!

HUH...?
DON'T MAKE A MOVE--NONE O'YA! YER ON PRIVATE PROPERTY, SEE!
I DUNNO HOW YA GOT UP HERE-- OR WHATCHA WANT --I'M JUST THE GARDENER. NO-BODY TELLS ME NOTHIN'.!

NOT THAT I RESENT THAT, SEE-- IT AIN'T MY JOB TA KNOW--
BUT I'M S'POZED TA KEEP PESTS OUTTA HERE-- AN' THAT INCLUDES YOU!
NORMALLY, I JUST SPRAY 'EM, SEE-- WITH POISON-- OR LEAD-- WHATEVER--
BUT I FIGGER THAT BOSS MIGHT LIKE TA INSPECT YOU FOUR PERSONALLY. C'MON... STEP LIVELY.

FOUND THIS BUNCH UP ON THE ROOF GARDEN, MR. SLECH...
HIT MEN!
WELL, THEY AIN'T A BARBERSHOP QUARTET. NICE WORK, SOD. I'LL MARK YOU DOWN FOR A BONUS.
NOW GET BACK UPSTAIRS, HUH. BACK TO YOUR PLANTS. YOU SMELL.

AWRIGHT, I BELIEVE IN BEING CIVILIZED ABOUT THESE THINGS, SO SUPPOSE WE JUST RELATE. TELL ME ALL ABOUT YOURSELVES.
WHO'S YOUR EMPLOYER? WHY'D HE SEND YOU? WHAT MADE YOU THINK YOU'D GET AWAY FROM HERE WITH YOUR LIVES?
I'LL BE THE ONE TO DECIDE IF YOU GO AT ALL. GET THAT STRAIGHT.
HECK, I WOULDN'T MIND KEEPIN' THIS CUTIE AROUND FOR A LONG TIME.
EUWGG

WE'RE NOT HERE TO... UH, LOOK, WE HONESTLY MEANT NO HARM... OR EVEN INCONVENIENCE.
REALLY, WE LANDED ON YOUR ROOF... BY MISTAKE. WE'LL GO PEACEABLY, IF--
I SUGGEST YOU KEEP YOUR TENTACLES TO YOURSELF, MR. SLECH. I DIDN'T HEAR THE YOUNG WOMAN ASK TO BE TOUCHED.
MY FRIEND MR. ASTRO DID, HOWEVER, REQUEST POLITELY OUR FREEDOM TO LEAVE.
WE'RE WAITING FOR YOUR ANSWER. AND IF IT ISN'T "YES," I'LL RIP THIS--
MEN--!

LET 'IM LOOSE, CHUBS-- OR SOMEBODY'S HEAD GETS BLOWN AWAY!
IF THAT IS A THREAT...
IT'S A PROMISE, PAL. WE'RE IN FOR A FIGHT.

FROM YONDU'S BOW: A YAKA ARROW, A SHAFT OF "LIVING METAL" THAT CUTS CLOVERLEAVES IN THE AIR AROUND AND ABOUT SLECH'S THUGS.

FROM ASTRO'S SKULL: BURSTS OF PURE PSYCHO-KINETIC FORCE, THE POWERS OF MIND, APPLIED DIRECTLY TO THE MATTER AT HAND.

I WARNED YOU, DIDN'T I, MR. SLECH? NOW LOOK AT ALL THE TROUBLE YOU'VE CAUSED YOURSELF.

"IT'S A **ZOO!**" NIKKI EXCLAIMS. "A **FREAK SHOW** WOULD BE MORE LIKE IT," ASTRO CORRECTS. "I **RECOGNIZE** THIS PLACE. IT'S ANCIENT NEW YORK-- TIMES SQUARE CIRCA 1980 OR SO-- WITH A FEW **MODIFICATIONS**."

VANCE ASTRO WAS **EIGHTEEN** THAT YEAR. HE'D LEFT HIS HOME IN SAUGERTIES TO ATTEND **COLLEGE** IN THE BIG--AND BY THEN, **THOROUGHLY** WORM-RIDDEN-- APPLE. WHEN SCHOLASTIC PRESSURES GREW TOO GREAT, WHEN THE COMPANY OF HIS FELLOW FRESHMEN GREW TOO **DRAB**, HE WOULD TAKE TO THE **SIDEWALKS**.

AND OFTEN, **SLUMMING**, HE WOULD FIND HIMSELF "HERE"-- AMONG THE BROKEN, THE WASTED, THE WEARY, THE CHEAP, THE GAUDY, THE FILTHY, THE UNLOVED AND UNLOVING.

PLUS: MASSAGE

DEEP KISS XXX

STARRING LINDA LOVECRAFT

EAT

NOW AS THEN, HE IS FASCINATED-- AND **APPALLED**.

I DO NOT UNDERSTAND, MAJOR. WHERE ARE WE GOING? WHY DID WE LEAVE THE OTHERS BEHIND...?
TO THE NEAREST HOBBY SHOP-- NOT THAT YOU'VE ANY IDEA WHAT THAT IS-- AND BECAUSE IT'S YOU I TRUST LEAST IN AN ENVIRONMENT LIKE THIS.
TRUST...?

TO SURVIVE. YOU'RE JUST A LITTLE TOO NOBLE A SAVAGE FOR THIS NEIGHBORHOOD.
'TIL WE FIND OUT JUST WHAT KIND OF WHACKO PLANET WE'VE LANDED ON, YOU'RE NOT LEAVING MY SIGHT.
MAY I HELP YOU...?

YOU CARRY RADIO PARTS, DON'T YOU? TRANSISTORS? I NEED ONE THAT'LL STAND UP UNDER A LOT OF CURRENT.
Y'DON'T SAY? YEAH. WE STOCK 'EM. ALL SIZES. WE GOT JUST WHAT YER LOOKIN' FOR.
ONLY I DON'T SEE NO POCKETS IN THAT FANCY-SHMANCY OUTFIT, MAC. SEE MY MEANING?
NO SALE

HOW YOU PLAN ON PAYIN' FOR THIS LITTLE GEM IF YOU DON'T CARRY A WALLET?
UH, I ...
'COURSE, IF YA WANT IT BAD ENOUGH, WE COULD MAKE A TRADE. THEM'S PRETTY NICE ARROWS YER BUDDY'S PACKIN'!
YONDU...?

I CANNOT, MAJOR. THE YAKA METAL FROM WHICH THEY ARE MADE IS FOUND ONLY ON MY HOMEWORLD, AND--
ARE YOU OUT OF YOUR MIND? SALVAGING THE WHOLE SHIP DEPENDS ON THIS!
GIMME!

IT'S A DEAL-- NOT THE BEST I'VE EVER NEGOTIATED, BELIEVE ME, BUT--!
SOME YA WIN, SOME YA LOSE. WHAT CAN I SAY? ALL'S FAIR IN LOVE AN' BUSINESS, RIGHT?

YOU HAD NO RIGHT, MAJOR ... AND YOU SETTLED FOR FAR LESS THAN THE ARROW'S TRUE WORTH.
YEAH, WELL ... THAT'S LIFE IN THE GREAT NEBULA. I MAJORED IN ASTROPHYSICS, NOT MARKETING.
IN FACT, I DON'T THINK E.S.U. EVEN OFFERED A COURSE IN BARTER.
SO CRITIQUE MY MORALS IF YOU WANT, BUT LEAVE MY BUSINESS ACUMEN ALO--
C'MON-- WHAT'RE YOU DRAGGING YOUR FEET FOR? WE'VE GOT A GALAXY TO SAVE, REMEMBER?
I AM GIFTED WITH AN EXCELLENT MEMORY, MAJOR...
"... ESPECIALLY WITH REGARD TO THE PROPERTIES OF THE METAL, YAKA. MORE THAN ONCE HAVE I FELLED A FOE NOT BY MY AIM...
"... BUT BY MY WHISTLE..."
WHEEEEE
... TO WHICH THE SHAFT RESPONDS AS IF TRAINED.
OH, NO...
DO YOU REALIZE WHAT YOU'VE DONE, YOU--YOU INDIAN-GIVER!?! WITH ONE SUSTAINED NOTE YOU'VE MADE US HUNTED MEN!
NOT I, MAJOR. I REPEAT: YOU HAD NO RIGHT TO BARGAIN WITH WHAT WAS NOT YOURS!
STOP-- THIEF!!
LOOK, WE'RE GONNA HAVE COPS ON OUR TAIL ANY MINUTE. WE'D BETTER SPLIT UP.
THAT WAY THEY'LL ONLY NAB ONE OF US AT MOST--YOU, HOPEFULLY!
MOVE, BLUEBOY --LAST ONE BACK TO CHARLIE'S A ROTTEN BADOON EGG!

...AMUSEMENT?! WHAT'S AMUSING ABOUT HAVING YOUR EAR-DRUMS PUMMELLED TO DEATH?! CHEESH!
I SUPPOSE IT'S THE KIND OF SOUNDS-- BELLS, BUZZERS, WHISTLES-- AS CONTRASTED TO THE DULL RUMBLE OF THE STREETS.

YOU'RE NEW AROUND HERE, AIN'TCHA, RED?
MAYBE. BUT I'M TOO OLD FOR YOU, BUSTER. WALK ON.
HUH? NOW, WAIT--DON'T GET THE WRONG IDEA.

SHE DIDN'T. AND NEITHER DID I. GET SCARCE, SHORT STUFF.
THE LADY'S WITH ME.
PHOTO
STREET BRUTES
'ZAT SO?

SNIK!
THEN YOU MUST BE NEW ON THIS CORNER, TOO, FATS.
OTHERWISE YOU'D KNOW-- NO LADY'S WITH NOBODY 'TIL THEY CLEAR IT WITH ME.

WE GOT RULES ON THIS BLOCK, SEE? AN' WE DON'T LIKE IT WHEN THEY GET--
UURK
-- BROKEN? WELL, I CAN CERTAINLY SYMPATHIZE.

PERSONALLY, I HATE TO SEE ALMOST ANYTHING GET BROKEN.
AAAGH

BUT I MAY BE A TRIFLE OVER-SENSITIVE ABOUT IT BECAUSE OF MY SIZE.
I'M HUSKY, SOMEWHAT CLUMSY-- DON'T REALLY KNOW MY OWN STRENGTH.
YAARRRGH!

YUMPIN' YIMINY, HE BAN CROOSHIN' BLACKIE'S FINGERS!
SACRE BLEU! LAY EENTO HEEM!
STREET BRUTES
AS CONFUCIUS SAY: LOB HIS FREAKIN' HEAD OFF!
A MOMENT LATER, THE MASSIVE JOVIAN FORM OF CHARLIE-27 IS BARELY VISIBLE 'NEATH THE MELTING POT OF "STREET BRUTE" BODIES DOGPILED UPON IT.
ANOTHER MOMENT LATER, IT'S THE GANG THAT'S DIFFICULT TO SEE. THEY'RE MOVING TOO FAST --REDUCED TO A MULTI-HUED BLUR --AS THE GUARDIANS' MUSCLEMAN TOSSES THEM ALL ASIDE WITH A SINGLE, MIGHTY SHRUG.
CHEEZE IT-- IT'S THE FUZZ!!
STREET BRUTES
AND ON THIS WORLD, AS ON MANY OTHERS, THE MINIONS OF THE LAW ARE APT TO CONFUSE VICTIM WITH CULPRIT--AND ACT ACCORDINGLY.
NEVER MIND THE SMALL FRY--GAS THE GREAT WHITE WHALE HERE!
HUNH--?! NO, WAIT, YOU'RE -- COFF BLECCH WHUHH
IF I KNOW MY HISTORY TAPES, CHUNKY'S HEADED FOR THE SLAMMER! I GOTTA GET OUTTA HERE!
AND SO THE YOUNG MERCURIAN MAKES HERSELF BUT ANOTHER OF THE DIVERSE PATCHES OF COLOR IN THE CRAZY QUILT OF THE CROWD.
THE POLICE NEVER SPOT HER. CHARLIE'S "RAMPAGE" WILL BE NOTED ON THE BLOTTER AS "UNPROVOKED."

ELSEWHERE, ANOTHER FUGITIVE GUARDIAN -- HIS WILDERNESS-BRED INSTINCTS SATISFIED THAT HE ELUDED ANY PURSUERS -- PAUSES TO OBSERVE A CULTURAL PHENOMENON.
HAPPY "200" YEARS
... ASSURED THAT I WILL NOT LEAD YOU INTO WAR, UNLESS A REALLY NICE COUNTRY IS THREATENED
ON THE DOMESTIC FRONT, PROSPERITY FOR ALL IS MY BICENTENNIAL PLEDGE. I...
WIN

PARDON ME... WHO IS THAT MAN ON THE SCREEN?
CRIPES, WHERE YOU BEEN? THAT'S THE PREXY HIS-SELF.
IS HE YOUR CHIEFTAIN -- YOUR LEADER?
HE IS OUR TALKER, BABY BLUE. WE AIN'T GOT NO LEADERS.

AH, THEN HE IS A WISE MAN, A GIVER OF TRUTH TO YOUR PEOPLE.
SHEESH WHERE'D YOU ESCAPE FROM? HE'S A DOPE, AN' HE LIES OUTTA BOTH SIDES OF HIS MOUTH!
AND YET YOU ENTRUST HIM WITH YOUR PEOPLE'S HIGHEST OFFICE?

WE DON'T "ENTRUST" NO-BODY WITH NUTTIN'!
WE JUST FIGGER: "HEY, HE CAN'T SCREW THINGS UP ANY WORSE'N THE NEXT SCHLEMIEL, RIGHT?"
TAXES GO UP, WARS FLARE UP, THE AVERAGE JOE GETS TOOK-- A SMART GUY COULDN'T HANDLE IT ANY BETTER'N A DUMB GUY. WHO CARES?
SEE YA AROUND, SIMP. HAW.

THE STENCH IN THE AIR... MUST POISON THE MINDS OF THE MEN WHO WALK THIS WORLD.
THEY HAVE GROWN ACCUSTOMED TO THE FOULNESS IN ALL ASPECTS OF THEIR LIVES.
THEY ARE... TO BE PITIED.

WHILE, IN ANOTHER PART OF THE CITY...
THE MORE I SEE OF THIS PLACE, THE CREEPIER IT FEELS.
PARALLEL EVOLUTION WAS A SCIENCE FICTION CLICHÉ WHEN I WAS A KID, BUT...
...A WRITER WHO TRIED TO PASS OFF A PLANET LIKE THIS, WITH ITS PLETHORA OF INTELLIGENT SPECIES, WOULD'VE BEEN CRUCIFIED BY THE CRITICS.
EVOLUTION DOESN'T WORK THAT WAY! IT--
OBOY...
WELL! IT SEEMS WE HAVE A LATE ARRIVAL!

ME? OH, NO. I WAS JUST PASSING THROUGH...!
IN THAT CASE, IT'S DESTINY. IF ANYONE EVER NEEDED TO GET IN TOUCH WITH HIS BODY, IT'S YOU!
WIGGLE OUT OF THOSE SHINY MUMMY WRAPPINGS. JOIN US IN THE SUN!

WE'RE HERE TO EXPLORE AND EXPAND OUR POTENTIAL-- TO HEIGHTEN OUR CONSCIOUSNESS OF ALL WE ARE--
--TO RELATE TO ONE ANOTHER OPENLY, CANDIDLY-- TO EXPERIENCE THE JOY OF STRETCHING, BENDING, TOUCHING --BEING ALIVE.
THAT'S... WONDERFUL!

UNFORTUNATELY, THOUGH... WELL, I'M OVER A THOUSAND YEARS OLD, AND IF I UNDRESS, I'LL CRUMBLE INTO DUST.
SO-O-O, MUCH AS I'D LOVE TO EXPLORE MY POTENTIAL, I'VE GOTTA TURN YOU DOWN. SORRY.

IT-- IT WASN'T NECESSARY TO CONCOCT A SAD STORY LIKE THAT, YOU KNOW. Y-YOU COULD'VE JUST ADMITTED YOU WERE UPTIGHT...!
YEAH... WELL, I GUESS I'M JUST NOT READY FOR TOTAL HONESTY YET.
GUESS I'M JUST ... SET IN MY WAYS. TAKE CARE, HON.

IN YET ANOTHER OF THE CITY'S ODD CORNER'S, HEAVY EYELIDS BLINK, NOSTRILS TWITCH, DRY LIPS PART...
THE FLATTENED FACE OF THE JOVIAN GUARDIAN SHOWS ALL THE SIGNS OF WAKING.
AND WHEN THE MIST AND TEARY MOISTURE HAVE LEFT THE EYES, THAT FACE DISPLAYS SOMETHING ELSE AS WELL--ARRANT SHOCK.
TWELVE MOONS OF--! WHERE AM I?!
IN THE CLINK, THE SLAMMER, THE BIG HOUSE, THE HOOSEGOW, THE CALA-BOOSE--
JAIL?!
JAIL.

JAIL. I, UH, GATHER YOU'RE NO NEWCOMER HERE, HUH?
YOU KIDDIN'? IF THIS PLACE RAN ON SENIORITY, I'D BE THE WARDEN!
BEEN HERE SINCE ME 'N MY GIRL STOLE A CAR AN' ROBBED A GAS STATION WHEN WE WAS SEVENTEEN.

HEY, JAKE--LOOKA ME--I MADE PAROLE! THEY'RE LETTIN' ME OUT, MAN!
:SIGH: MEBBE I'LL SEE YA ON THE OUTSIDE SOME-TIME, MAC. GOOD LUCK.

WHAT WAS HE IN FOR?
MURDER. THEM GUYS ALWAYS GETS OUT AFTER SEVEN YEARS OR SO.
THEY DO THIS BIG REPENTANCE NUMBER ON THE PAROLE BOARD...

SHUCKS, NOBODY FIGGERS A GUY'LL KILL TWICE. ROBBERY, THOUGH-- THAT'S TOO EASY TA SLIP INTO AGAIN.
HECK, WE PULLED THE FIRST ONE WITH A BLAMED CAP PISTOL...!
MM... WISH I COULD STICK AROUND AND SYMPATHIZE, OLD TIMER, BUT I'M PROBABLY LATE FOR AN APPOINTMENT. HAVE TO BE GOING...!
HUH? GOIN' WHERE? THIS'S JAIL, REMEMBER?
HOW COULD I FORGET?
I DON'T KNOW ...BUT I DID.
KROOM!

MEANWHILE, BACK AT THE "FREAK SHOW"...
OOOH, SISTER, YOU LOOK LOST. WHY DON'T YOU JOIN US? QUEUE UP AND BE SAVED.
THIS LINE LEADS TO FAITH, TO HOPE, TO TRUTH AND REDEMPTION! THAT'S WHAT YOU SEEK, ISN'T IT?
WEL-L-L.
THE APOCALYPSE WAITS JUST BEYOND MORNING, SISTER. IT'S NOW OR NEVER.
WHAT THE HECK... I GUESS IT'S NOW.
IT WOULDN'T BE IF I HAD ANY BETTER PROSPECTS, BUT...
THERE IS NO BETTER, SISTER. HE IS THE GOOD, THE ALL-KNOWING, THE WHOLE OF TRUTH...!
HE?
HE AND NONE OTHER!
ALL GLORIES TO THE SUBLIME ONE, TO THE WORD INCARNATE--
"...TO THE BIG BUDD, MASTER OF THE WORLD!"
KNEEL, DAUGHTER--AND LAY AT MY FEET ALL YOUR MATERIAL BURDENS THAT I MAY LIGHTEN YOUR SPIRIT.
YOU'VE GOTTA BE KIDDIN'!
I DON'T SINK TO MY KNEES FOR ANYBODY! AND EVEN IF I HAD ANY MATERIAL "BURDENS"--
-- WHY WOULD I HAND 'EM OVER TO A HOLIER-THAN-THOU BALL OF LARD?
-GASP- HERESY!! THE WOMAN IS AN AGENT OF SATAN!!

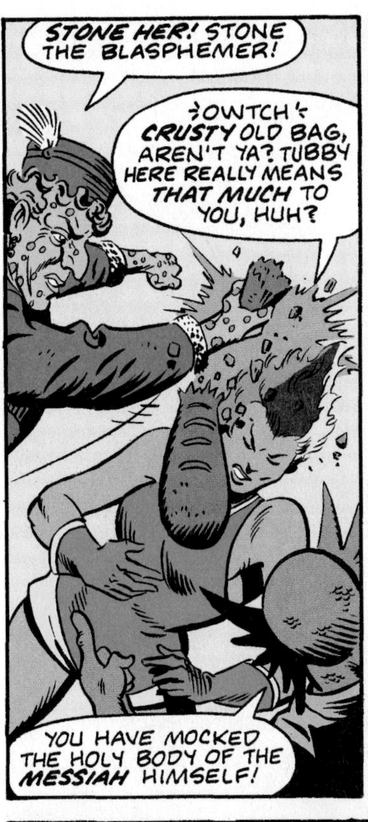
STONE HER! STONE THE BLASPHEMER!
OWTCH! CRUSTY OLD BAG, AREN'T YA? TUBBY HERE REALLY MEANS THAT MUCH TO YOU, HUH?
YOU HAVE MOCKED THE HOLY BODY OF THE MESSIAH HIMSELF!

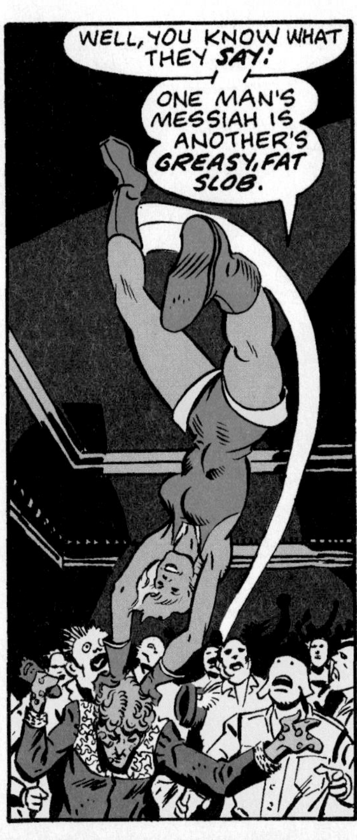
WELL, YOU KNOW WHAT THEY SAY:
ONE MAN'S MESSIAH IS ANOTHER'S GREASY, FAT SLOB.

JOIN THE GUARDIANS AND SEE THE GALAXY -- I MUST'VE BEEN OUT OF MY MIND!
I WAS BETTER OFF IN MY LITTLE ONE-WOMAN SPACESKIFF -- ALONE WITH MY TAPES!
UH-OH. THE SCENE'S JUST AS WEIRD OUT HERE. CONSTERNATION CITY!

MOMENTARILY, THE CAUSE OF THE DISTURBANCE BATTERS ITS WAY THROUGH THE MAZE OF BODIES...!
YOU!!
YOU!!
I'M ON THE LAM. HOW 'BOUT YOU?
MARVEL
HULK
TIMES

IF YOU MEAN, "AM I BEING PURSUED?" THE ANSWER IS YES.

BUT THIS SHOULD HELP RECTIFY THE SITUATION.
CRUUNCH

HAVE YOU SEEN ANYTHING OF VANCE?
NOT EVEN A LITTLE SPARKLE. AROUND HERE, HE DOESN'T EXACTLY STAND OUT IN A CROWD, Y'KNOW.
BUT UNLESS MY EYES DECEIVE ME, CHUCK-27, I'VE JUST SPOTTED--
--YONDU!!
WHAT--?
BY THE THREE SUNS!!
REFLEXIVELY, THE CENTURIAN'S HAND LEAPS TO HIS QUIVER. ALMOST FASTER THAN THE EYE CAN FOLLOW, THE BOW-STRING FINDS ITS NICHE, DRAWS BACK, AND LAUNCHES THE SHAFT INTO FLIGHT.
I THINK I JUST FIGURED OUT HOW THE ANCIENT CAVALRY WON.
DOES BLUENOSE REALLY PLAN ON TURNING BACK THIS MOB WITH ONE ARROW?!
CHARLIE GRINS.
"HE'S A PRIMITIVE, NIKKI--NOT A FOOL. DON'T UNDERESTIMATE HIM--
"--OR HIS ARROWS."
--GET BACK TO YOU WHEN YOU'VE LOCATED THE OTHERS. RIGHT NOW I'M PICKING UP ANOTHER SIGNAL.
UH ... SO AM I, PAL. STAY BY THE PHONE. I'LL BE IN TOUCH.

I KNEW IT-- I **KNEW** IT! OFF HIS LEASH FOR TWO HOURS IN A PLACE LIKE THIS AND HE MOVES A MOB TO **RIOT**!

WELL... HE'S GOTTA BE IN THE CROWD **SOME-WHERE**, ASSUMING THEY HAVEN'T MADE **PULP** OUT OF HIM.

JUST-- HAVE TO --GATHER-- MY WITS-- FOR **PSYCHO BURST** -- MAKE THEM--

--**SCATTER**!!

VANCE!!

EEEEEEEEEEEE

FOR CRYIN' OUT LOUD-- ALL **THREE** OF YOU? WHAT HAP--?

NO! DON'T ANSWER! JUST FOLLOW ME! THIS WAY! I'LL RADIO MARTY TO--

CHEESH
NOW WHAT'RE THEY SCREAMING ABOUT?

MADNESS *IS* THE EXPLANATION, MAJOR. MADNESS OF QUITE THE ***STANDARD*** SORT.

I AM DR. PAZZ-KO. MY PILOT-ASSOCIATE, DR. ROH-MA, AND I ARE CHIEF ***CARETAKERS*** OF THIS WORLD WHICH WE'VE COME TO CALL, SIMPLY, "***ASYLUM.***"

WE ***NAME*** IT THUS, MAJOR, BECAUSE THAT'S WHAT IT ***IS***-- A ***MENTAL INSTITUTION*** FOR THE MOST HOPELESSLY NEUROTIC SPECIMENS OF SOME ***FIFTY*** LOOSELY CONFEDERATED PLANETS IN THIS SECTOR OF THE GALAXY.

B-BUT THE CULTURE-- THE PARALLELS TO ***OLD EARTH***-- WHY DID YOU ARRANGE--?

WE ARRANGED ***NOTHING,*** MAJOR. WE'RE A VERY ***PROGRESSIVE*** INSTITUTION.

WE ALLOWED THE PATIENTS TO STRUCTURE ***THEIR OWN*** SOCIETY. WHAT YOU SAW--WAS ***THEIR*** CREATION, NOT OURS.

NORMALLY, VISITORS ARE STRICTLY ***PROHIBITED*** FROM THE PLANET'S SURFACE. WE ONLY SUSPECTED YOUR PRESENCE--

-- WHEN OUR ***SCANNERS*** SPOTTED YOUR DISABLED ***SHIP*** IN ORBIT.

WE ACTED ***IMMEDIATELY,*** OF COURSE--AND YOUR FRIEND MR. MARTINEX DETAILED YOUR SITUATION FOR US IN FULL.

I WON'T NEED THAT "TRANSISTOR" NOW, VANCE. THE DOCTORS PROVIDED--

YEAH. SO WE'VE HEARD. WILL SHE ***SAIL?***

SHORTLY. AS SOON AS THE HYPER-DRIVE ENGINES ***REGENERATE.*** I'M PATCHING UP THE NAVIGATIONAL CONSOLES NOW...

WHAT ABOUT YOU FOUR? ARE ***YOU*** IN ANY CONDITION TO GO GALAXY-SAVING?

WHY NOT? IT'S A MISSION FOR A ***CRAZY MAN*** IF EVER I'VE ***HEARD*** OF ONE.

NEXT: THE **HUB** OF **LIGHT!**

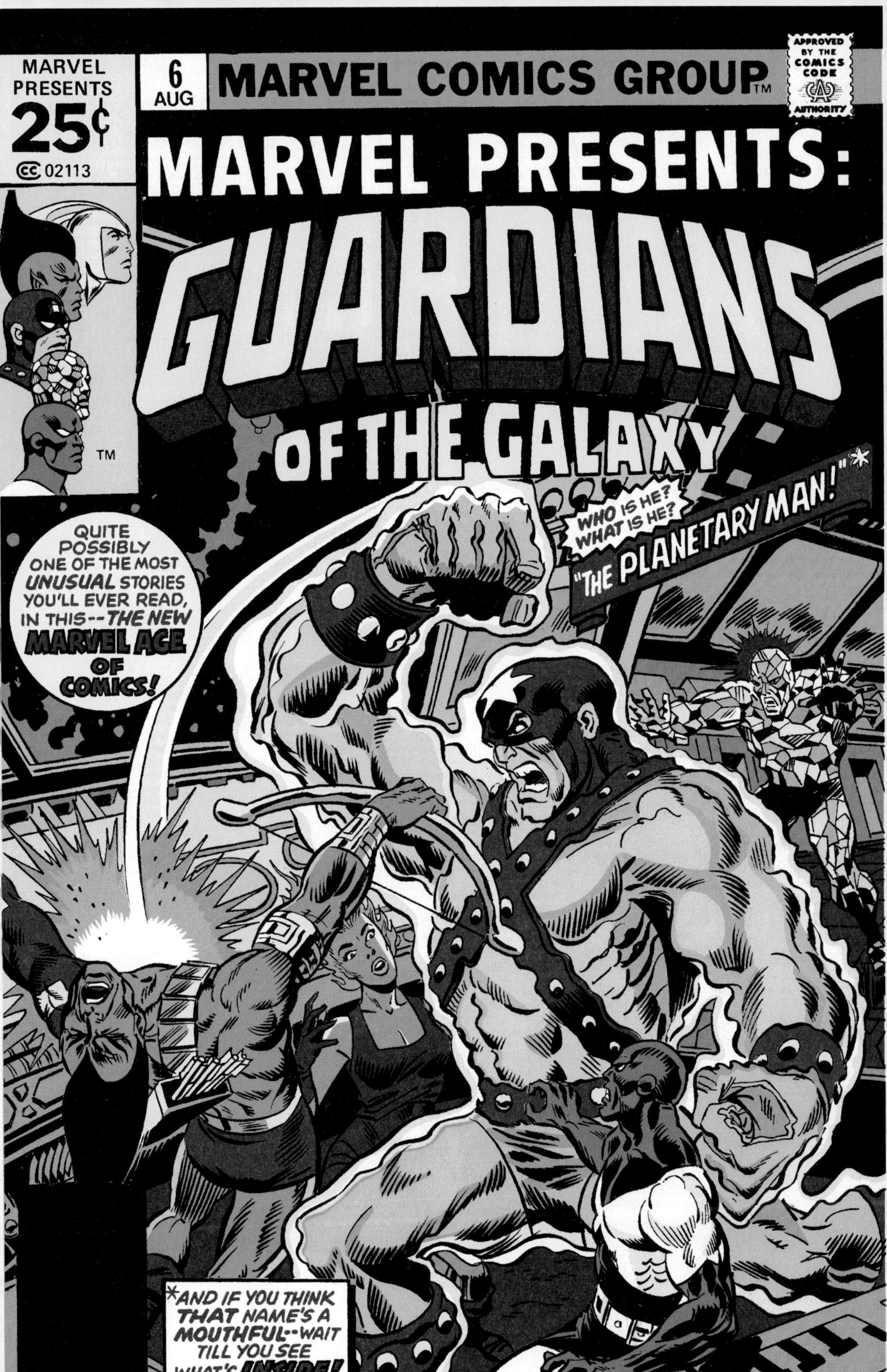
MARVEL PRESENTS
25¢
CC 02113
6 AUG
MARVEL COMICS GROUP
APPROVED BY THE COMICS CODE AUTHORITY
MARVEL PRESENTS:
GUARDIANS OF THE GALAXY
TM
WHO IS HE? WHAT IS HE?
"THE PLANETARY MAN!"*
QUITE POSSIBLY ONE OF THE MOST UNUSUAL STORIES YOU'LL EVER READ, IN THIS--THE NEW MARVEL AGE OF COMICS!
*AND IF YOU THINK THAT NAME'S A MOUTHFUL--WAIT TILL YOU SEE WHAT'S INSIDE!

Yondu, from Centauri-IV. Charlie 27, from Jupiter. *Martinex,* from Pluto. And Earth's thousand-year-old survivor, *Vance Astro.* Ten centuries from now, these last survivors of their worlds will see planet Earth from the grasp of the *Badoon.* Together with the mysterious being known as *Starhawk,* they roam the universe!

Stan Lee PRESENTS: THE GUARDIANS OF THE GALAXY!™

JV 334

STEVE GERBER WRITER / AL MILGROM ARTIST / TERRY AUSTIN INKER / IRV WATANABE, LETTERER / DON WARFIELD, COLORIST / ARCHIE GOODWIN EDITOR

...THOSE WHO WATCH, IN QUIET CONTEMPLATION, IN SILENT REVULSION, IN MUTE HORROR, AS THE CREATURE FEEDS AGAIN.
ELECTRONS DANCE ACROSS THE VIDEOSCREEN, WEAVING A TAPESTRY OF TERROR, A WORLD IN THE THROES OF UNBECOMING. ITS CULTURE, ITS TECHNOLOGY, ITS PEOPLE AND THEIR VERY SOULS CRUMBLING, DECAYING.
I CAN'T STAND IT! A WHOLE PLANET IS DYING DOWN THERE, WHILE WE "GUARDIANS" SIT IN THE BLEACHERS AND RUBBERNECK!
WHY DON'T WE DO SOMETHING?! THIS IS A STARSHIP! WE'VE GOT WEAPONS--
--NONE OF WHICH WERE DESIGNED TO COPE WITH A MENACE OF THIS NATURE.
WE ARE OBSERVING. OUR SENSORS ARE RECORDING. WE ARE DOING ALL WE CAN!
BUT MARTINEX--YOU SAID STARHAWK LEFT INSTRUCTIONS WITH YOU--A COURSE TO FOLLOW IN THE EVENT OF HIS DEATH.
WHAT DID HE TELL YOU?
TO IGNORE THIS CREATURE, VANCE--TO PROCEED ON OUR VOYAGE TO THE CENTER OF THE GALAXY, RESISTING ALL TEMPTATION TO INTERVENE ELSEWHERE!
THE PLUVIAN'S WORDS STRIKE YOUNG NIKKI LIKE A BLOW TO THE STOMACH. SHE REELS MOMENTARILY, AS IF BEREFT OF WIND...
...AND THEN CAN CONTAIN HER MERCURIAN TEMPERAMENT NO LONGER!
NIKKI--STOP!!

CHARLIE 27'S ADMONITION COMES TOO LATE. NIKKI'S FINGERS ARE AS FAST AND LITHE AND ACROBATIC AS THE REST OF HER.
AND BEFORE SHE CAN BE RESTRAINED...
SHE'S CHANGED COURSE-- AND ACCELERATED TO HYPERDRIVE!
NICE GOING, RED! WE'RE HEADED STRAIGHT FOR FROGGY'S TONSILS-- AND WE'RE MOVING TOO FAST TO TURN BACK!
BATTLE STATIONS, GROUP! WE'RE GONNA HAVE TA FIGHT!
APPARENTLY, I FAILED TO MAKE MYSELF CLEAR, VANCE. WE'VE NOTHING TO FIGHT WITH. OUR ION-FIRE HAS NO EFFECT ON THE CREATURE.
INDEED, AS WE APPROACH CLOSER, ALL OUR SYSTEMS GROW WEAKER.
WH-WHAT'S HAPPENING?! EVERYTHING'S SWIMMING-- CAN'T SEE STRAIGHT--!
PREDICTABLE. VISUAL DISTORTION EFFECT CAUSED, I WOULD POSIT, BY OUR PENETRATION OF THE CREATURE'S ENERGY FIELD!
CURIOUSLY, THOUGH...MY READINGS SEEM TO BE STABILIZING.
TERRIFIC. I'M THRILLED FOR YOUR READINGS.
HOW CAN YOU STAY SO BLASTED CALM WHEN--
I AM NOT EXPERIENCING THE SAME DISTORTION, VANCE. MY VISUAL RECEPTORS ARE QUITE DISSIMILAR TO YOUR OWN.
STILL... I'M ANYTHING BUT CALM. I FIND OUR LACK OF USEFUL INFORMATION EXTREMELY FRUSTRATING.

I AM A SCIENTIST, VANCE. I AM FASCINATED BY THE UNEXPLAINED-- BY THE CHALLENGE IT PRESENTS-- BUT I DO NOT ENJOY IT!
AND I AM AT A LOSS TO EXPLAIN ANY OF THIS-- EVEN TO GUESS WHERE WE ARE.
WHUMP!

TERRIFIC! JUST PEACHY KEENO! JUST WHAT I'VE ALWAYS WANTED--
--TO BE SHOT BULLETLIKE INTO THE MIRE OF IGNORANCE BY A CHARCOAL GRAY TEENYBOPPER WITH A CRUSADER COMPLEX!
WHAT IN HARKOV'S NAME WERE YOU THINKING OF? WERE YOU THINKING?
I--I'M SORRY!

I COULDN'T SIT ON MY THUMBS AND-- NOT AFTER SEEING MERCURY TRASHED BY THE BADOON--I--
LOOK, I'VE SPENT THE LAST SEVEN YEARS ALONE IN SPACE--'TIL YOU CLOWNS CAME ALONG, I THOUGHT THE WHOLE GALAXY WAS DEAD EXCEPT ME.
THE THOUGHT OF MY NIGHTMARE COMING TRUE--A WHOLE UNIVERSE EMPTY--WAS TOO MUCH TO BEAR.

SHE DID AS HER SPIRIT BADE HER, VANCE. NO ACT OF SPIRIT CAN BE WRONG AGAINST KARANADA.
UH-HUH. WELL, LISTEN, FLAG-HEAD, I'VE HAD IT UP TO HEAR WITH YOUR PRIMITIVE PHILOSOPHY, TOO!
I'M GAGGING ON YOUR WARRIOR'S WISDOM, Y' KNOW?

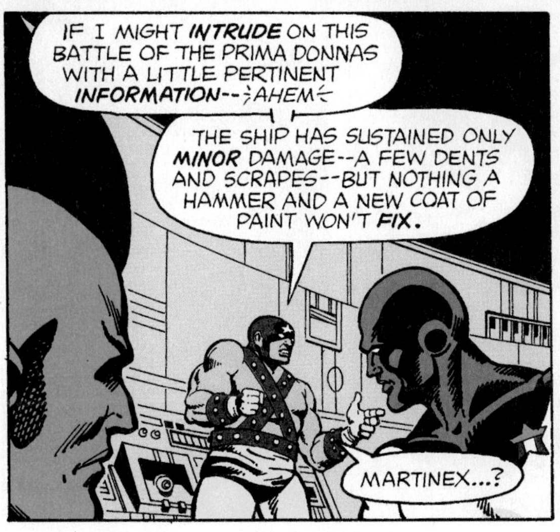
IF I MIGHT INTRUDE ON THIS BATTLE OF THE PRIMA DONNAS WITH A LITTLE PERTINENT INFORMATION-- ≯AHEM≮
THE SHIP HAS SUSTAINED ONLY MINOR DAMAGE--A FEW DENTS AND SCRAPES--BUT NOTHING A HAMMER AND A NEW COAT OF PAINT WON'T FIX.
MARTINEX...?

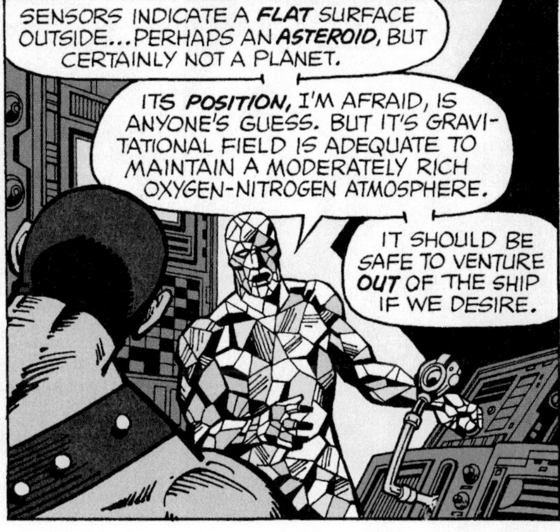
SENSORS INDICATE A FLAT SURFACE OUTSIDE...PERHAPS AN ASTEROID, BUT CERTAINLY NOT A PLANET.
ITS POSITION, I'M AFRAID, IS ANYONE'S GUESS. BUT IT'S GRAVITATIONAL FIELD IS ADEQUATE TO MAINTAIN A MODERATELY RICH OXYGEN-NITROGEN ATMOSPHERE.
IT SHOULD BE SAFE TO VENTURE OUT OF THE SHIP IF WE DESIRE.

VENTURE OUT? YOU SAW THE VIDEOSCREEN --THERE'S NOTHING BUT **WASTELAND** OUT THERE! WHY--?
PERHAPS...TO FIND **STARHAWK,** VANCE. IF THIS IS WHAT HAPPENED TO **US,** IT'S NOT UNREASONABLE TO POSTULATE THAT--
"NOT UNREASONABLE," HE SAYS!

NOTHING'S REASONABLE ABOUT OUR SITUATION, GUYS. **NOTHING!!** BUT IT LOOKS LIKE **I'M** THE ONLY ONE WHO FEELS THAT WAY. **SO-O-O...**
I AM GOING TO MY QUARTERS. I AM LEAVING THE DECISIONS TO YOU. ALL I WANT IS TO BE LEFT ALONE AND TO BE HAPPY.
GOOD **RIDDANCE!**

OOOH! THIS'S ALL **MY** FAULT! IF YOU DON'T NEED ME HERE--
--I'M GONNA GO PLAY **PEACEMAKER** FOR A MINUTE, OKAY?

SHORTLY, IN THE CUBICLE VANCE ASTRO HAS **REMODELED** TO RESEMBLE HIS BOYHOOD BEDROOM **SANCTUARY...**
UH...CAN I COME IN?
SURE. JUST DON'T EXPECT ME TO ACKNOWLEDGE YOUR **EXISTENCE.** I WANNA BE **HAPPY,** REMEMBER.
I **DID** PULL A PRETTY STUPID STUNT, DIDN'T I?

YOU? **NAH!** YOU JUST DID AS "YOUR SPIRIT BADE YOU." SEE, I'VE BEEN **ANALYZING** OUR PROBLEM FOR THE LAST THIRTY SECONDS OR SO...
...AND I THINK **I KNOW** NOW WHERE WE TRIPPED OURSELVES UP. WE'VE BEEN TAKING IT ALL TOO **SERIOUSLY!**
HA!!

WE'VE ALL BEEN-- HEE HEE SO **GRIM,** SO **EARNEST** HOHO-HO WHEN WE'VE BEEN PLAYING SECOND-THROUGH-SEVENTH BANANAS IN A GALACTIC **SLAPSTICK FARCE!** HAHAHA
THINK ABOUT IT--FIVE **MOTES** OF RAINBOW-COLORED FLESH TRYING TO SAVE THE YUK YUK GALAXY!
IT'S **FUNNY,** NIKKI-MOTE! TAKE IT FROM OLE VANCE-MOTE!
ARE YOU ALL RIGHT?

ARE YOU KIDDING? BEST I'VE FELT IN A THOUSAND YEARS! I AM SECURE IN MY MOTE-NESS! HOW 'BOUT YOU?
THE WAY I SEE IT, WE EITHER APPRECIATE THE HUMOR OF OUR PREDICAMENT, OR WE GO CRAZY. DON'T YOU AGREE?
I--I DON'T KNOW!

IT'S A PARTY, BABE--AN ALL NIGHT SAVE-THE-GALAXY BASH! THEY PUT ALL THOSE STARS OUT THERE JUST FOR OUR AMUSEMENT! IT'S FUN!
WHEN WAS THE LAST TIME YOU HAD FUN, NIKKI-MOTE? HOW LONG SINCE YOU'VE REVELLED IN YOUR COSMIC INSIGNIFICANCE?
HEY! LEMME DOWN, YA BIG LUG!

DO AS SHE SAYS, VANCE, IMMEDIATELY!
SHE CAME DOWN HERE TO MAKE AMENDS, NOT TO BE MANHANDLED.
OH, YEAH?

HERE--YOU WANT 'ER, TAKE 'ER! I CAN PARTY BETTER ALONE ANYWAY! YOU TWO WERE BORN TOO LATE TO KNOW HOW TO BOOGIE!
YOU'LL NEVER KNOW WHAT YOU MISSED--THE 1980'S--DANCING IN THE STREETS WITH THE OZONE AMPUTEES--OOH, WAH!
I DON'T THINK YOU'RE WELL, VANCE. YOU'VE LET THE TENSION OF THE SITUATION SET YOU OFF-BALANCE.

WE'RE GOING EXPLORING OUTSIDE. IT'S PROBABLY BEST THAT YOU REMAIN ABOARD...AT LEAST 'TIL YOU'VE COMPOSED YOURSELF.
WHATEVER ELSE OUR DILEMMA MIGHT BE, IT CERTAINLY ISN'T LAUGHABLE.

OH, YES IT IS...YES IT IS...YES-IT-IS... YES! IT! IS!
IT'S A CHUCKLE A MINUTE, YOU FRIGID-FACED, FAT SIMPLETON!
SLAM!

NO RADIO SIGNALS... AT LEAST NONE WITHIN OUR COMMUNICATOR'S RANGE.
LIFE-FORM READINGS...ARE UNLIKE ANY I'VE EVER ENCOUNTERED... DIFFUSE... UNFOCUSED... ENERGY WITHOUT FORM...
IS THAT WHY I FEEL LIKE I'M STEPPING ON SOMEBODY'S FACE WITH EVERY TWITCH OF A TOE?
THERE IS LIFE... EVERYWHERE IN THIS PLACE... STRIVING... TO SURVIVE...
IT IS A WORLD OF CHANGES ...SHAPES SHIFTING AS THE WIND ALTERS THE LANDSCAPE.
WAIT! THAT WAY--ACCORDING TO THE BIOCORDER--READINGS MUCH MORE INTENSE! LIFE-FORMS--AND A POWERFUL ENERGY SOURCE.
WELL, WHAT ARE WE WAITING FOR? LET'S INVESTIGATE.
BEATS WAITING AROUND FOR THE CACTUS TO SPROUT. BUT--
--YOU SURE YOU WANNA TRAIPSE OFF WITHOUT ASTRO? WILL HE BE OKAY ALONE?
HE'S A BIG BOY NOW, NIKKI. HE CAN TAKE CARE OF HIMSELF--
--IF HE DECIDES TO GROW UP AGAIN.
I'VE BEEN MEANING TO START A JOURNAL EVER SINCE I STEPPED OUT OF MY SHIP ON CENTAURI-IV.
MIGHT AS WELL BEGIN NOW. CAN'T IMAGINE WHEN I'LL EVER BE MORE ALONE WITH MY THOUGHTS.
WHAT TO WRITE, WHAT TO WRITE? "IT WAS THE BEST OF TIMES, IT WAS THE WORST..." NAH!
OW! MY LEG! WHAT--? FELT LIKE A MOSQUITO BITE! BUT TO GET THRU MY METAL SHEATHING, IT'D HAVE TO BE SOME--
--MOSQUITO.
oh, my God!

SOME TIME LATER...
HEY, GLOM THAT, WILLYA-- CIVILIZATION DEAD AHEAD!
AND JUST IN TIME. I DON'T LIKE THE WAY THE WIND IS WHIPPING UP. THERE'S A SANDSTORM BREWING. WE'LL NEED SHELTER.
CAN WE BE SURE THEY'RE REAL?
THE BIOCORDER SAYS THEY ARE. THEIR READINGS CORRESPOND TO THE ONES WE FOLLOWED HERE. AND YET--
NO, NEVER MIND, JUST APPROACH WITH CAUTION--AND LOOK FRIENDLY.
GREETINGS, MY FRIEND. WE ARE, EH, WANDERERS, LIKE YOURSELVES, AND WE ARE IN NEED OF HAVEN FROM THE GATHERING STORM.
WE DO NOT WISH TO IMPOSE, BUT--
WANDERERS YOU MAY BE... BUT IN NO WAY DO YOU RESEMBLE US! WHAT MANNER OF BEINGS ARE YOU?
SINCE THE GREAT UPHEAVAL WE HAVE DREADED THE COMING OF CERTAIN DEMONS, WHO--
DEMONS WE ARE NOT, I ASSURE YOU. INDEED WE CALL OURSELVES GUARDIANS! WE--
DIE, GEM-BODIED INFIDEL! DIE IN THE NAME OF ULLAH!
HAIEEEEE!!
WHAT--?
BEHOLD HER--DARK WITH THE GRIME OF THE INFERNAL PIT--HER HAIR RED WITH FLAME LIKE A DEVIL'S TONGUE!
KILL!!
JEESH! GRIME? TONGUE?? LISTEN, MAC, PERSONAL HYGIENE IS ONE OF MY FEW CLAIMS TO FAME!

I'D LIKE TO SEE YOU COME OUTTA THIS FIGHT--LET ALONE SEVEN YEARS IN SPACE--AS CLEAN AS I AM!

YONDU LISTENS TO THE YOUNG WOMAN IN SLIGHT WONDERMENT.

HIS PRIMITIVE'S MIND CANNOT COMPREHEND HER NEED TO BANTER IN THIS LIFE-OR-DEATH SITUATION.

UNLESS, HE REASONS, HER WORDS FUNCTION SIMILARLY TO HIS SHRILL, PIERCING WHISTLE...

WWHHEEEEEEEEEEEEEEEEEEEEEEEEEE

...WHICH NOT ONLY GUIDES HIS YAKA ARROW THROUGH ITS MANEUVERS, BUT TENDS TO UNNERVE HIS ENEMIES, AS WELL.

NNNUH

NNNGH

I HOPE YOU GENTLEMEN WEREN'T PLANNING ON LEAVING US.

THERE'S A STORM APPROACHING, YOU KNOW!

WELL--?
ALL I HAVE, WHATEVER YOU DESIRE, IS YOURS FOR THE ASKING.
COME! YOU SHALL BE MY PERSONAL GUESTS!
EVERYTHING YOU SEE--MY FOOD, MY JEWELS, MY WINE--ALL ARE YOURS FOR THE TAKING!
NO SONS, HUH?
I HAVE BUT ONE. HADJI! COME! GREET OUR GUESTS!

"AND," STARHAWK ADDS, "THAT IS AS TRUE FOR MAJOR ASTRO AS FOR OURSELVES."
NAUSEOUS-- TIRED--TAKING ALL MY ENERGY-- JUST--TO KEEP FROM--PASSING OUT--
WEAKER I GET--LARGER THE THING GROWS--NOURISHING ITSELF ON MY DESPAIR--
HAVE TO--CONCENTRATE --MAKE MY MIND WORK--OR I'M GONNA VOMIT--!

WITHIN THE BRAIN OF THE 1000-YEAR-OLD-MAN THOUGHT IMPULSES MASS, SWIRLING TOGETHER LIKE A BALL OF FIRE, UNTIL...
LET...
ME...
GO!!
...THEY ERUPT FROM HIS FOREHEAD AS A BOLT OF PURE MENTAL FORCE!

ITS PSYCHOKINETIC POWER PENETRATES TO THE CORE OF THE BEAST...

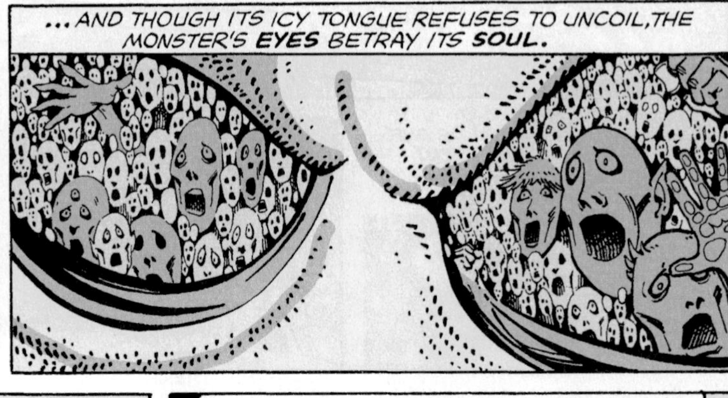
...AND THOUGH ITS ICY TONGUE REFUSES TO UNCOIL, THE MONSTER'S EYES BETRAY ITS SOUL.

FACES--THOUSANDS OF THEM--ALL AS HOPELESSLY CAPTIVE AS I--!
WHAT--DOES IT MEAN? --WHO ARE THEY? --MUST KNOW--

MUST--STAY ALIVE--TO--KNOW!!
IMPOSSIBLY, HE SUMMONS THE RAW STRENGTH OF WILL FOR ONE LAST POINT-BLANK SHOT.

EEEEEEYAARGH
SCREAM--DEAFENING--NOTHING YELLS LIKE THAT UNLESS IT'S DYING--!
RIGHT--YOU'RE EXPIRED, AREN'TCHA, LITTLE BUDDY--ALL DEAD AND READY FOR DISSECTION!
A SHORT TIME LATER, IN THE SHIP'S LABORATORY.
OKAY, FROGGY--PEEK-A-BOO!
I'VE WATCHED MARTINEX FIDGET WITH THIS TRISPECTRASCOPE A FEW HUNDRED TIMES--YOU'D THINK I'D REMEMBER HOW IT WORKS.
BUT, NO--I WAS TOO BUSY WATCHING THE PRETTY COLORED LIGHTS! IF THIS GADGET PERFORMS FOR ME, IT'LL BE PURE, DUMB LUCK!
"I SEE YOU!"
AND WHAT HE SEES CAUSES HIM TO BLINK REPEATEDLY--IN SHEER ASTONISHMENT. THE CREATURE'S BODY IS A HOLLOW HUSK OF PURE ENERGY ABOUT A SINGLE GLOWING GRAIN OF SAND!
IT'S...A MOTE!
ITS EXTERIOR IS NOTHING MORE THAN A FORCE MANIFESTATION THAT EXPANDS AS IT ENGORGES ENERGY.
IT'S POSSIBLE, THEN...THAT EVERY GRAIN OF SAND ON THAT DESERT OUT THERE IS...!
HAVE TO RADIO THE OTHERS ...AND FAST! THEY--
HUH?! SHIP--SHIFTING POSITION--HOW--OH, LORD--
IT'S AN EARTHQUAKE!!

--AN ACCURATE ENOUGH DESCRIPTION OF THE TREMOR--FOR THE **MOMENT!**

I SUGGEST WE CONTACT **MAJOR ASTRO,** AND--

I'M WAY **AHEAD** OF YOU.

SWEET! SO WE SAVE THE **SHIP!** WHAT ABOUT **US?!** I'VE GOT THIS THING ABOUT SELF-PRESERVATION!

WE SHALL COME TO NO HARM. YOU HAVE MY **WORD** AS--

YEAH, YEAH--"ONE WHO KNOWS"! **JEESH!**

START THE **ENGINES?!** BUT THE SHIP ISN'T **DESIGNED** FOR INTRA-ATMOSPHERIC FLIGHT!

SHE'S GOT THE AERODYNAMICS OF AN **ARMADILLO!** SHE'D SCUD ACROSS THE DESERT LIKE A DUNE BUGGY IN **HYPERDRIVE!**

THOSE WERE STARHAWK'S **INSTRUCTIONS,** VANCE. I'D ADVISE--

STARHAWK?!

HE'S HERE **WITH** US. NO TIME TO EXPLAIN. JUST **DO** IT.

AND, VANCE--GOOD **LUCK!** ALL IS **FORGOTTEN,** OKAY?

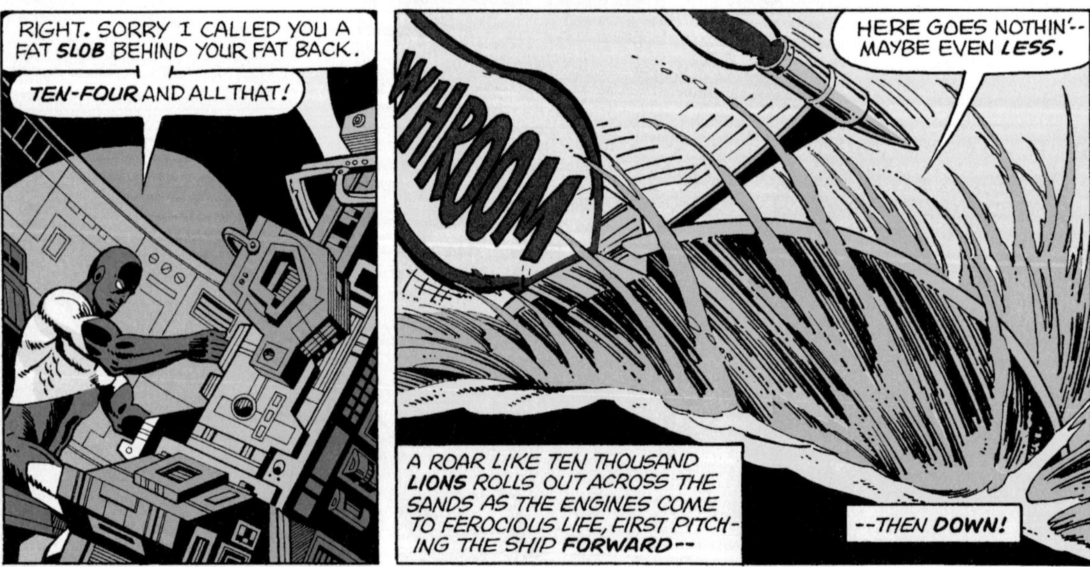

IT OCCURRED TO ME THE SHIP MIGHT TIP OVER WITH THE THRUST...
...BUT I NEVER FIGURED ON ITS VELOCITY BEING SO GREAT--
--IT'D KEEP ON GOING STRAIGHT THROUGH THE PLANET...
...AND OUT THE OTHER SIDE!
IT DAWNS ON HIM, TOO, THAT THIS IS THE FIRST TIME HE'S EVER HEARD THE STARSHIP'S ENGINES --THAT SOUND DOESN'T CARRY IN THE VACUUM OF SPACE--THAT THE HUM TO WHICH HE'D BEEN ACCUSTOMED--
BUT THEN, ADJUSTING THE VIEWSCREEN TO PEER AT THE WORLD HE'S ESCAPED, THAT SOUND AND FURY ASSUMES ALL THE SIGNIFICANCE OF A CANARY'S TWEET.
FOR WHAT HE SEES IS NOT THE FAMILIAR GLOBULAR SHAPE OF MOST OF THE GALAXY'S BILLIONS OF PLANETS... BUT SOMETHING ANTHRO-POMORPHIC!
A MAN--WITH AN ARM-SPAN OF SEVERAL LIGHT YEARS--WHOSE BODY'S SLOPES AND CURVES AND RIDES ARE FORMED NOT OF TISSUE AND BONE, BUT SAND AND STONE AND SOIL!
BENEATH ITS METAL SHEATHING, ASTRO'S FACE GOES PALE.

WHILE SOMEWHERE JUST ABOVE THE SMALL OF THE TOPOGRAPHICAL MAN'S BACK...
THE WIND IS DYING NOW... THE MOTION OF THE SURFACE IS SUBSIDING. IT SHOULD BE SAFE TO TRAVEL.
HAVE WE ANY PARTICULAR DESTINATION?
INDEED. THE MOUNTAINS, YONDER.
UH... Y'KNOW, THESE MOUNTS AREN'T OURS.
AH, BUT THEY ARE! A GIFT--FROM THE CHIEFTAIN'S SON!
THE CORNERS OF HIS MOUTH TURN HALF A DEGREE UPWARD, NIKKI NOTES. HE ALMOST--BUT NOT QUITE--SMILES AS HE LIFTS HIS SOLAR SAILS.
YOU ARE A SLY ONE, AREN'TCHA, HADJI?
I SHALL FLY AT THE VANGUARD. I ANTICIPATE NO PERIL--
--BUT SHOULD THE UNFORESEEN ARISE, I SHALL BE ABLE TO ALERT YOU.
UNREAL! HE --IT--ISN'T MANACLED BY THOSE STARS--HE'S FEEDING THEIR FUSION REACTION--
--ACCELERATING THEIR MATURATION--PUSHING THEM TOWARD NOVA--AND FAST!
AND IT AIN'T HARD TO RECKON WHY... NOW THAT I'VE DETERMINED OUR POSITION.
WE'RE SMACK AT THE HUB OF THE GALAXY, WHERE THE STARS ARE MOST DENSELY CLUSTERED. IF HE--
PARDON ME. MAJOR ASTRO--?
PLEASE DON'T BE ALARMED SIR. IT'S ONLY I--
--MAJOR VANCE ASTRO, CIRCA 1988.

THE FACE IS FAMILIAR. I USED TO HAVE ONE JUST LIKE IT.
BUT...I TEND TO THINK YOU'RE AN ILLUSION, PAL. OR SOME VISION OUT OF A TIME-WARP PHENOMENON.
WHATEVER, YOU'RE UNEQUIVOCALLY--
--UNREAL.
OH, NO.
THE SENSATION IS FAMILIAR THIS TIME--THAT'S SOME CONSOLATION--BUT NOT MUCH.
STARHAWK, THE NOMADS SPOKE OF SOMETHING CALLED THE "GREAT UPHEAVAL."
HAVE YOU ANY NOTION WHAT--?
NEITHER THE SANDSTORM NOR THE EARTH TREMOR, IF THAT IS WHAT YOU SUPPOSED.
THEY WERE REFERRING TO THE DISASTER WHICH DESTROYED THEIR HOME WORLD.
YOU MEAN--THEY'RE NOT NATIVES? I DON'T--
THE ANSWER YOU SEEK, JOVIAN, WAITS AT THE DEPTHS OF THE CAVERN.
WE SHALL HAVE TO MAKE THE DESCENT ON FOOT. THE PATH IS FAR TOO NARROW FOR OUR MOUNTS.
WHATEVER YOU SAY!
AS THE LIGHT AND THE GIVER OF LIGHT, I MAY ILLUMINE YOUR PATH, SERVE AS YOUR GUIDE.
BUT IF YOU ARE TO BE OF ANY USE TO ME, YOUR CONCLUSIONS MUST BE YOUR OWN.
HEAVY.

NEXT THE CATACLYSMIC CONCLUSION TO--JUST ABOUT EVERYTHING! THE STORY THAT COULD ONLY BE FILMED IN THE UNIVERSE, WHERE LIFE IS CHEAP!

MILKY WAY SNUFF!

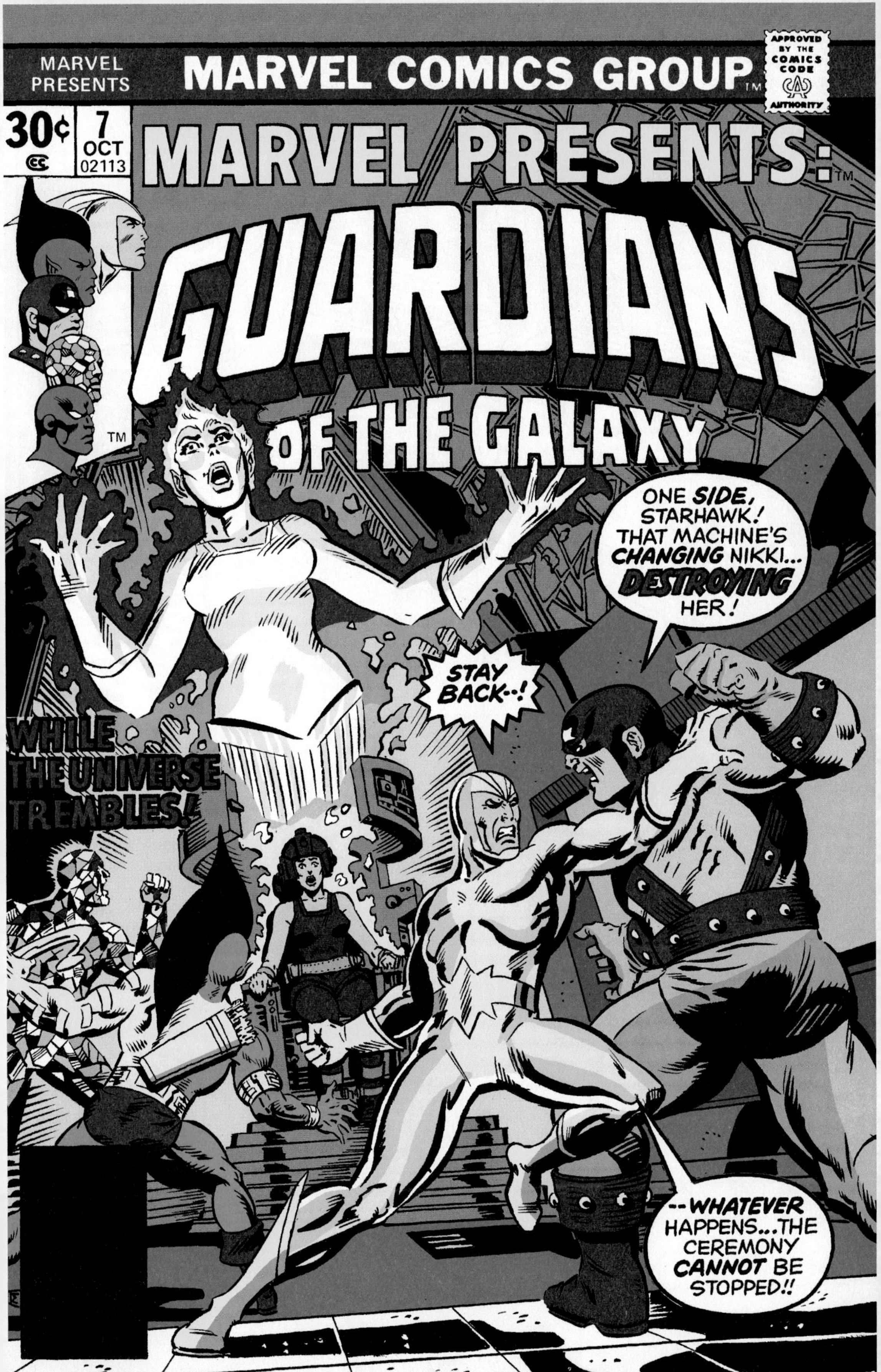

MARVEL PRESENTS
MARVEL COMICS GROUP
APPROVED BY THE COMICS CODE AUTHORITY
30¢
7 OCT
02113
MARVEL PRESENTS:
GUARDIANS OF THE GALAXY
ONE SIDE, STARHAWK! THAT MACHINE'S CHANGING NIKKI... DESTROYING HER!
STAY BACK--!
WHILE THE UNIVERSE TREMBLES!
--WHATEVER HAPPENS...THE CEREMONY CANNOT BE STOPPED!!

Yondu, from Centauri-IV. Charlie 27, from Jupiter. *Martinex,* from Pluto. And Earth's thousand-year-old survivor, *Vance Astro.* Ten centuries from now, these last survivors of their worlds will see planet Earth from the grasp of the *Badoon.* Together with the mysterious being known as *Starhawk,* they roam the universe!

Stan Lee PRESENTS: THE GUARDIANS OF THE GALAXY! ™

EMBRACE THE VOID!

WOW--CAKEWALKING DOWN A BEAM OF **LIGHT!** THIS, FOLKS, IS **SPELUNKING** IN **STYLE!**

IT IS BUT A **SMALL** WONDER, NIKKI, BESIDE THOSE WHICH AWAIT AT THE CAVERN'S **FLOOR--**

--IN THE **CONVENT OF LIVING FIRE!**

HAIL, STARHAWK! WE WHO SHARE YOUR DOOM BID YOU **WELCOME!**

STEVE GERBER WRITER	AL MILGROM PENCILLER	BOB WIACEK INKER	I. WATANABE, LETTERER P. GOLDBERG, COLORIST	ARCHIE GOODWIN EDITOR

YOUR COMPANIONS, MAN OF KNOWLEDGE, WHO--?
THEY ARE CALLED NIKKI, YONDU, MARTINEX, AND CHARLIE, MOTHER SUPERIOR.

OOOAOOAOOAA
AND LIKE YOU AND I, THEY ARE SELF-APPOINTED GUARDIANS OF THIS GALAXY.
TRULY? HOW SAD.
PSSST LISTEN! YOU GUYS HEAR--?

AOOAOOAOOAOOOOOAOOAOAOAO
THE SENSATION IS MORE THAN MERELY AUDITORY TO ME, NIKKI. MY ENTIRE CRYSTALLINE STRUCTURE IS VIBRATING!
WHAT IS THAT SOUND-- STARHAWK-- MOTHER SUPERIOR--?

IT IS PRAYER, MY FRIEND--

A SONG OF IMPECCABLE JOY, A CRY OF EXQUISITE ANGUISH.
THE WOMEN MOURN A DEPARTED SISTER AND REJOICE AT HER ENTRY INTO ETERNAL COMMUNION.

ANY OF YOU--ANALYSIS? I'M AFRAID MY TOO-LOGICAL MIND CAN APPRECIATE BUT NOT INTERPRET--!
DON'T LOOK AT ME! I'VE NEVER HAD A RELIGIOUS EXPERIENCE IN MY LIFE!
MAYBE SOMETHING IN NIKKI'S HISTORICAL BACKGROUND OR YONDU'S CENTAURIAN MYSTICISM--!

I CAN SPEAK WITH ASSURANCE ONLY ABOUT THE TEXTURE OF THE MOTHER SUPERIOR'S WORDS, CHARLIE.
I FIND A FAMILIAR QUALITY THERE-- AND AN UTTER ABSENCE OF EVIL INTENT.
IN OUR PRESENT CIRCUMSTANCES, FRIEND YONDU, "GOOD" AND "EVIL" ARE QUITE IRRELEVANT.

WE ARE DEALING WITH AN EVEN MORE BASIC CONFLICT: EXISTENCE VERSUS NON-EXISTENCE FOR A GALAXY WHICH CONTAINS ITS SHARE OF GOOD AND EVIL BOTH.
CHEEZ! GET A LOAD OF THE LIGHTING IN THIS PLACE!

WHAT IS IT? SOME KINDA MAGNESIUM SCULPTURE, YOU THINK? EVEN THROUGH THE FLAMES, THE FIGURES ARE SO REALISTIC!
BUT WHOEVER HEARD OF A CONVENT WITH A SPECIAL EFFECTS DEPARTMENT?!

DID YOU-- WERE YOU-- ADDRESSING ME, SISTER?
HUH?

THERE IS --SO MUCH-- I COULD TELL YOU--
--BUT SO LITTLE--
--TIME.

SHE--TURNED TO ASHES-- RIGHT IN FRONT OF ME!
LISTEN--I, UH, REALLY THINK I'M GONNA BE SICK!

WOULD THAT YOU COULD AFFORD THAT SELF-INDULGENCE, NIKKI, BUT NOW MOST OF ALL YOU MUST REFORTIFY YOUR STRENGTH OF WILL.
FOR IN ORDER TO SAVE THE GALAXY, YOU MUST ENTER THE FLAME STATE AND--
ME?!?

OH, NO! UH-UH! NOT THIS KID!! YOU'VE FLIPPED YOUR SUNBONNET, MAN! I DIDN'T SPEND SEVEN YEARS SURVIVING ALONE IN SPACE TO WIND UP A HUMAN CIGARETTE BUTT!

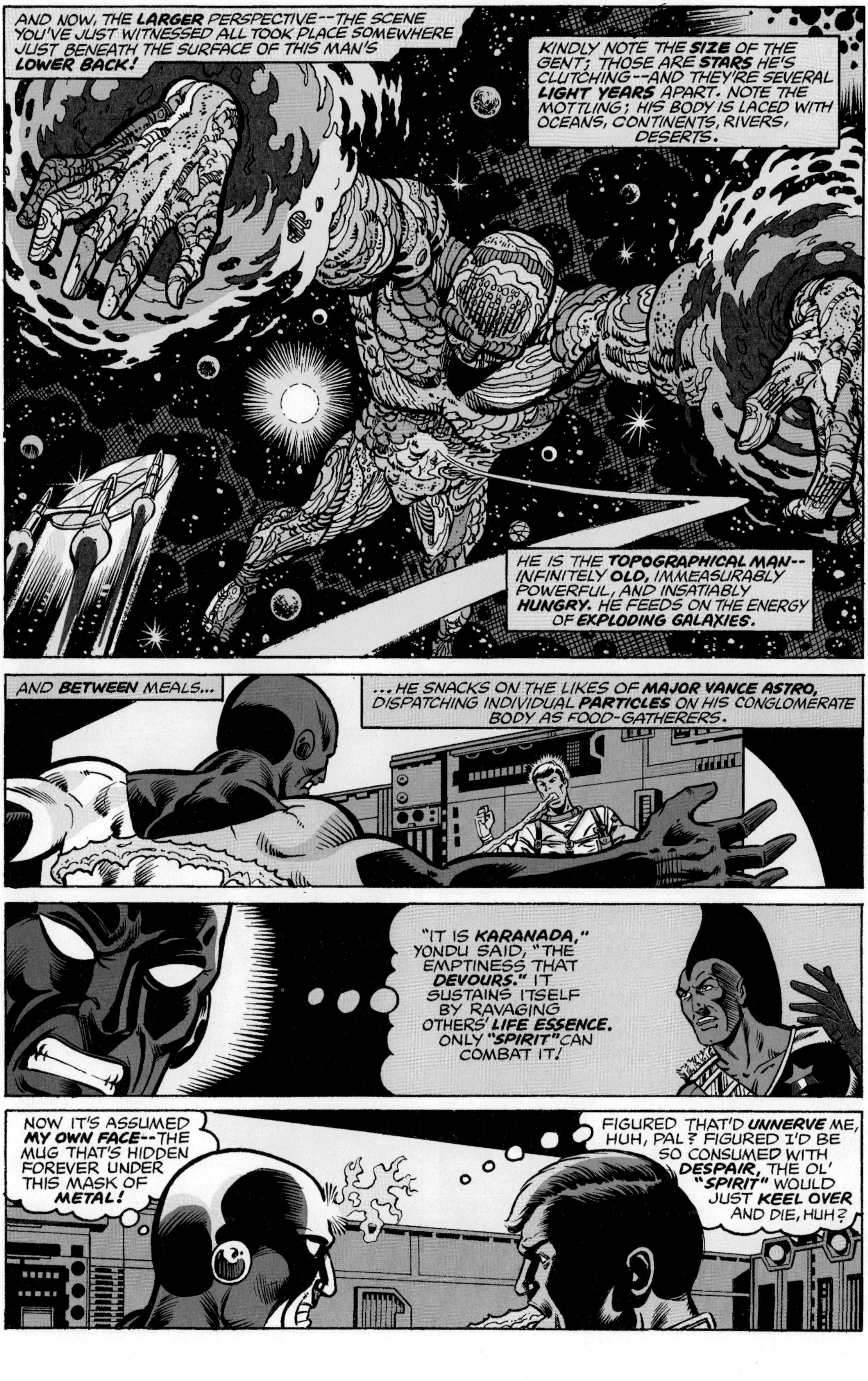

AND NOW, THE LARGER PERSPECTIVE--THE SCENE YOU'VE JUST WITNESSED ALL TOOK PLACE SOMEWHERE JUST BENEATH THE SURFACE OF THIS MAN'S LOWER BACK!

KINDLY NOTE THE SIZE OF THE GENT; THOSE ARE STARS HE'S CLUTCHING--AND THEY'RE SEVERAL LIGHT YEARS APART. NOTE THE MOTTLING; HIS BODY IS LACED WITH OCEANS, CONTINENTS, RIVERS, DESERTS.

HE IS THE TOPOGRAPHICAL MAN--INFINITELY OLD, IMMEASURABLY POWERFUL, AND INSATIABLY HUNGRY. HE FEEDS ON THE ENERGY OF EXPLODING GALAXIES.

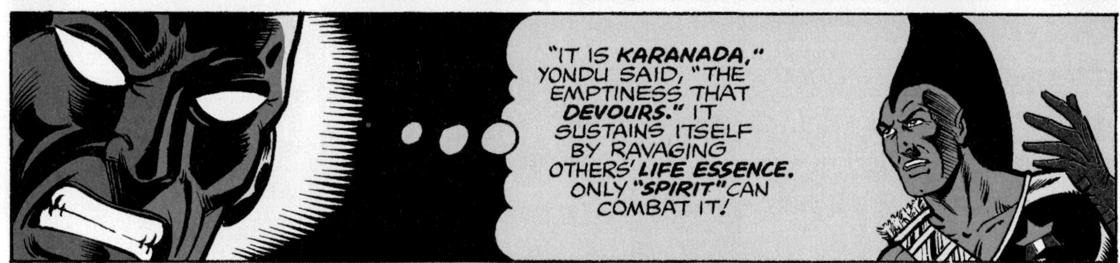

WELL, GUESS AGAIN, HANDSOME!! PAPA SHOULD'A WARNED YOU I'M SENSITIVE ABOUT BEING TOYED WITH!
AND THIS PSYCHE-BLAST OUGHTTA DRIVE THE POINT HOME!! THAT FACE IS MINE, AND YOU CAN'T HAVE IT!!

IT IS THE SINGLE MOST POTENT PSYCHOKINETIC BURST VANCE ASTRO HAS EVER HURLED. AND IT TAKES ITS TOLL.

THE MILLENNIUM-OLD GUARDIAN AND HIS ALTER EGO BOTH SINK TO THEIR KNEES.

THEN, ITS EYES DIMMING, ITS FACE A PORTRAIT OF FATIGUE, THE UNLIVING ASSASSIN RETRACTS ITS ICY TONGUE. BUT THE BATTLE IS NOT OVER!

THEY TOTTER ON THEIR KNEES, VYING WITH STARES. IT REMAINS A CONTEST OF WILLS. AND IT DOES NOT END...

...UNTIL, AFTER AN ETERNITY OR TWO, ONE COMBATANT FINALLY FALLS.

BUT FOR ALL ITS WEIRD TERRORS, THE HUB OF THE GALAXY, WHERE THE GUARDIANS' QUEST HAS LED...
...CAN CLAIM NO EXCLUSIVENESS ON THE FORCES OF DEATH AND DESTRUCTION.
THIS IS STARHAWK'S ASTEROID HOME, PARSECS DISTANT.

ITS PROTECTIVE DOME SHATTERED, THE COLD OF SPACE HAS INVADED THE PLACE.

ALONG WITH THE ARTIFICIAL ATMOSPHERE, SOUND, TOO, HAS FLED.

AND GRAVITY.

ON THE CYCLOPEAN COMPUTER SCREEN, THE WOMAN ALETA CRIES SILENTLY FOR TARA, SITA, JOHN--THE CHILDREN.
NO ANSWER COMES.

AFTER A TIME, THE SCREEN ITSELF MALFUNCTIONS AND EXPLODES.
AND THEN THERE IS DARKNESS DEEP ENOUGH TO MATCH THE COLD AND THE SILENCE.

WHILE, IN A CHAPEL UNDER THE CRUST OF THE TOPOGRAPHICAL MAN...!
AW, COME ON! I MEAN, I'M AS GUTSY AS THE NEXT CHILD...
...BUT YOU DON'T REALLY EXPECT ME TO TAKE THE CHAIR WITHOUT EVEN KNOWING THE RAP, DO YOU?!
IT IS NOT AN EXECUTION YOU FACE, NIKKI --BUT A SORT OF MARRIAGE.
THAT'S EVEN WORSE!

IT IS THE UNION OF WOMAN WITH THE GODHEAD--THE ULTIMATE SENSUAL EX-EXPERIENCE--A JOINING WITH ALL OF INFINITY.
AND FOR YOU, IT IS STILL MORE, CHILD. IT IS YOUR ROLE IN THE GALAXY'S SALVATION.
YOU REALLY KNOW HOW TO MAKE A GIRL FEEL GUILTY, DON'TCHA?
SIGH OKAY, WHAT DO I DO?

NOTHING. THE SISTERS SHALL DRAPE YOU IN THE RITUAL ROBING.
YOUR TASK IS BUT TO CLEAR YOUR MIND--LUXURIATE IN THE SOFTNESS OF THE GARMENT!
RIGHT. NEATO. BUT WHAT HAPPENS WHEN I PLUNK MYSELF IN THAT HOT SEAT?

THE DEVICE ACTIVATES A PORTION OF THE BACKBRAIN, CHILD--UNLEASHING A RESERVOIR OF ORDINARILY UNTAPPED PSYCHIC ENERGY.
THE RESULT IS QUITE DRAMATIC.
I'LL JUST BET.
THE WOMAN'S BODY BURSTS INTO FLAME...WHILE HER MIND IS EXPANDED TO THE FARTHEST REACHES OF THE UNIVERSE.

"MOST WOMEN ARE CONTENT TO REMAIN IN THAT STATE FOR THE REST OF THEIR LIVES--WHICH, OF COURSE, ARE DRASTICALLY SHORTENED BY THE VAST EXPENDITURE OF ENERGY."

SOME, HOWEVER, DO RETURN TO THIS SPHERE--THOSE WITH THE STRONGEST SENSE OF SINGULAR IDENTITY.
AH-HA! AND IF THERE WAS EVER A DESCRIPTION OF NIKKI--!

THE MOTHER SUPERIOR HERSELF IS ONE SUCH RETURNEE.
MY SECRET SORROW, AS IT WERE--FOR THOUGH I AM PRIVILEGED TO USHER OTHERS BEYOND THE PALE--
NEVER AGAIN SHALL I KNOW THE ECSTASY WHICH YOU ARE ABOUT TO EXPERIENCE.
AND SO IT BEGINS AGAIN: THE HAUNTING CHANT WHICH GREETED THE GUARDIANS ON THEIR ARRIVAL --THE SIREN SONG OF BEREAVEMENT AND DELIVERANCE.
OOOAOAOAOAOAO

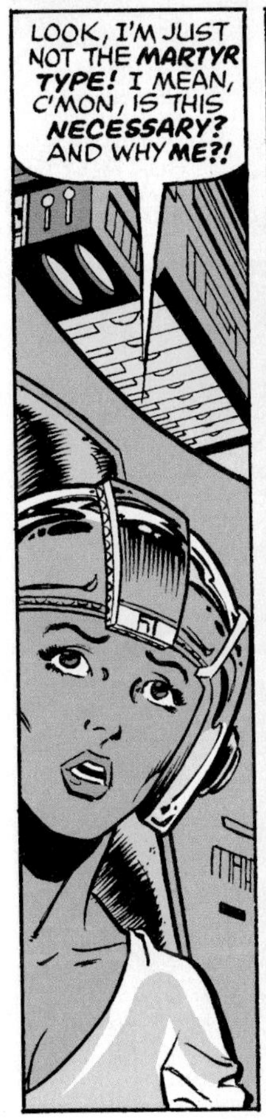
LOOK, I'M JUST NOT THE MARTYR TYPE! I MEAN, C'MON, IS THIS NECESSARY? AND WHY ME?!

BECAUSE ONLY A WOMAN MAY PARTAKE OF THE KNOWLEDGE THIS STRANGE JOURNEY OFFERS. I ASSURE YOU--YOU WILL SURVIVE--ON MY WORD AS--
"ONE WHO KNOWS"? SORRY, NOT IMPRESSED.
THERE'VE BEEN A FEW TOO MANY INCONSISTENCIES WITH THAT CLAIM ALREADY!

YONDU--OLD BLUE BUDDY--SAY SOMETHING! WHAT'S YOUR INTUITION TELL YA?
THAT--YOU MUST BE BRAVE!

THAT'S IT--MY LAST CARD. YOU MAY AS WELL START THE MOTORS, MAMA!

IT IS DONE!

RAW ENERGY JOUNCES THE YOUNG MERCURIAN'S FORM.
HER HEAD SNAPS BACK INVOLUNTARILY. HER SPINE ARCHES.
TREMORS RIPPLE THE LENGTH OF HER BODY. SHE TWITCHES, WRITHES, SPASMS, UNCONTROLLABLY.

BUT THE ONLY ANGUISHED CRY SPRINGS FROM THE LIPS OF--STARHAWK!
NO!!
NOT NOW!! NOT HERE!! YOU MUSTN'T! YOU--
AAARRGH!!

ENFOLDING HIMSELF IN HIS ARMS--LESS IN PAIN, APPARENTLY, THAN IN AN EFFORT TO PREVENT HIS RATTLING APART--STARHAWK LURCHES FOR THE CHAPEL DOOR.
I--CANNOT--REMAIN--DO NOT FOLLOW--NO ONE--CAN HELP!
WAIT! YOU CAN'T DESERT NIKKI! STOP, OR I'LL--

NO! STAY HERE! BOTH OF YOU! IF NIKKI WAKES SUDDENLY, YOURS ARE THE FACES SHE'LL WANT TO SEE!
AND I'M THE ONE BEST QUALIFIED TO HANDLE OUR ALLY'S AILING STOMACH!

HE'S RIGHT, OF COURSE, AS USUAL. HE CONSISTENTLY AMAZES ME WITH HIS OBJECTIVE APPRAISALS OF OTHERS' FEELINGS TOWARD HIM. HE--
HOLY HARKOV! YONDU--

LOOK!!

BUT NATURALLY, HE'D UNFOLD THOSE SOLAR SAILS OF HIS! WHATEVER CHANGES HE'S GOING THROUGH, HE WANTS THEM TO HAPPEN OUTSIDE THE CAVERN!
I CAN'T MATCH HIS SPEED, OF COURSE--

--BUT IF HE THINKS HE'S STRANDED ME HERE AT THE BASE OF THE TABLE ROCK, HE'S SADLY MISTAKEN!
SHOOM

A BRIEF APPLICATION OF HEAT FORMS SEMI-MOLTEN STONE--
IT'S YOUR BASIC INSTANT LADDER!

OAOAOAOA
INSIDE, THE TRANSITION PHASE OF NIKKI'S JOURNEY REACHES SUCCESSFUL COMPLETION.

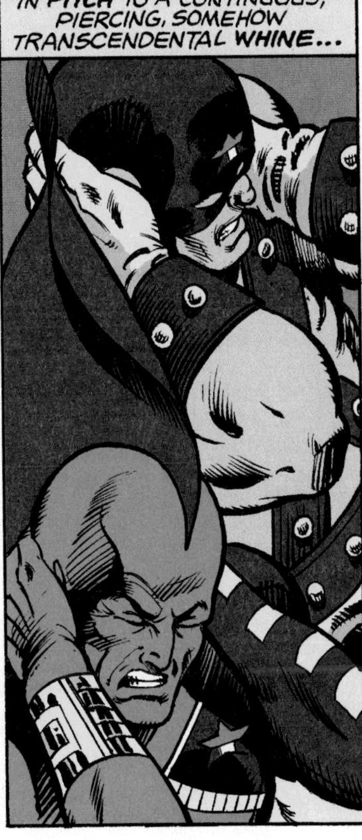
THE SISTERS' CHANT ESCALATES IN VOLUME, AND RISES IN PITCH TO A CONTINUOUS, PIERCING, SOMEHOW TRANSCENDENTAL WHINE...

...WHICH PENETRATES EVEN THE BARRIER OF THE WHITE FLAME TO NIKKI'S DEEPEST LEVEL OF CONSCIOUSNESS.
OAOAOA
AND THEN, EYES WIDE WITH WONDER, SHE JOINS IN THEIR SACRED SONG.

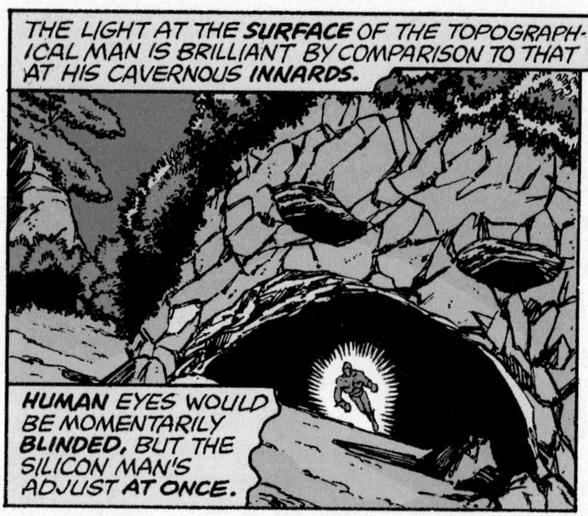
THE LIGHT AT THE SURFACE OF THE TOPOGRAPHICAL MAN IS BRILLIANT BY COMPARISON TO THAT AT HIS CAVERNOUS INNARDS.
HUMAN EYES WOULD BE MOMENTARILY BLINDED. BUT THE SILICON MAN'S ADJUST AT ONCE.

AND SO, THE SLEEK, GLEAMING FORM OF STARHAWK STANDS OUT (IF NOT UP) EVEN MORE CLEARLY AGAINST THE HARSH, RUGGED TERRAIN.
I--BEGGED YOU--NOT--TO FOLLOW!

I ASKED--ONLY--THAT NO SPECTACLE--BE MADE OF MY SUFFERING!
NAIVELY, I BELIEVED --THAT YOU, AT LEAST --MIGHT UNDERSTAND!
I IMPLORE YOU AGAIN, MARTINEX--TURN YOUR BACK!
GOOD LORD!
LEAVE ME--WITH MY--DIGNITY--INTACT!

STARHAWK?
N-NO... THE BODY IS MINE, NOW. FOR A TIME.

HE RENEGED ON HIS VOW, IGNORED MY SUMMONS!
HE ABANDONED US--ABANDONED THE CHILDREN!
YOU'RE TREMBLING. LET ME HELP.

HE ABANDONED THE CHILDREN--TO THE REAVERS OF ARCTURUS!!
HE MURDERED THEM--AS CALLOUSLY AS HE SLEW ME!

I SHOULD BE CELEBRATING: I WON MY FREEDOM FROM THAT FORM-FITTING FOIL JUST IN TIME TO CATCH THE DESTRUCTION OF THE GALAXY ON THE SHIP'S VIEWSCREEN.
OH, IT'S GREAT TO FEEL LIKE A MAN AGAIN INSTEAD OF A CANDY BAR. I ONLY WISH I UNDERSTOOD HOW IT HAPPENED.
...HOW I CAME TO BE KEELING OVER ONE MINUTE AND STARING DOWN AT MY OWN PRONE FORM THE NEXT.

AND I'D ALSO LIKE TO KNOW WHAT GOOD IT DOES ME--NOW THAT "TALL PAUL" OUT THERE HAS RAISED THOSE TWIN STARS TO NEAR-NOVA BRIGHTNESS.
WHEN THEY EXPLODE, THEY'LL INITIATE A CHAIN REACTION OF EXPLODING STARS THAT EVENTUALLY WILL LEAVE THE OLD MILKY WAY A VERY LARGE CINDER.
BUT I SUPPOSE IT'S JUST THE FINAL ACT OF THIS ZANY COSMIC FARCE WE'RE ENACTING.
I FEEL NEW STRENGTH, NEW VIGOR PULSING THROUGH ME--AND THERE'S ABSOLUTELY NO PLACE TO PUT IT!

AND THANKS TO THE SOLAR INTERFERENCE, I HAVEN'T EVEN BEEN ABLE TO CONTACT--
EH--? SHIP'S LIGHTS DIMMING. WHY...?

BETTER RUN A CHECK ON THE POWER LEVELS, SEE IF--
WHAT THE--?! MY SKIN!! I LOOK LIKE AN OVERRIPE LEMON!!

THE SAME HUE THE GIANT'S FOOD-GATHERER TURNED... JUST BEFORE IT WAS SATED WITH ENERGY! CAN IT BE ...WHEN THE THING TOOK MY FACE...

...I WAS SO ENRAGED THAT MY PSYCHIC BLAST DISPLACED MY IDENTITY INTO THE CREATURE??
YES!! I'VE BEEN ABSORBING THE SHIP'S POWER!! I'VE BECOME PART OF THE TOPOGRAPHICAL MAN!

"AND NOW... MY BODY... GOING FLUID... LOSING SHAPE, DEFINITION...
"I'M GOING HOME!"

BACK IN THE CHAPEL, UNAWARE OF VANCE'S BIZARRE PREDICAMENT, YONDU SENSES A SUDDEN INDEFINABLE SHIFTING OF SPIRITUAL FORCES.
"NIKKI'S VERY SOUL IS IN DANGER," HIS WILDERNESS-BRED INSTINCTS TELL HIM...!
...AND HE REACTS WITH SILENT SWIFTNESS!
HEY! WHAT'S GOT INTO YOU?!
BLIND PANIC JUST DOESN'T SUIT YOU! COOL DOWN!
FREE ME, MY FRIEND-- URGENCY, NOT PANIC PROPELS ME!
THE PATTERNS HAVE ALTERED! THE MACHINERY MUST HALT BEFORE--
BUT THE ODD INTERMINGLING OF TECHNOLOGY AND MYSTICISM HAS TAKEN YONDU TOO LONG TO PENETRATE ALREADY. NIKKI HAS REACHED THE SEPARATION STAGE. SHE SCREAMS.
AAAAAAA
HARKOY'S HOLY GHOST--I DON'T BELIEVE IT! WHAT--?!
WE ARE TOO LATE. HER WILL FLOATS FREE!
"THE TIES BETWEEN SPIRIT AND BODY HAVE BEEN SEVERED!"
SHE HAS ASCENDED.

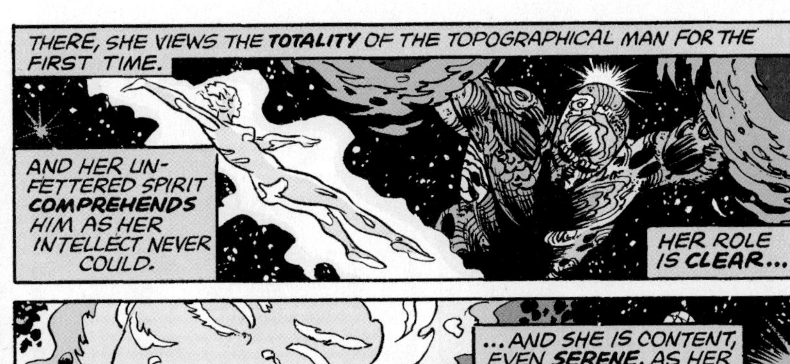

...AND SHE IS CONTENT, EVEN **SERENE,** AS HER ASTRAL FORM EXPANDS TO ENCOMPASS IT.

BUT, NO... THE GIANT **CANNOT** WAKE. IMPLICIT IN WAKING IS THE PRESENCE OF **LIFE,** AND THIS COLOSSUS IS LIFE'S OWN **OPPOSITE.** WHAT NIKKI HAS ROUSED IS ANOTHER BODILESS **SPIRIT...**

THE GIRL--
LEAVE HER! SHE HAS SERVED HER PURPOSE-- BY PRECIPITATING THE CATACLYSM!
HER BODY WILL PERISH IN JOYOUS UNION WITH--

NO!! SHE DID NOT CHOOSE TO DIE! YOU'VE NO RIGHT!!
YONDU! THE FLAMES! DON'T!

IF I MUST BEAR THE PAIN TO SAVE HER, I SHALL. SAY NO MORE.
ULP

ALL RIGHT, THEN--I'LL DO MY BEST TO CLEAR A PATH!
KRAM
I THINK YOU'RE OUT OF YOUR MIND... BUT I ADMIRE YOU FOR IT!

SOON, BEYOND THE CONVENT WALLS...
YOUR FOREARMS ARE IN LUCK, FRIEND! THE LIGHT-BRIDGE IS WAITING FOR US!

QUICKLY, YOU TWO! SHE CAN'T MAINTAIN THE BRIDGE FOR LONG!
SHE?? WHO'S--

--SHE ?!?
LATER! YONDU'S ABOUT TO PASS OUT! CARRY HIM, CHARLIE. I'LL TAKE NIKKI!

AND RUN! YOUR LIFE DEPENDS ON IT!

OUTSIDE, CHARLIE'S COMMUNICATOR ACTIVATES THE "CAPTAIN AMERICA" TELEPORT MECHANISM ...AND AS THE QUINTET VANISHES BACK TO THE SHIP...

THE DISINTEGRATION BEGINS!
THE BODY OF THE TOPOGRAPHICAL MAN FALLS AWAY IN FIERY CHUNKS...AND THE MULTITUDES OF PEOPLES WHO INHABIT HIS SURFACE EXULT!
MARTY! WHAT'S HAPPENING OUT THERE?! IS THE PLANET EXPLODING, OR--?
WE, UH--WEREN'T ON ANY PLANET, CHARLIE.
BUT YOU'LL HAVE TO SEE THIS YOURSELF TO BELIEVE IT.
"IT IS KARANADA'S END," YONDU INTONES SOLEMNLY, AS CHARLIE APPROACHES THE SCREEN, "AND NIKKI AND VANCE HAVE BROUGHT IT ABOUT THE ONLY WAY POSSIBLE--
"--BY FORCE OF SPIRIT ALONE--CAUSING THE DEMON TO ENGAGE IN AN ACT OF LOVE--AN AFFIRMATION OF ITS OWN OPPOSITE, WHICH IS LIFE!"
UH-HUH--THEREBY BUFFETING US HALFWAY BACK TO EARTH!!

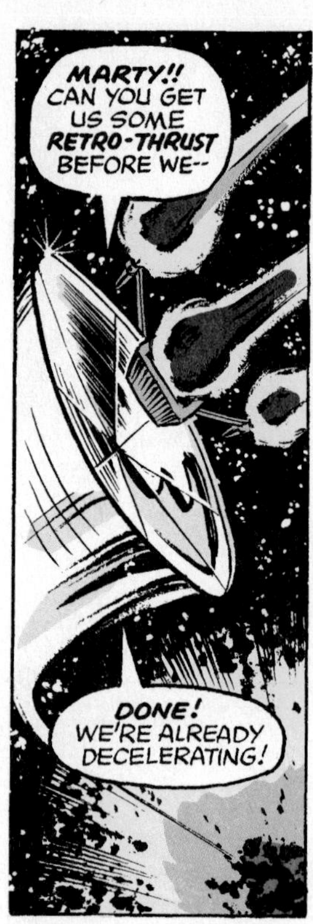

NEXT: THE REAVERS OF ARCTURUS!

MARVEL PRESENTS

MARVEL COMICS GROUP™

30¢ 8 DEC 02113

MARVEL PRESENTS:™

GUARDIANS OF THE GALAXY™

SPECIAL RETURN APPEARANCE-- THE SILVER SURFER!

THE SENTINEL OF THE SPACEWAYS PITS THE POWER COSMIC AGAINST THE GUARDIANS' GREATEST FOES!

BATTLE WITH THE BADOON!

Yondu, from Centauri-IV. Charlie 27, from Jupiter. *Martinex,* from Pluto. And Earth's thousand-year-old survivor, *Vance Astro.* Ten centuries from now, they roam the universe!

Stan Lee PRESENTS: THE GUARDIANS OF THE GALAXY!™

HAVING FINALLY **ENDED** THE GALAXY-ANNIHILATING THREAT OF THE **TOPOGRAPHICAL MAN,*** THE **GUARDIANS,** ONCE AGAIN ABOARD THE STARSHIP CAPTAIN AMERICA, ENCOUNTER A STRANGE AND INTERESTING OBJECT FLOATING IN DEEP SPACE...

WE **GOT** IT, MARTINEX!

SO WE HAVE, CHARLIE. STILL, I FAIL TO UNDERSTAND WHY YOU **INSISTED** ON ACCOMPANYING ME.

I COULD HAVE EASILY RETRIEVED THIS DEVICE BY MYSELF, AND **I** NEED NO SPACE SUIT.

HARKOV'S BONES, MAN! I USED TO BE A **MILITIAMAN,** REMEMBER? THERE WAS NOTHING IN **BASIC** TRAINING I ENJOYED BETTER THAN A GOOD OLD-FASHIONED **SPACE-WALK!** WHY, DO YOU KNOW--

HEY, YOU TWO! IF YOU'VE GOT THAT THING, CUT THE CHATTER AND GET BACK IN HERE... **ON THE DOUBLE!**

*LAST ISSUE --ARCHIE.

A TALE OF TWO TIMES-- AS TOLD BY

(30TH CENTURY) **ROGER STERN,** WRITER **AL MILGROM,** PENCILER **BOB WIACEK,** INKER **J. NOVAK,** LETTERS **G. WEIN,** COLORS

(20TH CENTURY) **STAN LEE,** WRITER **JOHN BUSCEMA,** PENCILER **JOE SINNOTT,** INKER **SAM ROSEN,** LETTERER

ARCHIE GOODWIN-- EDITOR OF SPACE AND TIME!

A STRANGE AURA OF ENERGY PULSES OUT FROM THE MENTO-CORDER, FLOODING THE GUARDIANS' MINDS WITH A SCENE FROM A MILLENIUM AGO...

...A SCENE OF A LONE BADOON STARSHIP HURTLING INTO EARTH'S ATMOSPHERE--UNDETECTED BY ALL BUT ONE BEING--

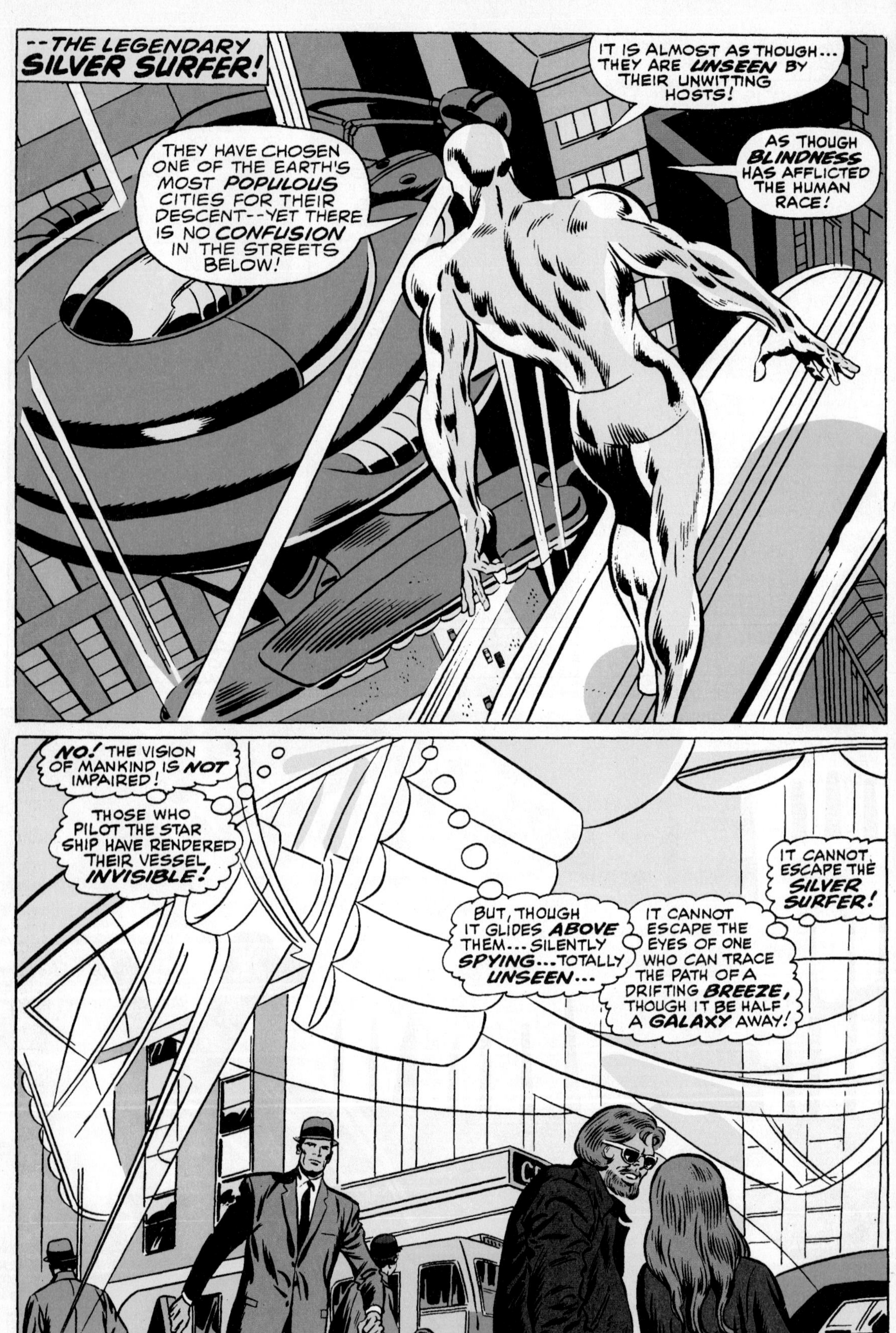
--THE LEGENDARY SILVER SURFER!
THEY HAVE CHOSEN ONE OF THE EARTH'S MOST POPULOUS CITIES FOR THEIR DESCENT--YET THERE IS NO CONFUSION IN THE STREETS BELOW!
IT IS ALMOST AS THOUGH... THEY ARE UNSEEN BY THEIR UNWITTING HOSTS!
AS THOUGH BLINDNESS HAS AFFLICTED THE HUMAN RACE!
NO! THE VISION OF MANKIND IS NOT IMPAIRED!
THOSE WHO PILOT THE STAR SHIP HAVE RENDERED THEIR VESSEL INVISIBLE!
BUT, THOUGH IT GLIDES ABOVE THEM... SILENTLY SPYING... TOTALLY UNSEEN...
IT CANNOT ESCAPE THE EYES OF ONE WHO CAN TRACE THE PATH OF A DRIFTING BREEZE, THOUGH IT BE HALF A GALAXY AWAY!
IT CANNOT ESCAPE THE SILVER SURFER!

AND SHORTLY, A PORTAL IN THE CRAFT OPENS, ADMITTING THE EARTH-BOUND SKY-RIDER.
STRANGER, BE NOT AFRAID! NO HARM SHALL BEFALL YOU!
THE SILVER SURFER KNOWS NO FEAR!
WHO ARE YOU? FROM WHENCE DO YOU COME? AND WHAT IS YOUR PURPOSE HERE?
WE ARE THE BROTHER-HOOD OF BADOON!
WE COME FROM BEYOND THE FURTHEST STAR ...AND FROM A WORLD SO ANCIENT IT HAS NO NAME!

WE COME IN PEACE...TO EXPLORE..TO LEARN..TO AID THE WEAK!
THEN WHY DO YOU CONCEAL YOUR-SELF FROM THE HUMANS?
YOU KNOW OF THAT?

YES! THOUGH I BEHOLD YOU... THEY CANNOT!
IT IS MERELY A PRECAUTION... TO INSURE OUR SAFETY!
COME! FOLLOW ME!

SEE OUR CONTROL APPARATUS...OPERATED BY DEDICATED TECHNI-CIANS, EAGER TO BRING THE BENEFITS OF OUR GREAT CULTURE TO OTHER, LESSER RACES!

NOW, NOTE OUR ENGINES...
THEY GENERATE THE POWER OF A GIANT EX-PLODING SUN!
THINK HOW POWER SUCH AS THIS CAN BRING UNTOLD WEALTH TO IMPOVERISHED PLANETS!

HARM? YOU SPEAK TO ME OF HARM?

WOULD WE JOURNEY A DISTANCE BEYOND IMAGINATION... ENDURE THE RIGORS OF END-LESS SPACE... MERE-LY TO HARM ANOTHER WORLD?

WHAT WOULD BE OUR MOTIVE?

I HAVE ALWAYS BEEN MYSTIFIED BY THE MOTIVES FOR EVIL!

NOW, SURELY YOU SEE THAT WE MAY BE TRUSTED!

I TRUST ALL MEN, UNTIL--

NO! YOU MUST NOT LISTEN... YOU MUST NOT BELIEVE!

THE VOICE OF A GIRL... A HUMAN!

THEY'RE HERE TO ENSLAVE US...TO DESTROY THE EARTH!
THEY'RE MONSTERS.. WITHOUT FEELING..WITH-OUT MERCY... WITHOUT SOULS!

WHO ARE YOU? WHAT ARE YOU DOING HERE? HOW DO YOU KNOW ALL THIS?
THEY CAPTURED ME...USED ME TO TEACH THEM OUR LANGUAGE..OUR CUSTOMS...BY SOME STRANGE TELEPATHY RAY..!

I HEARD THEM SPEAK...HEARD THEIR HORRIBLE PLANS! NONE OF US ARE SAFE... ANYWHERE IN THE GALAXY!!
BUT THE WORLD MUST BE WARNED..!

THERE'S STILL TIME TO... OHHH!
YOU'RE HURT!

SO THIS IS HOW YOU SILENCE THOSE WHO WOULD OPPOSE YOU!
THIS IS HOW YOU BRING THE BENEFITS OF THE BROTHER-HOOD OF BADOON TO OTHER WORLDS!

THEN LET THE TRUTH BE OUT! WHAT DOES IT MATTER?
THE FEMALE CAN NO LONGER SPEAK! AND, AS FOR YOU...
WE HAVE OBSERVED ENOUGH TO KNOW THAT MANKIND WILL NEVER BELIEVE YOU!

THUS, YOU POSE NO DANGER TO US! WE SHALL SET YOU FREE.. FOR OUR OWN PURPOSES!
SO YOUNG... SO FAIR... SO MUCH LIKE MY OWN BELOVED SHALLA BAL.. AN ETERNITY AWAY!

WHILE WE AWAIT THE COMING OF OUR MAIN FLEET, WE SHALL AMUSE OURSELVES BY HUNTING YOU, LIKE SOME CRAVEN BEAST OF PREY!
GLOAT WHILE YOU MAY, THING OF EVIL... BUT KNOW YOU THIS...
DESPITE YOUR WEAPONS... DESPITE YOUR POWER ...WE SOON SHALL SEE WHICH OF US IS THE HUNTED...AND WHICH THE HUNTER!

BEGONE, YOU PIOUS, WHIMPERING LACKEY!
YOU HAVE 24 EARTH HOURS TO LIVE... AND THEN --THE HUNT BEGINS!

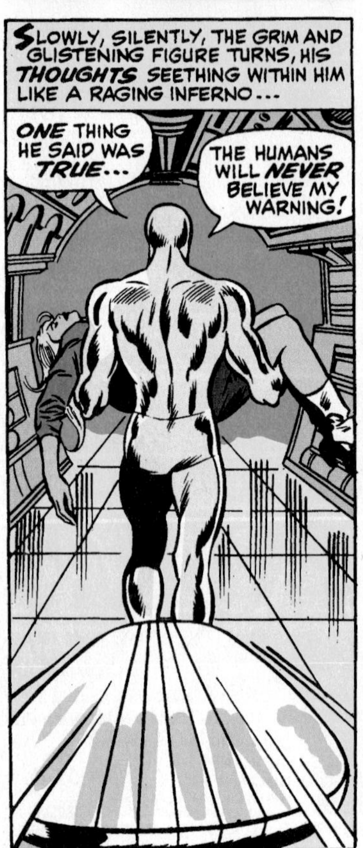
SLOWLY, SILENTLY, THE GRIM AND GLISTENING FIGURE TURNS, HIS THOUGHTS SEETHING WITHIN HIM LIKE A RAGING INFERNO...
ONE THING HE SAID WAS TRUE...
THE HUMANS WILL NEVER BELIEVE MY WARNING!

THEREFORE, IF EARTH IS TO BE SAVED... I MUST DO IT ALONE!
AND DO IT I WILL!

SOME TIME LATER...
I HAVE LOCATED OUR PREY, AS ORDERED, SIRE!
GOOD! THE HUMANS ARE FAR TOO WEAK TO AFFORD US ANY AMUSEMENT---
THEREFORE, IT IS TIME TO OCCUPY OURSELVES WITH THE SILVER SURFER!
...THOUGH WE MUST BE CAREFUL, LEST THE GAME END TOO QUICKLY!
AND NOW, LET THE ROCKET BE LAUNCHED! 
THE ATTACK BEGINS! 
BUT, IT SHALL END FAR, FAR DIFFERENTLY THAN THE BROTHERHOOD SUSPECTS!

THE ROCKET IS LIKE A LIVING THING!
TRY AS I MAY, I CANNOT ELUDE IT!
BUT, THERE IS AN EASIER WAY--!
I WILL LEAD IT BACK FROM WHENCE IT CAME!
THERE, IT CAN DESTROY THE SHIP OF... NO!
I DARE NOT!
SINCE THE ALIEN CRAFT IS BASED IN THE HEART OF THE CITY...
TOO MANY INNOCENT HUMANS WOULD BE AMONG THE VICTIMS!
THUS, WITH MY SPACE-BORN SKILL, I MUST FIND A BETTER WAY!
ALL I NEED DO IS HURTLE TOWARDS THE NEAREST MOUNTAIN!
THEN INSTANTLY DOUBLE BACK!!
IT IS DONE! THE ROCKET COULD NOT HOPE TO MATCH MY SPEED!

BROTHER ROYAL OF BADOON... I KNOW THAT YOU BOTH SEE AND HEAR ME!
THEREFORE, LISTEN WELL... FOR I AM THE POWER... AND YOU ARE THE PAWN!
YOU MAY SAVE YOURSELVES ONLY BY ABANDONING THIS PLANET... AND ORDERING THE FLEET WHICH APPROACHES TO DO LIKEWISE!
MOCKERY OF MOCKERIES!! HE DARES THREATEN ME!!
WE WAIT NO LONGER!!
NOW MUST THE SILVER SURFER PERISH!
UNLEASH THE WEAPON OF WEAPONS!!
GO! LET THE SILVER-SKINNED UPSTART FEEL THE MATCHLESS MIGHT OF...
THE MONSTER OF BADOON!

LIKE OURSELVES ... AND OUR SHIP... HE WILL ALSO BE INVISIBLE TO THE HUMANS!
BUT THE SURFER WILL SEE HIM... TO HIS LASTING REGRET!
FIRST, A MISSILE... AND NOW, A MONSTER ROBOT!
THEY MUST CONSIDER HIM FAR DEADLIER THAN THEIR PREVIOUS WEAPON!
HE GATHERS SPEED...
AND, UNLIKE THE MISSILE... HE IS CAPABLE OF THOUGHT!
BUTOOOM!
HAD I BEEN A MICROSECOND SLOWER...
HE WOULD HAVE FOUND HIS QUARRY!
MISS NORMAN... LOOK!!
THE POLICE!! CALL THEM... QUICKLY!
IT'S THE SILVER SURFER AGAIN! HE'S WRECKING THE CITY!
HE CLAIMED TO BE A FRIEND OF MANKIND'S!
WHAT'S HAPPENED TO HIM? WHY IS HE DOING IT?
THEY SHOULD JUST SHOOT HIM DOWN ...LIKE THEY WOULD A MAD DOG!

ONCE I MIGHT HAVE FELLED YOU WITH A SHRUG!
BUT, THOUGH I AM LESS THAN BEFORE... STILL AM I THE SILVER SURFER!
STILL IS MINE THE POWER COSMIC!
AS THE FURY OF THE BATTLE MOUNTS, ONE SMALL DETAIL CONTINUES TO ESCAPE THE SURFER--;
BATTLING FOR HIS LIFE, HE REMAINS UNAWARE THAT THE HUMANS CANNOT SEE HIS MONSTROUS FOE...
HE'S GONE CRAZY, I TELL YOU!
HE'S OUT TO KILL US ALL!
HE'S GOT TO BE STOPPED ...BEFORE IT'S TOO LATE!
STOP THE FLYING MURDERER!
THEY... WOULD HAVE ME FALL...
THOUGH THEIRS IS...THE FIGHT I FIGHT!
THUS, EVEN AS VICTORY DAWNS...
..IN MY HEART IS THE SORDID STENCH OF DEFEAT!

QUICKLY! RECALL THE MONSTER...
BEFORE THE SMOOTH-SKINNED DEMON DESTROYS IT!
HE WAS TO BE OUR WEAPON OF WEAPONS... AND HE SHALL BE STILL!
HE MUST NOT BE SACRIFICED TO THE ACCURSED SILVER SURFER!
MOLECULAR DISPLACEMENT RAY ACTIVATED, BROTHER ROYAL!
THE ROBOT DEMATERIALIZES... BEFORE MY VERY EYES!
HIS BASIC MOLECULAR STRUCTURE HAS BEEN INSTANTLY ALTERED!
WITHIN SECONDS... HE WILL BE GONE!
BUT, AS ONE PROBLEM SEEMS TO EVAPORATE, ANOTHER LIES A'BORNING...
TRIANGULATION CHECKS OUT! WE'VE GOT THE SURFER PIN-POINTED!
ALERT ALL UNITS, COLONEL! THIS TIME THE SURFER'S GONE TOO FAR!
WE HAVE OUR ORDERS...
THERE'S NOTHING MORE TO SAY!
WE'RE PUTTING ENOUGH FIRE POWER IN THE AREA TO LEVEL AN ENTIRE CITY!
BUT, GENERAL... HOW CAN WE BE CERTAIN..?
I JUST PRAY... WE'RE NOT WRONG... ABOUT OUR OBJECTIVE!

THE BADOON SPACE SHIP!
IS IT LEAVING?
...OR GIRDING FOR A NEW ATTACK?
A VESSEL SO LARGE... YET, NONE BUT I CAN SEE IT!

WAIT!
THE ROBOT MONSTER I FOUGHT...
CAN IT BE?
WHAT IF HE, TOO, WAS NOT VISIBLE TO THE UN-SUSPECTING HUMANS?
WOULD THEY NOT HAVE THOUGHT I WAS SEEK-ING TO SHATTER THEIR CITY?
HENCE THEIR FEAR ...THEIR SEETHING HATRED!
NOW... HOW CAN I EXPLAIN??

BUT, THE TIME FOR EXPLANATIONS, ALAS, IS ALL BUT GONE...
WHAT'S THAT? YOU SIGHTED HIM... HEADING THIS WAY?
THERE HE IS! IT'S THE SURFER!
LOOK ALIVE, MEN! THIS IS IT!
HE WON'T ESCAPE US THIS TIME!

BATTERY ONE... HUNTER MISSILES READY FOR LAUNCH!
ALL UNITS-- FIRE!
IT IS NOT POSSIBLE! IT CANNOT BE!
FIRST, OUR WEAPON OF WEAPONS IS FOUGHT TO A STANDSTILL..!
AND NOW...THEY BOMBARD US WITH ROCKETS!
OUR GREATEST WEAPON... INVISIBILITY... HAS FAILED! THEY SEE US!
NO EARTHLY MISSILE CAN HOPE TO MATCH MY SPEED!
BUT NOW THEY STRIKE THE BADOON...
...ALMOST PENETRATING THE ENEMY'S PROTECTIVE FIELD!
FULL SPEED STAR-WARD!
WE MUST FLEE THE SECTOR!

UNDER INTENSE MAGNIFICATION I CAN SEE HOW TORMENTED HE LOOKS!
BUT, I CANNOT FATHOM WHY!
FOR, THIS TIME HE IS THE VICTOR... AND WE THE LOSERS!
STILL, ETERNITY IS ENDLESS... AND THE BADOON CAN AFFORD TO WAIT!
SOONER OR LATER... WE SHALL RETURN!

BUT NOW... WE LEAVE THIS ACCURSED GALAXY... TO PLAN ANEW!
WHEN NEXT WE STRIKE, NOT EVEN THE SILVER SURFER SHALL HAVE POWER ENOUGH TO STAY OUR WRATH!
FOR, BY THEN... THE INCOMPREHENSIBLE HUMANS SHALL MOST PROBABLY HAVE SLAIN HIM---
...HIM, WHO MIGHT HAVE BEEN THEIR GREATEST DEFENDER!

NO! I'VE SEEN ENOUGH!
FRAM
ABRUPTLY THE IMAGES OF TIMES PAST BEGIN TO FADE FROM THE MINDS OF THE GUARDIANS.

VANCE, HAVE YOU GONE MAD?!? THERE'S NO TELLING HOW MUCH INFORMATION YOU'VE LOST US!
WE'VE LEARNED ENOUGH FROM THE BADOON, MARTY!

NEXT ISSUE THE ORIGIN OF STARHAWK!

READERS' SPACE

Dear Armadillo,

As you're probably noticed, this issue of MARVEL PRESENTS contains a partial reprint story — "When Lands the Saucer!", it was originally titled, I think — from SILVER SURFER #2. It's one of Stan's more interesting stories from the early sixties, one most reader's probably haven't seen, one they're sure to enjoy.

But it isn't the origin of Starhawk which we promised last issue, and for that reason, I feel I owe you (and our fellow Marvelites) an explanation.

By now, we've all heard of the Dreaded Deadline Doom — but for most readers, I suspect, it's still just a catch-phrase, a cute little bit of alliterative evasiveness. It's time we bared all, don't you think? Told the folks out there just how the ol' D.D.D. occasionally puts the screws to the best-laid Marvel machinations? Me, too.

It's this way, friends. This comic book, which you can read in, oh, fifteen minutes or so, takes an entire staff of creative and production personnel almost a month to produce. It begins with a story synopsis prepared by the writer ... which finds its way to the artist, who draws the story in pencil ... which drawings return to the writer for the completion of captions and dialogue ... and then make their way to a letterer, an inker, and finally the Marvel Bullpen for proofreading and correction.

Along the way, there are any number of SNAFUs possible. The synopsis gets lost in the mail. The artist comes down with a cold and keeps sneezing pages off the drawing board. The letterer's Rapidograph point snaps. The embellisher runs out of India ink late on a Saturday night.

But none of those happened this time.

This time, we created some whole new monkey wrenches to throw into the machinery.As you've no doubt heard, *HOWARD THE DUCK* is running for President this year. By choice, wise or otherwise, I've devoted a great deal of time to taking HTD's candidacy to the people. Radio guest-shots. Appearances at comics conventions. Meetings with Stan and Archie and Roger Stern and — just *and*. Writing press releases and Campaign Reports. Designing the HTD Button and Campaign Portrait. And pouring an inordinate amount of time and energy into shaping the Campaign Issues of the HOWARD THE DUCK magazine to something near ... I'd like to say "perfection," but the truth is, "satisfactory."

Meanwhile, natch, the jaws of Doom were chomping away at the GUARDIANS script.

Too, you may have read in the various rock magazines that Marvel has been working with the musical group KISS on a new and very revolutionary cooperative magazine project. Stan chose me to act as Marvel's envoy to the group and their management and — surprise! surprise! — this, too, consumed several weeks of precious, unrecoverable moments that might otherwise have been spent plotting and scripting the GUARDIANS OF THE GALAXY. To be sure, the KISS project will be worth every nanosecond Marvel and I have invested in it ... once it reaches fruition. But, though every moment is infinite — as Kurt Vonnegut maintains — the number of moments allotted to any human being is *decidedly* finite, and my number came up. Or, rather, the GUARDIANS' did.

And that's why there's a reprint in this issue.

Oh, sure, there are other reasons, too: writer's blocks, fatigue, occasional paralyzing exasperation with the Whole World, personal stuff (if MAN-THING were still being published, you'd probably get to read all about it there).

But the fact remains: there's a reprint in this issue, and howevermuch I try, I really can't justify it — only explain it. And apologize.

Next issue, of course, the New Stuff will be back. Al Milgrom's done a magnificent pencil job on "Breaking Up is Death to Do!", which begins the eerie tale of Starhawk's origin and his mysterious "partnership" with Aleta. And I intend to turn in a magnificent script, too, to match it. (But no promises. I'd hate to disappoint you.)

So cross your fingers and toes, keep faith in the future, and join us sixty days hence. Hopefully, we'll boggle your mind and tickle your spine and ... well, all that. And one promise I shall make, to my editors and publishers and readers alike: this won't happen again.

Thanks, Armadillo, for your indulgence.

Steve Gerber
Marvel Comics Group
575 Madison Avenue
New York, N Y 10022

P.S.: Please note that I was *so* contrite that nowhere in this letter did I mention that readers could obtain a HOWARD THE DUCK FOR PRESIDENT button for just $1.25 from — nnngh — hey! Cut it out! That paw — shredding my lower lip — aaaaagh!!

Dear Readers,

No need to worry! Steve is mending nicely already, and I'm sure he'll be back on his feet in plenty of time to finish MARVEL PRESENTS #9. And *that's* only sixty days away. Isn't modern medicine amazing? Oops! Heads up, Steve! Here comes the Night Nurse with your pill!

the Armadillo

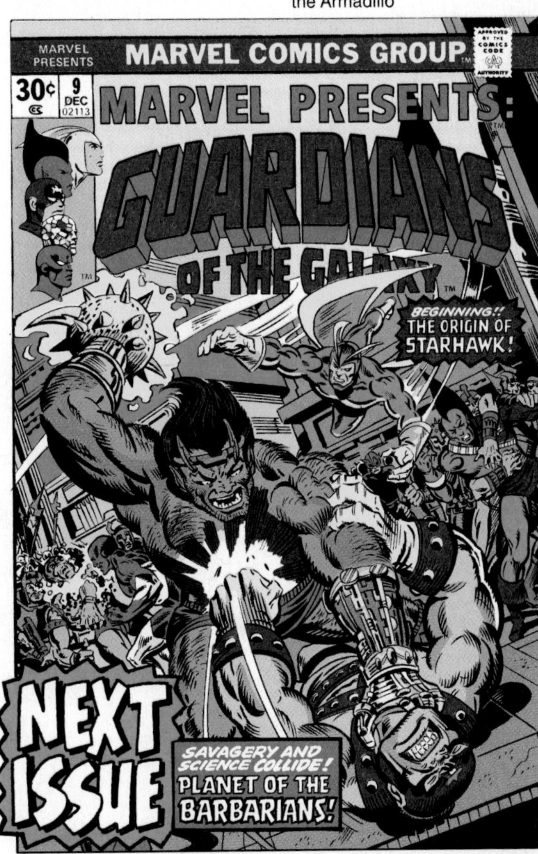

HOWARD THE DUCK CAMPAIGN UPDATE FINAL----Time is short, and so is our space. There's just enough room allotted us for this item:

----*DUCK SUPPORT SWEEPS COUNTRY!* Pie Town, New Mexico (UDI) City Father Harley D. Farnsworth last week declared his full support of the Duck. Speaking before a gathering of the West Central New Mexico Chapter of the Sons of the Sagebrush, Mr. Farnsworth said, "It's about time that this country had a candidate that truly respects the public. There's not a man among us that Howard wouldn't look up to. I say let's put him on a pedestal, and look up to him for a change!"

----For further news on the campaign, on the *Official HTD Button* and related paraphernalia, be sure to catch the next HOWARD THE DUCK letters page. And don't forget to vote!

MARVEL PRESENTS

MARVEL COMICS GROUP™

APPROVED BY THE COMICS CODE AUTHORITY

30¢

9

DEC

02113

MARVEL PRESENTS:™

GUARDIANS OF THE GALAXY™

BEGINNING!! THE ORIGIN OF STARHAWK!

SAVAGERY AND SCIENCE COLLIDE!

PLANET OF THE BARBARIANS!

Yondu of Centauri-IV. *Charlie 27* of Jupiter Colony. *Martinex* from Pluto. *Nikki* from Mercury. And Earth's thousand-year-old spaceman, *Vance Astro.* Over ten centuries from now, these last survivors of their worlds—together with the mysterious being known as *Starhawk* stalk the cosmos...this galaxy's self-appointed protectors!

HOLD IT DOWN, WILLYA, SWEETCHEEKS?! YOU'LL WAKE THE NEIGHBORS -- IN THE NEXT GALAXY!
BESIDES, IT'S NOT AS BAD AS ALL THAT!
MAYBE NOT.
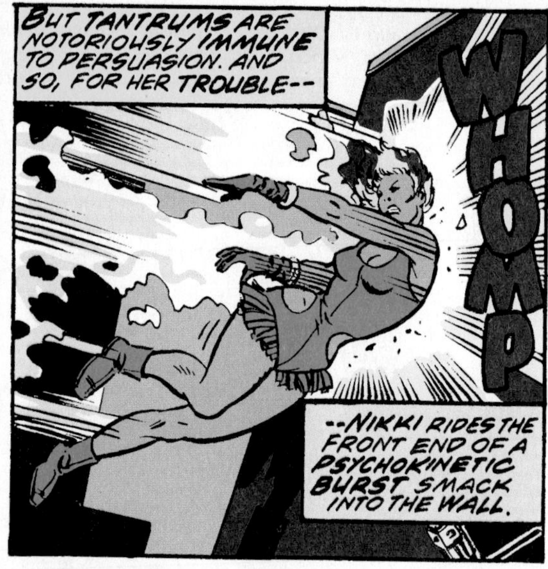
BUT TANTRUMS ARE NOTORIOUSLY IMMUNE TO PERSUASION. AND SO, FOR HER TROUBLE--
WHOMP
--NIKKI RIDES THE FRONT END OF A PSYCHOKINETIC BURST SMACK INTO THE WALL.

ONLY THEN, TYPICALLY, DOES RATIONALITY RETURN.
OH, LORD... WHAT HAVE I DONE?!
NIKKI--?

C'MON, YOU KNOW I DIDN'T MEAN-- I DIDN'T HIT YOU THAT HARD, DID I?
DID I??

NAH.
ANYONE EVER TELL YOU--YOU'RE BEAUTIFUL WHEN YOU'RE ANGRY?
NNNGPH!

YOU THINK THAT'S FUNNY?! THAT'S NOT FUNNY-- THAT'S CRUEL, BABE!
WHY? JUST CUZ YOU'D CRUMBLE WITH AGE IF YOU EVER TOOK OFF THAT GALVANIZED BODY SUIT?
I THINK IT'S ROMANTIC -- A GUY WHO'D TURN TO DUST FOR LOVE OF LI'L OLE ME!

LISTEN, YOU LITTLE TWIT -- YOU COULD HAVE SOME RESPECT FOR MY YEARS, IF NOT MY CONDITION!
SURE, GRAMPS! I-- HEY!!
WHAT THE--
THOOM!

WHO ROCKED THE BOAT?
I WAS JUST ABOUT TO FIND OUT!
MARTINEX! WHAT'S GOIN' ON UP THERE?
HAS THE SHIP BEEN HIT? OR IS CHARLIE JUST PRACTICING?

TELL HIM TO CUT THE COMEDY AND DRAG HIS BUTT UP HERE.
THERE'S YOUR ANSWER, VANCE! TO THE BRIDGE-- ON THE DOUBLE! AND BRING THE WOMEN WITH YOU!

LOOKS LIKE OUR SCENE FROM "VIRGINIA WOOLF" WILL HAVE TO WAIT, KIDDO.
SIGH
OKAY. BUT, VANCE...
... PENCIL ME IN FOR AFTER THE CRISIS, HUH?

SHORTLY, IN THE SHIP'S CORRIDOR...
WE'RE UNDER ATTACK, AREN'T WE? IT'S THE REAVERS OF ARCTURUS, ISN'T IT?
LADY, IT COULD BE BILL HALEY AND HIS COMETS FOR ALL I KNOW! WE WON'T FIND OUT...

"...TILL WE GET TO THE BRIDGE!"
THOOM!
WELL, GROUP -- THAT ONE DID IT. THEY'VE GOT US RIGHT WHERE I PRESUME THEY WANT US.

WHAT'S HE TALKING ABOUT? WHO'S GOT US?
I DIRECT YOUR ATTENTION TO THE SCREEN, MAJOR.
GERONIMO H. BALDHEADED CHRISTMAS! WHAT IS IT?
"THEY", MAJOR--
--THE REAVERS OF ARCTURUS!

WE'RE TRAPPED, VANCE --HELD FAST IN A SPHERE OF PULSATING ENERGY.
ITS RADIATION IS SLOWLY PENE-TRATING OUR HULL. ONLY A MATTER OF TIME BEFORE THE LEVELS BECOME LETHAL.
AND THERE'S NOTHING WE CAN DO TO PREVENT IT.

THE FLEET IS DISPERSING NOW... THE SHIPS ARE RETURNING TO THEIR PORTS.
BUT THE ENERGY-BUBBLE REMAINS.
WHY?

TO TEST YOUR SPECIES, MAJOR.
ONE VESSEL WILL STAY WITHIN SENSOR RANGE, MONITORING OUR LIFEFORMS, NOTING PRECISELY THE RADIATION DOSAGE REQUIRED TO KILL EACH OF US!

IT IS... THEIR STANDARD PROCEDURE FOR FIRST CONTACT WITH ANY ALIEN RACE.
KNOWING THAT -- YOU STILL INSISTED WE DETOUR TO THIS STAR-SYSTEM?
I HAD NO CHOICE.

BUT SHE'S OBVIOUSLY GOT MORE CONFIDENCE IN US THEN WE HAVE, GUYS.
YOU WEREN'T PLANNING A SUICIDE MISSION, WERE YA, HON?
NO.

IN ANY CASE, ALETA, I MUST NOW DEMAND THE FULL DETAILS OF YOUR STORY.
WHEN YOU, EH, CHANGED PLACES WITH STARHAWK, YOU MENTIONED RESCUING "THE CHILDREN." WHOSE CHILDREN? WHY?

FIRST OF ALL, MARTINEX, I DID NOT "CHANGE PLACES" WITH STARHAWK, I--
OOOH!
ALETA! WHAT IS IT? WHAT'S WRONG?

BUT THE MYSTERY WOMAN CANNOT REPLY.

ALL HER STRENGTH IS FOCUSED IN A SINGLE-MINDED, BUT FUTILE, ATTEMPT...

...TO RESIST THE OTHER.
STARHAWK!!

I DON'T GET IT! WHERE'D ALETA GO?!
NO HARM... HAS COME TO HER. SO LET US NOT DWELL UPON THE MATTER.
MERELY ACCEPT THE WORD... OF ONE WHO KNOWS.

YOU WILL NO DOUBT BE PLEASED TO LEARN THAT I HAVE BATTLED THE ARCTURANS BEFORE--
--AND THAT THEIR GLOBE OF FORCE CAN INDEED BE SHATTERED.
SO WHAT ARE WE WAITING FOR?!

PRECISELY MY POINT, MAJOR. WE CANNOT DELAY.

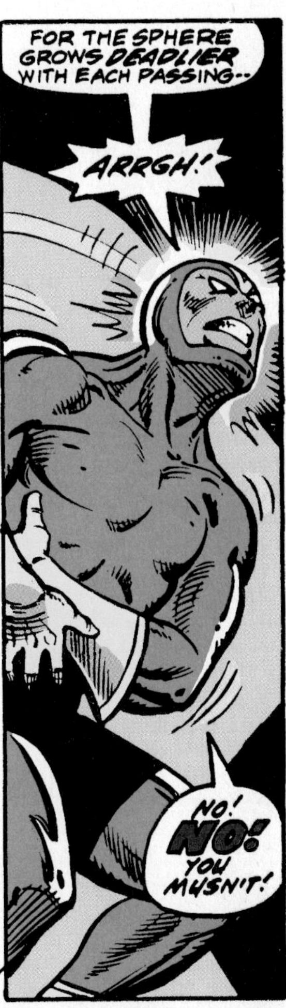
FOR THE SPHERE GROWS DEADLIER WITH EACH PASSING--
ARRGH!
NO! NO! YOU MUSN'T!

CHEEZ--NOT AGAIN! IF THIS WASN'T SO WEIRD, IT COULD ALMOST GET MONOTONOUS!
THIS IS MORE THAN JUST A RE-PEAT PER-FORMANCE, NIKKI. LOOK--

"STARHAWK'S NOT CHANGING. HE'S STILL THERE--BUT SO IS ALETA!"

AND NEITHER ONE'S A PICTURE OF HEALTH! GET 'EM TO SICK BAY!
FUNNY... HE'S LIGHT AS A FEATHER.

SICK BAY:
INCREDIBLE!
C'MON, C'MON--WHAT'S WRONG WITH 'EM? IT'S JUST LIKE THAT MALINGERING ONE-WHO-KNOWS-IT-ALL TO--

THEY'RE DYING--BOTH OF THEM--DUE TO INADEQUATE MOLECULAR DENSITY.
EACH POSSESSES ONLY HALF THE ATOMS OF A NORMAL HUMAN BODY. IT'S A WONDER THEY HAVEN'T GONE LIQUID ON US.
WOW. I'M ALL FOR TOGETHERNESS, BUT THIS IS RIDICULOUS.
ARE YOU SAYING--THEY NORMALLY SHARE THE SAME BODY?!

THE CHILDREN ...TARA...SITA... JOHN...YOU ABANDONED... THE CHILDREN...
SHE'S CONSCIOUS!

ALETA, LISTEN--YOU'RE SEPARATED FROM STARHAWK! YOU MUST TELL US--
CAN'T... WEAK...

DO NOT TRY TO SPEAK.
WE TOUCH--AS SPIRITS IN SPACE.
YES...

ABANDON THIS PLANE. COMMUNICATE WITH ME ABOVE... IN THE TIMELESS VOID.
I AM THERE...

I AM... WITH YOU...
WHAT...?
HE'S ENTERED A TRANCE STATE--HEARTBEAT REGULAR, BUT VASTLY SLOWED.

GONE TRANSCENDENTAL ON US AGAIN, HUH? TERRIFIC!

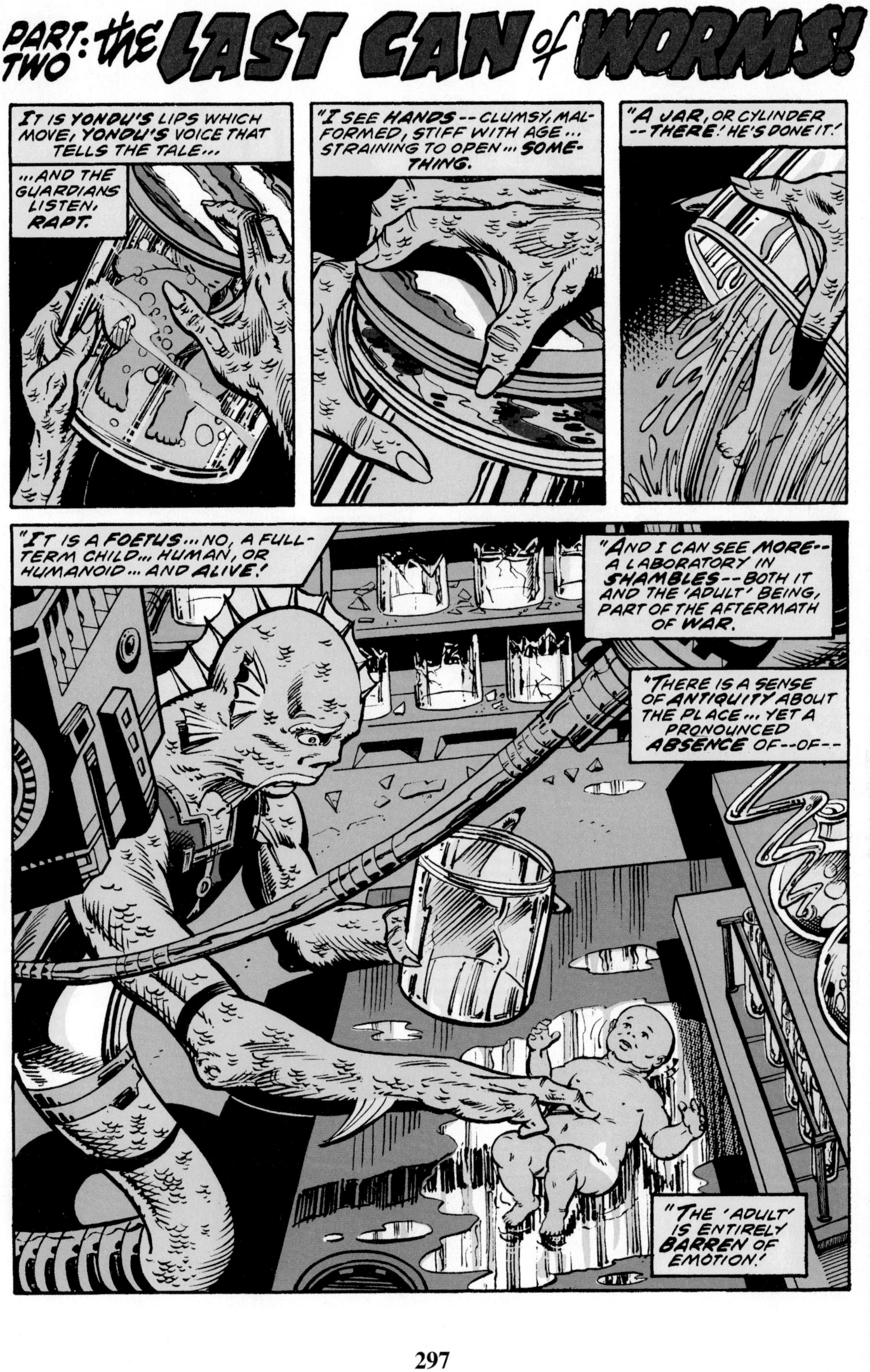

PART TWO: THE LAST CAN OF WORMS!

"IT IS A FOETUS... NO, A FULL-TERM CHILD... HUMAN, OR HUMANOID... AND ALIVE!

"AND I CAN SEE MORE--A LABORATORY IN SHAMBLES--BOTH IT AND THE 'ADULT' BEING, PART OF THE AFTERMATH OF WAR.

"THERE IS A SENSE OF ANTIQUITY ABOUT THE PLACE... YET A PRONOUNCED ABSENCE OF--OF--

"THE 'ADULT' IS ENTIRELY BARREN OF EMOTION!

"HE DEMONSTRATES NO SURPRISE, NO CONCERN, INDEED HIS INTEREST IN THE CHILD IS ALREADY SLIPPING AWAY!
"HE'S ABANDONING IT...

"... SLITHERING OUT OF THE LAB... INTO THE STREETS OF A CITY... NO! THE RUINS OF A CITY!
"THERE ARE OTHERS HERE-- UNLIKE HIM IN APPEARANCE... BUT WITH THE SAME EMPTINESS.

WHERE WERE YOU, SLEESE?
LOOKING AT THE BOTTLES.
WHAT DID YOU FIND?
NOTHING TO EAT. IT WAS ALIVE.

MAYBE IT DIED BY NOW. DID IT LOOK LIKE IT MIGHT DIE?
NO, IT LOOKED LIKE US.
SIGH THEN IT WILL PROBABLY LIVE FOREVER-- BUT I'LL CHECK.

"THERE IS A SOUND FROM ABOVE-- BUT SHE DOES NOT SEEM TO REACT!
"NONE OF THEM DO!

"THEIR CITY IS BEING INVADED--
"-- AND THEY SIMPLY DO NOT CARE!

"THE SKY-RAIDERS ARE SLAUGHTERING THEM, YET THEY MAKE NO ATTEMPT TO RESIST -- OR EVEN ESCAPE!
"THEY SEEM --RELIEVED!

"THESE ARE THE REAVERS OF ARCTURUS!

"AND THEIR SOLE PURPOSE HERE IS TO KILL!

"THEY TAKE JOY IN IT--

"--AS IF, BY SLAYING THESE PATHETIC CREATURES, THEY DESTROY SOME HATED PART OF THEMSELVES.

"THE CHILD! -- A REAVER LIFTS HIS BLADE! --
"--BUT HESITATES.

"HE MISTAKES THE INFANT FOR ONE OF HIS OWN KIND.

"OUTSIDE, THE DEVASTATION IS COMPLETE. THIS WILL BE THE REAVERS' LAST RAID ON THE RUINS.

WHERE WERE YOU, OGORD?
IN AN OLD LAB, COMMANDER.
WHAT'S THAT YOU'VE FOUND?
HE'S ALIVE, SIR!

"FLUSHED WITH PRIDE IN THEIR VICTORY, THEY BEGIN THE LONG MARCH HOME.

"AND THE CHILD BECOMES A SOUVENIR OF THE CAMPAIGN.
SALAAN! ALETA! I AM HOME! AND SEE THE BOOTY I'VE BROUGHT!

A SON, SALAAN-- A BROTHER FOR ALETA!
I TORE HIM FROM THE CLUTCHES OF A MUTANT WHO WOULD HAVE EATEN HIM ALIVE!
THE COMMANDER LET ME KEEP HIM, AS WE CAN HAVE NO SON OF OUR OWN.

WE'LL BE PROUD OF HIM, SALAAN! HE'S STRONG! HE ENDURED THE ARDUOUS TREK BACK WITHOUT SO MUCH AS A WHIMPER!!

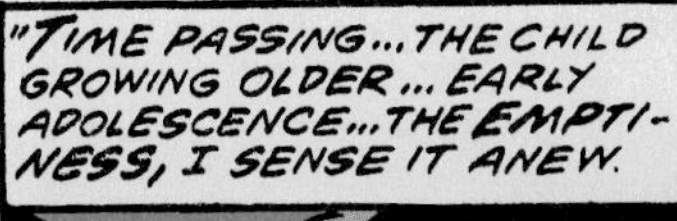
"TIME PASSING... THE CHILD GROWING OLDER... EARLY ADOLESCENCE... THE EMPTINESS, I SENSE IT ANEW.

"BUT WITH A DIFFERENCE. IT IS EMPTINESS BORN OF LONGING, OF ESTRANGEMENT.
"THE CHILD HAS BEEN A DISAPPOINTMENT TO OGORD.
STAKAR! WHAT ARE YOU LOOKING AT?

YOU SPEND SO MUCH TIME IN USELESS THOUGHT, SO LITTLE DEVELOPING YOUR BODY!
YOU'LL DIE FOR THIS FOOLISHNESS WHEN IT'S TIME FOR YOUR FIRST CONTEST!

THERE WILL BE NO FIRST CONTEST FOR ME, ALETA. HERE, LOOK.
HAVE YOU EVER WONDERED WHY THE RUINS ARE OFF-LIMITS TO US?

NO, I HAVEN'T. WE'RE NOT SUPPOSED TO WONDER. THERE'S NOTHING THERE, ANYWAY.
YOU ARE WRONG, ALETA. OUR HISTORY IS THERE--
--AND PERHAPS OUR FUTURE AS WELL.

I'M YOUR SISTER, AND I'M TELLING YOU YOU'RE GOING TO TRAIN!
I WON'T LET YOU EMBARRASS MOTHER AND FATHER FURTHER BY THROWING YOUR LIFE AWAY!
I APPRECIATE YOUR CONCERN, ALETA-- BUT IT'S MY LIFE!

HOW CAN MY BROTHER BE SO STUPID?!
I'M NOT YOUR BROTHER, ALETA-- AND ONE DAY I'LL PROVE IT TO YOU.

"AGAIN THE PASSAGE OF TIME... YOUNG MANHOOD... STAKAR FORSAKES TRADITION TO SEEK HIS OWN FIRST CONTEST...

"...THE CHALLENGE OF THE RUINS...

"...AND THEIR INNERMOST SECRETS.

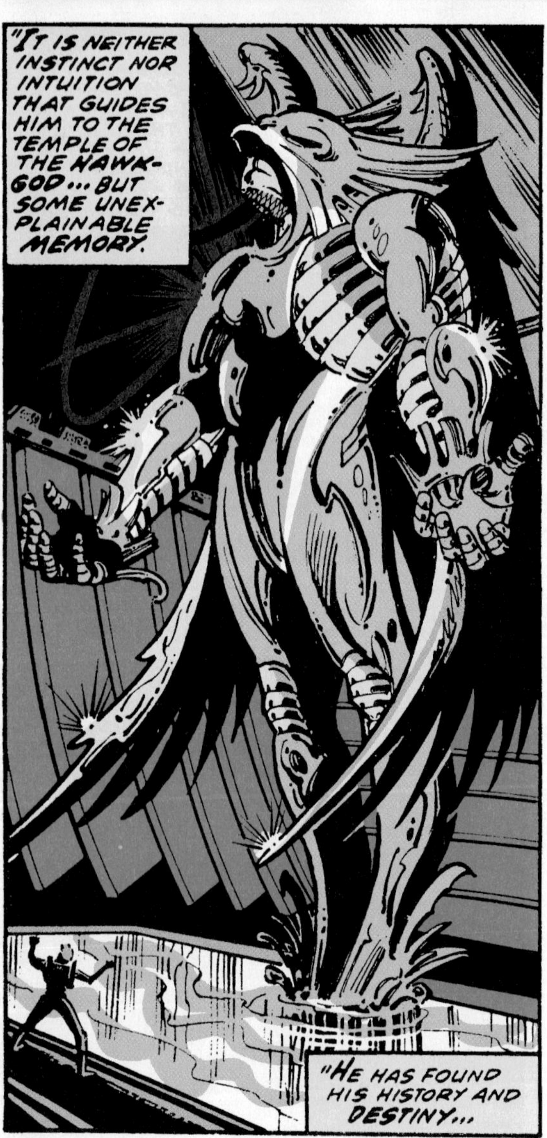
"IT IS NEITHER INSTINCT NOR INTUITION THAT GUIDES HIM TO THE TEMPLE OF THE HAWK-GOD... BUT SOME UNEXPLAINABLE MEMORY.
"HE HAS FOUND HIS HISTORY AND DESTINY...

"...AND THE WOMAN WHO WILL SHARE IT HAS FOUND HIM!
DO NOT MOVE, STAKAR.
ALETA!

I ASSUME ...YOU'VE COME TO KILL ME?
I SHOULD, YOU LITTLE FOOL-- BUT I ADMIRE YOUR COURAGE.
SO I'VE COME TO PROTECT YOU.

"THEY JOIN HANDS-- STAKAR SPEAKS--
"BUT I CANNOT HEAR--
"I CAN SEE NO MORE.

MY CONTACT IS BROKEN... THEIRS IS RE-ESTABLISHED.
THE TRUTH... HAS SOMEHOW SET THEM FREE.

TRUTH?! THAT SCIENCE FICTION CONFESSION MAG STORY?!
LOOK, FLAG-HEAD, I DUNNO WHAT THEY TOLD YOU AS A KID... BUT HOLDING HANDS DOESN'T MAKE BODIES MELT TOGETHER.
APPARENTLY, VANCE, SOMETHING DEEPER WAS COMMUNICATED --SOMETHING WE WEREN'T PRIVILEGED TO HEAR.

"AND WHATEVER CONFLICT IT RESOLVED BETWEEN ALETA AND STARHAWK...
"...IT SEEMS TO HAVE SAVED THEIR LIVES."

ALL OUR LIVES, PLUTONIAN--

--IF WE ACT SWIFTLY ENOUGH! FOLLOW ME-- TO THE TELEPORT CHAMBER.

SHORTLY...
LISTEN, PAL-- BEFORE YOU FADE AWAY-- I THINK I OWE YOU AN APOLOGY.
I NEVER DREAMED THAT BENEATH YOUR POMPOUS EXTERIOR LURKED A FELLOW FALLEN IDEALIST!

COMPUTE CO-ORDINATES FOR THE SHIP'S OUTER-HULL, MARTINEX...
...AND LOWER THE TUBE. I AM READY

"WE'RE BEING BOARDED!!"

NEXT ISSUE DEATH-BIRD RISING!

MARVEL PRESENTS

MARVEL® COMICS GROUP

APPROVED BY THE COMICS CODE AUTHORITY

30¢ 10 APR 02113

MARVEL PRESENTS:™ GUARDIANS OF THE GALA

™

Yondu of Centauri-IV. *Charlie 27* of Jupiter Colony. *Martinex* from Pluto. *Nikki* from Mercury. And Earth's thousand-year-old spaceman, *Vance Astro.* Over ten centuries from now, these last survivors of their worlds—together with the mysterious being known as *Starhawk*-stalk the cosmos...this galaxy's self-appointed protectors!

Stan Lee PRESENTS: THE GUARDIANS OF THE GALAXY! ™

DEATH-BIRD RISING!

SOME 36 LIGHT-YEARS FROM EARTH, THE **GUARDIANS** FIND THEMSELVES SURROUNDED BY AN ENERGY-BUBBLE OF HIGHLY **LETHAL** RADIATION!

AND AS IF THAT WEREN'T ENOUGH--

WE'RE BEING BOARDED!

ROGER STERN WRITER
AL MILGROM PENCILER
BOB WIACEK INKER
I. WATANABE LETTERER
JANICE COHEN COLORIST
A. GOODWIN EDITOR

BRUTAG CAN HANDLE THE BIG ONE! FRY THE REST!
SPREAD OUT! DON'T MAKE EASY TARGETS OF YOURSELVES!
ZZZZZZZZZZZK
YEOWW!

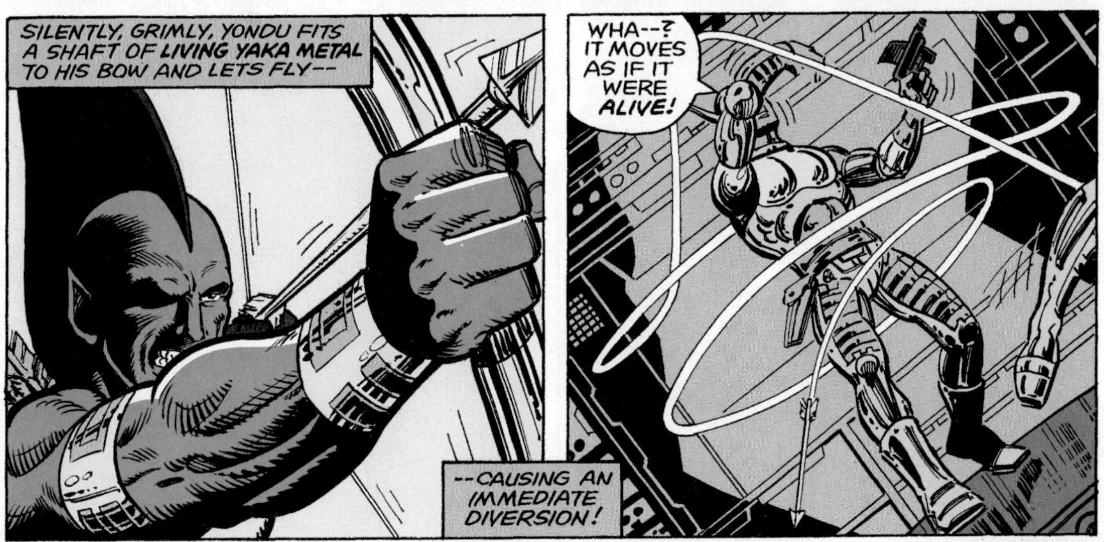
SILENTLY, GRIMLY, YONDU FITS A SHAFT OF LIVING YAKA METAL TO HIS BOW AND LETS FLY--
WHA--? IT MOVES AS IF IT WERE ALIVE!
--CAUSING AN IMMEDIATE DIVERSION!

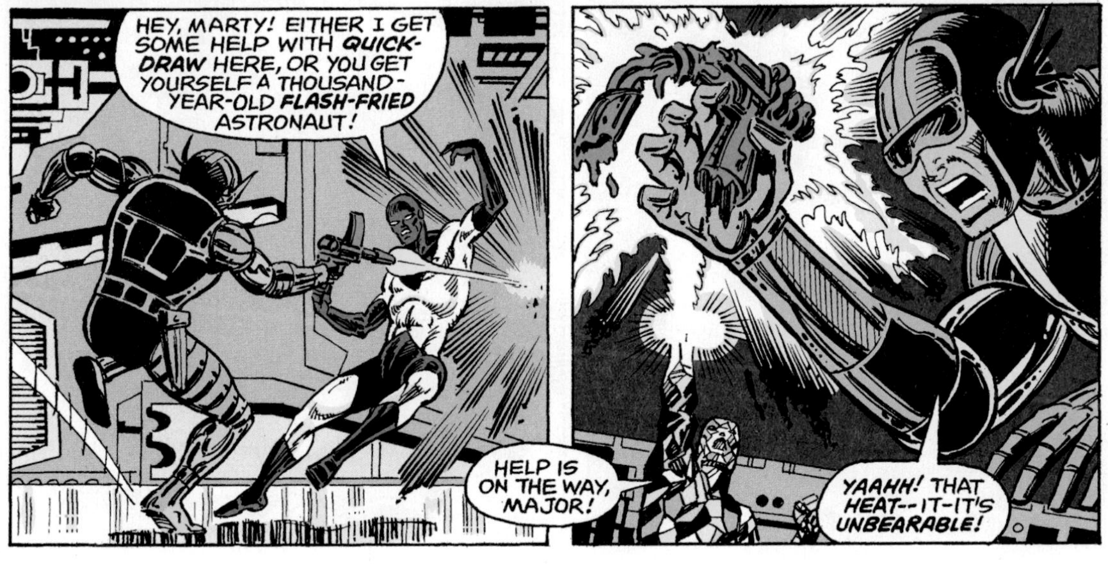
HEY, MARTY! EITHER I GET SOME HELP WITH QUICK-DRAW HERE, OR YOU GET YOURSELF A THOUSAND-YEAR-OLD FLASH-FRIED ASTRONAUT!
HELP IS ON THE WAY, MAJOR!
YAAHH! THAT HEAT--IT-IT'S UNBEARABLE!

OH, NO, YOU DON'T, SHINY! LI'L NIKKI DIDN'T SURVIVE ALONE IN THE VOID FOR SEVEN YEARS JUST TO BE WASTED BY THE LIKES OF YOU!
ULP!
AS THE NIMBLE MERCURIAN SPOILS THE INVADER'S AIM, HIS SHOT GOES WILD--
--STRIKING A SENSITIVE PIECE OF EQUIPMENT--
--WITH DRAMATIC RESULTS!
WE'VE LOST OUR GRAVITY!
MARTY, YOU HAVE A TALENT FOR STATING THE OBVIOUS! STILL, THIS LITTLE ACCIDENT DOES GIVE ME A CHANCE TO--

THAWAM!

--IT'S HOW TO BRACE MYSELF FOR FIGHTING IN FREE FALL!

OUR BACK-UP SYSTEMS ARE FINALLY KICKING IN. WE SHOULD BE BACK TO FULL G-FORCE ANY MOMENT!
NO SWEAT, MARTY--JUST AS LONG AS WE ALL REGAIN OUR FOOTING FIRST!

HMM. MOST PECULIAR! THIS ISN'T A MAN AT ALL! IT'S AN ANDROID--AND APPARENTLY ONE OF ANCIENT DESIGN!

YOU'RE KIDDING!
HARDLY, VANCE! WE'VE BEEN FIGHTING SYNTHETIC MEN! AND I'D HYPOTHESIZE THAT THE NEWEST ONE IS OLDER THAN YOU!

WELL, THAT EXPLAINS WHY "WARRIORS" WERE SENT INTO A SURE DEATH-TRAP, BUT IT STILL LEAVES A LOT UNANSWERED!
LIKE WHY DID ALETA BRING US OUT HERE TO RISK OUR NECKS AGAINST THE REAVERS OF ARCTURUS--AND WHY HAS STARHAWK LEFT US HERE TO DIE?
YEAH, ESPECIALLY--

"--SINCE THE TWO OF THEM ARE REALLY ONE BEING! JUST WHERE IS OUR BIG BLUE BOY SCOUT WHEN WE NEED HIM?"

AT THAT MOMENT, THE SUBJECT OF MAJOR ASTRO'S QUESTION IS HURTLING DEEP INTO THE ARCTURIAN SYSTEM.
ONCE HE WAS TWO SEPARATE ENTITIES--THE YOUTH STAKAR AND THE WOMAN CALLED ALETA. NOW HE IS SIMPLY THE 'ONE WHO KNOWS'.

STARHAWK!

HOW I'VE WAITED FOR THIS MOMENT! BEFORE THIS DAY IS OVER YOU SHALL FEEL THE FULL VENGEANCE OF ARCTURUS!

A THOUSAND YEARS IS A LONG TIME--EVEN TO THE LONG-LIVED ARCTURIANS WHO CELEBRATE THEIR BIRTHDAYS BY THE CENTURY.

IT WAS ABOUT A THOUSAND YEARS AGO THAT THE ARCTURIAN MUTANT STAKAR DISCOVERED THE THE TEMPLE OF THE HAWK-GOD, DEEP BENEATH A CITY'S RUIN.*

*LAST ISSUE--ARCHIE.

THIS BRAIN-WAVE HELMET JUST MIGHT BE THE ANSWER I'M LOOKING FOR.
STAKAR! A PATROL IS HEADED THIS WAY! IT'S ONLY A MATTER OF TIME BEFORE THEY FIND THIS PLACE. WE'VE GOT TO GET OUT OF HERE!

NO, I CAN'T LEAVE NOW! I'M RIGHT ON THE VERGE OF UN-LOCKING THE KNOWLEDGE OF THE ANCIENTS!

KNOWLEDGE? ARE YOU OUT OF YOUR MIND?! WHAT GOOD IS KNOWLEDGE AGAINST AN ELITE PATROL OF REAVERS?
HEY!

WE DON'T NEED KNOWLEDGE! WHAT WE NEED IS A WEAPON!
ALETA! DON'T--

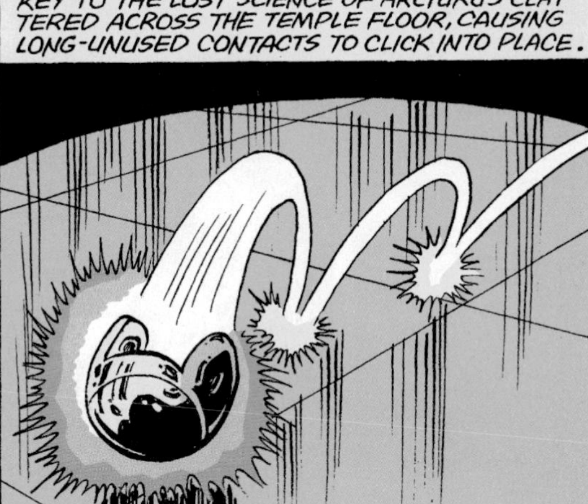
BUT STAKAR'S WARNING CAME TOO LATE! THE KEY TO THE LOST SCIENCE OF ARCTURUS CLAT-TERED ACROSS THE TEMPLE FLOOR, CAUSING LONG-UNUSED CONTACTS TO CLICK INTO PLACE.

AND AS IF IN PUNISHMENT FOR ITS RUDE TREATMENT--

--THE HELMET STRUCK BACK! BEFORE STAKAR'S DISBELIEV-ING EYES--

--ALETA'S BODY WAS CON-VERTED INTO PURE RADIANT ENERGY!

I-I HAVE POWER!

THE VOICE WAS ALETA'S--BUT IT HELD A FORCE AND AN EDGE THAT CHILLED STAKAR TO THE BONE.

POWER--DO YOU HEAR? I HAVE--I--NO! THE POWER--IT--IT'S--

--TOO MUCH! TOO MUCH POWER!!

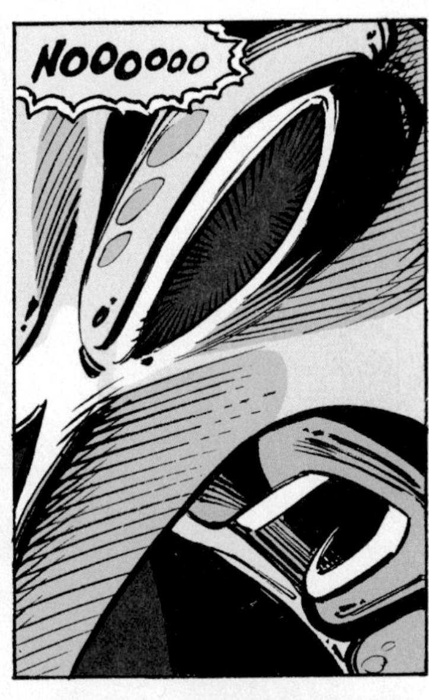
NOOOOOO

MUST GET OUT!
KERRAAM
ALETA!

MUST BE FREE!
LOOK!
WHAT THE DEVIL IS THAT?

NO, SIR! I DON'T KNOW WHERE IT CAME FROM! ALL I KNOW IS THAT THIS ENTIRE SECTOR COULD FALL--

"--IF WE DON'T GET IMMEDIATE AIR SUPPORT!"
BOGEY AT ELEVEN O'CLOCK! GO GET 'IM, BOYS!

BUT THE FLEDGLING AIR FORCE WAS IN NO WAY PREPARED FOR THE 'BOGEY' THEY FACED THAT DAY--A GLEAMING BEHEMOTH BUILT BY A LONG-DEAD, LONG-FORGOTTEN TECHNOLOGY. WITHIN MERE MINUTES, HALF OF THE ARCTURIAN PLANES WERE DESTROYED.

KAAHRREE!!
AND WITHIN THE HAWK-GOD'S METAL FORM, THE LIFE ESSENCE OF ALETA--DRIVEN TO THE BRINK OF MADNESS--CRIED OUT IN PAIN!

WHILE, ON THE GROUND...
ALETA... ALETA. IF ONLY I--

WAIT! THE HELMET! MAYBE I CAN CONTACT HER THROUGH IT!

STAKAR--HELP ME! I-I CAN'T CONTROL IT! CAN'T CONTROL--HELP!

AND IN THAT MOMENT, HE KNEW WHAT HE MUST DO!
DON'T NEED THE HELMET ANY MORE--I ONLY NEED ME! BUT I'VE GOT TO GET CLOSER!

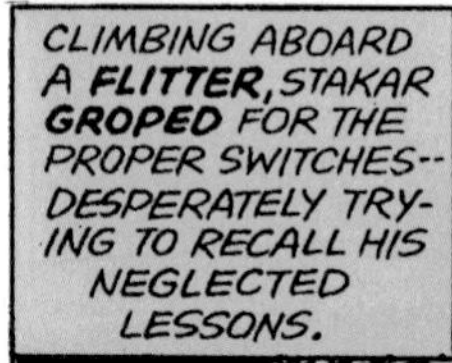
CLIMBING ABOARD A FLITTER, STAKAR GROPED FOR THE PROPER SWITCHES--DESPERATELY TRYING TO RECALL HIS NEGLECTED LESSONS.

AND THROUGH A COMBINATION OF MEMORY AND INSTINCT, HE MANAGED TO GET THE CRAFT AIRBORNE!

IN A MANNER OF SPEAKING...

NO! THAT BUILDING... COMING UP TOO FAST! I'M GOING TO HIT!

CRASH!
GLANCING OFF THE RUINED STRUCTURE, STAKAR FOUGHT THE CONTROLS FOR ALL HE WAS WORTH--

--AND LUCK BROUGHT HIM TO HIS GOAL.
VEER OFF! THAT CRAZY KID'S MORE DANGEROUS THAN THE BIRD-MAN!

ALETA! ALETA, THIS IS STAKAR!

ALETA! FIGHT IT-- YOU HEAR ME? YOU'VE GOT TO OPEN UP YOUR MIND AND FIGHT IT!
ST-STAKAR?

YES, ALETA! STAKAR! YOU MUST OPEN YOUR YOUR MIND TO ME AND LISTEN!

"THE POWER OF ARCTURUS IS IN THE HAWK-GOD, ALETA-- ALONG WITH THE KNOWLEDGE TO USE IT.
"BUT IT'S ALL WASTED-- ALL OF IT-- WITHOUT THE WISDOM TO CONTROL IT!"

WISDOM--YES! BUT HOW--?

"TOUCH YOUR MIND TO MINE, ALETA! I AM THE KEY!"
YES--I SEE IT ALL NOW! I CAN SEE IT ALL!

AND SUDDENLY, FOR THE FIRST TIME IN **CENTURIES**, THE ARCTURIAN SYSTEM WITNESSED A **MULTINUCLEAR EXPLOSION**--

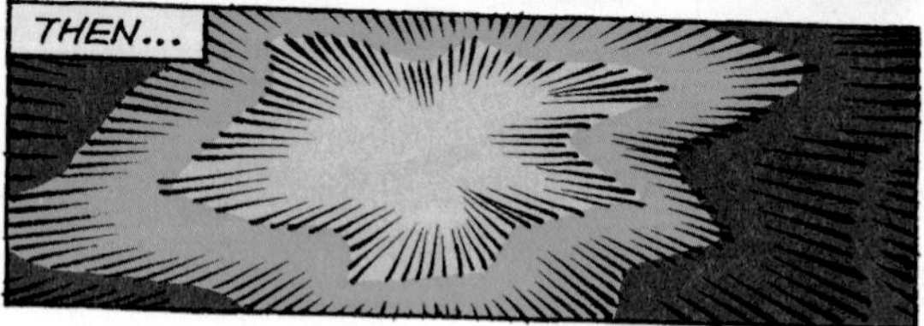

W-WHAT IS THIS? WHO--?
I AM...STARHAWK. I AM STAKAR AND ALETA, AND I AM MORE!
I AM THE WISDOM AND THE GLORY OF YOUR ANCESTORS. I AM THE LIGHT AND THE GIVER OF LIGHT. I AM YOUR HERITAGE AND YOUR DESTINY! I AM THE POWER THAT WAS ARCTURUS!
WHY--IF WHAT YOU SAY IS TRUE--THEN THE STARS ARE OURS FOR THE TAKING!
NO.
I SPEAK ONLY THE TRUTH--YET YOU STILL DO NOT UNDERSTAND! MY POWER SHALL NEVER BE USED TO CONQUER!
EH?
SOMEDAY YOU SHALL LEARN THE DEPTH OF YOUR FOLLY.
NOW I GO TO FIND MY PLACE IN THE STARS.
STARHAWK! COME BACK HERE!
"IF YOU ABANDON US NOW, I SWEAR I'LL NEVER REST UNTIL I HAVE YOUR HEAD!
"DO YOU HEAR ME, STARHAWK? DO YOU HEAR?"

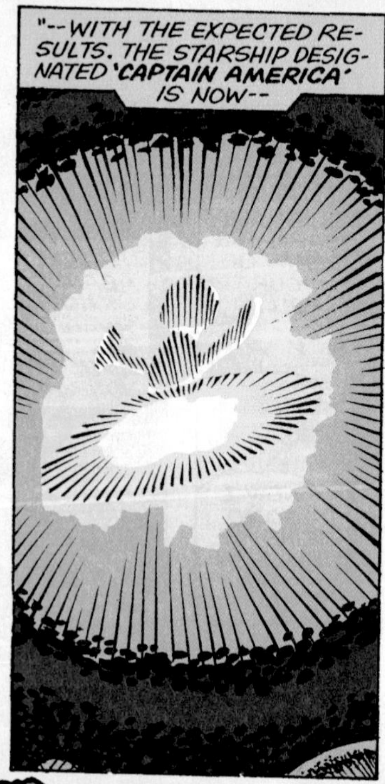

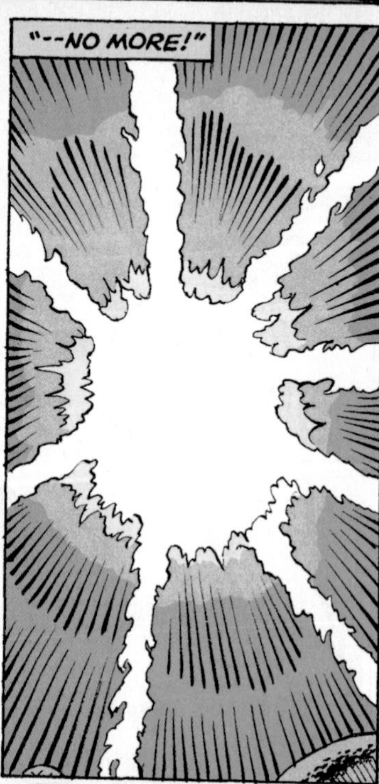

NEXT ISSUE: AT WAR WITH ARCTURUS!

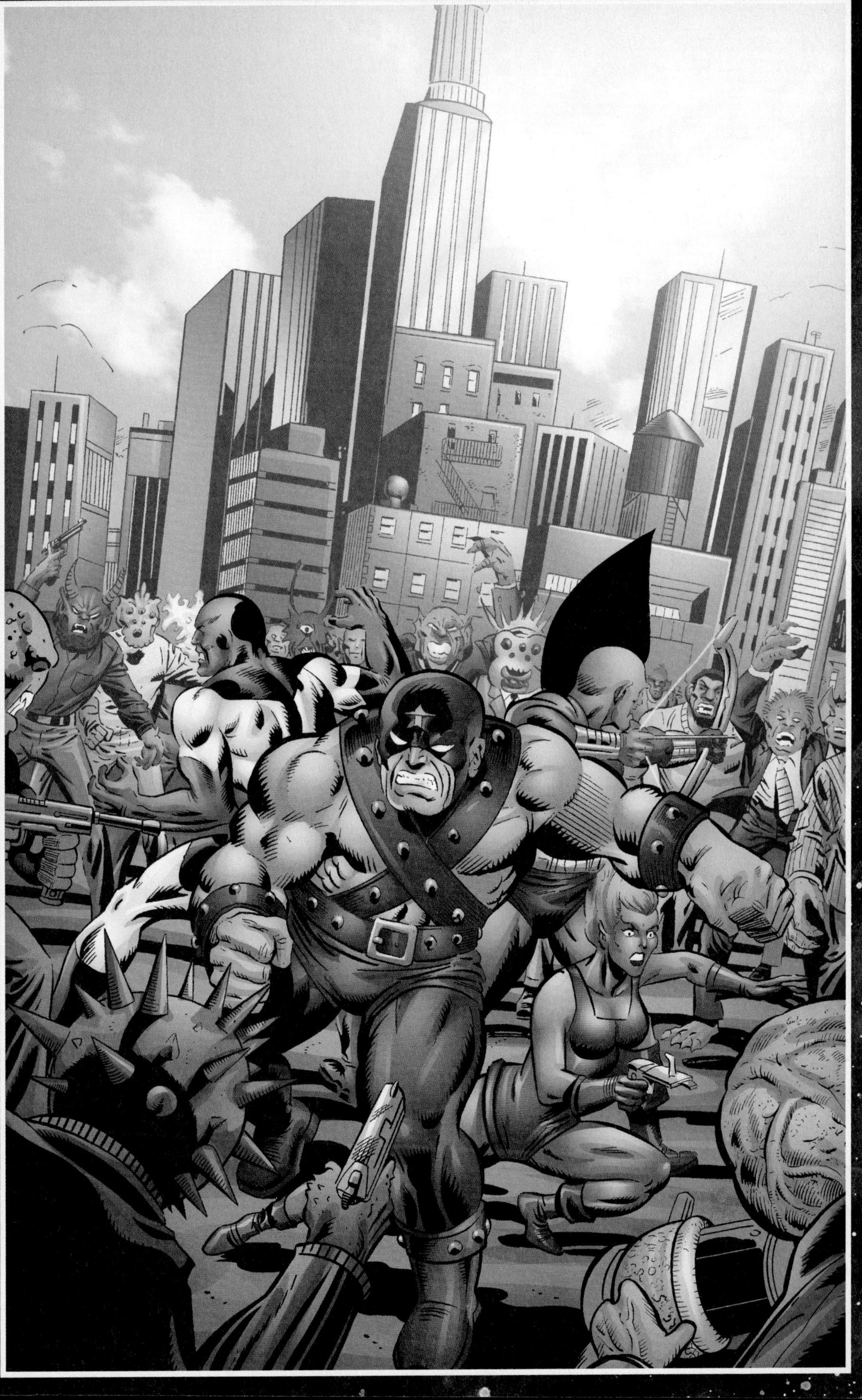

MARVEL PRESENTS™

MARVEL® COMICS GROUP

APPROVED BY THE COMICS CODE AUTHORITY

30¢ 11 JUNE 02113

MARVEL PRESENTS:™ GUARDIANS OF THE GALAXY™

THEY FEED ON THE LIFE FORCE OF LIVING BEINGS-- AND STARHAWK IS THEIR PREY!

THE PSYCHIC VAMPIRES OF ARCTURUS!

Yondu of Centauri-IV. *Charlie 27* of Jupiter Colony. *Martinex* from Pluto. *Nikki* from Mercury. And Earth's thousand-year-old spaceman, *Vance Astro.* Over ten centuries from now, these last survivors of their worlds—together with the mysterious being known as *Starhawk*-stalk the cosmos...this galaxy's self-appointed protectors!

Stan Lee PRESENTS: THE GUARDIANS OF THE GALAXY! TM

ONE-POINT-OH-SEVEN SECONDS AGO, THE GUARDIANS' STARSHIP, THE **CAPTAIN AMERICA,** WAS STRUCK BY A **PROTONUCLEIC DISRUPTOR PULSE** FROM THE ARCTURIAN SCOUT SHIP KAMMAR.

THE RESULTS OF THAT ATTACK ARE RATHER OBVIOUS.

AT WAR WITH ARCTURUS!

ROGER STERN · WRITER
AL MILGROM · PENCILER
BOB WIACEK · INKER
DENISE WOHL · LETTERER
PHIL RACHE · COLORIST
ARCHIE GOODWIN · EDITOR

REPEAT: THE STARSHIP CAPTAIN AMERICA IS NO MORE! ONLY WRECKAGE REMAINS!
VERY GOOD, KAMMAR--
"--PROCEED TO HOME ORBIT AND MAINTAIN COM-SILENCE. COMMAND OUT!"
BUT AS THE ARCTURIANS PREPARE TO GET UNDER WAY--
--ONE PARTICULAR CHUNK OF THE WRECKAGE SEPARATES FROM THE REST OF THE DEBRIS AND BEGINS TO DRIFT TOWARD THE KAMMAR--
PARDON THE INTRUSION, GENTLEMEN, BUT WE GUARDIANS THOUGHT WE'D RETURN YOUR LAST LITTLE VISIT!*
*LAST ISSUE--ARCHIE.

...UNNOTICED.
SWIFTLY, SURELY, THE STARSHIP FRAGMENT APPROACHES THE ARCTURIAN VESSEL, UNTIL IT GENTLY NUDGES AGAINST AN AFT AIRLOCK.
EH?
CLICK!
IN OTHER WORDS, WE'RE BOARDING YOU!
AWK!

I MEAN--WAR IS HARDLY EVER FOUGHT FAIRLY, BUT THOSE KILLER-ANDROIDS YOU SICCED ON US* JUST RUBBED ME THE WRONG WAY --UNDERSTAND?
*ALSO LAST ISSUE--A.

ATTABOY, CHUNKY! LET'S SHOW 'EM THAT NOBODY MESSES THE GUARDIANS OVER!

'SPECIALLY WITH DEAD-EYE NIKKI AROUND!

NOT BAD, YOUNGSTER! JUST LEAVE A LITTLE ACTION FOR THE REST OF US-- OKAY?

MAJOR ASTRO IS OVERLY MODEST, MARTINEX. IT WAS HIS PSYCHE-BLAST WHICH PROPELLED OUR ESCAPE MODULE TO THIS SHIP!
IF ANYONE IS LEFT OUT OF THIS ACTION, IT IS I!
STRANGE FEELING FOR A WEAPONS MASTER, EH?

STILL, IN A SITUATION LIKE THIS, IT'S ONLY NATURAL THAT WE HAVE CHARLIE LEAD THE WAY!
AFTER ALL, HE HAS THE MOST EXPERIENCE IN STARSHIP WARFARE!

OF COURSE, HE DOES TEND TO BE A BIT OVEREAGER.
OH, HIYA, FELLAS! GEE, THESE ARCTURIANS AREN'T MUCH OF A CHALLENGE AT ALL WITHOUT THEIR ANDROIDS.
UNNN!
OHHH!
UH-HUH.

THINK I TOOK CARE OF ALL OF 'EM--WITH THE EXCEPTION OF THE CAPTAIN HERE!
UH--YOU ARE THE CAPTAIN, AREN'T YOU?
Y-YES.

GOOD! SEEING AS HOW YOUR REAVER-BOYS SHREADED OUR SHIP, YOU CAN JUST SIT THERE AND PLAY CHAUFFEUR FOR US!
WATCH 'IM, NIKKI!
WILL DO, BIG MAN.

I'M SURE HE DOESN'T WANT ANY MORE TROUBLE. NOW, DO YOU?
OH... NO.

WELL, THESE BOYS DON'T SEEM TO BE IN THE MOOD FOR FIGHTING NOW! I'LL HAUL 'EM OFF TO THE BRIG AS THEY COME TO.
GOOD WORK, CHARLIE! WHILE YOU DO THAT--
--I'LL TRY TO FIND OUT JUST WHAT OUR 'HOSTS' WERE UP TO.

IF I CAN JUST... YES! I'VE TAPPED THE SHIP'S DATA BANKS. THE SCREEN'S FLASHING THE LAST READ-OUT THE REAVERS REQUESTED.

STAKAR
ALETA
RE: STARHAWK--COMPOSITE BEING FORMED BY THE CORPOREAL MERGER OF STAKAR AND ALETA OF THE HOUSE OF OGORD.

TIME: 1000 YEARS PAST. FEMALE SUBJECT ALETA, BY MEANS UNKNOWN, MERGED WITH HAWKGOD COMPUTER-ROBOT--A LONG-LOST ARTIFACT OF THE GENETICS WAR--AND ATTACKED FLEDGLING AIR-FORCE.

MALE SUBJECT STAKAR PURSUED THE HAWKGOD IN A STOLEN PLANE AND INITIATED MENTAL CONTACT WITH ALETA'S LIFE-FORCE WITHIN THE ROBOT--

--APPARENTLY CAUSING THE HAWKGOD'S HYPER-ENERGIZED FORM TO ACHIEVE FISSION.

POST-HOLOCAUST INVESTIGATION BY SUBJECTS' PARENT OGORD UNCOVERED THE CREATION OF A NEW BEING-- STARHAWK--WHO WAS BOTH STAKAR AND ALETA, WITH ALL THE POWER AND KNOWLEDGE OF THE HAWKGOD.

SUBJECT STARHAWK DISOBEYED ORDERS TO STAY AND AID ARMED FORCES--LEAVING ARCTURUS-IV TO ROAM THE STARS.

TIME: 500 YEARS PAST. EARLY ARCTURIAN STARSHIP ATTEMPTED A FIRST CONTACT SEIZURE OF AN ALIEN AIRCRAFT.

ATTEMPT WAS FOILED BY STARHAWK'S INTERVENTION.
STARHAWK'S DEATH WAS SUBSEQUENTLY DECLARED A FLEET IMPERATIVE.

TIME: 2 DAYS PAST. AN ELITE REAVER STARSHIP STUMBLED UPON STARHAWK'S ASTEROID LAIR AND DISCOVERED THE EXISTENCE OF HIS THREE CHILDREN.

THE CHILDREN WERE CAPTURED FOR DEBRIEFING UNDER DIRECT ORDERS FROM HIGH COMMANDER OGORD.

SUBSEQUENT TESTING SHOWED CHILDREN TO POSSESS LATENT POWER OF UNUSUAL STRENGTH. THROUGH IMPLEMENTATION OF MENTAL CONTROL, THEY HAVE BEEN PRESSED INTO IMPERIAL SERVICE.
SUCH POWER --IT-IT IS UN-THINKABLE!

"THEIR ASSIGNED TASK IS THE DEATH OF STARHAWK."
OMIGOD! I THINK THEY CAN ACTUALLY DO IT!

MEANWHILE, PARSECS AWAY, STARHAWK KNIFES THROUGH THE VOID, HIS SOLAR SAILS SWELL-ING WITH THE STAR WINDS.
DEEP WITHIN HIS SOUL, THE VOICE OF ALETA CRIES OUT-- "THE CHILDREN... SAVE THE CHILDREN!" --AND HIS ALREADY INCREDIBLE SPEED INCREASES.

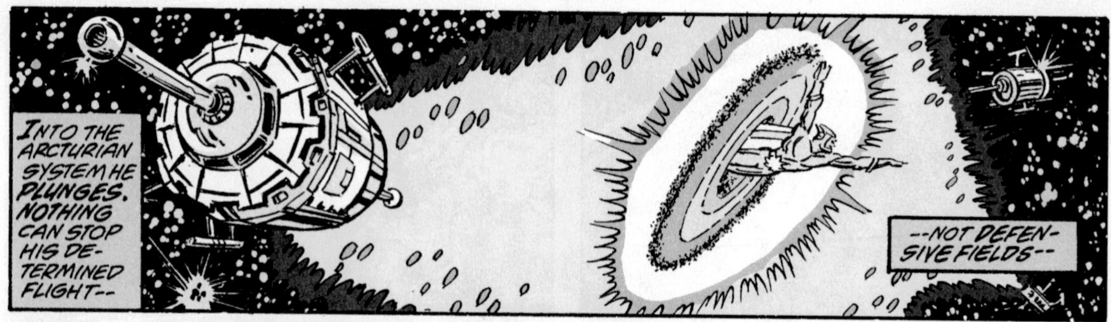
INTO THE ARCTURIAN SYSTEM HE PLUNGES. NOTHING CAN STOP HIS DETERMINED FLIGHT--
--NOT DEFENSIVE FIELDS--

--NOT SPACE MINES--

--NOT EVEN ELITE ARCTURIAN STARSHIPS! THE OBSTACLES BARRING HIS PATH EITHER FALL BEFORE HIS STAR-SPAWNED MIGHT, OR ARE SWEPT ASIDE EASILY.
PERHAPS-- HE CONSIDERS --TOO EASILY.

HA-HA-HA! THE GREAT STARHAWK! HE FLIES INTO A TRAP THAT A RECRUIT WOULD NOT FALL FOR.
WHY... YOU--!
VANCE! NO! HOLD YOUR ANGER! WE NEED HIM TO PILOT THIS SHIP!
WHAK!

BALONEY! IF MARTY CAN MAKE THAT COMPUTER SING, THEN HE CAN FIGURE OUT THE CONTROLS ON THIS HEAP!
AND WITHIN MOMENTS THE CAPTURED SHIP KAMMAR IS CAREENING ALONG STARHAWK'S TRAIL AT LIGHT-ANNIHILATING SPEED.
COME ON, WE'VE GOT US A GUARDIAN TO SAVE!

VANCE'S EMOTIONAL EXTREMES ARE BECOMING MORE PRONOUNCED. HE'S STARTING TO WORRY ME.
EASY, MARTY! WE WANT TO GET THERE IN ONE PIECE!
I'M DOING MY BEST, VANCE!
WITH A LITTLE LUCK WE'LL MAKE IT! I JUST HOPE I DON'T MAKE A MISTAKE WITH THESE UNFAMILIAR CONTROLS THAT GIVES US AWAY TO OTHER ARCTURIAN CRUISERS.

BUT IF APPROACHING ARCTURIAN SHIPS NOTICE ANYTHING ERRATIC IN THE FLIGHT OF THE KAMMAR, THEY PAY IT NO MIND--UNTIL IT IS TOO LATE.

NOR DO THE DRONE DEFENSE CRAFT ORBITING ARCTURUS-IV FARE ANY BETTER AGAINST THE IRRESISTIBLE FORCE OF STARHAWK'S COHERENT-LIGHT BURSTS.

DOWNWARD DIVES THE COSMIC GUARD-IAN. THE ATMOSPHERE FAIRLY SIZZLES AS HE HURTLES UNERRINGLY TO HIS GOAL.
OGORD! I HAVE RETURNED!
WELL! STARHAWK! BACK AGAIN, AFTER ALL THESE YEARS!
I HAVE NOT COME TO PLAY YOUR POWER GAMES, FATHER!
I WANT MY CHILDREN!
WHY, OF COURSE, YOU DO! AND I'VE BEEN TAKING VERY GOOD CARE OF THEM! HERE-- SEE FOR YOUR-SELF!
STARHAWK FREEZES! THERE IS SOMETHING WRONG HERE-- SOMETHING BEYOND EVEN HIS EXPERI-ENCE--
--SOMETHING ...SINISTER.

TARA... SITA... JOHN! DON'T YOU RECOGNIZE ME?
BUT OF COURSE THEY DO! WELCOME YOUR PARENT, CHILDREN!
WELCOME HIM WITH--
"--DEATH!"
HA-HA-HA! WEAKNESS ILL BECOMES YOU, OFFSPRING!
COULD IT BE THAT THE MIGHTY ONE-WHO-KNOWS WAS UNAWARE OF HIS OWN CHILDREN'S POWER?
OR DID YOU JUST REFUSE TO BELIEVE THAT THEY COULD EVER BECOME PSYCHIC VAMPIRES-- FEEDING ON THE LIFE-FORCES OF OTHERS!
YOU... DID THIS TO THEM?

THE POWER WAS ALREADY THEIRS, STARHAWK! I MERELY RELEASED IT. OH, YES--THE CHILDREN ARE VERY MUCH UNDER MY CONTROL--
--AND AT MY COMMAND, THEY SHALL BEGIN TO STEAL AWAY YOUR VERY SOUL!

TARA... SITA... JOHN... YOU WOULDN'T--!

OGORD'S RESPONSE IS LAUGHTER! "STRIKE HIM DOWN, YOUNG ONES! KILL STARHAWK!"

TOO WEAKENED TO FLEE, STARHAWK REELS UNDER THE FORCE OF A POWER HE CANNOT LONG ENDURE. IF HE WOULD LIVE, HE MUST DESTROY HIS OWN CHILDREN!

BUT AT THAT MOMENT, A FAMILIAR FORM DARKENS THE SKIES OUTSIDE...

SKAK! KRAM!

AND IF THE FIELD GROUND CREW WAS CAUGHT OFF GUARD BY THE KAMMAR'S SURPRISE LANDING, THEY ARE EVEN LESS PREPARED TO RESTRAIN ITS FIVE DISEMBARKING PASSENGERS...

I'VE GOT A READING ON STARHAWK! HE'S IN THAT COMPLEX JUST AHEAD!

LEAD ON, MARTY! WE'RE RIGHT BEHIND YOU!

AND INSIDE THAT COMPLEX...
CHILDREN-- NO! STOP!

HIS STRENGTH DRAINING AWAY, STARHAWK'S CONSCIOUSNESS BEGINS TO FADE--AND DEEP WITHIN HIS PSYCHE, ANOTHER PERSON FIGHTS TO TAKE OVER--
YOU... MUST LISTEN... TO ME! I... AM...

--CHANGING AND MOLDING THE BODY TO FIT THE MIND OF ALETA!
...YOUR MOTHER! TARA... SITA... JOHN... PLEASE! YOU... MUST REMEMBER--!

THE THREE CHILDREN DO NOT ANSWER--THEIR ENTRANCEMENT IS COMPLETE. THEY CAN ONLY STAND STOCK STILL--ZOMBIE-LIKE--LEECHING AWAY THE INCREDIBLE LIFE FORCE FROM THIS BEING WHO IS TRULY BOTH FATHER AND MOTHER TO THEM.

AND AS THEY ABSORB THAT POWER, THEY BEGIN TO CHANGE INTO THE BEINGS THEY MIGHT ONE DAY BECOME.

YOUTH YIELDS TO ADULTHOOD, AND 20 YEARS FALL AWAY IN MERE SECONDS.

BUT THEN...
CHOOM!
WHAT?
HEADS UP, PEOPLE! WE'RE HERE!

CHILDREN! CONTINUE YOUR ATTACK, BUT PROTECT YOURSELVES AT ALL COSTS!

AND AT THE COMMAND OF OGORD, A FORCE FIELD OF RADIANT ENERGY SPRINGS UP AROUND ALETA AND HER TORMENTORS.

C'MON, CHARLIE! WE'VE GOT TO GET LADY BLUE OUT OF THERE!
I'M TRYING, VANCE!

LOOKS BAD, MAJOR! NEITHER EXTREME HEAT NOR COLD ARE WEAKENING THE FIELD!
BUT WE MUST FREE HER! WE MUST! THIS CRIME MUST NOT CONTINUE!

AND WHILE THE GUARDIANS BATTLE VAINLY, STARHAWK-- WITH A LAST DESPERATE BURST OF WILL--RESUMES THE BODY.
GUARDIANS ...STAY BACK. IT IS... HOPELESS.

THE BLAZES IT IS! CHARLIE! LAY OFF THE FORCE FIELD! MAYBE WE CAN'T STOP THESE THREE STOOGES, BUT WE CAN GET THEIR BOSS!
HUH? WHERE?

OVER THERE! THE OLD GEEZER IN CHARGE-- OGORD! HE ISN'T PROTECTED BY ANY FIELD! LEAN ON'IM!
WILL DO, SQUIRT!
OH, NO.

NO--DON'T! STOP!

AT THE SOUND OF THE HASTY SHOUT, THE CHILDREN SUDDENLY STOP DEAD--THEIR PROTECTIVE FIELD FADING INTO NOTHINGNESS.

VANCE! THOSE HEAD-BANDS-- THEY ARE KEEPING THESE PEOPLE IN THRALL! I-I KNOW IT!

WELL, THEY WON'T MUCH LONGER!

AND WITH A BOLT OF ENERGY THAT MOVES WITH THE SPEED OF THOUGHT, VANCE ASTRO KNOCKS THE HEAD-BANDS OFF THEIR RESTING PLACES--

NEXT ISSUE THE GUARDIANS FACE DANGER AND DESTINY IN... The SHIPYARD of DEEP SPACE

MARVEL PRESENTS ™

MARVEL® COMICS GROUP

APPROVED BY THE COMICS CODE AUTHORITY

30¢ 12 AUG 02113

MARVEL PRESENTS: GUARDIANS OF THE GALAXY™

THE GUARDIANS' LAST STAND

Yondu of Centauri-IV. *Charlie 27* of Jupiter Colony. *Martinex* from Pluto. *Nikki* from Mercury. And Earth's thousand-year-old spaceman, *Vance Astro.* Over ten centuries from now, these last survivors of their worlds—together with the mysterious being known as *Starhawk*-stalk the cosmos...this galaxy's self-appointed protectors!

Stan Lee PRESENTS: THE GUARDIANS OF THE GALAXY!™

PROLOGUE:

STARHAWK'S CHILDREN ARE **DEAD**--REDUCED TO DUST BY THEIR OWN **VAMPIRIC POWERS** BEFORE THE EYES OF THE GUARDIANS. NOW, WITH STARHAWK CRITICALLY-- PERHAPS **MORTALLY**-- WEAKENED, THE GUARDIANS ARE FACED WITH THE TASK OF ESCAPING FROM **ARCTURUS-IV**-- A PLANET WHICH IS VIRTUALLY AN **ARMED CAMP.**

I'VE **GOT** HIM, YANCE!

TAKE IT **EASY** WITH HIM, CHARLIE! WE'LL KEEP YOU **COVERED!**

LET'S GET **OUT** OF HERE! THIS PLACE GIVES ME THE **CREEPS!**

A **ROGER STERN-ALLEN MILGROM** CO-PRODUCTION
INKED BY **BOB WIACEK**
LETTERED BY **I. WATANABE**
COLORED BY **PHIL RACHE**
EDITED BY **ARCHIE GOODWIN**

C-CHILDREN? YOU **CAN'T** BE DEAD! WE--WE HAVE A **UNIVERSE** TO CONQUER!

THROUGH DESERTED STREETS AND ALLEYWAYS THE FIVE RUN-- THE PITIFUL WAILINGS OF HIGH COMMANDER OGORD, THE CHILDREN'S DERANGED GRANDFATHER, ECHOING WITH THEIR FOOTSTEPS.

AT THE EDGE OF THE ARCTURIAN AIR FIELD, A HOME GUARD OF ELITE REAVERS STANDS READY TO RESIST THIS LAST CHARGE OF THE GUARDIANS--

--BUT NOT FOR LONG!

SO IT IS THAT, QUITE SHORTLY, THE GUARDIANS REACH THEIR COMMANDEERED SHIP--
HEY, PEOPLE--IT LOOKS LIKE THE REAVER CREWMEN HAVE ESCAPED!
GOOD! CHECK FOR BOOBY TRAPS AND LET'S SPLIT!

--AND LIFT OFF FROM THE SOMEWHAT RUINED AEROSPACE FACILITY.*
*RUINED JUST LAST ISSUE BY THE GUARDIANS' HASTY LANDING--ARCH.

WHY ARE WE JUST STANDING AROUND? WHY DON'T WE TRY TO STOP THEM?
STOP THEM WITH WHAT? THEY'VE ROUTED THE HOME GUARD, BROKEN THE HIGH COMMANDER--

--AND DECIMATED THE FLEET! YOU WANT TO STOP THEM? BE MY GUEST! AS FAR AS I'M CONCERNED, THEY CAN'T GET FAR ENOUGH AWAY!

AND SO, THE SCOUT-SHIP KAMMAR-- WITH THE LAST FRAGMENT OF THE STARSHIP CAPTAIN AMERICA STILL DOCKED AMIDSHIPS--LEAVES THE ARCTURIAN SYSTEM WITH RELATIVE EASE.

BUT, ABOARD SAID VESSEL...
LOOK, MARTY, WHY DON'T YOU LET ME RELIEVE YOU AT THE CONTROLS? I CAN FLY THIS HEAP!
ALL RIGHT, CHARLIE--YOU PROBABLY ARE THE BETTER PILOT. JUST KEEP HER ON A HEADING FOR SOL, AND GIVE HER ALL THE SPEED YOU CAN.

I, IN THE MEAN-TIME, MUST HELP YONDU CARE FOR STARHAWK.
HOW IS HE?
NOT GOOD. HE'S FADING.

ISN'T THERE ANYTHING WE CAN DO, CHARLIE?
VANCE, RIGHT NOW OUR BEST OPTION IS TO SEND OUT A WIDE-BAND DISTRESS CALL--

--AND PRAY.

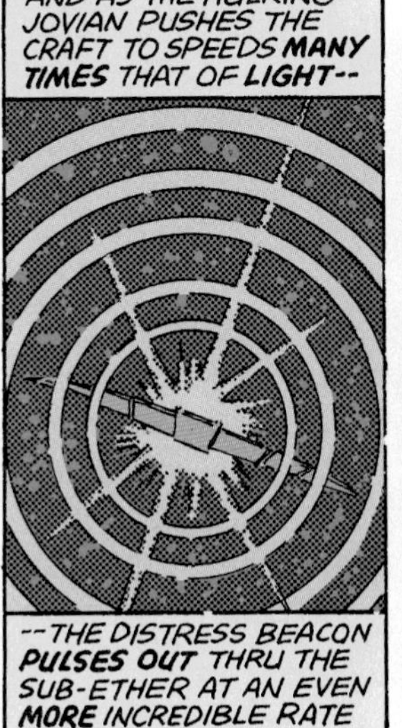
AND AS THE HULKING JOVIAN PUSHES THE CRAFT TO SPEEDS MANY TIMES THAT OF LIGHT--
--THE DISTRESS BEACON PULSES OUT THRU THE SUB-ETHER AT AN EVEN MORE INCREDIBLE RATE

UNTIL FINALLY...
HEY! WHOA! WE'RE GETTING A RESPONSE!
WHAT'S THE READING, NIKKI?
ONE-OH-FIVER! WE MUST BE RIGHT ON TOP OF IT!

FUNNY! THE SIGNAL SEEMS TO BE COMING FROM THAT PLANET BELOW-- BUT SENSORS DON'T SHOW ANY SIGNS OF LIFE!
WAIT-A-MINUTE! COMING UP OVER THE HORIZON--! IT'S--BUT IT CAN'T BE!
IT-IT'S DRYDOCK!
DRY- WHAT?
DRYDOCK, NIKKI-- THE FEDERATION STARSHIP-YARD! I SPENT MOST OF MY BASIC TRAINING THERE! BUT WHAT'S IT DOING OUT HERE? IT WAS REPORTED LOST DURING THE WAR!
PUTTING HIS QUESTIONS ASIDE, CHARLIE FIRES THE SHIP'S RETRO-BANKS, SLOWING THE KAMMAR.
WE'RE IN LUCK--

THE SHIPYARD OF DEEP SPACE!
--THE AUTOMATIC DOCKING CYCLE'S BEEN ACTIVATED! HANG ON, WE'RE GOING IN!

JUST WHAT ARE WE GOING TO **FIND** HERE, CHARLIE?
HOPEFULLY, A FUNCTIONING **SICK BAY**, VANCE. DRYDOCK IS UNDOUBTEDLY A **DERELICT**, OPERATING ON AUTOMATIC PROGRAMMING.

OF COURSE, I COULD BE **WRONG!**
COME ON, SOLDIER! **MOVE IT!**
WESNER! FOLLOW ME--ON THE **DOUBLE!**

THE COMMANDER'S OFFICE IS JUST DOWN THIS CORRIDER. I'M SURE YOU'LL... AH, BUT I'M FORGETTING MYSELF! YOU'D PROBABLY LIKE TO FRESHEN UP AFTER YOUR JOURNEY!
WELL...
PLEASE FEEL FREE TO MAKE USE OF THESE AUTO-VALET CHAMBERS. I'LL BE BACK FOR YOU SHORTLY.

COMING, VANCE?
NO...NO, THAT'S ALL RIGHT. I'LL SIT THIS ONE OUT. MY SKIN CONDITION-- REMEMBER?
OH... YEAH.
JUST HANG OUT! WE WON'T BE LONG.

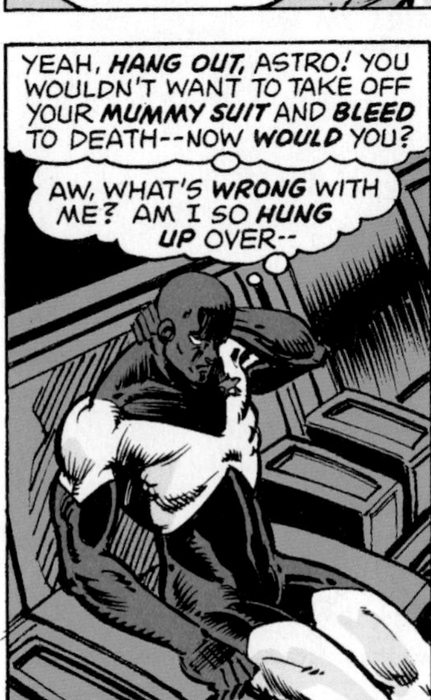
YEAH, HANG OUT, ASTRO! YOU WOULDN'T WANT TO TAKE OFF YOUR MUMMY SUIT AND BLEED TO DEATH--NOW WOULD YOU?
AW, WHAT'S WRONG WITH ME? AM I SO HUNG UP OVER--

TA-DAH!
HUH? NIKKI!

IN THE FLESH! HOW DO YA LIKE THE NEW THREADS?
THEY DON'T LOOK ALL THAT DIF-FERENT FROM YOUR OLD ONES.
WELL, WHY KNOCK A WINNING COMBO?

DOES THAT MEAN I SHOULD HAVE PASSED UP MY NEW DUDS?
HEY-HEY! GET A LOAD OF CHUNKY!

HAH! YOU LOOK JUST LIKE A FOOTBALL PLAYER!
FOOTBALL? WHAT'S THAT, VANCE?
WHO CARES? YOU LOOK GREAT, BIG MAN! WHY'D YOU EVER PUT ON A MASK?

WELL, GEE...'CAUSE I LIKE IT, I GUESS. GIVES ME A LITTLE CLASS, Y'KNOW!
YEAH-- ALL LOW!

HEY, YOU TWO! KNOCK IT OFF! WE'VE--
UH... MAJOR? IF YOU'RE READY, THE COMMANDER WILL SEE YOU NOW.

AND SO...
SIR? MAJOR ASTRO AND HIS PARTY ARE HERE!
VERY GOOD, KIRTLEY! YOU MAY GO.

I HOPE YOU'LL EXCUSE ME FOR NOT BEING ON HAND TO GREET YOU UPON DOCKING, GENTLEMEN ...LADY.
HEY, YOU'RE--!

HOLLIS-12, COMMANDER OF DRYDOCK. DON'T ACT SO SURPRISED, MISTER. YOU WEREN'T THE ONLY JOVIAN IN THE MILITIA, YOU KNOW!
ULP... SIR! I'M SORRY... I--!

BELAY THAT, SOLDIER! THE WHOLE SERVICE IS PROUD OF THE COMBAT RECORD OF CHARLIE-27!
I--UH-- THANK YOU, SIR!

BAH! ENOUGH OF FORMALITIES! I SUPPOSE YOU'RE WONDERING JUST WHAT DRYDOCK IS DOING OUT HERE IN THE MIDDLE OF NOWHERE.
WELL, IT DID CROSS OUR MINDS.

ACTUALLY, WE'RE HERE BY ACCIDENT. WHEN THE BADOON ATTACKED IN THE EARLY DAYS OF THE WAR, WE WERE IN THE MIDST OF DEVELOPING A NEW WARP-DRIVE. SO, RATHER THAN LET IT BE CAPTURED--
YOU USED IT TO BLAST DRYDOCK OUT OF THE SOLAR SYSTEM! BRILLIANT!

WELL...NOT TOO BRILLIANT! THE NEW DRIVE WAS DEFECTIVE. IT BURNT OUT AND STRANDED US HERE-- IF YOU GET MY DRIFT.
STRANDED... DRIFT--? OH, NO! HA-HA-HA!

HAH! COMMANDER HOLLIS, YOU ARE...
NOT REAL?

WHAT THE **TANJ** IS GOING **ON** HERE? YOU'RE NO **JOVIAN!** YOU'RE JUST A--

--HOLO GRAMM

CHARLIE!

ALL **RIGHT,** HOLLIS! YOU'VE GOT JUST **FIVE SECONDS** TO RELEASE CHARLIE AND **EXPLAIN** YOURSELF!

I **AM** SORRY ABOUT THIS, MAJOR--

"--BUT I'M AFRAID YOU'RE IN **NO** POSITION TO MAKE **DEMANDS.**"

SSSSSSS

BUT AS THE **ANESTHETIC GAS** TAKES EFFECT ON VANCE AND NIKKI--

PTANG

--CHARLIE'S MIGHTY **JOVIAN MUSCLES,** CONDITIONED BY A GRAVITY **ELEVEN TIMES** THAT OF EARTH'S, SNAP HIS BONDS--

--**TOO LATE!** BEFORE HE CAN GRAB FOR A **HANDHOLD,** CHARLIE FINDS HIMSELF PLUNGING DOWN A **CENTRAL UTILITY SHAFT.**

WHOOOAA

ALL HIS YEARS OF TRAINING COME TO THE FORE AS, TWISTING AND TURNING, THE GUARDIAN TRIES TO STOP HIS FALL--

AH, BUT YOU'RE PUZZLED ABOUT ME I SEE. IT'S NO GREAT MYSTERY. ALL I TOLD YOU ABOUT THE NEW WARP-DRIVE WAS TRUE-- BUT IT DID HAVE ONE ADDITIONAL FAULT.

"BUT THE MAJOR AND THE GIRL WILL SERVE A MORE IMMEDIATE PURPOSE. THEY'LL BE DISSECTED AND CLONED. SOON I SHALL HAVE THOUSANDS OF COMPANIONS!"

MISTER, YOU ARE CRAZY! WHAT'S MORE, YOU'RE MESSING WITH THE GUARDIANS OF THE GALAXY--AND AS LONG AS ONE OF US IS FREE, YOU'VE GOT A FIGHT ON YOUR HANDS!

OH, YOU'RE MISTAKEN! I'M NOT CRAZY-- I'M NOT EVEN HOLLIS! YOU SEE, I AM DRYDOCK!
AND YOU, MY FRIEND, WILL SOON BE TOO DEAD TO FIGHT!
HUH?

YEOW! LASERS!
I'D ALMOST FORGOTTEN ABOUT DRYDOCK'S INTERNAL DEFENSE SYSTEMS. AND NOW THERE'S A MANIAC COMPUTER CONTROLLING THEM!

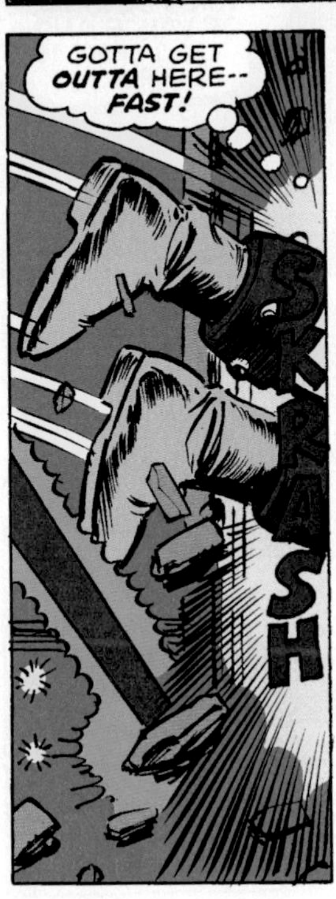
GOTTA GET OUTTA HERE-- FAST!

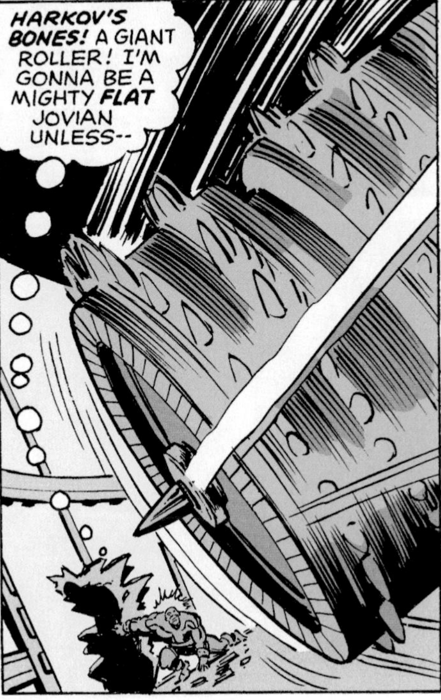
HARKOV'S BONES! A GIANT ROLLER! I'M GONNA BE A MIGHTY FLAT JOVIAN UNLESS--

I CAN RIP UP ENOUGH OF THIS BULKHEAD!

SCREEE
--LIKE SO!
JAMMED BY THE THICK SLAB OF METAL, THE GIANT ROLLER SLOWLY GRINDS TO A HALT--

--ENABLING CHARLIE TO DISPOSE OF IT IN HIS OWN DISTINCTIVE WAY.
KA-PLANG
I HAVE TO QUIT FIDDLIN' AROUND DOWN HERE. IF I DON'T GET TO SICK BAY SOON, THERE WON'T BE ENOUGH OF VANCE AND NIKKI LEFT TO SAVE!

BUT BEFORE HE CAN TAKE MORE THAN A HALF-DOZEN STEPS--
UMMPH!
--CHARLIE IS CAUGHT IN THE GRIP OF A MIGHTY CONSTRUCTION PRESS.

HUNH--CAUGHT ME FLATFOOTED. BUT I CAN'T LET THIS STOP ME! I CAN'T! I--

KA-THRAK
--CAN'T!

REACHING AN OUTER CORRIDOR, CHARLIE BEGINS TO RUN WITH A SPEED BELIED BY HIS MASSIVE FRAME.
GOTTA MOVE UP THRU THE BASE BEFORE IT CAN THROW SOMETHING ELSE AT ME!
I NEED TO STRIKE BACK SOMEHOW--BUT HOW DO YOU SURPRISE A COMPUTER?

WELL, AT LEAST I'VE GOT ONE ADVANTAGE-- I REMEMBER MOST OF THE LAYOUT OF THIS PLACE FROM MY CADET DAYS. THIS CORRIDOR SHOULD GAIN ME SOME TIME.
SO INTENT ON HIS PROGRESS IS CHARLIE, THAT HE FAILS TO NOTICE THE FAINT CRACKLE OVERHEAD--THE WARNING RATTLE OF--

--ELECTRO-CABLES!
YAAHHH!

LIKE GREAT SNAKES, THE CABLES TWINE ABOUT THE HUGE GUARDIAN--EACH ONE SENDING COUNTLESS KILOVOLTS THROUGH HIS BODY!
NNNGGH!

G-GOD! WHOLE B-BODY FEELS LIKE IT'S ON F-FIRE! C-CAN'T TAKE MUCH M-MORE. ONLY CHANCE IS TO B-BREAK CIRCUIT!

FORCING HIS HALF-PARALYZED MUSCLES TO WORK, CHARLIE STRAINS AT ONE OF THE CABLE MOORINGS UNTIL...
CREEEE

CRACK!
D-DID IT!

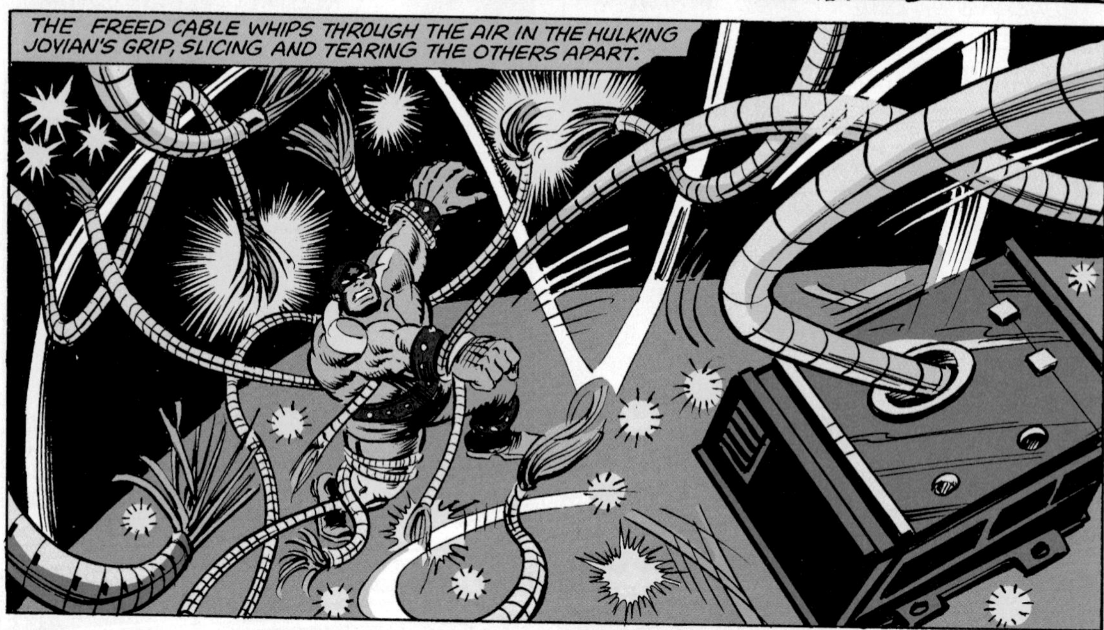
THE FREED CABLE WHIPS THROUGH THE AIR IN THE HULKING JOVIAN'S GRIP, SLICING AND TEARING THE OTHERS APART.

WHEW! THAT WAS THE CLOSEST CALL YET! NEED TO REST, BUT I DON'T DARE.
THE GUARDIANS'LL BE DEAD MEAT IF I DON'T MAKE IT TO SICK BAY IN TIME!

BUT HOW AM I EVER GONNA GET THERE IF I HAVE TO FIGHT AN ENTIRE SPACE STATION? UNLESS--!

UNLESS I DON'T STAY IN THE STATION!
LET'S SEE, THERE OUGHTA BE A STORAGE LOCKER RIGHT THRU HERE!
WHAM

AND SHORTLY...
HAH! THERE'S NO NEED TO WASTE TIME GOING THRU DRYDOCK--

WHEN I CAN GO OUTSIDE AND WORK MY WAY AROUND IT! I'D LIKE TO SEE THAT COMPUTER STOP ME NOW!

WHOOP! CONSTRUCTION-ROBS! THEY'LL TEAR ME APART IF I GIVE 'EM HALF A CHANCE!

BLAST! EVERY SECOND I SPEND WALTZING AROUND WITH THESE ROBOTS BRINGS VANCE AND NIKKI CLOSER TO THE KNIFE! BUT IF I LET UP, THEY'LL TOTAL ME! ONLY ONE WAY TO STOP THEM!

IF I'M LUCKY, I'LL SURVIVE.
THIS IS IT! I'M COMIN' THRU!
AND WITH THAT, CHARLIE SLAMS THE ROBOTS AGAINST THE OUTER HULL WITH SUCH FORCE--

--THAT IT GIVES WAY-- CAUSING THE ENTIRE COMPARTMENT TO EXPLODE OUT INTO THE VACUUM!

RIPPED FREE FROM DRY-DOCK, THE ROBOTS DRIFT SI-LENTLY AWAY, LEAVING CHARLIE ALONE--

--AND ALIVE!
BOY! GOT MY HELMET SEALED JUST IN TIME!
BETTER SET MY MAGNO BOOTS ON AUTO-MATIC AND GET TO WORK.

NOW FOR THE HARD PART. COMPUTER'LL THINK I'M DEAD FROM DECOMPRESSION. BUT IF I GET CLOSE TO THE HULL SENSORS, IT'LL BE TIPPED OFF, SO--
--THEY'VE GOTTA GO!

HAVE TO WORK FAST NOW!

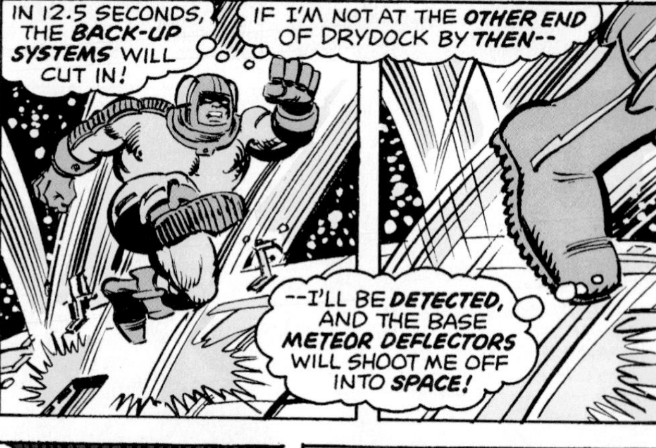
IN 12.5 SECONDS, THE BACK-UP SYSTEMS WILL CUT IN!
IF I'M NOT AT THE OTHER END OF DRYDOCK BY THEN--
--I'LL BE DETECTED, AND THE BASE METEOR DEFLECTORS WILL SHOOT ME OFF INTO SPACE!

SHORTLY, IN DRYDOCK'S SICK BAY...
GEEZ! DON'T I AT LEAST GET AN ANES-THETIC?
I-ASSURE-YOU-MA'AM-IT-WILL-ALL-BE-OVER-BEFORE-YOU-KNOW-IT.

SEZ YOU!
SQUEEEEE
CHARLIE!

BOY, YOU'RE A SIGHT FOR SORE EYES! HOW--?
NO TIME, SQUIRT! GET EVERYONE FREE! I'VE GOT THINGS TO DO!

AND A QUICK DASH DOWN THE CORRIDOR TAKES CHARLIE FROM THE SICK BAY--

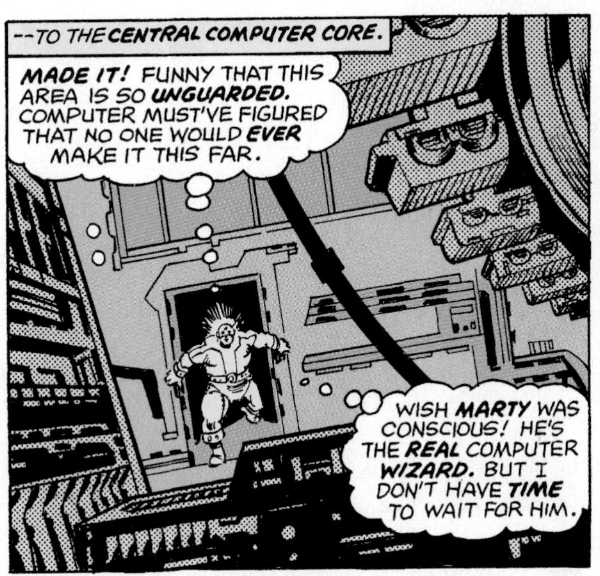
--TO THE CENTRAL COMPUTER CORE.
MADE IT! FUNNY THAT THIS AREA IS SO UNGUARDED. COMPUTER MUST'VE FIGURED THAT NO ONE WOULD EVER MAKE IT THIS FAR.
WISH MARTY WAS CONSCIOUS! HE'S THE REAL COMPUTER WIZARD. BUT I DON'T HAVE TIME TO WAIT FOR HIM.

JUST HAVE START TRASHING CIRCUITS! THIS IS AS GOOD A PLACE TO START AS ANY.
WHAM

THEN...
CHARLIE--DON'T! YOU-YOU'LL KNOCK OUT THE LIFE SUPPORT SYSTEMS--KILL YOUR FRIENDS!
MALARKEY!

I KNOW THIS BASE, MISTER! LIFE SUPPORT HAS ITS OWN BACK-UP SYSTEM! NOTHING I DO HERE WILL EFFECT IT!
NO! NOT THAT ONE!

CHARLIE--PLEASE STOP! DON'T DESTROY ME! I-I CAN DO GREAT THINGS FOR YOU! LOOK--I CAN BE ANYONE YOU WISH! EVEN--

--YOUR FATHER!
D-DAD?

OF COURSE, SON! I WAS IN THE MILITIA, TOO--REMEMBER? ALL MY RECORDS ARE ON FILE. THE WHOLE FAMILY CAN BE TOGETHER AGAIN!
PLEASE... STOP IT.

COME ON, CHARLIE BOY! IT CAN BE JUST THE WAY IT USED TO BE! REMEMBER HOW I USED TO RIDE YOU ON MY SHOULDERS WHEN YOU WERE A BOY?
PLEASE...DAD... IT'S BEEN SO LONG. I-- I--!

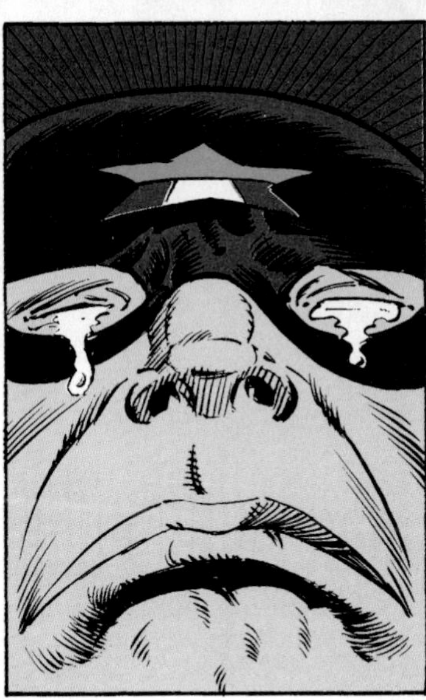

THE END-- FOR NOW!

BE WATCHING FOR THE NEXT APPEARANCE OF THE GUARDIANS IN THE THOR ANNUAL ON SALE IN JULY!

GUARDIANS OF THE GALAXY

by Steve Gerber

FROM FOOM #21 (SPRING 1978)

As I recall, it was my idea to revive the Guardians of the Galaxy strip. Initially we did a five-issue story in *The Defenders*, co-starring the Guardians, which started out in an issue of *Giant-Size Defenders*. It was more or less a trial appearance to find out if anyone was interested in the strip. We had Dave Cockrum redesign the costumes, we created a new starship for them to pilot and we revised the premise of the strip, so that they were no longer fighting the Badoon on earth, and sent them off among the stars."

"Most of the comics series I was scripting then were set in the present. I wanted to do something that combined the standard super-hero elements with something a little different, so that I could give my imagination a bit more play. There had only been one other story of the Guardians done previously, and that was almost five years earlier. As a result, we assumed that most of the readers hadn't even seen the original Guardians story (although I think it was later reprinted, between the time the *Defenders*' stories and the time when they received their own comic). But we wanted to expand and enlarge upon what had been done. I didn't feel that the characters in the original story had much meat on their bones in terms of characterization. I wanted to make Vance Astro a little crazier than he had been, after having been locked up in that space capsule for 200 years—and I wanted to make Charlie a little more militaristic, make Yondu more spiritual and Martinex more the scientist. Nikki was thrown in as an X-factor. The conception was, I think, half mine and half Mary Skrenes'. I wanted to do a girl—a Mercurian—because there wasn't one in the group. So she was our token female and our token Mercurian. We devised the name, we devised the character, and I think it was Mary who came up with the explanation that she had learned history from all these old tapes, most of which stopped after 1940. So she spent all her time wandering around the cosmos listening to all those tapes over and over again, until she wound up with a speech pattern somewhere between Humphrey Bogart and a teeny-bopper. And that was basically the idea of Nikki."

"Although there were various themes in the particular stories. I did not have a theme as a whole. Yet these five exiles would really be as much outsiders on earth as they would be among the stars. So if there was a theme, ultimately, that was it. Ultimately, their rationale for leaving earth was the fact that everyone else was normal, except for this last Jovian, last Plutonian, and last Mercurian—and Vance was the one and only, a human candy-bar wrapped in aluminum."

"As for explanation of the Guardians' proper place within the Marvel Universe, it entailed virtually an entire issue of *The Defenders* to explain the future history of earth from 1980 to the year 3015. Then a corollary explanation that this was only one possible course of history—that it need not necessarily be the only one, and that the events of the present could alter it—but that it was still the future, at least as the Guardians would experience it. That's a confusing enough paradox, as it stands. I really didn't want to delve into the rest of the Marvel continuity—I didn't want to talk about Iron Man, who died in 1998, or go into the Guardians meeting the Kree of the Skrulls or the Watcher or whatever—basically because I didn't want to put anyone into the position where they would ever have to explain this whole mess again. Therefore, it seemed better to create new nemeses and new races for them to encounter."

"There's no particular reason I used satire in the strip. I think, for better or worse, it's a world view that I have, and I can't keep it out of my writing—no matter what I do. In the particular instance of the Cosmic Consummation experienced by Nikki and the Topographical Man in #7, both Al Milgrom and I knew we could get our heads chopped off for dealing with such a controversial subject—but there was a very valid reason for presenting that scene the way we did. It seemed that was the only real way to conclude that story. Any other ending seemed false. It had nothing to do with going out of my way to be controversial. A lot of people wrote in about it, and appreciated it – and the funny thing was, we couldn't print the letters! They were too explicit!"

"Basically, Al Milgrom and I worked together the same way I have with almost every other artist. I typed up a plot and sent it to him, he drew it—and if he had any questions, he'd contact me and we'd work 'em out. Al and I are friends, and we had a basic conception of the Guardians that pretty much matched up. But other than that, we didn't work together particularly closely. I let him do the artwork, and I worried about the words."

"I don't think science-fiction is basically my inclination, actually. The Guardians of the Galaxy was something I wanted to do, because I have never done a project like it—and because Marvel didn't have a comic like it at the time. I think the Cosmic Consummation has to be the highlight of the series for me. I don't know how I could top that. The logical thought behind it was that this was the supreme affirmation of life—as opposed to the Topographical Man who was the embodiment of anti-life."

GUARDIANS OF THE GALAXY

by Roger Stern

FROM FOOM #21 (SPRING 1978)

The Guardians of the Galaxy was basically my first title for Marvel. I picked it up under circumstances that have since become a trademark for Marvel—it was already late, and not only that, but my first issue was to be the conclusion of a two-part tale about the origin of Starhawk. When Steve brought in the pages of the preceding issue, I said, 'Gee, this is really bizarre, Steve! How does it end?' And Steve revealed that he hadn't really figured that out yet."

"I was thunderstruck."

"There was a lot of pressure on me, since the comic was so late, so I re-read everything there was on the Guardians. And suddenly it occurred to me that these Arcturians were the same ones—or ancestors of the ones—who appeared in Steve's *Morbius, the Living Vampire* series. So I got the whole idea for what became of Starhawk's children and an inkling of how I was going to complete the origin. I was over at Chris Claremont's for dinner one evening, and we tossed ideas back and forth. Chris was a big help. And, basically that's how I worked out the conclusion of the origin story as it appeared in *Marvel Presents #10*. Of course, Al Milgrom was a great help, too! And Jim Starlin helped quite a bit, because he was doing an issue of Captain Marvel at the same time as Al Milgrom was doing an issue of Guardians, while out on the West Coast. Starlin helped him lay out the Guardians story, and I just recently got a chance to thank him for that in a *Doctor Strange* letters page, because the original letters page that was to appear in that issue got dropped because that issue worked out to be an 18-page story."

"I supposed people could take me to task for killing off Starhawk's kids, but I'm proud of it. I've always had this thing about super-hero offspring—unless they've got a good purpose for being there, they're in the way. You've got this ultra-cosmic character, Starhawk, both male and female, roaming the galaxy for a thousand years—and suddenly, about six or seven years ago, he decides to have kids. So, by artificial test-tube means, he has three kids. Once in a while he visits them on the environmentally self-contained asteroid. The whole contradiction annoys me. You've got this character, 'One Who Knows,' who every so often goes off and plays 'Ozzie and Harriet.' And, if anyone really remembers the *Morbius, the Living Vampire* stuff, then I'm sure they're secure in the knowledge that the kids aren't gone forever, because they know how the kids can be brought back, quite easily. And I'll just let it go at that."

"Working on a science-fiction comic was a new experience for me. There was very little to connect the Guardians with the regular Marvel Universe. Eventually they would have come back to earth to see what was going on, because there have been some other Marvel time-travel tales that have touched on the 31st Century. In fact, Siseneg, from *Doctor Strange*, came from the 31st Century, and said that sorcery in his original time period had undergone a big renaissance. Almost everyone had been getting into sorcery. So that would have been a storyline I would eventually have touched on."

"The foundations that Steve had set up were very good. Nikki was—and still is—a great character to write. The whole relationship between her and Vance is a great thing to play off. Starhawk was an enigmatic cosmic character with the unique male/female identity. But a thing that always bothered me, of course, was that any story about the future is of necessity going to be a possible future story. Steve had constructed a general history to explain the existence of Killraven and Deathlok and all relationships leading up to the 31st Century. Generally, I followed Steve's outline, but I went a bit further and set up a separate outline for myself, going back to the year 10,000 BC, because the Caretakers from Arcturus were involved in the storyline. It became a lot like E.E. 'Doc' Smith's *Lensmen* series, so I did a tremendous amount of research to track things down. John Byrne did a little astronomical studying and discovered that in the year 2001 Mars would be in position that would put it equidistant from both earth and counter-earth. Going on that theory, I assumed that the Deathlok and Killraven stories were based on counter-earth, which accounted for the absence of super-heroes in those storylines. There was still an inconsistency, though, because the Guardians had heard legends from both earth and counter-earth, so I developed a hypothesis about the Day of Earth-Merger. Perhaps sometime in the middle of the 22nd Century, there was a cataclysmic, cosmic calamity that caused the two earths to merge—and because of this intense upheaval, records were lost, things were destroyed and people were left very dazed afterwards. What caused it, I don't know—but that more-or-less explained it for me at that point"

"My approach to Guardians was very different from Steve's. His stories were very psychological and mine were more space-opera. Purely by coincidence, Al Milgrom and I happened to live in the same apartment building at the time, on the same floor, and there were many nights when we were trying to crack the old deadline doom, passing pages back and forth across the hall. He'd finish one page and hand it back to me, and as I was writing, he'd work on another. It was a lot of fun, and I have a lot of good memories of that time."

DEFENDERS #26 PAGE 9 ART BY SAL BUSCEMA AND VINCE COLLETTA

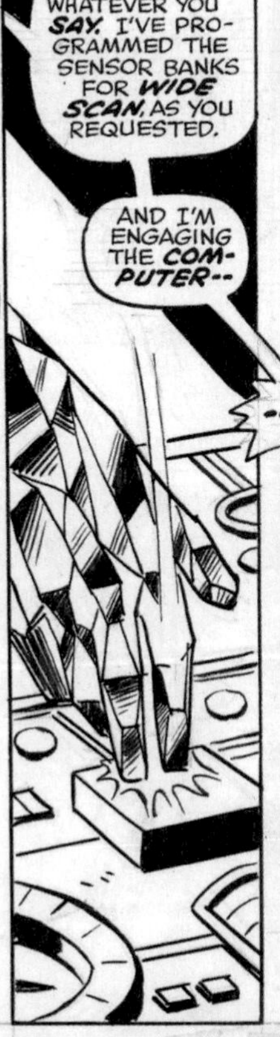

23

CONTINUED AFTER NEXT PAGE

DEFENDERS #27 PAGE 14 ART BY SAL BUSCEMA AND VINCE COLLETTA

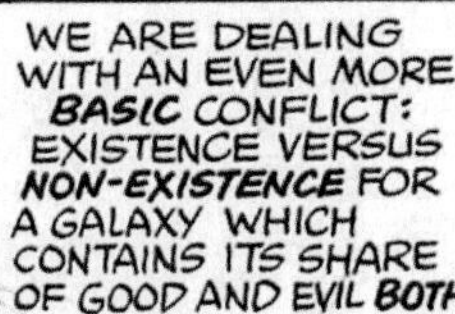
WE ARE DEALING WITH AN EVEN MORE BASIC CONFLICT: EXISTENCE VERSUS NON-EXISTENCE FOR A GALAXY WHICH CONTAINS ITS SHARE OF GOOD AND EVIL BOTH.

CHEEZ! GET A LOAD OF THE LIGHTING IN THIS PLACE!

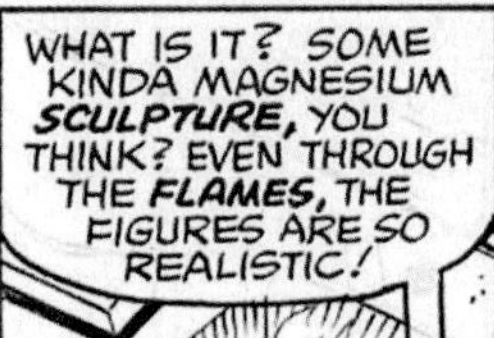
WHAT IS IT? SOME KINDA MAGNESIUM SCULPTURE, YOU THINK? EVEN THROUGH THE FLAMES, THE FIGURES ARE SO REALISTIC!

BUT WHOEVER HEARD OF A CONVENT WITH A SPECIAL EFFECTS DEPARTMENT?!

DID YOU-- WERE YOU-- ADDRESSING ME, SISTER?
HUH?

THERE IS --SO MUCH-- I COULD TELL YOU--
--BUT SO LITTLE--
--TIME.

SHE--TURNED TO ASHES--RIGHT IN FRONT OF ME!
LISTEN--I, UH, REALLY THINK I'M GONNA BE SICK!

WOULD THAT YOU COULD AFFORD THAT SELF-INDULGENCE, NIKKI, BUT NOW MOST OF ALL YOU MUST REFORTIFY YOUR STRENGTH OF WILL.
FOR IN ORDER TO SAVE THE GALAXY, YOU MUST ENTER THE FLAME STATE AND--
ME?!?

OH, NO! UH-UH! NOT THIS KID!! YOU'VE FLIPPED YOUR SUNBONNET, MAN! I DIDN'T SPEND SEVEN YEARS SURVIVING ALONE IN SPACE TO WIND UP A HUMAN CIGARETTE BUTT!

AND WHILE THE GUARDIANS BATTLE VAINLY, STARHAWK--WITH A LAST DESPERATE BURST OF WILL--RESUMES THE BODY.
GUARDIANS... STAY BACK. IT IS... HOPELESS.
THE BLAZES IT IS! CHARLIE! LAY OFF THE FORCE FIELD! MAYBE WE CAN'T STOP THESE THREE STOOGES, BUT WE CAN GET THEIR BOSS!
HUH? WHERE?
OVER THERE! THE OLD GEEZER IN CHARGE--OGORD! HE ISN'T PROTECTED BY ANY FIELD! LEAN ON 'IM!
WILL DO, SQUIRT!
OH, NO.
NO--DON'T! STOP!
AT THE SOUND OF THE HASTY SHOUT, THE CHILDREN SUDDENLY STOP DEAD--THEIR PROTECTIVE FIELD FADING INTO NOTHINGNESS.
VANCE! THOSE HEAD-BANDS--THEY ARE KEEPING THESE PEOPLE IN THRALL! I-I KNOW IT!
WELL, THEY WON'T MUCH LONGER!
AND WITH A BOLT OF ENERGY THAT MOVES WITH THE SPEED OF THOUGHT, VANCE ASTRO KNOCKS THE HEAD-BANDS OFF THEIR RESTING PLACES--